ESTABLISHING JUDICIAL AUTHORITY IN INTERNATIONAL ECONOMIC LAW

A central development in international law is the intensified juridification of international relations by a growing number of international courts. With this in mind, this book discusses how international judicial authority is established and managed in key fields of international economic law: trade law, investor-state arbitration, and international commercial arbitration. Adopting a unique legal-centric approach, the analysis explores the interplay between these areas of economic dispute resolution, tracing their parallel developments and identifying the ways they influence each other on processual mechanisms and solutions. Drawing together contributions from many leading scholars across the world, this volume considers issues such as the usage of precedent and the role of legitimacy, suggesting that the consolidation of judicial authority is a universal trend which impacts on state behaviour.

JOANNA JEMIELNIAK is Associate Professor at the Centre of Excellence for International Courts at the University of Copenhagen. She specialises in international business law and arbitration, and in the theory of legal interpretation and argumentation.

LAURA NIELSEN is Associate Professor at the Centre for Company Liability and an associate member of the Centre of Excellence for International Courts at the University of Copenhagen. She is an international trade law expert, but specialises also in the broader area of international economic law.

HENRIK PALMER OLSEN is Professor of Jurisprudence at the University of Copenhagen. He co-founded the Centre of Excellence for International Courts in 2012 and is a leading expert in legal theory.

CAMBRIDGE INTERNATIONAL TRADE AND ECONOMIC LAW

Series Editors

As the processes of regionalisation and globalisation have intensified, there have been accompanying increases in the regulations of international trade and economic law at the levels of international, regional and national laws.

The subject matter of this series is international economic law. Its core is the regulation of international trade, investment and cognate areas such as intellectual property and competition policy. The series publishes books on related regulatory areas, in particular human rights, labour, environment and culture, as well as sustainable development. These areas are vertically linked at the international, regional and national levels, and the series extends to the implementation of these rules at these different levels. The series also includes works on governance, dealing with the structure and operation of related international organisations in the field of international economic law, and the way they interact with other subjects of international and national laws.

Books in the series

Establishing Judicial Authority in International Economic Law
Edited by Joanna Jemielniak, Laura Nielsen, and Henrik Palmer Olsen

Trade, Investment, Innovation and Their Impact on Access to Medicines: An Asian Perspective
Locknie Hsu

The Law, Economics and Politics of International Standardisation
Panagiotis Delimatsis

The WTO and International Investment Law: Converging Systems
Jürgen Kurtz

Export Restrictions on Critical Minerals and Metals: Testing the Adequacy of WTO Disciplines
Ilaria Espa

Optimal Regulation and the Law of International Trade: The Interface between Societal Values and WTO Law
Boris Rigod

The Social Foundations of World Trade: Norms, Community and Constitution
Sungjoon Cho

Public Participation and Legitimacy in the WTO
Yves Bonzon

The Challenge of Safeguards in the WTO
Fernando Piérola

General Interests of Host States in International Investment Law
Edited by Giorgio Sacerdoti, Pia Acconci, Mara Valenti, and Anna De Luca

The Law of Development Cooperation: A Comparative Analysis of the World Bank, the EU and Germany
Philipp Dann

WTO Disciplines on Subsidies and Countervailing Measures: Balancing Policy Space and Legal Constraints
Dominic Coppens

Domestic Judicial Review of Trade Remedies: Experiences of the Most Active WTO Members
Müslüm Yilmaz

International Organizations in WTO Dispute Settlement: How Much Institutional Sensitivity?
Marina Foltea

Public Services and International Trade Liberalization: Human Rights and Gender Implications
Barnali Choudhury

The Law and Politics of WTO Waivers: Stability and Flexibility in Public International Law
Isabel Feichtner

African Regional Trade Agreements as Legal Regimes
James Thuo Gathii

Liberalizing International Trade after Doha
David Gantz

Processes and Production Methods (PPMs) in WTO Law: Interfacing Trade and Social Goals
Christiane R. Conrad

Non-Discrimination in International Trade in Services: "Likeness" in WTO/GATS
Nicolas Diebold

The Law, Economics and Politics of Retaliation in WTO Dispute Settlement
Edited by Chad P. Bown and Joost Pauwelyn

The Multilateralization of International Investment Law
Stephan W. Schill

Trade Policy Flexibility and Enforcement in the WTO: A Law and Economics Analysis
Simon A.B. Schropp

ESTABLISHING JUDICIAL AUTHORITY IN INTERNATIONAL ECONOMIC LAW

Edited by

JOANNA JEMIELNIAK, LAURA NIELSEN, AND HENRIK PALMER OLSEN

CAMBRIDGE
UNIVERSITY PRESS

CAMBRIDGE
UNIVERSITY PRESS

University Printing House, Cambridge CB2 8BS, United Kingdom

Cambridge University Press is part of the University of Cambridge.

It furthers the University's mission by disseminating knowledge in the pursuit of education, learning and research at the highest international levels of excellence.

www.cambridge.org
Information on this title: www.cambridge.org/9781107147102

First published 2016

A catalogue record for this publication is available from the British Library

Library of Congress Cataloging-in-Publication data
Jemielniak, Joanna, editor. | Nielsen, Laura, (Jurist), editor. | Olsen, Henrik Palmer, editor.
Establishing judicial authority in international economic law / Edited by Joanna Jemielniak, Laura Nielsen and Henrik Palmer Olsen.
New York : Cambridge University Press, 2016.
LCCN 2015041405 | ISBN 9781107147102
LCSH: International economic relations. | International courts. | Jurisdiction. | International commercial arbitration.
LCC K3820 .E88 2016 | DDC 343.07–dc23
LC record available at http://lccn.loc.gov/2015041405

ISBN 978-1-107-14710-2 Hardback

CONTENTS

FIGURES

TABLES

CONTRIBUTORS

David A. Gantz, Samuel M. Fegtly Professor of Law, James E. Rogers College of Law, the University of Arizona

Joanna Jemielniak, Associate Professor, iCourts, Faculty of Law, University of Copenhagen

Chang-fa Lo, Justice, Constitutional Court, Taiwan, and Part-time professor, National Taiwan University College of Law

Krista Nadakavukaren Schefer, Professor of Law, University of Basel, Switzerland

Laura Nielsen, Associate Professor, CEVIA, Faculty of Law, University of Copenhagen

Henrik Palmer Olsen, Professor and Vice-Dean for Research, Faculty of Law, University of Copenhagen

Joost Pauwelyn, Professor of Law, Graduate Institute of International and Development Studies, Geneva, and Georgetown University Law Centre

Krzysztof J. Pelc, William Dawson Scholar Associate Professor, Department of Political Science, McGill University, Canada

Stefanie Pfisterer, Senior Associate, Homburger AG, Zurich, Switzerland

Benedikt Pirker, Senior Lecturer, Institute for European Law, University of Fribourg, Switzerland

Amos Saurombe, Professor of International Economic Law, Head of Graduate Studies, Research & Innovation in the College of Law at the University of South Africa

Anton K. Schnyder, Professor of Law, Faculty of Law, University of Zurich, Zurich, Switzerland

Gregory Tereposky, Partner, Borden, Ladner, Gervais, LLP, Ottawa

Ingo Venzke, Associate Professor, University of Amsterdam

ACKNOWLEDGEMENTS

We would like to thank the editors of the book series for accepting our book, as well as the anonymous peer reviewers for their helpful suggestions. We would also like to thank the very professional staff at CUP, Kim Hughes and Rebecca J. Roberts, for helping us through the publication process. In addition, we would like to thank "Dreyers Fond" in Denmark for supporting the conference in December 2013 which this publication developed from. Finally, we thank our student assistants Kristoffer Krohn Schaldemose, David Steen Skovsted and Amalie Munch-Jensen, and in particular Christina Blaunfeldt, LL.M., for their help with formatting the footnotes in the entire book.

Introduction

JOANNA JEMIELNIAK, LAURA NIELSEN AND HENRIK PALMER OLSEN

The idea behind the book

The past two decades have seen a significant increase in the political reach and influence of international law.[1] A central element in this process has been an intensified juridification of international relations and, more specifically and importantly, a steep growth in international judicialization through a steadily growing population of international courts (ICs).[2] Nearly 90 per cent of the total historical output of legal decisions made by ICs was issued during this period, and ICs are gaining more autonomy from nation states: more ICs have compulsory jurisdiction, many allow agents other than states to initiate litigation before them, and several have the authority to review state compliance with international rules.[3] This development is best described as a shift from what might be called a *pacta sunt servanda* regime of synallagmatic relations between sovereign states to a more dynamic and self-sustaining regime of "living law", in which courts exert an increasing influence on legal development through their interpretation of international legal documents. This development has resulted in a number of universalizing tendencies in legal interpretation[4] and in engagement with a dynamic approach to legal regulation, whereby

[1] See Anne Marie Slaughter, *A New World Order* (Princeton: Princeton University Press, 2004); Karen J. Alter, *The New Terrain of International Law: Courts, Politics, Rights*, (Princeton: Princeton University Press, 2014).

[2] *Ibid.*

[3] *Ibid.*;*The Oxford Handbook of International Adjudication* (Cesare Romano, Karen Alter, and Yuval Shany (eds.)) (Oxford: Oxford University Press, 2014).

[4] See Joanna Jemielniak and Przemysław Mikłaszewicz, "Capturing the Change: Universalising Tendencies in Legal Interpretation" in Joanna Jemielniak and Przemysław Mikłaszewicz (eds.), *Interpretation of Law in the Global World: From Particularism to a Universal Approach* (Heidelberg: Springer, 2010).

the most influential ICs participate more actively in developing and adapting the law to majoritarian preferences.[5]

Understanding how and why ICs become frequent interpreters of international law with impacts on state behaviour (and why some do not) is important for understanding this development. One important dimension of this issue is the institutional, political and social context in which an IC operates. A recent study of this topic showed how this context influences the capacity of ICs to translate formal legal authority into authority in fact.[6] Hence, issues such as access to an IC, the existence of alternatives to international litigation and whether an IC makes decisions on technical issues or issues of high political importance influence the ability of ICs to establish authority in fact and thereby operate as an important agent in defining the law within its subject matter jurisdiction. Applying these general findings specifically to a study of the authority of the WTO Appellate body (AB), another recent study explained the widening of the WTO-AB's authority[7] by showing how the changes to the WTO dispute settlement system that went into effect in 1995[8] combined with various political factors (most fundamental, the fall of the Berlin Wall and, with it, the collapse of Soviet economic model and the subsequent international rise of neo-liberalist economical thinking, but coupled to other important politico-economic developments that happened around the same time[9]) rapidly transformed the WTO-AB into an IC with extensive authority in international trade law.

This book departs from the above-mentioned studies in two ways. First, the focus of this study is neither on ICs in general nor on the WTO-AB alone. Rather, this study's focus is on how *international judicial authority* is established and managed in the field of international economic law, which we define here as encompassing international trade

[5] See Miguel Poiares Maduro, *We, the Court: The European Court of Justice and the European Economic Institution* (Oxford: Hart Publishing, 1998); Alec Stone Sweet and Thomas L Brunell, "Trustee Courts and the Judicialization of International Regimes", *Journal of Law and Courts*, vol. 1 (2013), 61–88.

[6] See Karen J. Alter, Laurence R. Helfer, and Mikael Rask Madsen, "How Context Shapes the Authority of International Courts", *Law & Contemporary Problems*, vol. 79: 1 (2016).

[7] See Gregory Schaffer, Manfred Elsig, and Sergio Puig, "The Extensive (but Fragile) Authority of the WTO Appellate Body", *Law & Contemporary Problems*, vol. 79: 1 (2016).

[8] See Manfred Elsig and Jappe Eckhardt, "The Creation of the Multilateral Trade Court: Design and Experiential Learning", *World Trade Review* (forthcoming 2015).

[9] See Schaffer, Elsig, and Puig, "The Extensive (but Fragile) Authority of the WTO Appellate Body".

law, investor-state arbitration and international commercial arbitration. Second, the focus of the book is not exclusively on the political and social contexts and their shaping effect on international adjudicative institutions but rather on the institutions themselves: their (legal) history, their (legal) culture and their (legal) behaviour. Originating from a conference that was organized by the Centre of Excellence for International Courts (iCourts) and Copenhagen Centre for Commercial Law (CCCL) of the Faculty of Law of the University of Copenhagen and was entitled "Establishing Judicial Authority in International Trade Law" (Copenhagen, 12–13 December 2013), in which leading international economic law scholars from around the world participated and discussed the topics that are now collected in this volume, the ambition has been to study how various aspects of legal culture affect judicial authority in international economic law. This investigation is accomplished through three interlinked parts with the following themes: (1) emergence, (2) precedent and (3) legitimacy. These three issues together provide an important supplementary perspective to existing research in the field, in that this approach seeks to show how the institutional history, the instrument of legal precedent and the perceived legitimacy underpinning the agency of these institutions shape judicial institutions in international economic law.

Economic law and the other fields of international law

When focusing in particular on (public) international trade law, it is important to note that this area is different from other subsystems of international law. The interests of states in facilitating the trading system result in a process that seems much more predictable and enforceable than the processes that occur in human rights law, international criminal law or international environmental law. Most significantly, in the trade area, states "make money" in the sense that private stakeholders within their jurisdictions acquire financial benefits, generate wealth, ensure and create jobs, and so on. In contrast, for example, international environmental law is often viewed as an area that "costs" money (even though this view is a very rough generalization). On the other hand, human rights and international criminal law are areas that by their nature reach into the core of sensitive domestic politics. These areas are very value sensitive and will therefore often be dominated by politics.[10]

[10] See also Alter, Helfer, and Madsen, "How Context Shapes the Authority of International Courts".

Comparing this characteristic to trade, it is important to note that international trade law is detached from current politics, at least to a certain degree, in the sense that it follows primarily economic trends. A popular saying when teaching trade law is that if you want to know why public international controversies have arisen, "follow the dollar sign"; in other words, states typically do not engage in WTO cases unless there is a real loss of trade and thus national jobs and profits. Jobs and enterprise benefits are in the end a major factor when evaluating the factors that get politicians re-elected. However, this simple fact also informs why such a broad (even if sometimes denounced as "fragile")[11] judicial authority is vested in the WTO's dispute settlement mechanism, as well as in other types of dispute resolution in the economic area. Another comparison between human rights and international criminal law on one side and international trade law on the other is that, in the trade area, no country really holds an absolute position in this field because all countries engage in trading and investing across the border. Some countries do so to a greater extent than others, and some countries do so with greater success than others, but there is no decisive divide in trade views between East and West, the new world and the old world, or the European Union and the United States, as there would be had we picked another and more politically sensitive topic, such as human rights and international criminal law.[12] The same pragmatic difference in modus operandi can also be traced in the functioning of the WTO. Unlike the United Nations, where political battles are fought, diplomats strive to keep political battles out of the WTO.[13] Whereas the conflicts between some countries that are played out in the United Nations may cause the world tremble because those countries may be nuclear powers and on the verge of entering into an armed conflict, the very same states may have remained allies in the

[11] See Schaffer, Elsig, and Puig, "The Extensive (but Fragile) Authority of the WTO Appellate Body".

[12] It is worth emphasizing that the role of global trade in diminishing the traditional North-South divide between the developed and developing world, while controversial, also certainly escapes bipolar categorizations, especially when the key role of such powerful economies as India and China (characterized as the "Southern engines of growth") in the global economic landscape is considered. See Gouranga Gopal Das, "Globalization, Socio-Institutional Factors and North–South Knowledge Diffusion: Role of India and China as Southern Growth Progenitors", *Technological Forecasting and Social Change*, vol. 79 (2012).

[13] The most political stance was probably taken when Israel blocked an observer and Egypt reacted by blocking all observers, *see e.g.*, Craig vanGresstek, *The History and Future of the World Trade Organization*, 164–166, available at www.wto.org/english/res_e/booksp_e/historywto_05_e.pdf.

trade area due to shared economic interests. An exception is of course when states use economic and trade sanctions against each other.

This background is particularly important in the context of Part I of this volume, concerning the *establishment* of the judicial authority, where the historical perspectives and the differences between various parts of the world are outlined. The need for countries to have a predictable trading system is the most important explanation for why a "World Trade Court" with mandatory and compulsory jurisdiction was set up with the WTO dispute settlement mechanism. The same holds for the decisions of that court, which, at least to a considerable extent, are enforceable and have some "teeth" in comparison to other fields, in which a dispute settlement mechanism is missing altogether, is not compulsory or is in place in areas where only a smaller number of states participate.

Another aspect that differentiates this area from other fields of international law is that the international and regional trading system includes several layers of dispute resolution systems: the WTO DSM is the "world trade court", many regional trade agreements maintain separate mechanisms, and private companies also engage in commercial arbitration and investor-state dispute resolution. The spheres of economic interest of the states and private actors in this area are also not completely different, as the latter players are important stakeholders that directly affect a country's trade policies in market economies. Moreover, as discussed in detail *infra*, the procedural and institutional standards that are developed in the private field of commercial arbitration and in the public-private field of investment treaties influence trade dispute settlement in a variety of ways (from forum shopping strategies to specific procedural solutions). This characteristic is also unique to international economic law in comparison to for example, human rights, international criminal law, or international environmental law, where only rarely, if ever, will there be an underlying case that involves private parties seeking the resolution of a dispute before several fora and perhaps via parallel proceedings before dispute resolution bodies of different types.[14]

[14] Whereas the phenomenon of forum shopping has also been identified in the area of human rights, in our opinion, the unique feature of international economic dispute resolution is forum shopping *across* different orders and types of bodies (or, in other words, *across* layers of underlying disputes, as illustrated by Figure I.1 in this chapter). Cf. Laurence R. Helfer, "Forum Shopping for Human Rights", *University of Pennsylvania Law Review*, vol. 148 (1999), 285–400.

The definition of international economic law

For the purposes of this volume, we assume a broad definition of international economic law, which encompasses trade law and its various dispute settlement mechanisms, investor-state relations and dispute settlement and international commercial arbitration. The inclusion of all three of these areas is necessary to fully understand the systemic and functional character of economic law, with a special focus on how disputes in this field actually arise and to what degree private social actors participate directly or indirectly in shaping the law. The volume thus seeks to break with the tradition of presenting each of these fields as separate and unrelated phenomena.

As will be discussed in this book, the above-mentioned shift from the *pacta sunt servanda* regime of synallagmatic contractual relations towards an increasingly judicialized regime of "living law" can be traced not only in international trade dispute settlement but also in the resolution of international investment and commercial disputes. While rarely considered together, these three areas of international economic dispute resolution disclose not only a number of significant, parallel developments but also mutual inspiration and the "borrowing" of procedural mechanisms and solutions, as well as an overlap in experts and even fora, which is observable on the procedural, institutional and personal levels.

This chart is inserted to illustrate the different "layers" of disputes in the field of international economic law.

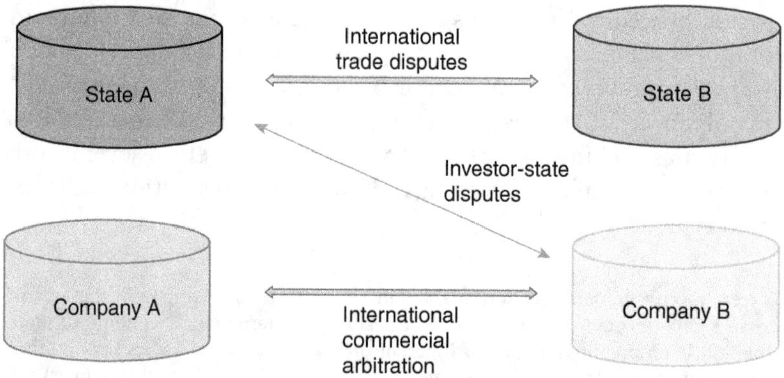

Figure I.1 Different "layers" of disputes in the field of international economic law

The top layer represents international law disputes, in which state-to-state controversies in the field of international trade law are handled either through dispute settlement of a free trade agreement or via the multilateral system of the WTO. Within this layer, private participation is usually not discussed, as the states are the acting parties, although nearly all disputes are driven heavily by the affected industry, and one can therefore often speak about private parties that stand immediately behind the government litigating the case; in some instances, such private parties effectively manage the case for the government. On the other hand, the affected industry is the direct party in the underlying dispute, which can be channelled through a commercial arbitration, handled as an investor-state dispute or both.

To exemplify situations in which all three cases can arise *in casu* concerning the same private companies in two countries, one can imagine the scenario where a private company B enters into a contract with private utility company A about setting up a power plant in state A. When the construction is nearly finished, state A changes its legislation so that the power plant can no longer generate the same revenue for its production of energy because state A wants to favour green energy and therefore enacted a rule that obstructs the importation of certain parts used in the production and running of the conventional power plant in conjunction with heavy taxes on conventional energy production. When this happens, company A can no longer honour the contract with company B and wants to either have the power plant substantially transformed to produce more environmentally friendly energy or simply rescind the contract and not pay the rest of the instalments. Therefore, company B brings an international commercial arbitration case against company A to force company A to honour the original agreement. In addition, company B brings an investor-state case against state A in which it seeks compensation for its loss associated with the extra cost involved with having to purchase some parts domestically that can no longer be imported. Finally, company B convinces the government of state B to bring a WTO complaint that addresses the import restrictions and any potential discriminatory aspects of the legislation. The WTO case is added at the top level to have the measure itself removed. Although the WTO dispute may require several years to resolve, this strategy may nevertheless be a good investment for the company to sponsor (building up the case legally with its own counsel) or in other ways assist the government (or simply lobby the government into taking action) because this approach can pave the way for more business in state A in years to come.[15]

On a more abstract level, the three layers interact in several other ways. For example, one can imagine the scenario where a company (and/or a state) has two or more parallel proceedings in different venues and a ruling in one venue becomes persuasive for the ruling in another venue. However, the scenario can be even more abstract so that the interpretation from one layer of the disputes can be borrowed in an entirely unrelated dispute in another venue that concerns altogether different parties.[16]

Judicial authority

The substance of the book centres on the theme of "establishing judicial authority". An important element in establishing judicial authority, whether in international trade law or in any other field of law, is the building up of legitimacy for the body that has been granted the competence to manage this authority. Solid authority cannot be built from scratch without legitimacy, and authority that is not consistently supported by legitimacy will erode and disappear.[17] However, this statement does mean that legitimacy and authority coincide. If this were true, then the more authority an institution has, the more legitimate it must be. However, that is not always the case. ICs may very well acquire extended authority (for instance, authority over more legal issues, authority to issue more binding decisions and authority to commission more evidence during trial) without necessarily becoming or appearing more legitimate to all agents. On the contrary, increasing authority may well lead to decreasing legitimacy because authority attaches to responsibility. Hence, if an institution increases its authority, it also becomes more blameworthy for events over which it has a

[15] The issue of parallel proceedings in investor-state proceedings and the WTO is outlined by Tereposky and Nielsen in Chapter 4.

[16] In addition, Jemielniak and Nielsen in Chapter 10 also discuss the possibility of states opting for arbitration mechanisms that were developed in a commercial (and not investment) setting rather than resorting to, for example, the WTO to solve their state-to-state disputes, highlighting the complexity of forum shopping and the interplay between the types of dispute settlement even further.

[17] Alter, Helfer, and Madsen apparently find that "authority in fact without legitimacy" is possible, see Alter, Helfer, and Madsen, "How Context Shapes the Authority of International Courts". However, they do not explain how this is possible.

say or in which it is involved.[18] Still, studying international judicial authority in international economic law is in part, a study in legitimacy; it is a study of the practice of building continued support for the international bodies that have been empowered to adjudicate trade law issues. On a very practical level, it is worth noting that one factor that has certainly boosted the legitimacy of the WTO DS system is the extensive *usage of* and *adherence to* the system from very early on by members.[19]

By analogy, had investor-state and international commercial arbitration not had both legitimacy and authority on a transnational level (although drawn from different sources and secured by different means), those systems would not have been used and relied on so often by private parties.[20] However, the diffusion processes in the area of dispute resolution in international economic law are also to be seen in such widely discussed phenomena as the judicialization of commercial arbitration[21] and its consolidation as a *sui generis* transnational legal order,[22] exceeding the limits of a mere *a casu ad casum* settlement of controversies and transforming into a system of administration of justice. This evolution of commercial arbitration adds yet another layer of considerations to the above-described strategies of possible forum shopping, but it is also indicative of the complex interplays among the three layers

[18] See e.g.Birgit Peters and Johan Karlsson Schaffer, "The Turn to Authority beyond States", *Transnational Legal Theory*, vol. 4 (2013), 315; Michael Zürn et al., "International Authority and Its Politicization", *International Theory*, vol. 4 (2012), 69.

[19] See also Alter, Helfer, and Madsen, "How Context Shapes the Authority of International Courts"; Schaffer, Elsig, and Puig, "The Extensive (but Fragile) Authority of the WTO Appellate Body". As of 31 March 2016, 504 disputes were filed; see http://www.wto.org/english/tratop_e/dispu_e/dispu_status_e.htm (last visited on 31 March 2016). This has resulted in 123 adopted Appellate Body reports and only 20 22.6 awards (retaliation i.e., noncompliance) reports issued, concerning a total of 9 cases (as some concern the same case), see www.worldtradelaw.net (last visited on 31 March 2016).

[20] The sources of the transnational legitimacy of arbitration have been identified as a delegation of the powers extended by the individual states (in a traditional, monolocal approach); the general legitimation granted by the international community of states (in the Westphalian or pluralistic model); or the autonomous standing of arbitration as a *sui generis* transnational legal phenomenon, which is largely emancipated from the original consensus of the states. See in detail:Emmanuel Gaillard, *Legal Theory of International Arbitration* (Leiden: Martinus Nijhoff Publishers, 2010), 15ff.

[21] cf. e.g. Richard B. Lillich and Charles N. Brower, *International Arbitration in the 21st Century: Towards "Judicialization" and Uniformity?: Twelfth Sokol Colloquium* (New York: Transnational Publishers, 1994); Fali S. Nariman, The Spirit of Arbitration: The Tenth Annual Goff Lecture, Arbitration International vol. 16 (2000).

[22] See Gaillard, *Legal Theory of International Arbitration*.

of international economic dispute resolution, which the book aims to unveil and address, as we believe that these issues should no longer be treated as separate and isolated developments. Because legitimacy is a key issue in the discussion of judicial authority, we found it useful to dedicate the entire third part of this book to a detailed discussion of this topic, particularly to the question of the legitimacy of decision-making.

However, before arriving at this issue, we first aim to show how the establishment of judicial authority in international economic law rests on three very diverse historical developments, a diversity that shows itself very clearly by focusing, as we do in Part I of the book, on regional differences in the development of judicial authority. Following this discussion, we move to what is legally speaking at the heart of disseminating judicial authority: the use of precedent in legal argumentation.[23] As was noted by Chang-fa Lo at the Asia WTO Research Network (AWRN) at 10, NTU, Taiwan, 14–15 June 2015, WTO cases have been used to encourage trade negotiations,[24] something that would not have been possible but for precedent. As a consequence, precedent with a certain authority can influence countries' negotiating positions. A similar theme is that governments are sometimes seen to use reference to international law as leverage for making unpopular changes domestic law after a WTO ruling against such a change.[25] Precedent is therefore covered in Part II of this book.

[23] For an overview of precedent in all three layers of disputes, *see* Giorgio Sacerdoti, "Precedent in Settlement of International Economic Disputes: The WTO and Investment Arbitration Models", *Contemporary Issues in Int'l Arbitration and Mediation: The Fordham Papers* (2011). For a more general introduction to how precedent is used in the legal decisions made by international courts, see Marc Jacob, *Precedents and Case-based Reasoning in the European Courts of Justice* (Cambridge: Cambridge University Press, 2014). Although it is a study of precedent use in the CJEU, we believe that many of the findings reflect a similar situation in other active international courts.

[24] Citation confirmed with the author. The email is on file with the editors.

[25] Similarly, the European Union had to reform the sugar area after the *EC – Sugar* case, *see* European Communities – Export Subsidies on Sugar, Report of the Appellate Body, WT/DS265/AB/R, WT/DS266/AB/R, WT/DS283/AB/R, 28 April 2005. Another type of "compliance" is described by Shaffer as compliance with the rules "outside the dispute settlement decisions", i.e., the implications for national regulatory governance, see Gregory Shaffer, "How the WTO Shapes the Regulatory State", School of Law, University of California, Irvine, legal Studies Research Paper Series No. 2015-10, available at http://papers.ssrn.com/sol3/papers.cfm?abstract_id=2480664&download=yes (last visited on 19 February 2015).

Part I – Courts in international economic law: emergence, interplay and proliferation

Part I of the volume explains how international trade "courts" have emerged and how different regions have developed differently. It does so by asking questions in the area of the legal-historic and socio-legal fields: Who created these courts? Who supported them and what shaped them? How do they function in practice? Whilst the primary focus of such accounts is typically the ideologies and political strategies of the United States and the European Union in finalizing the multilateral foundation of the dispute resolution mechanism of the GATT and subsequently the WTO, it is evident that regional dispute resolution mechanisms have also shaped the establishment of judicial authority in the trade field. However, regional judicial authority is not distributed equally around the world. This volume therefore addresses this aspect and provides insight into the special developments in Asia and Africa, including their special conditions and cultural and political explanations for the developments that are particular to those regions.

After an account of the development towards establishing judicial authority in the multilateral and regional trade "courts", the book moves on to illustrating how investor-state dispute resolution relates to dispute resolution in the trade field. It does so by adopting a functional approach described from the practitioner's perspective (focused on navigating procedural aspects of economic dispute resolution) and by explaining, inter alia, which litigation tactics the complaining party can use in parallel proceedings and how the different types of tribunals could potentially refer to interpretations rendered by another tribunal. The trade proceedings before the WTO are used to illustrate this problem. However, it should be noted that references to "external" precedent could also happen in regional systems, for example, where a decision stemming from a tribunal in one region could be relied on or "inspire" a certain interpretation in another region. This fact alone also shows the magnitude of the practical and theoretical issues that arise from parallel proceedings, as the interrelationship could easily be addressed differently by different tribunals. Moreover, understanding the practitioner's very practical perspective (or functional approach) raises a multitude of other practical and theoretical questions that are at the heart of this volume, such as: How does it affect the development of precedent and the predictability and accountability that investor-state arbitration is generally performed on an ad hoc basis? Which is different from the more established trade "court" of the WTO? Whether and how should or could one ruling dictate or influence the other (i.e., the issue of precedents being exchanged between different institutions)? These issues would equally apply to international commercial arbitration.

Chapter 1 is written by David A. Gantz and entitled "Assessing the Impact of WTO and Regional Dispute Resolution Mechanisms of the World Trading System". The chapter provides an analytic and historical overview of the different dispute resolution mechanisms that have emerged around the world. This chapter includes an overview of the WTO DSM and a range of RTA dispute resolution mechanisms from different regions of the world, including NAFTA, ASEAN, Mercosur, the Andean Community, the EU, COMESA, SADC and SACU, and analyses the effectiveness, advantages and deficiencies of those mechanisms. The history naturally starts with the largely unknown story of the stillborn international trade organization (ITO), which was intended to be the third Bretton Woods Institution, alongside the World Bank and the International Monetary Fund. This discussion offers additional insight into the processes that drove the development of the ITO, which was crafted primarily by the United States alongside Britain whilst World War II was still raging in Europe. By 1948, President Truman announced that he would not be able to submit the ITO to the Senate for its advice and consent. As a result, the General Agreement on Tariffs and Trade (GATT) 1947, which is an international agreement that did not establish an international organization, became the founding document for the functioning of the GATT dispute resolution. Over time, this mechanism evolved from the original diplomatic model of working parties into the increasingly legalistic model with panels on which today's system is based, primarily driven by the United States, which supported a more legalistic model. Similarly, the United States was the strongest proponent for the changes that were established with the Uruguay Round and the WTO DSM as we know it today. With that backdrop, this chapter offers additional insights into why parties to RTAs prefer the WTO system over the regional dispute resolution that is built into many FTAs and highlights apparent cultural differences, most importantly the seemingly non-litigious attitude in the Asian region, which the author and many others refer to as the "ASEAN way".

Chapter 2 is written by Chang-fa Lo and is entitled "Establishing Permanent Regional Good Offices for Trade Disputes in Asia". The chapter picks up where Gantz left off in Chapter 1 and goes straight to the heart of the issue of why Asian countries include legalistic dispute resolutions in their trade agreements but seem to resort to those resolutions to a much lesser extent than the rest of the world. The author notes that China is relatively active in WTO DSM but that, overall, Asian countries' reliance on dispute resolution in the trade area does not correspond with the trade volume in Asia. He posits several explanations for this phenomenon. Perhaps most interestingly, the author suggests that the historical preference for a diplomatic model is no longer present, a suggestion that can be evidenced by the fact that most Asian FTAs include detailed and legalistic rules for dispute resolution. The author continues by explaining that with its roots in Confucius' philosophy, there is a more pragmatic and non-confrontational or non-litigious attitude in Asia. Consequently, mediation and conciliation are preferred methods of dispute resolution in many jurisdictions in Asia. After an introduction to the philosophy and cultural background the lead to the existence of a less litigious attitude on an entire continent, the author points to an additional and very simple explanatory factor: the language difficulties that Asian countries encounter in WTO disputes.[26] Finally, the author adds insight into some strategic considerations that Asian countries may face when determining whether to instigate a case against a country, such as the United States. The chapter concludes by suggesting the establishment of a permanent regional good offices mechanism for trade disputes in Asia. By comparing the European experience with a variety of well-functioning courts, the author offers insights into why such a good offices process might be the ideal solution for trade disputes in Asia. This is also a timely suggestion that enhances the ongoing debate of whether FTA disputes ought to be litigated in the WTO or whether we will in time be faced with several "appellate bodies" in international trade law and thus risk regional differences in the interpretation of similar or identical legal rules, which is a type of fragmentation of international trade law.[27] Such a suggestion cannot avoid giving food for thought for those imagining that fragmentation emanates only

[26] The far-reaching linguistic diversity in Asia could perhaps also be seen as one of the factors that explain the difficulty of establishing a regional DSB in this part of the world.

[27] The International Law Commission issued a report on the fragmentation of international law that covered many different aspects of the fragmentation of international law; *see* United Nations, General Assembly, International Law Commission, Fragmentation of International Law: Difficulties Arising from the Diversification and Expansion of International Law, Report of the Study Group of the International Law Commission, Finalized by Marrti Koskenniemi, 13 April 2006, A/CN.4/L.682, available at http://legal.un.org/ilc/documentation/english/a_cn4_l682.pdf.

from "traditional" rulings by a court-like entity, such as yet another appellate body. Usage of the permanent good offices may thus result in more fragmentation if those results are to be included in the pool of decisions that are evaluated for traits of fragmentation. On the other hand, if those results are not included, this approach will lead to less fragmentation because it will result in fewer "court" cases (i.e., because more settlements via consultation or mediation will lead to less actual litigation).

Chapter 3, which was written by Amos Saurombe and entitled "African Regional Judiciaries and Their Jurisprudence in Trade Law Matters", concerns the special developments in Africa, including the African trade courts and their special challenges. As the author points out, the fact that many of the regional courts do not function as intended often leads people to assume that there is a special "no litigation" culture in Africa. Following the previous chapter about special Asian cultural traits that manifest themselves in attitudes towards litigation, it is fascinating to explore whether comparable cultural traits may explain the lack of usage of the courts in Africa and the issue of why such courts are established when they are not being used. However, the author quickly points out that the main problem in Africa is linked to the dysfunctional nature of the underlying political systems, where legal obligations are often disregarded, so the system itself is without authority when the African states fail to implement the treaty obligations to which they have consented. This issue very much relates to the issue of the authority and legitimacy of the systems, as outlined above and is further developed in Part III of this book.

Saurombe also points to problematic states, such as Zimbabwe, as a reason why some tribunals, such as the SADC, seem to have simply dissolved. What is also noticeable in the African context is the focus on integration and the willingness to set up supranational entities that model largely on the European Union rather than a lesser degree of integration, as would be found in free trade agreements. This point was also noted by David Gantz in Chapter 1. The reason for the heavy inspiration from Europe is probably due to the historically close colonial ties and perhaps even development aid in various forms, which combine to encourage the adoption of the European model. However, when adding other issues to the agreements, these issues may be attached to massive political disagreement, which can ultimately supersede the trade agenda and hence undermine the establishment of judicial authority. The suspension of the SADC Tribunal following the Campbell case (which revolved around a human rights issue) is a clear example of this idea.[28] COMESA is yet another example of African integration extending beyond the free trade agreement. In COMESA, citizens of the member states may under some circumstances bring cases to the COMESA court, a process that generally goes well beyond what would be the case in a traditional FTA tribunal. As a logical consequence, the author points out that COMESA has relied on ECJ jurisprudence concerning the issue of rights and obligations that emanate from the treaty to private citizens. After covering a similar issue with the EAC, the author concludes that the African regional courts have not truly assumed the supranational powers that were originally intended.

Saurombe is nevertheless optimistic in his concluding remarks, where he sees the potential for African member states that have adhered to the different regional organizations, in the sense that by having signed these "hard" law treaties, member states may in time adhere to the rules. However, he also cautions that without the states tackling their underlying poverty and development problems, the courts may not truly become relevant actors. These factual differences from the case of Asia and other parts of the world are of course very important to keep in mind when discussing the challenges to authority that trade courts face in many parts of Africa.[29]

Chapter 4, which is entitled "Coordinated Actions in International Economic Law as Illustrated by Investment Treaty Arbitration and World Trade Organization Disputes" and written by Greg Tereposky and Laura Nielsen, links trade dispute resolution to that of investor-state dispute resolution in a very practical way. This chapter provides the practitioner's perspective (or a functional approach) when planning cases and determining litigation strategy and tactics. The chapter uses the WTO case *Mexico – Taxes on Soft Drinks* to illustrate how previous parallel proceedings have taken place. Parallel to that WTO case, no less than three investor-state cases were launched against Mexico by three different private companies. This in itself might seem slightly overwhelming to the government being sued, particularly because the damages sought were in excess of half a billion US dollars.

[28] For an analysis, see the final sections of Henrik Palmer Olsen, "Fidelity to International Law: On International Courts and Politics" in P. Capps and S. Pattinson (eds.), *Ethical Rationalism and the Law* (Oxford: Hart Publishing, forthcoming 2016).

[29] This is one dimension of the political context of ICs that has not been given much attention by Alter, Helfer, and Madsen in "How Context Shapes the Authority of International Courts".

The chapter also gives rise to broader theoretical issues. The *Mexico – Taxes on Soft Drinks* case itself illustrated how issues of forum shopping within trade tribunals arise. In this case, the Appellate Body confirmed that the WTO panel could not decline jurisdiction even though the case could also be heard by a NAFTA Chapter 20 panel. This is in fact a landmark case in illustrating the trend of cases that could be resolved under a bilateral tribunal being brought instead before the WTO if the substantive obligations are comparable; the WTO is simply the preferred venue.

In terms of issues that arise from parallel proceedings, the chapter illustrates how the timing with which decisions in the different tribunals are issued may affect the course of the proceedings. In this case, the WTO report was released before the investor-state decisions, and inputs therefore flowed from the WTO proceedings to the investor-state proceedings. One may therefore speculate how the reverse situation would have affected the WTO case, if at all. The chapter also describes how investor-state proceedings may be inspired by particular interpretations of WTO law and concepts similar to those that occur in investor-state proceedings, but it also sets out why this can be problematic. Finally, the chapter explores the emerging issue of using the WTO Appellate Body as a type of world economic appellate court that also hears investor-state cases and the kinds of problems that are associated with this issue.[30]

Part II – The development and usage of precedents in international economic law

Part II of the volume addresses the issue of the framework conditions, status and role of case law in different areas of international economic law. In particular, the question of whether an accumulating body of case

[30] The postulate of introducing a permanent appellate body for investor state *and* commercial arbitration in cases in which public interest is involved has also recently been raised by the arbitration community. Cf. Kun Fan's presentation at the Queen Mary School of International Arbitration's 30th anniversary conference (London, 19–21 April 2015). References to this discussion date further back in the trade community, where the discussion probably originated from a discussion about whether the TPP needed a secretariat and whether the WTO could provide that; *see* Simon Lester, "Do We Need a WTO Secretariat", at http://worldtradelaw.typepad.com/ielpblog/2014/11/do-we-need-a-tpp-secretariat.html. This evolved into the WTO providing an Appellate Body for regional trade agreements during e.g., a conference at the Ministry of Foreign Affairs, Denmark, The Post-Bali WTO in May 2014 in light of the regional and sectoral trade negotiations, with Greg Tereposky, Simon Lester, Lorand Bartels, and Laura Nielsen as speakers. Confirmation of such discussions is on email with the editors.

law can be treated as de facto precedent has been raised and is being addressed. In none of the three fields of international economic law do the outcomes of adjudication formally enjoy a binding force for other proceedings. However, in all of those fields, different types of influence that are exerted by previous rulings onto new rulings can be identified and traced. In this part, the book aims to explore this influence and its conditions, to diagnose its scope (including the problem of having too much, sometimes conflicting, precedent), and to discuss its adequacy under the existing procedural and institutional frameworks. This part also examines the consequences for the involved actors and the impact on their forum shopping and procedural strategies.

In Chapter 5, which is entitled "Minority Rules: Precedent and Participation before the WTO Appellate Body", Joost Pauwelyn confronts the officially proclaimed lack of binding precedent in the WTO system with the appellate structure of its dispute resolution mechanism, which augments the call for a review and reference to formerly adopted decisions. As this two-tiered system has been purposefully established as a safeguard for the consistency and predictability of the application of WTO law, reliance on former rulings could also be seen as a direct consequence of such a design. The author seeks to answer the questions of the existence and historical development of de facto precedent in Appellate Body adjudication, as well as to explore the issue of the weight of specific Appellate Body reports in terms of the influence (or lack thereof) they exert on subsequent decisions. To address these questions, the author employs empirical methods to identify explicit cross references among 108 Appellate Body Reports that were issued over the years 1996–2013 and to map those cross-references using network analysis tools. The empirical findings from this project offer strong evidence that the de facto rule of precedent has been significantly present in Appellate Body adjudication from its very beginning (since the very second report), with a total number of 2,957 cross references (27.4 cross references per report, on average). Further analysis discloses such trends as the tendency for referencing to increase over time and the high density of the network, which reveals cross-references to virtually all reports. This analysis also discloses the most cited reports, in terms of the overall number of references to them and in terms of indegree centrality (with multiple references to the same report as one). This extensive empirical material provides the author with a basis for formulating caveats related to a rule of precedent having become too strong. In particular, as Pauwelyn argues in the context of the multiparty WTO structure, the risk is that decisions that are influenced by minority stakeholders (and especially by the particularly active litigants, who might undertake such action as a deliberate strategy) become general rules, shaping the legal positions taken by third parties.

The issue of the purposeful involvement of governments into the WTO de facto precedent system is also discussed by Krzysztof J. Pelc in Chapter 6, which is entitled "The Welfare Implications of Precedent in International Law". Pelc proposes an empirical test to verify whether the member states indeed choose to behave as if the *stare decisis* rule was binding under the WTO dispute settlement mechanism (based on the assumption that if the courts follow the rule of precedent, it also affects the behaviour of other actors). As the author argues, the governments of WTO member states indeed *systematically invest in precedent.* Having assumed the existence of de facto precedent in the WTO system, which is reflected in the behaviour of the involved actors, he then turns to a discussion of the reasons for governments' acceptance of this development despite the widely shared scepticism of the international community towards rule-making through judicial activism. The creation of "minority rules", as discussed in the preceding chapter (see above), and the notion of "democratic deficit" are frequently indicated as rationales for wariness about the general acceptance of precedent. However, Pelc argues that these considerations are outweighed by the strategic need to empower international courts, which would otherwise easily fall prey to political demands (and the resulting loss of credibility of international commitments would have an overall, undesired negative spillover effect). In his view, the growing acceptance of de facto rules of precedent in the WTO dispute settlement system is indicative not merely of the emancipatory tendencies of its adjudicating bodies but also of a deliberate strategy of the involved governments to empower international trade "courts". The adoption of precedent allows members of the panels and the AB to shift part of the liability for their decision onto the set of rules that is created through existing case law, ostensibly limiting their discretionary powers. However, in fact, as Pelc argues, this change increases their authority during confrontations with the political power of governments that are involved as parties in a specific dispute.

A comprehensive, comparative perspective on the mechanisms for international economic dispute resolution in relation to the rule of precedent is offered as a closing chapter for this part in Chapter 7 by Anton K. Schnyder and Stefanie Pfisterer, entitled "Features of Trade Law Adjudication and Their Impact on the Development of Legal

Concepts and Precedents". In this chapter, the authors examine how specific institutional and structural settings of different types of trade "courts" affect the processes of development of legal concepts and doctrines in all three areas of international economic dispute settlement: trade law, investment treaty arbitration and commercial arbitration. Schnyder and Pfisterer's analysis is divided into two main parts. First, the authors offer a structured, comparative discussion of particular features of international economic adjudication mechanisms (such as the design of the "courts", including the selection of the members and the usual lack of appeal; the status and role of adjudicators; the procedural characteristics; the nature and substance of disputes; and the orientation of legal interpretation). With this institutional and procedural comparative analysis, the authors demonstrate how some types of dispute settlement mechanisms offer a setting that is more "precedent-friendly" than others, such as international commercial arbitration; however, the development of legal doctrines through case law can also be traced in the latter field. Such issues as, inter alia, the presence of repeat-players with international backgrounds as adjudicators, the tradition of offering reasoned rulings (even if there is no formal requirement thereof), the publication of decisions and influence of a multicultural and multilingual environment, and the question of a main object of adjudicatory interpretation are all considered to enhance or limit the space for the development of de facto precedent in the resolution of economic controversies. In the subsequent part of their chapter, the authors turn to the issue of interrelations between the three areas of economic dispute settlement by offering comments on the role of international arbitration in international trade law adjudication. In particular, the authors examine conditions in which international arbitration is being successfully sought as a replacement for typical public law mechanisms of resolution of trade controversies, as illustrated by the case of two arbitrations that were held under the auspices of the London Court of International Arbitration in *Softwood Lumber*.

Part III – Legitimating decisions in international economic law

While in legal affairs, legitimacy is closely connected to legality, legality does not in and of itself produce or sustain legitimacy.[31] The reason is that legality, as it is broadly understood, is a predominantly formal

[31] The first part of this section relies on Henrik Palmer Olsen and Stuart Toddington, "The End of an Era: Static and Dynamic Interpretation in International Courts", *International Criminal Law Review*, vol. 14 (2014).

feature of the social practice we know as law. Hence, legality is the practice of rendering public decisions in accordance with pre-existing rules, and in that way, legality is associated with the autonomy of law (from morality and politics). In fact, a great deal of legal theory emphasizes the autonomy of law to explain two key aspects of legal order as opposed to other forms of social normativity. One aspect is the distinctness of a legal rationality (i.e., an allegedly special type of justificatory reasoning that is closely connected to the idea that legal decisions must always be grounded in pre-existing legal norms that are identifiable by belonging to a specific limited domain of normative sources); the other aspect is law's place in society as normatively dominant or supreme (by which theorists refer to the "pre-emptive" and "exclusionary" quality of legal norms). Legitimacy through legality, then, is obtained when the decisions issued by a public body are presented and perceived as deriving from pre-existing norms and hence as being neutral in the sense of not being influenced by morality or politics. It is precisely this neutrality that yields legitimacy; by being beyond morality and politics and instead relying on pre-existing legal norms (which may therefore be presented as *facts* rather than as *norms*, precisely because they are pre-existing) that are applied to a given fact situation, the decisions are rendered valid through a process of reasoning that assimilates inferential logic, even though they often involve discretion because the rules do not fit perfectly onto the facts. Consequently, law's autonomy is only relative. Gerald Postema explains this issue by saying that the norms that are identified through the legal sources[32]:

> are authoritatively interpreted and applied, and the system of norms is maintained, by adjudicative institutions. Moreover adjudicative institutions are authorized to settle issues left unsettled by the set of source based legal norms available at any point in time. Since, in such cases, by hypothesis, the existing legal considerations are silent, indeterminate, or in conflict, the Court' settling of them is determined not by appeal to the law, but by appeal to considerations outside its limited domain.

Legal norms are applied and interpreted by courts, and it is in this capacity that there is sometimes scope for courts to operate outside the limited domain. The line between applying, interpreting, adjusting, modifying, adapting and altering the law is fine; effectively, social

[32] See Gerald Postema, "Law's Autonomy and Public Practical Reason" in R.P. George (ed.), *The Autonomy of Law: Essays on Legal Positivism* (Oxford: Oxford University Press 1999), 93.

normativity is being re-coded (transformed) and dynamically (creatively, pragmatically) fashioned into legal normativity from material that exists – or might plausibly be purported to exist – both within and without the limited domain.

It is in this "grey zone" of the law that judicialization takes place. It is here that courts, in their case law, articulate legally what is sometimes referred to as judicial politics (i.e., they manufacture precedent). In effect, through dynamic judicial activity, courts synthesize new law, which can be absorbed by the pliable framework of doctrine and the constituting principle behind the existing positive law. This process of dynamic judicialization, in contrast to what in theoretical retrospect appears increasingly as the static logical ideal of a "limited domain", leads to judicial discretion, normative ambiguity and doctrinal predictability into synthesis through a process that brings to bear on a range of interests in the selection of the analogical content of increasingly focused and thus increasingly determinate "argumentation frameworks".

The assertion that judges are not constrained by "doctrine" but rather respond to "fact situations" is a very important, but only partial, truth. This assertion underestimates and under-theorizes the complex process of the movement, coding and delimitation of argument that lies behind the response to "the situation". It is trite to say that this process inevitably must involve political and moral choices. Alec Stone Sweet captures the character of this process in his article on the law's "path dependence". He says about judges that[33]:

> First, they work to enhance their legitimacy vis-à-vis all potential disputants by portraying their own rule-making as meaningfully constrained by, and reflecting the current state of, the law. Second, they work to enhance the salience of judicial modes of reasoning vis-à-vis disputes that may arise in the future ... Judges may also seek to enact their own policy preferences through their decisions. Yet the more they do so, the more likely judges will be to attempt to hide their policy behavior in legal doctrine. Once policy is packaged as doctrine, it will operate as a constraint on future judicial law-making

There is, then, an intimate relationship between the precedent-driven development of law and the creation of legitimacy. Portraying a legal decision as emerging from within "the law" as opposed to being policy-led is more likely to produce the desired outcome in the form of clarifying

[33] Martin M. Shapiro and Alec Stone Sweet, *On Law, Politics, and Judicialization* (Oxford; New York: Oxford University Press, 2002), p. 128.

the law; insofar as this approach is seen as the operation of the expected and revered "autonomy of law", it renders the decision more "legitimate". However, this scenario does not mean that the essence of legality and thus of legitimacy is automatically to be located in this inner, doctrinal "packaging", as Stone Sweet has labelled it. In fact, if the decision is perceived as a "bad" decision, courts, as the juridical representative of the wider regulation of social, economic and cultural interaction, become the focus of criticism for being either overly "legalistic" and mechanical in their reasoning or out of touch with the rest of society. Either way, the existence of these forms of judicial critique serves as a reminder that the "autonomy of law" and the idea of a "limited domain" are merely artificial orientations to the complex flux of competing normatives that weigh in on legal institutions.

In this third section of the book, we explore various dimensions of legitimacy that are separate from but connected to the issues discussed above (i.e., legitimacy through legality/law's autonomy from politics and morality). In Chapter 8, which is entitled "Judicial Ethics in International Economic Law: What Standards of Independence and Impartiality Apply to Arbitrators and Panellists?", Krista Nadakavukaren Schefer discusses how standards of independence and impartiality apply to arbitrators and panellists. The independence and impartiality of decision-makers is a classic feature of legitimacy and connects to legality in that independence and impartiality are generally thought to assure that decisions are not based on the decision-maker's private reasons or interests. In other words, the requirement for independence and impartiality serves to bolster legality and thereby enhance legitimacy. However, as Schefer points out, in international trade law (and more generally in international economic law), legitimacy takes on a political dimension that goes beyond what one would find in domestic contexts. With their competence to issue decisions that often result in a demand for changes to national legislation, decisions by international courts and tribunals in the field of trade and economy must strive to maintain states' acceptance of their authority to issue such judgements, even where adherence to a decision is viewed as an infraction on sovereignty.

Precisely because these decisions involve sovereign powers of nation-states, these decisions are seen as particularly sensitive and therefore particularly deserving of attention to avoid accusations that decision makers are not neutral. To gain and sustain their judicial authority, international trade courts and tribunals therefore rely on the perceived legitimacy of the decision-makers themselves. That is, the tribunal members as individual persons and their behaviour, both inside and outside the institution that gives them decision-making power, become integral factors in the perceived legitimacy of international dispute settlement as an institution. In addressing this important issue under the heading of "Judicial Ethics", Schefer investigates the norms of judicial independence as applied in international law and compares those norms to the standards of investment arbitration tribunals and the WTO's dispute settlement panellists. Because the expressed standards are practically the same across all international fora, her chapter proposes that *how these standards are discussed by tribunals and scholars are as interesting as the definition of the standard itself.* Interestingly, Schefer therefore connects the scholarly debate about the general international law standards for judicial independence that stem from the right to a fair trial and the need for legitimacy in the overall international system of law to the discussion of arbitrator ethics that is on-going in the context of investor-state dispute settlements. She then proceeds to the context of the WTO to compare that body's approach to panellist ethics to both international law norms and the practice of investment tribunals.

Closely related to Schefer's discussion of Judicial Ethics, in Chapter 9, which is entitled "Judicial Authority and Styles of Reasoning: Self-presentation between Legalism and Deliberation", Ingo Venzke ventures towards an inquiry into the self-understanding of international judges (and arbitrators, panellists, etc.). Hence, where Schefer discusses the ethical standards that are associated with independence and impartiality, Venzke moves this discussion problematically towards a socio-psychological perspective on legal reasoning. According to Venzke, in striving for the very same acceptance that produces legitimacy, international judges engage with what he calls techniques of impression management. Because judges are aware that the legitimacy of their decisions depends on how they and their decisions are perceived, they deliberately try to shape how others (i.e., the recipients of their decisions, their audience) perceive them (i.e., the judges and their decisions).

Pitching judicial decision-making between two well-known extremes (i.e., judicial formalism (or legalism) on the one hand and judicial normativism (or dynamism) on the other), Venzke sets out to understand styles of reasoning as a strategy of impression management. Rather than seeing legitimacy from the outside in (i.e., focusing on the requirements of independence and impartiality), Venzke focuses on legitimacy from the inside out (i.e., in terms of the performance pressure that judges perceive themselves to be under). More specifically, Venzke considers how formalism may often be seen as a safe haven for judges who wish to meet the expectations of their audiences when they face or (more often and more relevantly in this context) anticipated critique. Venzke points out in this regard that the appeal to formalism as a place of refuge actually depends on the predilection of audiences and that not all audiences are equally appreciative of formalism.

Alternatively, judges may opt for the more decidedly normative approach, which Venzke portrays as grounded in an exercise of discourse-theoretical reconstruction of judicial reasoning in relation to the sources of law (Venzke speaks, with reference to Habermas, of judges carrying out legal interpretation as a way of "completing the legislative program"). This approach might be seen to offer an opportunity for judges to connect more broadly with their audiences. Replacing formalism with normativism gives judges an opportunity to connect more broadly and dynamically with their audiences and obtain support for their decisions by connecting them to a more substantial social normativity than what is available through formalism. Although in international law, "legislative programs" are non-existent, one could easily see how such programs may be substituted for surveys of legal practices in member states.[34] In fact, a recent study by Stone Sweet and Brunell suggested that both the CJEU and the WTO AB operate in this manner.[35]

The third contribution in this section, Chapter 10, which is entitled "'Global Citizens' in International Commercial Arbitration and WTO Dispute Resolution" and written by Joanna Jemielniak and Laura Nielsen, picks up precisely where Venzke's chapter ends. Having discussed at length the importance of audiences, Venzke takes a step back from his own analysis and asks: "Which are the relevant audiences for international judges?" He points out that in international law, drawing attention to the role of judges' audiences in the construction of their authority and styles of reasoning may highlight and explain how international law is sometimes pushed in directions that follow the interests and inclinations of specific regimes. This observation prompts Venzke to follow up with a more normative issue:

> The question then is whether inclusive publics emerge that contest those moves. Evidence suggests that they do. In trade law, jurisprudence and styles of reasoning have, for instance, shifted visibly and significantly in

[34] See Maduro, *We, the Court: The European Court of Justice and The European Economic Institution.*

[35] See Alec and Brunell, "Trustee Courts and the Judicialization of International Regimes".

> reaction to widespread criticism to decisions seemingly categorically ruling out that unilateral trade-restrictive measure could be justified by the environmental objectives they pursued. Public contestation played its role in changing that ... While much is at present in flux in the field of investment arbitration, it is safe to say that public contestation has drawn it out into the open where the argumentative space has already shifted.

This theme of public contestation and its role in relation to legitimacy is precisely what preoccupies Jemielniak and Nielsen in their contribution. They point out that one of the most important developments in international trade law in recent decades has been the gradual opening up of judicial proceedings to a critical public. International economic law is no longer an issue that is relegated to diplomatic negotiations between leading state officials; this field is of general political concern due to the wide political consequences that flow from this kind of regulation. This development has been visible in politics for a long time but has now also reached international adjudication in trade law. Jemielniak and Nielsen show how this trend towards increased public attention to and interest in trade law issues translates into demands for procedural inclusiveness and openness of dispute settlement mechanisms, thereby allowing the participation of persons or groups that are not immediate parties to the dispute.

Theoretically, Jemielniak and Nielsen invoke the concepts of global citizenship as a platform for discussing the participatory potential for international trade disputes and for questioning the often-debated transparency deficit of arbitral decision-making. They argue that commercial arbitration is not devoid of components that support the development of global citizenship. To the contrary, and perhaps surprisingly, they find that arbitration offers a successful incarnation of the transnationalization of law and that the institutional and procedural network of arbitration supports the development of a new class of global citizens. In other words, the proliferation of arbitration is seen as a way of empowering actors who would not otherwise have access to influence the politics of international trade. Through the circulation of arbitral knowledge, actors in trade disputes can indirectly influence more state-oriented dispute resolution fora, such as the WTO.

However, Jemielniak and Nielsen also point out that the models of global citizenship that are supported by the projects of reform of the WTO dispute settlement mechanism are different. As a way of understanding this difference, they set out to analytically distinguish between two different ways of understanding what "citizenship" entails. Jemielniak and Nielsen propose that one model – the model that seems to be behind WTO reform proposals – relies on the Aristotelian and republican ideal of *civic and political participation* as a key virtue (i.e., participation in a predefined politico-legal process). Arbitration, which is a private means of resolution based on agreement, fulfils a more contemporary liberal ideal of citizenship as primarily a sphere of freedom in which participants are allowed to shape their own interrelations. A key part of their chapter is dedicated to the exploration of the interplay between these two models, as applied to international trade law dispute settlement procedures, and to an estimation, in light of this analysis, of the consequences for both WTO and arbitral decision-making that flow from an increased demand for transparency and openness. This demand seems to be the driving force in raising broader public support and, hence, ultimately represents a broader foundation for the legitimacy of judicialized decision-making in the field of trade law.

The book closes with Benedict Pirker's chapter entitled "Proportionality Analysis and International Commercial Arbitration: The Example of Public Policy and Domestic Courts". Balancing tests and proportionality analysis are at the heart of much international law, and it is precisely through these tests that courts are challenged on their legitimacy. An example will highlight what is at stake: GATT Article XX contains a list of so-called general exceptions. Trade infringing measures that are seen to be covered by these exceptions are permitted and therefore not illegal. However, to be permissible, the measures must be "necessary" to protect public morals, intellectual property and the life and health of humans, animals and plants and to comply with other conditions. This quite obviously is a very open standard, and decision-making under such a standard may very easily delegitimize the authority of the judicial body making the decision because there are no authoritative sources that the court can invoke as a basis for its decision. To reduce the burden of justification that is associated with making decisions within such an open norm, judicial bodies will seek to develop formal criteria that may operate as a pre-set paradigm for decision-making in these types of cases. This issue is precisely what has led some international courts to proceed with a strategy whereby they measure quantitatively the value consensus on a disputed issue among states that accept and use the court in question and use this consensus measurement to render the discretion during necessity analysis/proportionality testing more factual.[36]

Pirker contributes to our understanding of these tests, first and foremost by pointing out how contextual institutional arguments enter the reasoning process during balancing testing. Pirker explains that contextual elements (by which he means "the history, political economy or institutional features of treaty regimes") should be used by adjudicators to determine the most central values that are to be protected by a particular legal regime with judicial review. In addition, in relation to International courts and tribunals, he suggests that balancing tests should be developed to reflect their institutional context:

> Ideally, they should reflect upon the central values they are called to protect as the justification of their judicial review, and then adapt a balancing test as to how they can best counter severe violations of these values in their specific institutional context, while avoiding second-guessing e.g. legislative policy-choices where it is not required.

In as far as legitimacy can and should be discussed as a matter of independence and impartiality (Schefer), of meeting the expectation of audiences (Venzke) and of providing mechanisms that promote inclusiveness in judicial (and para-judicial) proceedings (Jemielniak and Nielsen), there is in the end no escaping the issue of a judiciary's duty to protect the values it is "called to protect", as Pirker phrases it. Ultimately, to be a judge is to render judgement, and to do so, one needs to conscientiously apply one's full capacity for reason and sentiment to the case at hand in order to provide a just and hence justified decision. Legitimacy is carved out of the institutional setup that is provided to further such sound judgement.

[36] *Ibid.*

PART I

Courts in international economic law: emergence, interplay, and proliferation

1

Assessing the impact of WTO and regional dispute resolution mechanisms on the world trading system

DAVID A. GANTZ

I Introduction

The General Agreement on Tariffs and Trade (GATT) 1947 created a bare-bones process for third-party resolution of disputes over the interpretation and application of GATT obligations, modified and expanded over the following decades.[1] Five years later, the initial parties to what is now the European Union (EU) created the Court of Justice of the European Union (CJEU), with jurisdiction over a range of trade and nontrade disputes.[2] For four decades, the evolving GATT panel process with its hybrid judicial/diplomatic approach and the European Court of Justice's (ECJ) judicial approach were the only effective third-party trade dispute settlement mechanisms available to disputants who were parties to one or both agreements. It was only in 1995, when the Agreements Establishing the World Trade Organization and the WTO's Dispute Settlement Understanding (DSU)[3] became effective that what is in retrospect the most successful trade dispute settlement mechanism (probably the most effective international dispute settlement mechanism of any kind) was created and implemented. As such many of the newer free trade agreement (FTA) mechanisms have patterned themselves after the

[1] See Section II (A).

[2] See "General Presentation," Court of Justice of the European Union, accessed October 29, 2014, curia.europa.eu/jcms/jcms/Jo2_6999/. The General Court (formerly the Court of First Instance) was established in 1989.

[3] Understanding on Rules and Procedures Governing the Settlement of Disputes [hereinafter "DSU"], Annex 2 of the Marrakech Agreement Establishing the World Trade Organization, April 15, 1994, 33 I.L.M. 1226 (1994), accessed November 14, 2007, www.wto.org/english/docs_e/legal_e/28-dsu.doc.

DSU system, while others, particularly in Africa, are patterned after the CJEU.

While third-party dispute settlement mechanisms were incorporated into some regional trade agreements (RTAs) beginning in the 1980s, with few exceptions they were of little practical value, usually because they were not mandatory; they required both disputing parties to agree to submit the case to arbitration after the dispute had arisen, or required a political body to approve arbitration requests. Efforts to implement mandatory trade dispute settlement mechanisms have had relatively little success in Asia, Africa, and Latin America from that time until the present. The Andean Group and Mercosur mechanisms have each addressed a handful of cases but their effectiveness in dealing with trade disputes generally has been modest. ASEAN remains committed to the "ASEAN Way," a diplomatic approach without mandatory arbitration or compliance. The relatively recent FTA among the ASEAN (Association of Southeast Asian Nations) members, Australia, and New Zealand (AANZ)[4] is one of the first Asian regional agreements with relatively effective (at least on paper) dispute settlement mechanisms. The courts created under the Southern African Development Community (SADC), East African Economic Community, the Economic Community of West African States, and the Common Market for Eastern and Southern Africa (COMESA) have produced few meaningful results in the trade area, but have had somewhat more success with human rights matters.[5]

It was only with North American Free Trade Agreement (NAFTA) in 1994 and the series of FTAs concluded subsequently by the United States[6] and Canada[7] that the inclusion of obligatory third-party dispute resolution became a common practice in a significant number of RTAs, yet none including the NAFTA mechanism has enjoyed frequent use. Regional mechanisms other than the ECJ have been far overshadowed in terms of significance and effectiveness by the WTO's Dispute

[4] ASEAN – Australia – New Zealand Free Trade Agreement (2009) [hereinafter AANZ], accessed September 12, 2013, www.asean.fta.govt.nz/preamble/.

[5] See James Thuo Gathii, *African Regional Trade Agreements as Legal Regimes* (Cambridge: Cambridge University Press, 2011), 264–297. The book discusses the four African regional trade courts.

[6] Bilateral FTAs with Australia, Bahrain, Chile, Jordan, Korea, Morocco, Oman, Panama, and Peru plus CAFTA-DR (Costa Rica, Dominican Republic, El Salvador, Honduras, Guatemala, and Nicaragua).

[7] See e.g., Canada – Chile FTA (1996), ch. N, sec. II, accessed October 29, 2013, www.sice.oas.org/trade/chican_e/chcatoc.asp.

Settlement Body (DSB), and it is evident that the parties to most RTAs prefer the DSU to the regional mechanisms in situations where parallel jurisdiction exists.

This chapter examines the reasons for the success of the WTO and EU dispute settlement mechanisms, the modest success of NAFTA, and the absence of effective mechanisms in most other FTAs. It provides an historical overview of the creation of the GATT/WTO and major regional mechanisms including insight into who those nations and their stakeholders were and what motivated their support, and an analysis of the structure and jurisprudence (or lack thereof) of each, and consideration of the reasons for success or failure. The result will hopefully provide a fuller understanding of why RTA dispute mechanisms generally have produced such limited positive results.

The chapter is structured as follows. Section II considers the GATT/WTO dispute settlement system, including the strengths and weaknesses. These issues have been exhaustively covered in recent literature[8]; the section thus focuses primarily on the historical derivation of the system than its operational features. Section III addresses RTAs (usually FTAs rather than customs unions), with a focus on NAFTA and the other US FTAs; the ASEAN FTA; and the AANZ. Section IV deals with common market courts of justice, including the CJEU, Mercosur and the Andean Court in South America, and several of the African common market courts. Section V discusses the reasons why the DSU seems to be generally preferred to the regional courts in situations where there is parallel jurisdiction, along with the challenges that have faced the regional courts and other dispute settlement mechanisms. Section VI comments briefly on means through which the effectiveness of regional systems could be improved.

II GATT/WTO system

A Dispute settlement under GATT

Professor John Jackson suggests that with regard to the preparatory conferences and negotiations during the 1946–1948 formative period,

[8] See e.g., Ross Becroft, *The Standard of Review in WTO Dispute Settlement* (Cheltenham: Edward Elgar, 2012); Mitsuo Matsushita, Thomas J. Schoenbaum, and Petros C. Mavroidis, *The World Trade Organization, Law, Practice and Policy* (Cambridge: Cambridge University Press, 2003), 18–51; Raj Bhala, *International Trade Law, Interdisciplinary Theory and Practice* (Newark: LexisNexis, 2008), 143–166.

the United States took the primary initiative. These efforts reflected the Reciprocal Trade Agreements Act under which more than thirty-two bilateral tariff reduction agreements had been concluded between 1934 and 1945.[9] These agreements were particularly significant because, as Jackson notes, "Almost all of the clauses in GATT can be traced to one or another of the clauses contained in these trade agreements."[10] The US initiative was based in significant part politically on the view that economic starvation makes people "all too ready to follow the first dictator who may rise up and promise them all jobs. Trade conflict breeds non-cooperation, suspicion and bitterness."[11]

As Gilbert Winham further explains:

> During the [Second World] war, officials in Washington and London commenced Negotiations for a post-war economic system since it appeared unlikely that the informal arrangements of the nineteenth century would reappear on their own. These negotiations were based around a compromise between the American position, which promoted multilateralism along with a bias toward liberal economic policy, and the British position, which was more concerned with historical ties to the Commonwealth and the capacity of governments to intervene in and manage the domestic economy.[12]

The two powers, with the United States very much in the lead, "generally agreed that economic recovery from wartime destruction and dislocation depended on restoring former levels of international trade and, if possible, expanding them."[13] They sought to provide a legal and economic framework to govern international trade, investment, and finance through the Bretton Woods Agreements, which created the International Bank for Reconstruction and Development (World Bank), the International Monetary Fund (IMF), and the Havana Charter contemplating the creation of the International Trade Organization (ITO). In the United States, these efforts were supported

[9] John H. Jackson, *World Trade and the Law of the GATT* (New York: Bobbs-Merrill, 1969), 36–37.

[10] *Ibid.*, 77.

[11] *Ibid.*, 38, quoting Harry Hawkins, director of the Office of Economic Affairs, Department of State (1944).

[12] Gilbert Winham, "The Evolution of the World Trading System – The Economic and Policy Context" in Daniel Bethlehem, Donald McRae, Rodney Neufeld, and Isabelle Van Damme (eds.), *The Oxford Handbook of International Trade Law* (Oxford: Oxford University Press, 2009), 5, 14.

[13] Robert E. Hudec, *Enforcing International Trade Law: The Evolution of the Modern GATT System* (London: Butterworth, 1993), 4.

by Congress, which in 1945 enacted a three-year renewal of the 1930's reciprocal trade agreements legislation.[14] It is also evident from the Congressional hearings that many in Congress were taking a proactive role, in part because of the concerns that nontariff barriers were nullifying tariff concessions and thus should be addressed in new trade agreements.[15] In other words, the efforts of the United States were not solely driven by the Executive Branch.

The World Bank and IMF charters entered into force, but the ITO died when President Truman and his State Department announced in 1948 that it would not be submitted to the Senate for advice and consent to ratification. In addition to opposition from many in Congress who believed the Havana Charter was too favorably inclined to state intervention in the economy, a general turn toward protectionism was taking place, particularly in the US Senate. Also, some officials in the Truman administration felt that support for the charter might detract from other priorities such as the Marshall Plan to reconstruct Europe.[16] As a result, the GATT 1947, incorporating extensive rules governing trade in goods but no secretariat or mechanism for application and enforcement, served as a somewhat makeshift framework for governing the international trading system from 1947 to 1995.[17] This bare-bones framework of GATT 1947 was modified, tariffs were reduced, and the membership expanded through various meetings of the contracting parties (CPs), including eight major multilateral negotiating "rounds" over more than four decades.

One of the consequences of the abandonment of the Havana Charter was the loss of a more comprehensive system for resolution of disputes. The GATT 1947 contained only two bare-bones articles on the subject. It called for consultation when requested by any CP "with respect to any matter affecting the operation of this Agreement."[18] Further, in a provision entitled "nullification or impairment," GATT provided that:

[14] John H. Jackson, "The Evolution of the World Trading System – The Legal and Institutional Context" in Bethlehem et al. (eds.), *Oxford Handbook of International Trade Law*, 31, 33.

[15] *Ibid.*, 39–40.

[16] See e.g., Andreas F. Lowenfeld, *International Economic Law* (Oxford: Oxford University Press, 2002), 25–26.

[17] *Ibid.*, 26.

[18] GATT 1947, Article XXII. Eighteen other provisions in the GATT also call for consultation among the CPs. Jackson, *World Trade*, 164.

> If any contracting party should consider that any benefit accruing to it directly or indirectly under this Agreement is being nullified or impaired or that the attainment of any objective of the Agreement is being impeded as the result of
> (a) the failure of another contracting party to carry out its obligations under this Agreement, or
> (b) the application by another contracting party of any measure, whether or not it conflicts with the provisions of this Agreement, or
> (c) the existence of any other situation,
> the contracting party may, with a view to the satisfactory adjustment of the matter, make written representations or proposals to the other contracting party or parties which it considers to be concerned. Any contracting party thus approached shall give sympathetic consideration to the representations or proposals made to it.[19]

Should the matter not be resolved, the CPs were authorized to investigate the matter and make recommendations to the CPs or issue a ruling on the matter, as appropriate, and in serious circumstances authorize the suspension of concessions by the complaining CP.[20] However, the agreement provided no structure or procedures for implementing the dispute settlement process.

As Petros Mavroidis notes, GATT dispute settlement reflected prior state practice, with diplomatic negotiations as the sole means of addressing controversies evolving into the use of "working parties" appointed from the CPs for purposes of conducting investigations.[21] Reports were referred to the GATT Council for recommendations.[22] Utilization of the GATT dispute settlement process began early. Professor Robert Hudec reports that fifty-three legal complaints were filed between 1948 and 1959.[23]

The dispute settlement process was addressed again in late 1960s, the 1970s, and the 1980s. In the 1960s both the new European Community and the United States supported an "anti-legalism" approach, arguing that "trade restrictions must be approached gradually, and with careful attention to social realities."[24] Hudec goes so far as suggesting that GATT more or less suspended its legal system during the period while negotiating over accommodation of new members and the organization's new agenda.[25]

[19] *Ibid.*, Article XXIII(1). [20] *Ibid.*, Article XXIII(2).
[21] Matsushita et al., *World Trade Organization*, 20. [22] *Ibid.*
[23] Hudec, *Enforcing International Trade Law*, 11. [24] *Ibid.*, 12. [25] *Ibid.*, 13.

The 1970s, which saw the completion of the Tokyo Round of GATT negotiations, was a decade during which the GATT legal system began a rebuilding process. By this time the United States had abandoned its anti-legalist approach, because of a need, presumably driven in part by Congress and private stakeholders, to devise a system which would result in better enforcement of US trade agreement rights.[26] This was not limited to an overhaul of the GATT dispute settlement process but included the conclusion of a number of multilateral trade negotiation "Codes" imposing on their members (not all GATT CPs) disciplines in such areas as antidumping, subsidies, and customs valuation. Some thirty-two cases had been decided during the decade.[27]

Approximately 115 complaints were filed in the 1980s with forty-seven of those producing reports, more than in all of the previous thirty years combined.[28] The volume of complaints, with many governments increasing their demands on the GATT legal system, necessarily led to a consensus (apparently including the United States despite the disenchantment noted below) favoring the creation of a legal office within the GATT Secretariat to address them, along with improvements in the legal skills that were applied by the secretariat to resolving the disputes.[29] The panel reports and recommendations evolved from a heavily diplomatic to a more rules-oriented and legal approach to dispute resolution.[30] It was only during the Tokyo Round, with what Robert Hudec calls a "legal rebuilding," that dispute settlement took a "central place" in GATT affairs, with thirty-two new cases brought during the decade.[31] The United States, in particular, had embraced the need for stronger enforcement of GATT obligations. Petros Mavroidis and his coauthors suggest that compliance was relatively high, not because of the threat of trade sanctions but because ignoring recommendations by the losing party "would threaten the entire legal order on which the GATT system was based" and make it much more difficult to prevail in situations where the losing party in one case was the complainant in another.[32]

Still, problems were emerging relating in part to the consensus required for approval of panel reports. For example, all five panel reports rendered under the Tokyo Round Subsidies Code were blocked.[33] According to Hudec, this led in the late 1980s to a rise of "unilateralism"

[26] *Ibid.* Discusses the political pressures that brought about this change. [27] *Ibid.*
[28] *Ibid.*, 14. [29] *Ibid.*
[30] Matsushita et al., *World Trade Organization*, 20. Discusses the evolutionary process.
[31] *Ibid.*, 13. [32] *Ibid.*, 21. [33] Hudec, *Enforcing International Trade Law*, 14.

in the United States supported by both the Executive Branch and Congress, with sufficient success that some CPs were concerned that the United States might abandon efforts toward GATT legal reform.[34] This was manifested in part through increasing use of Section 301 of the Trade Act of 1974, as amended by the Trade Act of 1988 (in which the Reagan administration managed to fend off even more draconian provisions suggested by Congress).[35] However, three years later, many of the concerns expressed earlier about the United States did not materialize, and the United States continued to support the "Dunkel Draft" version of a largely judicialized DSU.[36]

B *The WTO's dispute settlement understanding and dispute settlement body*

By the time the Uruguay Round negotiations were initiated in 1986, dissatisfaction with GATT dispute settlement was widespread, but probably strongest in the United States (which was increasingly resorting to unilateral efforts to enforce trade agreement rights as noted above). The principal concerns were: (1) the responding party to a complaint could often delay the process indefinitely because there were no time limits for forming a panel or rendering a report, or for implementing a panel recommendation; (2) once a report was rendered adoption could be blocked by the responding party due to the consensus requirement applicable within the GATT system; (3) retaliation through suspension of benefits was fraught with uncertainties and delays; (4) in the absence of an appellate mechanism the ad hoc panel process could produce conflicting interpretations of GATT provisions; and (5) the Tokyo Round Codes with their separate dispute settlement provisions were a source of confusion as well as having the major disadvantage of binding only to a minority of the GATT CPs. US authorities evidently perceived the benefits of a system that would force other trading partners to follow the rules, including the all-important ones restricting government subsidies, to be more important than the dangers of being forced by those other parties to observe the provisions of trade agreements themselves.

The DSU sought to resolve the shortcomings of the GATT system and provide detailed procedures for dispute settlement; in retrospect it likely

34 *Ibid.*, 14–15.

35 Omnibus Trade and Competitiveness Act of 1988, P.L. 100–418 (1988).

36 See Hudec, *Enforcing International Trade Law*, 14. Discusses US support for the Dunkel Draft.

succeeded except perhaps with regard to (3) above. Ultimately, it received the strong backing of the United States. As the Uruguay Round Statement of Administrative Action (the Executive Branch document transmitting the WTO agreements to the Congress for approval) observed:

> The new [Dispute Settlement] Understanding responds to long-held U.S. concerns regarding international trade disputes. As the country that has used the GATT dispute settlement more often than any other country, the U.S. has a strong interest in having an effective process to enforce U.S. rights under the Uruguay Round Agreements. Under the prior system, U.S. efforts to enforce its rights were often frustrated when other GATT parties delayed the dispute settlement process and blocked adoption of GATT panel reports. To address this problem, Congress made the negotiation of a more effective GATT dispute settlement system a principal U.S. negotiating objective in the Uruguay Round.[37]

This statement, with its reference to the "negotiating objectives" set out by Congress with Executive Branch concurrence in the "fast track" legislation authorizing the Uruguay Round negotiations, demonstrates as well that the objective of a stronger dispute resolution system was shared by the Executive Branch and the Congress. It also suggests that in the dichotomy between protecting US sovereignty and protecting US interests in trade disputes the balance had tipped toward the latter goal in the Uruguay Round.

The dispute settlement process is one of the most important aspects of the WTO system. As the DSU states, "The dispute settlement system of the WTO is a central element in providing security and predictability to the multilateral trading system."[38] Members of the WTO undoubtedly "enjoy one of the most successful systems for dispute settlement in the international sphere."[39] Over an eighteen-year period, sixty-four WTO members (including several EU members in their individual capacities) have participated in at least one WTO proceeding.[40]

After mandatory consultations,[41] the complaining party may request the formation of a panel, which request cannot be delayed by more than about thirty days,[42] effectively making the use of the system compulsory.

[37] Statement of Administrative Action, Uruguay Round Agreements Act, 103d Cong., 2d Sess., House Doc. 103-316, vol. 1, September 27, 1994, at 1008.

[38] DSU, Article 3.2.

[39] *WTO Annual Report 2013*, 76, accessed September 9, 2013, www.wto.org/english/res_e/booksp_e/anrep_e/anrep13_e.pdf.

[40] *Ibid.*, 86. [41] DSU, Article 4

[42] *Ibid.*, Article 6.1; the respondent could block panel formation at the first meeting of the DSB where it was requested, but not subsequently.

The DSU also establishes time limits for rendering of panel and Appellate Body reports,[43] although in practice those limits are commonly exceeded, beginning in 1995 in the case of panel reports and in more recent years by the Appellate Body, meaning that some proceedings require far more than those contemplated in the DSU.[44] Panel reports are subject to an appeal by right to the Appellate Body, a group of seven independent trade law experts who serve staggered four year (once renewable) terms.[45] Once the panel and, if requested, Appellate Body review, have been completed, the DSB (a committee of the entire WTO membership) approves the reports unless there is a consensus *not* to provide approval,[46] which has not happened in the almost eighteen years since the DSU system has been in operation. DSB recommendations, if not complied with within a "reasonable period of time," can be enforced with the suspension of trade benefits, although the type and magnitude of such suspensions is subject to arbitration.[47]

Perhaps the strongest evidence of the respect for the DSU system is the fact that it is almost certainly the busiest of any international dispute settlement system in history. The year 2012 was one of the most active in recent history for the DSU, including the work of the Appellate Body. Twenty-seven new requests for consultations were lodged, bringing the aggregate total between January 1, 1995 and August 30, 2013 to 456

[43] See DSU, Article 12.8–9, 17.5. Establishes time limits of six to nine months for the panel process and sixty to ninety days for the appellate process.

[44] From the date of formation of the panel (typically three months or more from the request for consultations), six to nine months for the panel report, sixty days for filing an appeal, sixty to ninety days for the Appellate Body report, and thirty days or less for consideration by the DSB. Thus, while it is theoretically possible for the DSB to approve the reports within fifteen months, in practice it takes far longer, particularly in complicated cases and particularly in recent years. For example, in *Canada – Measures Affecting the Export of Civilian Aircraft*, Appellate Body Report, WT/DS70/AB/R (adopted August 20, 1999), the request for consultations was received on March 10, 1997 and the Appellate Body report was adopted August 20, 1999, a relatively quick twenty-eight months. Accessed September 9, 2013, www.wto.org/english/tratop_e/dispu_e/cases_e/ds70_e.htm. In *Philippines – Taxers on Distilled Spirits*, Appellate Body Report, WT/DS403/AB/R (adopted January 20, 2012), where consultations were requested on January 14, 2010, the process was completed in approximately twenty-four months. In contrast, in complicated cases with many issues and a voluminous record, the time required for panels and the Appellate Body to complete their reports may be far longer. For example, in *United States – Measures Affecting Trade in Large Civil Aircraft (Second Complaint)*, Appellate Body Report, WT/DS353/AB/R (adopted March 23, 2012), the request for consultations was received on June 27, 2005, nearly seven years earlier.

[45] DSU, Article 17.1. [46] *Ibid.*, Articles 16.4, 17.14. [47] *Ibid.*, Articles 21.3, 22.6–7.

(including 10 in 2013).[48] Requests averaged thirty-seven per year from 1995 to 1999, and declined only modestly to 27.8 average from 2000 to 2004, before falling much further to an average of 15.6 from 2005 to 2009 and to 12.5 from 2010 to 2011.[49] The 2012 data also constitute a 200 percent increase from 2011, when only eight new requests for consultation were filed. During 2012, the DSB adopted seven reports from the Appellate Body (excluding Article 21.5 compliance reports, none of which were issued in 2012).

C *Strengths and weaknesses*

One of the reasons that the DSU system has proven so popular compared to mechanisms in RTAs is the relatively high level of consistency of the Appellate Body, due to its consistent devotion to precedent. While there is no formal requirement that the Appellate Body act consistently with prior reports, in practice it takes pains to do so.[50] The result, despite the inability of the ministers or the General Council to make authoritative interpretations, is a system that is generally predictable. Add to this compulsory nature of the process, the time limits, and certainty that panel and Appellate Body reports will be adopted automatically – most of which are not present in the majority of RTA mechanisms – it is no surprise that the system is the mechanism of choice.

Still, after eighteen years it is evident that the system has flaws. Among others, separate compliance procedures can easily add two additional years to the process with both panel and Appellate Body reports.[51] The costs of litigation are prohibitively high for members who do not have their own in-house international trade litigators, as they must either hire expensive outside counsel or seek the somewhat lower cost assistance of the not-for-profit Advisory Centre on WTO Law.[52] Other

48 "Chronological list of Disputes Cases," World Trade Organization, accessed September 9, 2013, www.wto.org/english/tratop_e/dispu_e/dispu_status_e.htm.

49 Kara Leitner and Simon Lester, "WTO Dispute Settlement 1995–2011 – A Statistical Analysis," *Journal of International Economic Law* (2012), 315–316.

50 See e.g., Appellate Body Report, *Japan – Taxes on Alcoholic Beverages*, WT/DS8, DS10, DS11/AB/R (adopted November 1, 1996); Appellate Body Report, *Korea – Taxes on Alcoholic Beverages*, WT/DS75, DS84/AB/R (adopted February 17, 1999); Panel Report, *Chile – Taxes on Alcoholic Beverages*, WT/DS/87, DS109, DS110 (adopted January 12, 2000).

51 See DSU, Article 21.5.

52 See "The ACWL Provides Advice, Support and Training to Developing and Least Developed Countries," accessed September 9, 2013, www.acwl.ch/e/index.html.

difficulties include the inability of smaller and poorer developing country members to take advantage of their right to impose trade sanctions on the EU or United States[53]; there is no alternative at present for a monetary payment. Most significant perhaps is the fact that since trade sanctions are not retroactive, a member violating a provision of one of the covered agreements effectively has a free ride for two to three years or more from the time consultations are initiated until the DSB approves the reports.

Some members have argued for increased transparency, including disclosure of pleadings and hearings open to the public. Others have focused on facilitating the use of private counsel, a necessity for many smaller members, and improvement of the consultation phase by making written records and shortening the time frame to one month instead of two.[54] Unfortunately, with the demise of the Doha Round it is evident that reform of the DSU may be some years away.

III FTA dispute settlement mechanisms with limited jurisdiction

A NAFTA, CAFTA-DR, and other US FTAs

This section is devoted primarily to NAFTA, given that the provisions of subsequent FTAs differ only modestly from NAFTA's Chapter 20.[55]

1 Introduction and overview

The North American Free Trade Agreement (NAFTA)[56] and its two parallel agreements on labor and on the environment[57] incorporate

[53] See e.g., Appellate Body Report, *European Communities – Regime for the Importation, Sale and Distribution of Bananas*, WT/DS27/AB/R (adopted September 27, 1997). Ecuador was eventually authorized to impose retaliation in the service sector amounting to $201.6 million per year. See WTO case summary, accessed September 6, 2013, www.wto.org/english/tratop_e/dispu_e/cases_e/ds27_e.htm. Ecuador deferred retaliation and the case was eventually settled through a "mutually satisfactory solution" in November 2012.

[54] See Bhala, *International Trade Law*, 168–169, 175–177.

[55] It draws on Gantz, "The United States and Dispute Settlement under the North American Free Trade Agreement: Ambivalence, Frustration and Occasional Defiance" in Cesare P.R. Romano (ed.), *The Sword and the Scales: The United States and International Courts and Tribunals* (Cambridge: Cambridge University Press, 2009).

[56] North American Free Trade Agreement, December 17, 1992, 32 I.L.M. 289 (1993) [hereinafter NAFTA], implemented by the North American Free Trade Agreement Implementation Act, 19 U.S.C. §§ 3312 et seq. [hereinafter NAFTA Implementation Act].

[57] North American Agreement on Environmental Cooperation, September 13, 1993, 32 I.L.M. 1482 (1993) [hereinafter NAAEC]; North American Agreement on Labor Cooperation, September 13, 1993, 32 I.L.M. 1502 (1993) [hereinafter NAALC]. Both agreements make it very difficult for formal arbitration to take place. Under the NAAEC,

a broad and sometimes confusing variety of mechanisms for resolving the disputes that relate to the interpretation and application of certain NAFTA provisions in specific situations.

Essentially, there are six distinct dispute resolution procedures within the larger NAFTA framework:

- interpretation and application of the agreement generally (Chapter 20);
- appeals of antidumping and countervailing duty (unfair trade) actions by administrative agencies (Chapter 19);
- those relating to foreign investment and investor-state disputes (Chapter 11);
- financial services (Chapter 14, a variation on Chapter 20);
- failure to enforce environmental laws (North American Agreement on Environmental Cooperation, or NAAEC);
- and failure to enforce labor laws (North American Agreement on Labour Cooperation, or NAAEC).

The focus on this section is Chapter 20, followed by briefer discussions of Chapter 19. Investment dispute resolution under Chapter 11 and the never used mechanisms under the financial service chapter and the labor and environmental side agreements are not discussed.

It is evident that this impressive package was accepted with some ambivalence by the US government; each of these mechanisms was incorporated for a variety of mostly pragmatic and diplomatic, as well as legal, reasons. NAFTA, it should be recalled, was negotiated at a time when the GATT Uruguay Round negotiations were largely stalled (1991–1992), but after three years of more or less satisfactory operation of the United States – Canada Free Trade Agreement (CFTA).[58] During the NAFTA negotiations the three parties had no assurance that the Uruguay Round's DSU would ultimately be adopted. Should the

arbitration is only available where there is a persistent pattern of failure by that other party to effectively enforce its environmental law (Article 22) Under the NAALC, arbitration is mandated only where there is a persistent pattern of failure by the other party to effectively enforce such standards (Article 27.1) ("Such" standards are limited to occupational safety and health, child labor, or minimum wage technical labor standards.) In each case, two of the three NAFTA parties must agree to move forward with arbitration. Thus, no arbitration is possible for violations which do not reach the "persistent pattern" stage.

[58] United States – Canada Free Trade Agreement, December– January 1998 [US–Canada], 27 I.L.M. 281 [hereinafter CFTA].

Uruguay Round have failed, the alternative was to resort either to the flawed GATT dispute settlement system or to a mechanism incorporated in to NAFTA. The fact that the DSB now provides a superior alternative could not be relied on in the NAFTA negotiations. Here, as in the WTO negotiations, Jeffrey Dunoff has observed:

> U.S. government support for judicialized dispute settlement in international trade is based less on an abstract commitment to the rule of law in international relations than on pragmatic, short-term and highly contextual calculations that this mechanism serves U.S. interests better than alternative arrangements.[59]

Also important was the recognition of the three NAFTA governments that disputes regarding NAFTA implementation were inevitable and that third-party binding mechanisms for their prompt resolution were essential. Moreover, the WTO system does not effectively extend to certain areas covered by NAFTA, such as energy, temporary visas for business travel, monopolies, some aspects of customs administration, labor and environmental issues, foreign investment, and land transportation services, among others.[60]

The NAFTA mechanisms share some common threads. All have evolved from previously existing dispute settlement procedures. Chapters 19 and 20 were cut and pasted, with minor modifications, from Chapters 19 and 18 of the CFTA, which preceded NAFTA by five years, and the NAFTA negotiations by three years. Likewise the provisions guaranteeing certain rights including mandatory investor-state dispute settlement to foreign investors were derived from various US bilateral investment treaties negotiated in the 1980s,[61] although the CFTA did not provide for mandatory investor-state arbitration.[62]

NAFTA did not create any permanent judicial dispute resolution body, akin to the CJEU or the Court of Justice of the Andean Community. On this issue, Canada and the United States had been divided since the days of the negotiations of the CFTA. Canada had advocated a strong dispute settlement mechanism, preferring a permanent tribunal; as several of those involved in the negotiations observed:

[59] Jeffrey L. Dunoff, "Does the U.S. Support International Tribunals? The GATT/WTO Case" in Romano, *The Sword and the Scales.*

[60] See NAFTA, Chapters 11 (foreign investment) and 12 (cross-border trade in services), esp. Annex I (regarding transportation services); DSU.

[61] See Department of State, United States Bilateral Treaties, accessed October 29, 2013, www.state.gov/e/eb/ifd/bit/117402.htm.

[62] CFTA, Chapter 16.

> As the smaller of the two countries and more liable to be affected by the exercise of power by the other, Canada had a relatively greater interest in effective dispute settlement. Only with the development of procedures and institutions based on jointly agreed principles and rules would the power disparity be attenuated.[63]

However, the United States preferred the arbitration approach similar to that used in the GATT, in part because of a reluctance to create new international institutions, and perhaps because of some unhappiness with Chapter 20's predecessor, Chapter 18 of the CFTA.[64] Eventually, during NAFTA negotiations a compromise was reached to create a mechanism that incorporates some elements of both courts and arbitral panels.

In addition to US resistance to a NAFTA "court," the complexity and breadth of the matters covered by NAFTA encouraged the use of highly specialized dispute resolution mechanisms and expert panelists. It is also notable that none of the three mechanisms is equipped with an effective appellate review mechanism, even though the "Dunkel Draft" with the text of the DSU was available to the NAFTA negotiators.[65] Still, the approach is "rule-based" and "juridical" with determinations that are legally binding.[66] While all three mechanisms provide for some sort of soft diplomatic procedures (i.e., consultation and conciliation), by and large they are garden-variety international arbitral mechanisms designed to issue awards that either are legally binding on the parties or for practical purposes mandate a solution to the controversy.

2 Government-to-government disputes under Chapter 20

Given that state-to-state settlement of international trade disputes has a long history under GATT, it was no surprise that during NAFTA negotiations the issue was not whether there should be such a mechanism but

[63] Michael Hart, Bill Dymond, and Colin Robertson, *Decision at Midnight: Inside the Canada – US Free Trade Negotiations* (Vancouver: UBC Press, 1994), 208.

[64] A senior former USTR official who was directly involved in the negotiations of Chapter 18 of the CFTA and Chapter 20 of NAFTA suggested both reasons. (Memorandum of Conversation, May 31, 2005 on file with author.) [Hereinafter "Senior USTR Official".]

[65] GATT Trade Negotiations Committee, "Draft Final Act Embodying the Results of the Uruguay Round of Multilateral Trade Negotiations, GATT Document MTN.TNC/W/FA," December 20, 1991; see also John H. Jackson, *The Jurisprudence of GATT and the WTO* (Cambridge: Cambridge University Press, 2000), 440. Notes that the Dunkel Draft of December 1991 included an agreement with revised dispute settlement procedures.

[66] *Ibid.*, 165.

rather how it should be structured. As noted above, Chapter 18 of the CFTA was driven more by Canada than by the United States, reflecting long-running dissatisfaction with efforts to resolve trade disputes between Canada and the United States, including but not limited to trade in softwood lumber.[67] Procedures under Article XXIII of the GATT as evolved over the years provided one model for negotiations that were concluded during the mid-1980s.[68] While the NAFTA negotiators carefully reviewed the "Dunkel Draft" of the DSU, there appears to have been relatively little direct "borrowing" from the DSU in NAFTA Chapter 20, perhaps in part because of the desire of both Canada and the United States to avoid wholesale renegotiation of CFTA, Chapter 18.[69]

The CFTA general dispute settlement system was considered to offer "a significant improvement to the traditional, pre-WTO GATT proceedings" by making the formation of a panel mandatory on the request of either party and for providing deadlines for each stage of the process. Yet, the rulings there, as in GATT, were only recommendations, leaving the prevailing party the option of retaliation.[70] The scope of Chapter 20 is broader than CFTA Chapter 18. This is largely because NAFTA itself is broader than the CFTA (and in some respects broader than the scope of the WTO Agreements, covering, inter alia, financial services, investment, intellectual property, standards, sanitary and phytosanitary measures, and, to some degree, the environment.[71]) Chapter 20 of NAFTA applies "with respect to the avoidance or settlement of all disputes between the Parties regarding the interpretation or application of this Agreement or wherever a Party considers that an actual or proposed measure of another Party is or would be inconsistent

[67] Hart et al., *Decision at Midnight*, 206–207.

[68] GATT Article XXIII; see Cunningham and Smith, "Section 301 and Dispute Settlement in the World Trade Organization in The World Trade Organization," *ABA Journal* (1996). See also DSU.

[69] Chapter 20 did take a similar approach to that of the DSU in seeking to put a limit on the level of retaliation by the prevailing party in a dispute, through providing for additional panel review, never used to date, if the retaliation levels were manifestly excessive (Article 2019).

[70] Jeffrey P. Bialos and Deborah E. Siegel, "Dispute Resolution under NAFTA: The New and Improved Model" in Judith H. Bello et al. (eds.), *The North American Free Trade Agreement: A New Frontier in International Trade and Investment in the Americas* (1994), 315, 323; CFTA, Article 1807.

[71] See e.g., NAFTA, Article 104 (environmental agreements), Chapter 7 (sanitary and phytosanitary measures), Chapter 9 (standards), Chapter 14 (financial services), Chapter 17 (intellectual property).

with the obligations of this Agreement or cause nullification or impairment."[72]

Like the WTO's DSU, Chapter 20 calls first for consultation between the parties, followed by conciliation before the "Free Trade Commission" (the trade ministers of the three NAFTA countries), the convening of binational panels (arbitration), and, ultimately, implementation of the arbitral report.[73] The arbitral decision is not automatically applicable, and in that sense (alone) is not "binding." Rather, once the decision is rendered, the parties "shall agree on the resolution of the dispute, which *normally* shall conform with the determinations and recommendations of the panel."[74] However, the prevailing party may retaliate with trade sanctions thirty days after the issuance of the panel report, if the parties do not earlier reach an accord.[75]

The arbitral panel process depends for its effectiveness on the use of a standing roster of international legal experts, ten designated by each NAFTA party, although during some periods it is questionable whether there has been agreement among the parties on roster members.[76] For each proceeding, a group of five arbitrators is to be chosen, primarily from the rosters; the chairperson is to be chosen by the two governments by agreement, with the choice by lot if there is no agreement.[77] Interestingly, in a unique "reverse selection process,"[78] one party chooses the two national arbitrators of the *other* party (e.g., in the dairy products case, discussed below, the two Canadian panelists were selected by the United States from candidates offered by Canada).

In many instances – except for certain environmentally related matters including those arising under the standards provisions of NAFTA[79] – the

[72] *Ibid.*, Article 2004; matters covered by Chapter 19 (antidumping and countervailing duty actions) are excluded. Private parties have no standing under Chapter 20, although those with political influence may be able to induce their respective governments to litigate on their behalf, as is evident from the cases.

[73] *Ibid.*, Articles 2006–2017. [74] *Ibid.*, Article 2018(1); emphasis supplied. [75] *Ibid.*

[76] Unlike the Chapter 19 rosters, the Chapter 20 roster members are not posted on the NAFTA Secretariat website, so their status is difficult to confirm.

[77] NAFTA, Article 2011. Article 2011(1)(c), provides that "[w]ithin 15 days of the selection of the chair, each disputing Party shall select two panelists who are citizens of the other disputing party."

[78] According to the senior USTR official this approach was suggested by Guillermo Aguilar, one of the principal Mexican NAFTA negotiators, in the belief that it would encourage governments nominating members of the standing rosters to be very careful about picking truly independent and objective individuals. Canada and the United States accepted the proposal, Senior USTR Official, *supra* fn. 65.

[79] NAFTA, Article 2005(3–4).

NAFTA parties have a choice between resorting to NAFTA, Chapter 20, or the WTO procedures, a logical approach given that the NAFTA parties' existing rights and obligations under GATT are explicitly reaffirmed and/or incorporated by reference in NAFTA.[80] Inevitably there will be disputes over NAFTA or other FTA provisions that have no direct parallel within the WTO system and cannot be litigated there, such as the disputes over cross-border trucking or sugar under specific NAFTA provisions or side letters. However, certain disputes among the NAFTA Parties, such as disagreements over the consistency of national antidumping or countervailing duty laws with the WTO Agreements, must be resolved through the WTO's dispute settlement procedure.[81]

Procedurally, Chapter 20 offers both disadvantages and advantages in comparison with the WTO's procedures. The inclusion of nationals of the disputing parties on NAFTA arbitral panels does not occur under GATT/WTO procedures; this may be an advantage, but it might also raise questions of bias toward the panelist's own government. Nor does the NAFTA mechanism provide a process for appeals, and the decision of the arbitrators may be more difficult to enforce given the lack of an independent international organization and secretariat such as the WTO. Each government created a national section of the NAFTA Secretariat to provide assistance to the NAFTA Free Trade Commission and to panels established under Chapters 19 and 20.[82] However, there is no independent secretariat comparable to that of the WTO to ensure that panels are promptly appointed and that delays in the process are avoided,[83] or legal staff to assist with the drafting of orders or decisions. This can help to explain why governments and NAFTA panelists regularly fail to comply with the relatively short deadlines provided in Chapter 20[84] and why it is possible for a recalcitrant party to stonewall a request of the others for the formation of a panel.

[80] *Ibid.*, Articles 103(1), 303 (incorporating GATT, Article III), 309 (incorporating GATT, Article XI).

[81] There is no Chapter 20 jurisdiction over such matters under NAFTA Article 2004, and only new national antidumping or countervailing duty laws may be challenged by the parties under NAFTA Article 1903.

[82] NAFTA, Article 2002(3).

[83] See David A. Gantz, "Dispute Settlement under the NAFTA and the WTO: Choice of Forum Opportunities and Risks for the NAFTA Parties," *American University International Law Review*, vol. 14 (1999), 1025, 1083–1095.

[84] For example, article 2011(1) provides that if the disputing parties cannot agree on panelists within fifteen days, the panel members will be chosen by lot from the roster. This has never happened, since there is no formal roster. Article 2016(2) provides for the panel to

During the first seven years of NAFTA, Chapter 20 was used on a regular basis but it has fallen into disuse since 2001. To date, there have been only three regular Chapter 20 panel decisions and one non-NAFTA proceeding using Chapter 20 rules,[85] *Dairy Products*, [86] *Broom Corn Brooms*[87] and *Cross-Border Trucking Services.*[88] Insofar as the author has been able to determine, at least ten other matters have reached at least the consultation stage under Chapter 20, involving (a) uranium exports (United States v. Canada, 1994).[89] Some, such as uranium, sportfishing, and potatoes, were resolved through consultations; others, such as sugar (Canada and Mexico) and tomatoes, were resolved among the governments in other contexts. Others, such as restrictions on small package delivery and Helms-Burton, appear to have been abandoned; there are no "active" Chapter 20 proceedings listed on the NAFTA Secretariat website.[90]

There appear to be several reasons for the declining use of Chapter 20. The US government had not been satisfied with the results under CFTA, Chapter 18; several of the five cases decided under those proceedings were thought to be poorly reasoned decisions, and there was no reason to believe that Chapter 20 would work better. Thus, even from the outset,

render its initial report within ninety days after the selection of the last panelist. This also has never occurred; in some instances the period required for briefings and a hearing have consumed almost the ninety days allotted for the entire process.

[85] The Softwood Lumber Agreement, May 29, 1996, 35 I.L.M. 1195, that sought (unsuccessfully in retrospect) to resolve a long-running dispute between Canada and the United States over Canada lumber exports to the United States, contained an ad hoc dispute settlement mechanism that is based in part on NAFTA Chapter 20 (Article V). An arbitral panel was convened in November 1998 to address an alleged violation of the agreement as a result of British Columbia's reduction of certain charges for harvesting timber from government-owned lands in the proceeding entitled, "In the Matter of British Columbia's June 1, 1998 Stumpage Reduction." The panel, operating generally under the NAFTA Chapter 20 Rules of Procedure, reviewed briefs submitted by the Parties, held a hearing and drafted a decision, but the case was settled by the Parties one day before the decision was due. See Exchange of Diplomatic Notes dated August 26, 1999.

[86] Tariffs Applied by Canada to Certain U.S.-Origin Agricultural Products, Case no. CDA-95-2008-01 (December 2, 1996), accessed September 10, 1996, www.nafta-sec-alena.org /Default.aspx?tabid=95&language=en-US.

[87] U.S. Safeguard Action Taken on Broomcorn Brooms from Mexico, Case no. USA-97-2008-01 (January 30, 1998).

[88] In the Matter of Cross-Border Trucking Services, Case no. USA-MEX-1998-2008-01 (February 6, 2001).

[89] For a discussion of these cases, see David A. Gantz, "Government-to-Government Dispute Resolution under NAFTA's Chapter 20: A Commentary on the Process," *American Review of International Arbitration*, vol. 11 (2002), 456–549.

[90] See Status Report of Panel Proceedings, Active NAFTA Panel Reviews

there was healthy skepticism of the process.[91] Second, some of the major trade-related issues within the region – including post 9/11 security and immigration – are not easily addressed under NAFTA. NAFTA contains a "national security" exception in Article 2102 similar to Article XXI of GATT, which would make formal dispute settlement under Chapter 20 problematic. In fact, the NAFTA parties appear to have been successful in addressing issues of border security through negotiations and planning without resorting to dispute settlement.[92] Also, some issues, such as those involving dumping and subsidies, effectively require resolution by the WTO's DSB.[93]

The apparent preference of the NAFTA parties for WTO dispute settlement is at least partially a result of the lengthy delays in several cases, notably *Cross-Border Trucking Services*, that reflect the inability of the parties to agree promptly on panelists.[94] There is also a feeling among some US government officials that it is better to have nonnationals than nationals of the parties as arbitrators.[95] Canada and Mexico, on the other hand, may well believe that when they are seeking changes in US trade law measures and policy it helps to have support from other members of the WTO, as discussed in Section V.

The US reluctance to use Chapter 20, compared to that of the other NAFTA Parties, is probably best illustrated by the Mexican sugar/corn syrup dispute, concerning US market access to Mexican sugar, which Mexico considered directly related to a dispute over Mexican taxes on high fructose corn syrup. The Chapter 20 case technically remains pending, but the US authorities refused for more than four years to appoint

[91] Discussion with senior USTR negotiator, Senior USTR Official, *supra* fn. 65.

[92] See "Fact Sheet: Security and Prosperity Partnership of North America," The White House (2005), accessed March 21, 2006, www.whitehouse.gov/news/releases/2005/03/200503234.html. Commits the NAFTA parties, inter alia, to develop a common security strategy to further secure North America.

[93] NAFTA, Article 1901(3) provides that, "[N]o provision of any other Chapter of this Agreement shall be construed as imposing obligations on a Party with respect to the Party's antidumping law or countervailing duty law."

[94] See Gantz, "Dispute Settlement under the NAFTA and the WTO," 1084. In Cross-Border Trucking Services, for example, there was a delay of approximately fifteen months between the formal request by Mexico for a panel and agreement by Mexico and the United States on the panelists.

[95] The author recalls a conversation with one of the US NAFTA negotiators some years ago in which the view was expressed that the foreign (e.g., Canadian or Mexican) nationals on the panel would tend to favor their own governments, while the US national panelists would make every effort to be absolutely objective without regard to nationality. This is despite the fact that in all three cases to date the panel decisions were unanimous.

panelists, a refusal that was effectively supported by a WTO panel.[96] A few years later, in the continuing controversy over the US embargo in imports of tuna from Mexico, the United States argued (probably correctly) that the matter should be referred to Chapter 20 because it involved environmental issues. Mexico, presumably because of the fiasco over delays with the sugar/corn syrup matter, refused and the matter was adjudicated at the WTO.[97]

3 NAFTA Chapter 19 – dumping and countervailing duties

The most innovative dispute settlement mechanism in NAFTA is Chapter 19, relating to antidumping and countervailing duty actions brought in one NAFTA member country against imports from another NAFTA country.[98] Numerous antidumping (AD) and countervailing duty (CVD) actions have been brought by national industries against the products of other NAFTA countries, in steel and steel products; beef, swine, and other agricultural products; high fructose corn syrup; cement; and softwood lumber, among others,[99] with more than 131 actions initiated. This is not surprising considering the volume of unfair trade cases brought by domestic industries in the NAFTA nations against imports from NAFTA partners, and the fact that "interested parties" in the various AD and CVD cases, as opposed to the governments, have effective control over whether actions are filed with binational panels.

The principal motivation for Chapter 19 was the adamant refusal of the United States to provide Canada with an exemption from US AD/CVD laws, a position that threatened to block agreement on

96 In *Mexico–Tax Measures on Soft Drinks and Other Beverages*, Appellate Body Report, WT/DS308/AB/R (adopted March 24, 2006), the Appellate Body upheld a panel decision rejecting Mexico's request that the panel and appellate body decline to exercise WTO jurisdiction because the matter was "inextricably linked to a broader dispute" which only a NAFTA [Chapter 20] panel could properly decide. The Appellate Body concluded that once it was established that a WTO panel had jurisdiction, it could not refuse to exercise it. See paras.10, 40, 57.

97 See Appellate Body Report, *United States – Measures Concerning the Importation, Marketing and Sale of Tuna and Tuna Products*, WT/DS381/AB/R (adopted May 16, 2012) [hereinafter *US – Tuna II* Appellate Body Report].

98 For a more extensive (but dated) discussion of the operation of Chapter 19 under NAFTA, see David A. Gantz, "Resolution of Trade Disputes under NAFTA's Chapter 19: The Lessons of Extending the Binational Panel Process to Mexico," *Law and Policy in International Business*, vol. 29 (297) (1998).

99 See NAFTA Secretariat, Status Report – NAFTA and FTA Panel Proceedings, accessed November 1, 2013, nafta-sec-alena.org/Default.aspx?tabid=94&language=en-US.

CFTA.[100] The United States agreed to the Chapter 19 process at Canada's behest, and Canada temporarily abandoned demands for special trade remedy laws – distinct from those available in the WTO/GATT system – to be applicable as between the United States and Canada.[101] The CFTA Chapter 19 mechanism also gave the parties an opportunity to challenge each other's proposed changes in their unfair trade laws with regard to consistency with NAFTA and GATT/WTO principles.

The factors that prompted Canada to insist on the Chapter 19 mechanism included the costs and delays of the appellate process in AD and CVD appeals to the US courts, and, ultimately, the belief that these courts had been overly deferential to the determinations of the Department of Commerce and the US International Trade Commission. Chapter 19, significantly, removed AD/CVD appeals from the jurisdiction of the federal courts of the United States and Canada, and substituted a panel process assuring that at least two Canadians would sit on any five-person binational panel reviewing a US agency decision, essentially as a surrogate for the federal courts of the parties.

Since the United States was no more willing in NAFTA than it had been in the CFTA to adopt more favorable AD and CVD rules for the FTA, Canada insisted on carrying over the mechanism; it would have been politically impossible for Ottawa to give up the hard-won mechanism that had secured the CFTA only a few years earlier.[102] Mexico

[100] One of the US NAFTA negotiators, Jean Anderson, has suggested that there was some sympathy in the US government for the argument that with the elimination of import duties and nontariff barriers for intraregional trade, the need for antidumping actions to control international price discrimination would be reduced or eliminated, although this was not the controlling view. There was little sympathy, however, on the US side for eliminating countervailing duty actions existing and possible future federal and provincial subsidies in Canada. Conference remarks, "The Future of NAFTA Chapter 19 Dispute Settlement," D.C. Bar (May 11, 2005) [hereinafter "D.C. Bar Conference"] (notes on file with author).

[101] See US General Accounting Office, US-Canada Free Trade Agreement, Factors Contributing to Controversy in Appeals of Trade Remedy Cases to Binational Panels, June 1995; *American Coalition for Competitive Trade* v. *United States*, D.C. Cir. No. 97-1036 (brief for intervenor the Government of Canada at 4) (September 5, 1997). Canada advocated, and later adopted in its 1996 FTA with Chile a position that there was no need for antidumping actions within FTAs, since there could be no international price discrimination where tariff and nontariff barriers had been abolished. Similar arguments were made for antisubsidy actions, with less economic justification in the absence of a centralized anticompetition authority, which NAFTA and most other FTAs lack.

[102] Conference Remarks of Douglas Waddell, former assistant deputy minister of trade, International Trade Canada, D.C. Bar Conference.

favored Chapter 11 for reasons basically similar to those articulated by Canada.[103] Mexico, as part of the package, agreed to make major procedural reforms in the administration of its AD and CVD laws, and to create a general right of judicial review of AD and CVD determinations.[104] In the author's personal experience, at least, these changes have been beneficial for US, Canadian, and other exporters to Mexico.

Chapter 19 jurisdiction extends only to decisions of administrative agencies of the three countries in AD and CVD cases; those relating, for example, to US, Canadian, or Mexican customs service rulings on classification, valuation, origin of merchandise, etc., are not subject to panel review[105] but remain with the federal courts. Under Chapter 19 a binational panel replaces the federal courts of the party imposing AD or CVDs. Appeals from the administrative agencies are referred to five-person arbitral panels, made of trade experts who are nationals of the two countries whose citizens are involved in antidumping or countervailing duty actions before the administrative agencies.

The binational panelists are citizens of the NAFTA parties selected from standing rosters of at least twenty-five individuals designated by each.[106] While they may be judges, the Panelists are normally trade practitioners or law professors serving on an ad hoc, part-time basis, paid very modest compensation.[107] However, unlike international tribunals, they do not apply international law (e.g., the provisions of the GATT and the WTO Agreements governing AD or CVD actions) except to the extent international trading rules are incorporated directly into national law. Panel procedures are in large part governed by tri-national rules and the Article 1904 Rules of Procedure as agreed by the three NAFTA parties, but with reference to national law where the rules do not apply.[108]

[103] Conference Remarks of Beatriz Leycegui, former member of the Mexican Secretariat of Commerce and Industrial Development (SECOFI), D.C. Bar Conference. Mexico was not seeking elimination of AD/CVD actions, but saw Chapter 19 as a means of fairly and definitively resolving such actions at reduced time and cost compared to litigation before the US Court of International Trade and the Court of Appeals of the Federal Circuit.

[104] NAFTA, Annex 1904.15 (Schedule of Mexico); the former government official suggests that US exporters subject to Mexican unfair trade proceedings have relied more on the Mexican writ of *amparo* than the binational panels for relief in difficult cases.

[105] NAFTA, Article 1904(1), limits Chapter 19 review to antidumping and countervailing duty determinations.

[106] *Ibid.*, Article 1901.2(1).

[107] CDN$400 per day until 2002, when the amount was increased to CDN$800 per day, roughly at par with the US dollar at current (November, 2013) exchange rates.

[108] See 59 Fed. Reg. 8,686 (1994).

Most observers would probably argue that Chapter 19 panel process has been on balance a success. As of September 2013, 131 Chapter 19 actions had been filed, thirty-three by US exporters, fifty by Canadian exporters, and forty by Mexican exporters.[109] Of these, more than a third were terminated by the request of the parties, and well over fifty decisions had been rendered.[110] Of the panel decisions rendered, a 2005 study determined that over 80 percent resulted in unanimous rulings regardless of panel member nationality.[111]

4 Subsequent US FTA dispute settlement provisions

All post-NAFTA FTAs have included a Chapter 20 or its equivalent, usually with only minor modifications.[112] For example, in Chapter 22 of the United States – Chile Free Trade Agreement, the basic Chapter 20 system consisting of consultations, mediation by the Commission and arbitration is reproduced with only a few significant changes.[113] One of these provides that six members of the twenty-person roster "shall be selected from among individuals who are non-Party nationals,[114] with the apparent hope innovation would facilitate panel selection, thereby avoiding the delays that have plagued the NAFTA Chapter 20 process. If the roster is appointed in a timely manner, chairpersons from neutral countries will effectively have been pre-approved, and, in appropriate circumstances, the entire (three-person)[115] panel can be chosen from non-American, non-Chilean nationals.

The United States – Chile FTA also provides greater specificity in the postreport phase of the proceedings. Provision is made for the adoption of a "mutually satisfactory action plan to resolve the dispute,"[116] along with detailed provisions, patterned after the DSU, to address situations where the disputing parties disagree over whether the prevailing party

[109] NAFTA Decisions and Reports (Chapter 19), accessed September 10, 2013, www.nafta-sec-alena.org/Default.aspx?tabid=95&language=en-US.

[110] *Ibid.* [111] Beatriz Leycegui.

[112] The dispute settlement provisions of the FTA with Jordan provide a more abbreviated section on dispute settlement compared to the rest, reflecting a bare-bones agreement (eighteen articles instead of 20–22 chapters). The dispute settlement process is compulsory but the report is nonbinding and the text contains no mention of trade sanctions. See United States – Jordan Free Trade Agreement, October 24, 2000, Article 17, accessed September 10, 2013, www.ustr.gov/sites/default/files/Jordan%20FTA.pdf.

[113] United States–Chile FTA, Articles 22.4–22.6. The principal additional changes relate to greater transparency and more detailed mechanisms for challenging the adequacy of postarbitration compliance or sanctioning by the parties.

[114] *Ibid.*, Article 22.7(1). [115] Instead of five, *ibid.*, Article 22.9(1)(a).

[116] *Ibid.*, Article 22.14(3).

proposed suspension of benefits is "manifestly excessive" or whether the responding party has eliminated the nonconformity of the measures complained against.[117] In such instances the original panel is to be reconvened.

Another innovation found in a series of subsequent US FTAs provides differing penalties for panel decisions relating to compliance with the labor and environmental chapters (which subsequent to NAFTA are incorporated in the body of the agreements rather than in side agreements). Here, instead of trade sanctions, labor and environmental violations are subject to monetary penalties in the earlier agreements.[118] In those with Colombia, Panama, Peru, and South Korea labor and environmental disputes are subject to the same penalties as trade disputes.[119]

None of the subsequent US FTAs (or those concluded by Canada or Mexico) contains a Chapter 19 or its equivalent; those provisions remain unique to NAFTA.

B *The ASEAN FTA and the "ASEAN Way"*

ASEAN as now constituted comprises more than 500 million persons, a land area of 4.5 million square kilometers, total trade of $850 billion (internal and external), and a GDP of approximately $700 billion.[120] The group encompasses several of the most dynamic trading nations in the world – Singapore, Malaysia, Thailand, Indonesia, and Vietnam – as well as several of the most restrictive nations – Laos and Myanmar – along with Brunei, Cambodia, and Indonesia. The wide differences in the levels of development, receptiveness to foreign investment and openness of the markets, among other factors, have led to a "least common denominator" effect. This means that the slowly reached accords among the ten members inevitably represent significant compromises by the bolder, more open member governments. Moreover, ASEAN

117 *Ibid.*, Article 22.15(3).

118 *Ibid.*, Article 22.16. The distinction between labor and environmental disputes and trade disputes with regard to penalties was eliminated beginning with the United States– Peru Trade Promotion Agreement, April 12, 2006, ch. 21, accessed September 10, 2013, www.ustr.gov/trade-agreements/free-trade-agreements/peru-tpa.

119 See e.g., United States–Peru Trade Promotion Agreement, US – Peru, April 12, 2006, Chapter 12, accessed February 17, 2014, www.ustr.gov/trade-agreements/free-trade-agreements/peru-tpa/final-text.

120 "Overview: Association of Southeast Asian Nations," ASEAN Secretariat, accessed June 28, 2012, aseansec.org/147.htm.

members have historically faced political and security challenges that discouraged and delayed greater economic integration, such as border clashes between Thailand and Cambodia,[121] so that maintaining peace and security in a violent region has historically been much more important than in crafting a western-style, rules-based model dispute settlement mechanism.

ASEAN and the 1994 ASEAN Free Trade Agreement (AFTA) consist of literally dozens of legal agreements and declarations, often overlapping and/or in conflict,[122] some of which remain un-ratified after many years. As a general rule, the treaties are only loosely enforced. As an ASEAN secretariat official has noted, "[e]ach member state is still very jealous of its own sovereignty and decision-making power."[123] Reluctance exists on the part of some of the member governments to accept firm commitments and to adopting functioning, and binding, legal rules and structures. The "ASEAN Way" traditionally has been a synonym for a vague consensus-based means of resolving differences among the members, resulting as often as not in delayed action or paralysis.

The first serious (although ultimately unsuccessful) effort at crafting a dispute settlement mechanism was in the 1976 Treaty of Amity, Chapter IV of which was devoted to "Pacific Settlement of Disputes" and was in significant part a nonaggression treaty. It created a High Council of ministerial level representatives of the members. The council was to take cognizance of a matter where direct negotiations were not successful in resolving the dispute, and offer its good offices, or mediation, but only with the consent of the parties.[124] The voluntary, politically oriented rather than legally oriented nature of this process is evident. Apparently the High Council was never utilized for dispute settlement even though a number of non-ASEAN members ultimately signed on.[125]

121 See e.g., Neil Chatterjee, "ASEAN Summit Fails to Resolve Thai–Cambodia Conflict," *Reuters* (Electronic ed.), May 8, 2011. Reports on ongoing border skirmishes.

122 See Table of Treaties/Agreements and Ratifications, ASEAN Secretariat, accessed June 28, 2012, aseansec.org/Ratification.pdf. Provides a list of 205 instruments that does not include dozens of ministerial and other declarations. This table is probably the best available source of the status of ratification of the various ASEAN and AFTA agreements.

123 See Thomas Fuller, "Wary Neighbors Turn into Partners in a Quickly Developing Southeast Asia," *The New York Times*, July 5, 2012 (quoting Secretary General Surin).

124 Treaty of Amity, Articles 15–16.

125 See Alyssa Greenwald, "The ASEAN-China Free Trade Area: A Legal Response to China's Economic Rise!," *Duke J. Comp. & Int'l L.*, vol. 16 (2006), 193, 205.

ASEAN recognition of the need for better dispute settlement was slow in coming. For example, at the time AFTA was created in 1992, the constituting agreement contained no dispute settlement provisions. A companion agreement provided only that "Any differences between the Member States concerning the interpretation or application of this Agreement or any arrangements arising therefrom shall, as far as possible, be settled amicably between the parties. Whenever necessary, an appropriate body shall be designated for the settlement of disputes."[126] The members left until later the creation of an "appropriate body."

In 1996, the ASEAN members, obviously mindful of the WTO's new dispute settlement mechanism, concluded a Protocol on Dispute Settlement.[127] The mechanism provides for the usual bilateral consultations, followed by the availability of good offices, conciliation or mediation provided (if the parties agree) by the "Meeting of Senior Economic Officials" (SEOM). If the dispute is not resolved within sixty days, the SEOM *may* establish a panel or refer the matter to a special body in charge of any special or additional rules and procedure (unspecified).[128] The panel would function in a manner similar to panels under the DSU.[129] The results are subject to appeal, not to a quasi-judicial body but to the politicians, the ASEAN Economic Ministers (AEM). The economic ministers participate in the deliberations but do not vote. Perhaps most significantly, where the AEM (or the SEOM if there is no appeal) makes a decision it is by simple majority, *not* by consensus.[130] The compliance, compensation and suspension of concession obligations also generally follow the DSU.[131]

In 2004, ASEAN adopted an "Enhanced Dispute Settlement Mechanism."[132] The revised mechanism, perhaps reflecting operational difficulties under the 1996 Protocol, moves closer to a rules-based, quasi-judicial, system. While a political body, the SEOM, is still responsible for establishing a panel, the SEOM no longer has discretion as to whether to do so. Rather, a panel *must* be established unless there is

(The author observes that China, India, Japan, Pakistan, Russia, Korea, New Zealand, and Australia ultimately became members.)

126 Economic Cooperation Framework Agreement, Article 9.

127 Protocol on Dispute Settlement Mechanism [hereinafter "Dispute Settlement Protocol I"], accessed November 2, 2007, www.aseansec.org/7813.htm

128 *Ibid.*, Articles 2–4. 129 DSU, Articles 11–12.

130 Dispute Settlement Protocol I, Articles 7–8. 131 DSU, Articles 21–22

132 ASEAN Protocol on Enhanced Dispute Settlement Mechanism, November 29, 2004, accessed November 2, 2007, www.aseansec.org/16755.htm.

a consensus not to do so.[133] The 2004 Protocol also provides for the creation of an Appellate Body by the AEM along WTO lines, with the members to be experts in law and international trade, not political operatives.[134]

The 2010 protocol designed to transform ASEAN into a rules-based system but was actually a regression; it is more a political than a legal mechanism.[135] In particular, arbitration is not mandatory, but occurs only when both parties give their consent or the ASEAN Coordinating Council directs the parties to go to arbitration, and no sanctions are available for noncompliance.[136]

C ASEAN – Australia – New Zealand FTA

Dispute settlement in the AANZ, in contrast to ASEAN, is much closer in form and language to the post-NAFTA US arbitration-based model, with some significant elements of the DSU also incorporated. Apparently, no arbitral proceedings have been brought during the four years since the treaty entered into force. The AANZ system contemplates consultation and compulsory arbitration on the request of the complaining party regarding "any measure affecting the operation, implementation or application of this Agreement" where there is nullification or impairment of benefits or an objective of the agreement is being impeded.[137]

AANZ provides for compliance within a reasonable period of time, usually within fifteen months, reflecting the DSU.[138] Provision is made for the convening of a Compliance Review Tribunal.[139] Absent compliance compensation is contemplated, with trade sanctions if no agreement on compensation can be reached. Where there is disagreement regarding whether the responding party has complied with the report of the panel, or whether the amount of retaliation is proper, the arbitral tribunal is to be reconvened.[140] Given that the ASEAN group has avoided mandatory dispute settlement in its own trade agreements, it can be reasonably assumed that the mechanism encompassed by the AANZ reflects the practice of New Zealand and Australia in other trade

133 *Ibid.*, Article 5(1). 134 *Ibid.*, Article 12.

135 Protocol to the ASEAN Charter on Dispute Settlement Mechanisms, April 8, 2010, accessed September 11, 2013. cil.nus.edu.sg/rp/pdf/2010%20Protocol%20to%20the%20ASEAN%20Charter%20on%20Dispute%20Settlement%20Mechanisms-pdf.pdf.

136 *Ibid.*, Articles 9, 10. 137 AANZ, Chapter 17, Article 2.

138 *Ibid.*, Chapter 17, Articles 15.2–15.3; see DSU, Article 21.3.

139 *Ibid.*, Chapter 17, Article 16. 140 *Ibid.*, Chapter 17, Article 17.

agreements. For example, the United States – Australia FTA contains government-to-government dispute settlement provisions highly similar to those found in NAFTA,[141] and those in the AANZ are in fact very similar to those in the United States – Australia FTA, with the usual consultation, mediation and binding arbitration approach.[142]

D *Andean court of justice*

The Andean Community was originally created in 1969 with the Cartagena Agreement by Bolivia, Chile, Colombia, Ecuador, and Peru "in order to jointly improve their peoples' standard of living through integration and economic and social cooperation."[143] Chile withdrew in 1976, Venezuela in 2006; Peru withdrew in 1992, but Chile later became an associate member. Until the 1980s the community followed an import substitution model and advocated a closed system with a substantial degree of state involvement in the economy. In 1989, at the end of the "lost decade" in Latin America this approach was replaced by an open model focusing on expanding trade and a market system. The free trade area was ultimately formed in 1993.[144] Subsequent discussion of forming a customs union in the first decade of the twenty-first century apparently did not result in such an institution. Given the greater interest by Colombia and Peru in other arrangements, such as the recently formed Pacific Alliance,[145] and Ecuador's interest in the antitrade Bolivarian Alliance,[146] the community is largely moribund.

The original Cartagena Agreement creating the Andean Group in 1969 did not provide for any binding dispute settlement mechanism. Rather, disputes were to be referred to the Andean Commission for informal, political-level resolution. If that process was ineffective in resolving

141 See United States – Australia Free Trade Agreement, US – Australia, May 18, 2004, 43 I.L.M. 1248 (2004), Chapter 21, accessed February 25, 2014, www.ustr.gov/trade-agreements/free-trade-agreements/australian-fta/final-text

142 See AANZ, Chapter 17

143 "Who Are We," Andean Community Secretariat, accessed April 4, 2011, www.comunidadandina.org/ingles/quienes/brief.htm 4/. See Cartagena Agreement, consolidated June 25, 2003, accessed October 31, 2013, www.sice.oas.org/trade/JUNAC/Decisiones/dec563e.asp.

144 See *ibid.*

145 See Alianza del Pacifico, accessed October 31, 2013, alianzapacifico.net/. The members in addition to Colombia and Peru include Chile and Mexico.

146 Alianza Bolivariana Para Los Pueblos de Nuestra America, accessed October 31, 2013, www.alianzabolivariana.org/. Other major members include Cuba, Honduras, Nicaragua, and Venezuela.

a dispute, it was to be resolved under the Latin American Free Trade Association's Dispute Settlement Protocol.[147] Presumably because this combined system was ineffective the Andean Court of Justice was created in 1979 and formed four years later.[148] It consisted of five independent magistrates who were to serve full-time for six-year terms.[149] The court's principal jurisdiction was over nullification actions filed by member countries, community institutions, or private natural or legal persons,[150] or noncompliance actions by the community institutions (the Board) or a member country when a member country fails to comply with its obligations under community treaties.[151] Also, "It is up to the Court to issue a pre-judicial interpretation of the rules comprising the legal system of the Cartagena Agreement, in order to ensure its uniform application in the territories of Member Countries" and judges of national courts may request advisory opinions on matters of community law from the court.[152]

One example of noncompliance actions was *Perú* v. *Secretaría General* (2003). In that proceeding Peru charged the community's General Secretariat of failing to comply with its obligations by failing to decide a claim Peru had made earlier involving Ecuador's import restrictions on certain goods originating within the community. The court upheld Peru's claim and issued an order directing the General Secretariat to comply with its obligations within ten days.[153] Professor Porata-Doria has assessed the court's activities as follows:

> A review of a representative sample of judgments of the Court shows a careful attention to detail, learned analysis, and sound judicial judgment. Accordingly, the Court constitutes an appropriate, efficient, and effective dispute resolution organism for the Andean Community. The Court's failure to recognize the validity of WTO norms that might conflict with Community norms, however, is a troubling fragmentation of international trade law.[154]

[147] 7 ILM 747 (1968).

[148] Treaty Creating the Court of Justice of the Cartagena Agreement [hereinafter "CJ Treaty"], May 28, 1979, accessed October 31, 2013, www.sice.oas.org/Trade/Junac/Tribunal/indexcar.asp.

[149] CJ Treaty, Articles 7–9. [150] *Ibid.*, Articles 17–19. [151] *Ibid.*, Articles 23–24.

[152] *Ibid.*, Articles 28–29.

[153] Rafael A. Porrata-Doria Jr, "Andean Community of Nations," "Court of Justice" in *Max Planck Encyclopedia of Public International Law*, 2010. Accessed October 31, 2013, www.mpepil.com.

[154] *Ibid.*

As with Mercosur, discussed infra, the Andean Group members, almost certainly influenced by the relative success of the GATT dispute mechanism and of the European Communities, including its Court of Justice in the 1970s, appear to have been willing to embrace a judicialized approach to dispute settlement, unlike the ASEAN group.

IV Common market courts of justice

A European Union

The EU is world's largest trader, accounting for approximately 20 percent of the world's exports and imports.[155] After sixty years, and despite the Eurozone crisis,[156] the EU remains the world's most successful customs union, having expanded from the original six members (France, Germany, Italy, Belgium, the Netherlands, and Luxemburg) to twenty-eight by July 2013. Tariffs and almost all nontariff barriers have long since been eliminated; most border controls no longer exist in the "single market." EU legislation ("regulations" and "directives") dominate in such areas as international trade regulation, intellectual property, competition law, and environmental law. With some exceptions, the EU has made major advances in the free movement of labor and capital as well as goods and services. After the entry into force of the Treaty of Lisbon in December 2009,[157] the commission's and European Parliament's authorities were again expanded. The commission's powers now encompass, inter alia, responsibility for foreign investment by the members in third countries and an office that is the equivalent of a foreign ministry, and the parliament has acquired a broader role in the legislative process and the budget, although little discussion has occurred in recent years considering the future of Europe's common security and military policies.[158]

155 "Trade," EU Commission, accessed September 16, 2013, europa.eu/pol/comm/index_en.htm.

156 See Jacob Funk Kirkegaard, "The Euro Area Crisis: Origin, Current Status and European and US Responses," October 27, 2011. Testimony before the House Committee on Foreign Affairs Subcommittee on Europe and Asia. Accessed June 27, 2012, www.piie.com/publications/testimony/kirkegaard20111027.pdf.

157 Treaty of Lisbon amending the Treaty on European Union and the Treaty establishing the European Community, December 13, 2007, *O.J.* C 306, December 17, 2007, accessed December 13, 2012, eur-lex.europa.eu/JOHtml.do?uri=OJ:C:2007:306:SOM:EN:HTML.

158 See Judy Dempsey, "Values Slide from Top of Merkel's List," *The New York Times*, November 26, 2012. Discusses the current focus of German foreign policy exclusively on economic issues.

The CJEU had its roots in the European Coal and Steel Community Treaty, which included among its organs a seven-member court of Justice and rendered 137 decisions in its seven years of existence.[159] The inclusion of a court to interpret the provisions of the treaty could have been anticipated. As George Berman and his collaborators have observed, "Given the Member States' [originally Belgium, Netherlands, Luxemburg, France, Germany and Italy] traditional commitment to the rule of law, it is not surprising that the European Community has also evolved into a highly structured and principled legal environment."[160] Martin Shapiro has noted that a constitutional or reviewing court is desirable whenever states "delegate authority to a designated agent" as they did in the ECSC. While there are many varieties of dispute settlement mechanisms, "the western political and legal tradition specifies one kind called Court." Further, "If a court was chosen it was in large part because the judicial institution had accumulated sufficient legitimacy and authority over time to promise an effective mode of resolving sub-set of the conflicts anticipated."[161] Shapiro further suggests that while the court was "a relatively minor matter in the intergovernmental supra-government conflict over the [ECSC] High Authority and Council," the court's judicial review would cover both the organs and the member states, "given the ambitions of France and Germany and the fears of the small states."[162]

The inclusion of the Court of Justice in the ECSC treaty was also consistent with concepts of European federalism extant in the late 1940s and early 1950s. For example, the European Union of Federalists insisted in 1947 that a federal authority aimed at unification of western Europe should include not only a government responsible to the people rather than to the federated states and an armed police system under the control of the federal government, but also "a Supreme Court capable of resolving possible disputes between state

[159] D. Lasok and J.W. Bridge, *Law and Institutions of the European Communities*, 4th edn (London: Butterworths, 1987); see Treaty Establishing the European Coal and Steel Community, April 18, 1951, Articles 31–45, accessed February, 2013, www.ab.gov.tr/files/ardb/evt/1_avrupa_birligi/1_3_antlasmalar/1_3_1_kurucu_antlasmalar/1951_treaty_establishing_ceca.pdf.

[160] George A. Berman, Roger J. Goebel, William J. Davey, and Eleanor M. Fox, *Cases and Materials on European Union Law*, 2nd edn (St. Paul: West Group, 2002).

[161] Martin Shapiro, "The European Court of Justice" in Paul Craig and Grainnne de Burca (eds.), *The Evolution of EU Law* (Oxford: Oxford University Press, 1999), 327–328.

[162] *Ibid.*, 329.

members of the federation."[163] (One could argue that the government responsible to the people remains to be achieved if at all and it is evident that the concept of a federal police force was not pursued.) Of the six original members, five had codified civil law systems based on the French (Napoleonic) model. Thus, it was predictable that the ECSC treaty and those that followed would incorporate a Court of Justice based on the French Conseil d'Etat (French Supreme Administrative Court).[164]

As some have suggested, the ECJ (to assure that the treaty would be complied with), along with the commission, the assembly (later the parliament), and the council and the Court of Justice were institutional arrangements, which, at the time, were the most remarkable features of the EEC Treaty.[165] Perhaps one of the driving forces then and now, as ECJ Judge Constantinos Kakouris has suggested, is that the ECJ is responsible not only for interpreting the treaties but accepting the guidance of the unwritten, superior "Law," that is attributable directly in the people. For example, in his view the effect of *Van Gend en Loos* was to "take community law out of the hands of the politicians and bureaucrats and to give it to the people."[166]

The EU's court system, with the CJEU and General Court (GC) (the ECJ and Court of First Instance, respectively, before the entry into force of the Treaty of Lisbon in 2009), is by far and away the busiest of any comparable institution in the world. For example, during the four-year period 2008–2012, approximately 630 new actions were submitted to the CJEU each year, including direct actions, appeals, references for a preliminary ruling, applications for or concerning interim measures, and opinions.[167] For the lower GC, the number of new cases was about the same, consisting of actions for annulment, failure to act, enforcement

[163] See "European Union of Federalists: Resolutions of the Montreux Conference, August 1974" in W. Lipges and W. Loth (eds.), *Documents on the History of European Integration*, vol. 4 (Berlin: De Gruyter, 1991), 35–36. Reproduced in Damian Chalmers, *European Union Law 6–7*, vol. 1 (Dartmouth: Ashgate, 1998).

[164] See Walter Cairns, *European Union Law 9* (London: Cavendish Publishing, 1997).

[165] *Ibid.*, 18.

[166] Harm Schepel and Erhard Blankenburg, "Mobilizing the European Court of Justice" in Grainne de Burca and J.H.H. Weiler (eds.), *The European Courts of Justice* (Oxford: Oxford University Press, 2001), 9–11. The authors quote Judge Kakouris, F. Mancini, D. Keeling, and others.

[167] *Court of Justice of the European Community, Annual Report 2012*, January 1, 2013, Chapter 1-D, table 2, accessed September 2013, curia.europa.eu/jcms/upload/docs/application/pdf/2013-04/192685_2012_6020_cdj_ra_2012_en_proof_01.pdf.

of arbitration clauses, intellectual property, staff matters, appeals, appeals concerning interim measures, and special forms of procedure.[168]

The jurisdiction of these courts is thus broad, much more so than any trade courts or other mechanisms under other RTAs or the WTO's DSU, loosely comparable only to the jurisdiction of the federal courts in the United States.[169] The aspect of CJEU jurisdiction most analogous to the dispute settlement mechanism found in FTAs such as NAFTA provides that "A Member State which considers that another Member State has failed to fulfill an obligation under the Treaties may bring the matter before the Court of Justice of the European Union."[170] Should the court find that the member state has failed to comply with one of the treaties, the state is required to comply with the court's judgment; the court may impose a "lump sum or penalty payment" on the offending member.[171]

However, given the fact that the entities of the EU, particularly the commission and the council, exercise substantial independent or shared powers, CJEU jurisdiction extends, inter alia, to situations where the commission (rather than another government) seeks enforcement of a determination that a member state has failed to comply with an obligation under the treaties.[172] The CJEU's jurisdiction extends as well to review of the legality of legislative acts as well as most acts of the council, commission, and European Central Bank, or situations in which any of the four entities has failed to act.[173] It may also give advisory rulings on questions relating to the interpretation of the EU treaties or the validity and interpretation of acts of the institutions of the EU when requested to do so by a court of one of the member states.[174] The GC's jurisdiction also extends to "direct actions brought by natural or legal persons against acts of Community institutions (addressed to them or directly concerning them as individuals) or against a failure to act on the part of those institutions, for example, a case brought by a company against a Commission decision imposing a fine on that company."[175]

[168] *Ibid.*, Chapter 2-C, table 3.

[169] See e.g., Gerald Paul McAlinn, Dan Rose, and John P. Stern, *An Introduction to American Law* (Durham: Carolina Academic Press, 2010), 141–153. The article discusses the jurisdiction of the federal courts.

[170] Consolidated Version of the Treaty on the Functioning of the European Union, O.J. 26.10.12, C 326/46, Article 259.

[171] *Ibid.*, Article 260. [172] *Ibid.*, Article 258. [173] *Ibid.*, Articles 263, 265.

[174] *Ibid.*, Article 267.

[175] "The European Court of First Instance – Background Guide," EU Business, November 26, 2009, accessed October 31, 2013, www.eubusiness.com/topics/eulaw/court-first-instance/.

For purposes of this chapter, the obvious question is whether the EU dispute settlement experience, and in particular the CJEU, is transferrable to any other customs union or common market. The answer is almost certainly "no." While the CJEU may be copied in terms of structure and even procedures, the outcomes are likely to be very different, as experience in Latin America and Africa demonstrates. The CJEU system works in large part because all of the member states have a high level of respect for the rule of law (even though it flags from time to time) and a shared history of economic and political cooperation (again with some slippage here and there) for over sixty years. Politically and economically the EU system has been challenged in recent years, and the willingness of some members to act for the greater good has been sorely tested, but these controversies do not seem to have significantly affected the CJEU or threatened its future as a highly competent, independent judicial entity.

B *African customs unions: COMESA, SADC, and SACU*

Africa is no stranger to RTAs; there are broad networks of accords in many areas of the continent.[176] Some twenty-eight RTAs, including seven customs unions and the rest FTAs, exist.[177] The continent has been fragmented into at least fourteen regional economic communities with overlapping membership.[178] One of the newer efforts designed to deal with these problems is a proposed agreement that would combine the SADC, the COMESA and the SACU, thus "ameliorating the problem

[176] Parts of this section are drawn from Gantz, *Liberalization of International Trade after Doha*, Chapter 10.

These include, in addition to SACU, the African Union; Central African Economic and Monetary Community; the Common Market for Eastern and Southern Africa; the East African Economic Community; Economic Community of Central African States; Economic Community of West African States; West African Economic and Monetary Union; and the South African Development Association. See USTR, *2007 Comprehensive Report on U.S. Trade and Investment Policy Toward Sub-Saharan Africa and Implementation of the African Growth and Opportunity Act*, May 2007, 29–30, annex C, accessed July 11, 2012, www.ustr.gov/sites/default/files/asset_upload_file762_11294.pdf.

[177] "Regional Trade Agreements Information System," WTO, accessed December 7, 2012, rtais.wto.org/UI/PublicMaintainRTAHome.aspx.

[178] Peter Draper, "Africa's Tripartite Preferential Trade Agreement and the PTA-WTO Coherence Debate: Yin and Yang" in ICSID, *Trade and Development Symposium: Perspectives on the Multilateral Trading System*, December 2011, accessed July 11, 2012, www.ictsdsymposium.org/en/events/trade-and-development-symposium.

of overlapping memberships among the three constituent RECs (regional economic communities)."[179] The result if implemented would be a simplification of trade and applicable legal rules, particularly conflicting rules of origin, which would presumably make the trade regulation process a good deal more transparent and less confusing for importers, both within and outside the tripartite agreement nations. This could be an important step toward the expressed pan-African objective of creating a single African Economic Community by 2025,[180] an objective that generates considerable skepticism among those who have followed the current lack of significant accomplishment.

Such consolidation would, inter alia, require conforming the dispute settlement mechanisms that currently exist in each of the regional organizations (typically with overlapping membership). Most have not developed a significant body of jurisprudence on trade issues, although investment issues as well as those relating to human rights matters have been brought before some of the tribunals.[181] As Professor Gathii notes, "the African RTA judiciaries are not simply custodians of the trading arrangements – in fact, they do much less dispute settlement around trade issues compared to the broad range of cases they have assumed jurisdiction over. Many of these judiciaries . . . have also entertained cases that are well beyond their treaty-defined jurisdiction bases."[182] This section discusses the judicial entities of each of the three RTAs noted above for which consolidation is being planned, along with one of the most active tribunals, the East African Court of Justice (EACJ), all of which except the SACU reflect to some extent the CJEU's influence on the structure.

1 COMESA's court of justice

COMESA's court of justice (COJ) is established in the COMESA treaty, which created one of the largest African RTAs, with nineteen members.[183] The COJ is to "ensure the application of law in the interpretation and

[179] *Ibid.* [180] *Ibid.*

[181] This section draws on Gathii, *African Regional Trade Agreements*, Chapter 12.

[182] *Ibid.*, 264.

[183] Treaty Establishing the Common Market for Eastern and Southern Africa, December 21, 1981, Article 7, accessed October 7, 2013, www.comesa.int/attachments/article/28/COMESA_Treaty.pdf. The members include Burundi, the Comoros, the Congo, Djibouti, Egypt, Eritrea, Ethiopia, Kenya, Libya, Madagascar, Malawi, Mauritius, Rwanda, Seychelles, Sudan, Swaziland, Uganda, Zambia, and Zimbabwe, a group that includes a handful of relatively well-functioning states as well as others that are failing or failed.

application of this treaty" and matters within the ambit of the court are to be subject to no other method of settlement.[184] As with the CJEU, member states may seek preliminary rulings from the COJ[185]; COJ decisions have precedence over national court decisions.[186] In certain instances the COJ is open to natural and legal persons in addition to governments, as well as to disputes between COMESA and its employees, but disputes between COMESA's secretariat and the member states require special arrangements.[187] Based on the COJ's website the operations of the COJ are still in the implementation stage.[188]

2 South African Development Community Tribunal

The SADC Tribunal illustrates the supreme challenges of operating an international tribunal among states where the rule of law is weak or nonexistent. The tribunal is designed to "ensure [. . .] adherence to, and proper interpretation of the provisions of, the SADC Treaty and subsidiary instruments, and adjudicates upon disputes referred to it."[189] It was established under the SADC Treaty[190] and a protocol to the treaty that has apparently not been fully ratified.[191] The tribunal is to consist of at least ten members, five regular and five to effectively serve as substitutes, appointed from the nationals of the member states.[192] In addition to jurisdiction between states over the interpretation and application of the treaty and protocols, the tribunal may give advisory opinions when requested by certain SADC organs such as the summit and council.

After the tribunal issued several rulings against the Government of Zimbabwe, the tribunal was suspended in August 2012![193] The principal ruling that led to the suspension involved an action by land-owners in Zimbabwe challenging the government's expropriatory land reform

[184] COMESA Treaty, Articles 31, 34. [185] *Ibid.*, Article 30. [186] *Ibid.*, Article 29.

[187] *Ibid.*, Articles 26–28.

[188] "About COMESA," COMESA Court of Justice, accessed October 7, 2013, about.comesa.int/index.php?option=com_content&view=article&id=83:comesa-court-of-justice&catid=43:institutions&Itemid=133.

[189] "SADC – Toward a Common Future," SADC Tribunal, accessed October 7, 2013, www.sadc.int/about-sadc/sadc-institutions/tribun/. The members include Angola, Botswana, Congo, Lesotho, Madagascar, Malawi, Mauritius, Mozambique, Namibia, Seychelles, South Africa, Swaziland, Tanzania, Zambia, and Zimbabwe.

[190] Treaty of the Southern African Development Community, August 17, 1992, accessed October 7, 2013, www.sadc.int/files/9113/5292/9434/SADC_Treaty.pdf.

[191] Gathii, *African Regional Trade Agreements*, 285. [192] Protocol, Article 3.1

[193] "SADC – Toward a Common Future," SADC Tribunal, accessed October 7, 2013, www.sadc.int/about-sadc/sadc-institutions/tribun/.

program.[194] Jurisdiction was considered questionable since none of the SADC documents provide protection for human rights, but the tribunal reasoned that its mandate to develop its own jurisprudence under rules of public international law gave it the necessary authority to exercise jurisdiction.[195] The matter also became embroiled in a conflict over jurisdiction with the High Court of South Africa and with the High Court of Zambia, relating to the same expropriations. While the claimants prevailed both before the tribunal and in the High Court of South Africa, Zimbabwe did not of course comply and apparently succeeded few years later in bringing about the suspension of the tribunal; the highest organ of the SADC, the summit, was responsible for the suspension and would have been charged with enforcing the tribunal's decision.[196]

3 Southern African Customs Union Tribunal

The 2002 SACU Agreement[197] called for the establishment of an ad hoc tribunal. The three-member tribunal is charged with settling "Any dispute regarding the interpretation of application of this Agreement, or any dispute arising thereunder at the request of the Council."[198] Decisions are by majority vote and are final and binding. It is contemplated that the council will create an approved roster of potential tribunal members from which the parties to the dispute will choose three persons to form each tribunal. Rules of procedure are to be determined by the tribunal itself, an approach that would permit different procedures for different disputes. The obvious weakness in this system is the requirement that a dispute must be referred by the council (a political body) to the tribunal. Since the council acts by consensus, any party to a dispute could block referral to the tribunal simply by refusing to go along with the consensus. The existence of the council/tribunal mechanism of dispute resolution explicitly does not preclude direct consultations between two or more

[194] *Mike Campbell (Pvt) Ltd. and 78 Others* v. *The Republic of Zimbabwe*, SADC(T), Case no. 2/2007 [2008] SADCT 2, November 28, 2008, discussed in Gathii, *African Regional Trade Agreements*, 288.

[195] Gathii, *African Regional Trade Agreements*, 290.

[196] *Ibid.*, 290–297. Discusses the various legal actions.

[197] 2002 Southern African Customs Union (SACU) Agreement [Bots.-Lesotho-Namib.-S. Afr.-Swaz.] [hereinafter "SACU Agreement"], October 21, 2002, accessed October 7, 2013, www.sacu.int/main.php?include=docs/legislation/2002-agreement/main.html. See also David A. Gantz, *Regional Trade Agreements: Law, Policy and Practice* (Durham: Carolina Academic Press, 2009), 441–442.

[198] *Ibid.*, Article 13.

parties with the objective of finding a solution.[199] It is too early to determine whether the tribunal will function effectively although there is good reason for skepticism; as of mid-2013 the provisions of the SACU Agreement creating the tribunal had not been implemented.[200]

4 East African Court of Justice

The EACJ was established under the East African Community (EAC) Treaty.[201] The treaty gives the court "jurisdiction over the interpretation and application of the Treaty ... [as well as] ... such other original, appellate, human rights and other jurisdiction as ... determined by the Council."[202] Here as elsewhere in Africa, the tribunals have jurisdiction going well beyond trade and investment issues. The court is divided into a First Instance Division and an Appellate Division, presumably adapting the CJEU and the EU General Court to local requirements.[203] To date, however, the court does not have jurisdiction to hear appeals from the high courts of the member states.

A ten-year report on the court by its registrar, John Eudes Ruhangisa, suggested that the court had successfully issued rules of procedure and for arbitration, and been accessible to "a range of stakeholders from State level to that of a simple individual."[204] However, delays of justice had also taken place in the form of the granting of ex parte orders, unnecessary adjournments, and delays after hearings in issuing judgments.[205]

The first ruling issued by the court determined on a highly technical basis that the actions of one of the community's organs, the Council on Legal and Judicial Affairs, in assuming control over certain bills before the assembly had been ultra vires because the council had not been

199 *Ibid.*, Article 15.

200 See "Tribunal," SACU, accessed October 7, 2013, www.sacu.int/main.php?id=388. This section states that the tribunal has yet to be established.

201 Treaty Establishing the East African Community, November 30, 1999, accessed October 7, 2013, www.eac.int/index.php?option=com_content&view=article&id=49&Itemid=66. The members are Burundi, Kenya, Rwanda, Tanzania, and Uganda, nations with a relatively strong rule of law by African standards.

202 EAC Treaty, Article 27; see Gathii, *African Regional Trade Agreements*, 268–279. Discusses the court structure and jurisprudence.

203 "The East African Court of Justice," EAC, accessed October 7, 2013, www.eacj.org/.

204 John Eudes Ruhangisa, "The East African Court of Justice (Achievements and Challenges)," November 2011, 3. Accessed October 7, 2013, http://eacj.huriweb.org/wp-content/uploads/2013/09/EACJ-Ten-Years-of-Operation.pdf

205 *Ibid.*, 5.

constituted solely of ministers, but also of attorneys general.[206] (The treaty was subsequently amended to validate participation of the attorneys general.)

Among the rulings issued by the court was a determination that the court had no jurisdiction over questions relating to the membership of the East African Legislative Assembly, opining that, because the issue involved Tanzanian representatives, jurisdiction lay with the High Court of Tanzania.[207] In a similar case, complainants challenged Kenya's process of election Kenya's members of the East African Legislative Assembly on grounds that the rules of the Kenyan National Assembly, the body responsible for choosing the Kenyan representatives, had infringed the EAC Treaty. The court ruled that the procedures for such elections are determined by the respective national assembly and not by another body.[208]

It is suggested, perhaps optimistically, that:

> The functionalist approach to integration departs from the assumption that violence and power become obsolete as a means by which to achieve ends and aspirations. It claims that group conflict is not inherent in humans once they realize that everyone shares common social goals and values. The establishment of courts of justice within regional groupings follows from this approach to integration and therefore always responds to the need for a mechanism of peaceful settlement of disputes when they occur. Arguably, in this regard the jurisdiction conferred upon the EACJ is wide enough to enable the peoples of East Africa to access the justice mechanism put in place by the EAC Treaty.[209]

However, Dr Ruhangisa cautioned that in addition to broad jurisdiction the court needed to "build users' confidence in its justice through fair and impartial decisions,"[210] noting that to date, despite some intimidation, the court "has so far proved to be an independent and impartial body."[211] One interesting aspect of the EACJ is that under the applicable treaties it shares jurisdiction over human rights matters with the African Union's Court on Human and Peoples' Rights,[212] confirming that African RTA courts at least in theory exercise jurisdiction that is far

[206] See *ibid.*, 10–11. Discusses *Callist Andrew Mwatella and 2 Others* v. *EAC*, Reference no. 1 of 2005.

[207] See ibid., 12–15. Discusses *Christopher Mtikila* v. *The Attorney General of the United Republic of Tanzania and the Secretary General of the East African Community*. Reference no. 8 of 2007.

[208] *Ibid.*, 12–13; see also Gathii, *African Regional Trade Agreements*, 269–270.

[209] Ruhangsia, "The East African Court of Justice," 14. [210] *Ibid.* [211] *Ibid.* [212] *Ibid.*

broader than that of the typical trade tribunal under RTAs in most other parts of the world.

C *Mercosur*

Mercosur (Argentina, Brazil, Paraguay, Uruguay, and Venezuela)[213] represents one of the most ambitious and important RTAs ever concluded, at least on paper. As Mark Keller has observed, "Mercosur remains an economic and political force in the region, uniting South America's two largest economies and providing a potential springboard for Latin American integration."[214] In the aggregate, the five current Mercosur member nations have more than 275 million inhabitants and an aggregate GDP of $3.3 trillion, about 75 percent of which is attributable to Brazil.[215] Brazil itself is the world's sixth largest economy and until 2012 was one of the most dynamic in Latin America because of factors that have little to do with Mercosur per se, including China's demand for soy and iron ore exports in the past decade and preparations for the FIFA (soccer) World Cup in 2014 and the Olympics in 2016.[216] Mercosur with its current five members represents 47.5 percent of Latin America's population and 59 percent of its GDP.[217] From 1990 to 1997, intra-regional trade increased from $4 billion to $20 billion. Since that time, between the Brazilian devaluation in 1999 and the Argentine devaluation and economic crisis of 2001, the customs union has foundered.[218]

Mercosur may hold more promise in the longer term for trade liberalization among the member states and within South America, but progress toward a completed customs union after twenty years has been unimpressive. The members (particularly Argentina and Brazil) are becoming more, rather than less, protectionist,[219] not only toward the

[213] With Bolivia and Guyana in discussions to join as of late 2013.

[214] Mark Keller, "Explainer: What Is Mercosur?," Americas Society/Council of the Americas, August 2, 2012, 9, accessed August 16, 2012, www.as-coa.org/articles/explainer-what-Mercosur-0.

[215] IDB, "Venezuela, a Mercosur Member," *INTAL Monthly Newsletter*, August, 2012; see also, "Mercosur Trade," EU, accessed June 27, 2012, trade.ec.europa.eu/doclib/docs/2006/september/tradoc_113488.pdf.

[216] See "US. Export Fact Sheet," International Trade Administration (US Dept. of Commerce), September 11, 2012. Extolls the benefits for US enterprises of exporting to Brazil.

[217] *Ibid.* [218] See Keller, "Explainer: What Is Mercosur?," 9.

[219] See Ed Taylor, "Brazil Increases Excise Tax on Car Imports," *International Trade Report*, vol. 28 *(BNA)* 1546 (September 22, 2011).

outside world but also internally. This lack of ability to move forward is reflected as well in the dispute settlement mechanism.

The initial dispute settlement provisions (Annex III of the Treaty of Asuncion) provided only for direct negotiations, followed by referral of the matter to the Common Market Group (CMG) for recommendations to the disputing parties. It was anticipated that a permanent dispute settlement mechanism would be adopted by 1994.[220] The first step in this direction was almost immediately taken through adoption of the Protocol of Brasilia for the Settlement of Disputes.[221] The Brasilia Protocol contemplated a more extensive, although still politically rather than judicially oriented, mechanism. Under the Brasilia Protocol, if consultations and review by the CMG were not successful in resolution of the controversy, either party could refer the dispute to binding international arbitration under rules similar to those in NAFTA, Chapter 20. Each party to the Brasilia Protocol accepted ipso facto the jurisdiction of the arbitral tribunal.[222] There was no requirement that the arbitral decision be reviewed or approved by the CMG and the prevailing party was authorized to adopt trade sanctions if the other did not comply with the arbitral ruling.[223]

One innovation went well beyond NAFTA Chapter 20. The dispute settlement process authorized aggrieved private parties to challenge, albeit indirectly, "the adoption or application, by a State Party, or legal or administrative measures of a restrictive or discriminatory nature or leading to unfair competition, in violation of the Treaty of Asuncion, the agreement concluded within the framework thereof, decisions of the Council of the Common Market or resolutions of the Common Market Group."[224] Such challenges were to be referred by the private party first to the National Section of the CMG. Should the National Section accept the claim, it could either enter into direct negotiations with the corresponding National Section, or submit the claim to the CMG.[225] The CMG had the authority to convene a Group of Exports to provide a report for the CMG. Based on the expert report, any state party (presumably the challenging Party) could request the other party to take "corrective measures." If such measures were not taken within fifteen days, arbitration under the procedures described earlier could be instituted.[226]

[220] Treaty of Asuncion, annex III, paras. 1–2.

[221] Brasilia Protocol, December 17, 1991, 36 I.L.M. 691 (1997).

[222] *Ibid.*, Articles 7–9.

[223] *Ibid.*, Articles 22–23.

[224] *Ibid.*, Article 25.

[225] *Ibid.*, Articles 27–28.

[226] *Ibid.*, Article 32.

Apparently because of the limited effectiveness of the Brasilia Protocol the Mercosur parties upgraded the regional dispute settlement mechanism in 2002, with the Protocol of Olivos for the Settlement of Disputes.[227] The Olivos Protocol explicitly permits the requesting party to choose between the Mercosur mechanism and the WTO's DSB for resolving a dispute.[228] It incorporates provisions for direct negotiations, involvement of the CMG and, ultimately, binding arbitration.[229] The major innovation is the creation of a Permanent Review Tribunal (PRT), patterned to a considerable extent after the Appellate Body of the WTO.[230]

The specter of national judges in four nations interpreting and applying community law in an inconsistent manner due to the lack of any supranational judicial system has stimulated further discussion of a Mercosur court. The decision not to create a truly supranational court was intentional. While Uruguayan interests favored such an institution Brazilian negotiators reportedly believed that the conditions in 2002 were not yet ripe and that enforcement of the decisions would in any event not be considered consistent with the Brazilian Constitution.[231] Brazilian views prevailed, then and now.

Still, the Olivos Protocol addresses the issue by making provision for the issuance by the PRC of advisory opinions to national courts under regulations that were to be issued by the CCM.[232] Insofar as I have been able to determine, no advisory opinions have been requested nor issued to date. This may be explained at least in part by the fact that under the regulations, except where the request emanates from national supreme courts, unanimity among the member states is required. Thus, any member state with an objection may block the request.

Whether these Olivos Protocol mechanisms are adequate depends to some extent on what they are judged against. By FTA standards, the government-to-government dispute settlement mechanisms in the Olivos Protocol compare favorably to those in other agreements, such as NAFTA Chapter 20 and the AANZ FTA. The protocol also contains detailed procedural rules and affords decision-making by a quasi-judicial body rather than a political one. By comparison to the EU, a standard to which Mercosur aspires in so many areas, it has significant shortcomings. As Professor Porrata-Doria has pointed out, the Olivos Protocol is not

[227] Olivos Protocol, February 18, 2002, 42 I.L.M. 2 (2003). [228] *Ibid.*, Article 2.
[229] *Ibid.*, Articles 4–16. [230] See DSU, Articles 17–18. [231] *Ibid.*, 7–14.
[232] Olivos Protocol, Article 3.

effective in protecting individual party rights under community law, and provides no jurisdiction under which the Mercosur institutions themselves can enforce state compliance with Mercosur norms.[233] The PRC thus falls well short of the EU's court system, in particular because it is an arbitral body rather than a permanent group of professional judges.[234]

V Why is DSU preferred by most parties over RTA mechanisms?

It is apparent from the volume of actions before the WTO's DSU and the relatively few state-to-state actions before all of the RTA dispute mechanisms except the unique Court of Justice and General Court of the EU, that WTO members prefer to bring trade actions to the WTO whenever the subject matter permits them to do so. On the political side, there are benefits for complainants in operating under the DSU, where other like-minded members can be encouraged to become involved as third participants, lending political as well as legal weight to DSU proceedings. For example, in the most recent chapter of the dispute between the United States and Mexico over US restrictions on tuna exports by Mexico to the United States – a matter the United States sought to have resolved under NAFTA, Chapter 20 – fifteen other WTO members intervened as third participants, almost all in support of Mexico.[235] Had the action been brought under NAFTA's Chapter 20 only one other nation – Canada – could have supported Mexico's legal positions.

Similarly, even though El Salvador, Costa Rica, Honduras, Guatemala, and the Dominican Republic are all parties to the CAFTA-DR with its NAFTA-like government-to-government dispute settlement mechanism,[236] the complainants chose to bring a safeguards-related claim against the Dominican Republic under the WTO's DSU.[237] Six other WTO members participated in the proceedings as third parties, including

[233] Rafael A. Porrata-Doria Jr, *Mercosur: The Common Market of the Southern Cone* (Durham: Carolina Academic Press, 2005), 39–40.

[234] *Ibid.*, 40.

[235] *US – Tuna II* Appellate Body Report. The third participants were Argentina, Australia, Brazil, Canada, China, Chinese Taipei, Ecuador, EU, Guatemala, Japan, Korea, New Zealand, Thailand, Turkey, and Venezuela.

[236] The United States – Central America – Dominican Republic Free Trade Agreement, U.S.-CAFTA-DR, August 5, 2004, Chapter 20, accessed February 26, 2014, www.ustr.gov/trade-agreements/free-trade-agreements/cafta-dr-dominican-republic-central-america-fta/final-text.

[237] See Panel Report, *Dominican Republic – Safeguard Measures on Imports of Polypropylene Bags and Tubular Fabric*, WT/DS 415, 416, 417, 418 (adopted February 22, 2012).

the United States, the EU, Columbia, Panama, Turkey, and China, most of which made oral presentations at the hearing.[238] (Some of the third parties' comments supported the claimants in part, while others supported the Dominican Republic.)[239] If either the complainants or the respondent were seeking solidarity and support, they found a level in the WTO system that would not have been available under CAFTA-DR.

Also, as discussed earlier, compared to most of the regional dispute settlement mechanisms, the DSU system has several critically important advantages in addition to provision for third party status: (1) the proceedings, including the appointment of panelists, are usually relatively prompt because an independent secretariat is primarily responsible for choosing panelists, minimizing the opportunities for delay; (2) those same secretariats are staffed with expert trade lawyers who assist both the panelists and, if appropriate, the parties, in key phases of the proceedings; (3) an Appellate Body and its own expert secretariat assure a high level of predictability and consistency among reports where complainants choose to appeal; and (4) despite some flaws enforcement through trade sanctions has been well-established. Detailed legal rules, many of which have been interpreted and applied by the Appellate Body in earlier proceedings, also tend to assure predictable outcomes in most instances.

No RTA dispute settlement mechanism other than the *sui generis* CJEU meets or exceeds the standard established by the DSU system over eighteen years.

This is not to suggest that the DSU process is ideal. The challenges include the costs of litigation, particularly for poorer countries; delays in reaching a final decision where any findings of inconsistency of a measure with one of the covered agreements are not retroactive; the Appellate Body's lack of remand authority, which assures that many cases are not finally resolved because the Appellate Body lacks the necessary factual record to "complete the analysis"; the second round of panel and appellate body proceedings necessitated when agreement is not reached on whether compliance has taken place; and the absence of a monetary payment as an alternative to trade sanctions which many members may not find it economically viable to apply against large economy members such as the EU and the United States. Nor does there seem any reasonable likelihood that the DSU can be revised given the demise of the Doha Development Round.

[238] *Ibid.*, paras. 1.6, 1.10.

[239] *Ibid.*, paras. 7.41–7.49. Not all third parties submitted comments.

The problems of RTA mechanisms beyond the CJEU are also legion. Even with NAFTA, Chapter 20, a deficient mechanism for assuring that panels once requested are promptly appointed has soured all three parties on the Chapter 20 system. While political interference appears to be at worst a minor problem in systems such those of Mercosur and the Andean Community, there is less assurance that reports once issued will be complied with. Elsewhere, particularly in ASEAN, there is effectively no compulsory dispute settlement; rather if disputes are to be resolved it is through diplomatic consultations rather than third-party arbitration. In Africa, despite a few successes, the courts either have not been constituted at all, have overstepped their jurisdiction and thus been reigned in or dissolved, or have been ignored when venturing into highly charged political disputes.

In the author's view it is also fair to suggest, particularly with Asia and Africa, that where there is a weak level of respect for the rule of law generally it is unreasonable to expect that regional arbitral bodies or courts will function in a legally sound manner. Here and elsewhere, there are all too many nations that attach more importance to concluding an agreement than to assuring that its provisions are faithfully implemented. Many of the developing countries in Africa, Latin America, and Asia have also inherited from the colonial powers, particularly the United Kingdom and France, legal systems which in structure are relatively well-designed but are difficult to implement where strong interest in building well-functioning, corruption-free legal institutions is lacking, including but not limited to dispute settlement mechanisms.

VI Improving the effectiveness of regional dispute settlement mechanisms

Under these circumstances, what can be done to make RTA dispute settlement mechanism work better? Unfortunately, the problem is much more likely to be a lack of political will than the shortage of viable legal solutions. With mechanisms such as NAFTA, Chapter 20, the parties need to commit themselves to following existing Chapter 20 legal provisions that provide for prompt choice of panelists (essentially by lot) when the involved parties cannot agree on the panelists in direct negotiations. Ironically, choosing panelists under Chapter 19 has generally been less controversial in these proceedings that effectively involve private interested parties who are challenging the validity of national administrative agencies, although staff shortages in the NAFTA secretariat have significantly contributed to delays, particularly in actions against US administrative agencies.

With the knowledge that WTO members have of the mechanics of the DSU, it is obvious that effective dispute settlement requires that panels be instituted at the request of the complaining party, without any need for approval by a political body that includes in its membership the responding party, or requires approval before a report finding inconsistency with a party's obligations is implemented, or made subject to trade sanctions. An appointing authority is also a virtual necessity to avoid delaying tactics by the responding party. In most instances, a much higher level of transparency would likely make it more difficult for any party to delay the process. It is, for example, ironic that the identities of NAFTA, Chapter 20 roster members are not publicly available (in contrast to the Chapter 19 members, whose names appear on the secretariat's website).

In some instances effective RTA mechanisms are discouraged by such factors as the lack of an independent secretariat (even in NAFTA) or insufficient staffing. It is probably unrealistic to expect that a professional secretariat will be created and maintained for a bilateral or trilateral FTA where the number of state-to-state disputes is likely to be miniscule. This excuse does not, however, apply to larger groupings, such as ASEAN, AANZ, or, if completed, the Trans-Pacific Partnership. It would probably make sense legally and practically to create a centralized secretariat for the many bilateral or trilateral RTAs, but such a result is likely unacceptable politically for many nations. Nor, as noted above, is it reasonable to establish a well-functioning binding arbitral mechanism among nations where respect for the rule of law and the independence and education of judges is deficient.

2

Establishing permanent regional good offices for trade disputes in Asia

CHANG-FA LO

I Introduction

Asia is geographically wide and culturally diverse. In general, Asia is also economically vigorous. Many countries in Asia have long and intimate relations among themselves in various contexts. These countries form cooperative arrangements, including regional trade agreements, to enhance their ties. However, many countries in this region still have complicated problems with their neighbouring countries. Hence, it is difficult to identify common interests or positions for the whole region in a range of areas.

However, with respect to the area of trade, the perspective could be quite different. Certain common practices or attitudes in the field of international trade can be traced and some common interests can be identified. One of these common interests is the existence of a stable environment for business activities, and one of the mechanisms to ensure a stable environment is the establishment of an effective but acceptable dispute settlement mechanism for the region.

If one looks at the practice of Asian countries with respect to the settlement of disputes in international trade, a diverse picture is revealed. Asian countries do not generally exclude detailed and binding rules for settling possible trade disputes from the multilateral, regional and bilateral trade agreements to which they are parties. However, Asian countries do not usually resort to the settlement of trade disputes under such detailed and binding rule-based dispute settlement mechanisms. There are some possible interpretations or reasons for this phenomenon, including the general attitude, the philosophy and the needed capacity. Some of these possible interpretations might not reflect the current situation. However, some other interpretations might still play a role in the practice of these countries. Based on this background, there should be proper grounds to argue that some kind of balance between detailed rules and a practical forum for trade disputes might be more desirable at this stage.

In addition to the introduction of the issue in this part, Section II of this chapter will explain the phenomenon of Asian countries' acceptance of the inclusion of detailed dispute settlement rules in the multilateral, regional and bilateral trade agreements to which they are parties. Section III will then explain Asian countries' lack of enthusiasm about engaging in detailed rule-based dispute settlement procedures. Section IV attempts to interpret this lack of enthusiasm from various perspectives, including the trade volumes among Asian countries and with countries in other regions, the generally resistant attitude towards power-oriented regimes, the generally non-litigious philosophy, and the capacity, experiences and resources of Asian countries. The chapter will argue in Section V that having some kind of mechanism with the elements of neutrality, lower resource demands and less legality could help Asian countries to manage their trade relations. Consistent with these arguments, the creation of some kind of permanent regional good office that provides an efficient but non-contentious and pragmatic solution for trade disputes might be a desirable option at the present time. It should be noted at this juncture that the author does not argue that confrontational and litigious proceedings should never be an option for Asian countries to resolve their disputes or would always lead to an adverse effect on their relations. It is argued here that building trust through the professional but more amicable resolution of disputes could be a first step that could lead to a more legalistic and rule-based approach to resolving disputes among Asian countries.

II Asian countries' acceptance of detailed dispute settlement rules

Asian countries' general position about the existence of detailed dispute settlement rules to govern trade disputes is reflected in their overall acceptance of the Understanding on Rules and Procedures Governing the Settlement of Disputes (DSU) under the World Trade Organization (WTO). When the DSU was negotiated, Asian countries expressed no apparent opposition against or serious concerns about the adoption of the new understanding to replace the previous broad and less detailed rules under Articles 22 and 23 of the General Agreement on Tariffs and Trade (1947; GATT). Even in the Doha round of the current DSU negotiations, no clear position was adopted by Asian countries to make the rules less detailed, less binding or less rule-oriented. The Asian countries that negotiated the reform of the DSU did not challenge the system of the DSU as a whole. Instead, those countries focused more on some technical issues. For instance, Japan and Korea raised a "sequencing issue" during the negotiations; China suggested the enhancement of third-party participation; and Malaysia proposed ideas concerning the costs of participating in the proceedings for developing countries.[1] These facts demonstrate the general acceptance of a detailed rule-based regime at the multilateral level.

Asian countries' position on detailed rules is also reflected in the wide practice of having detailed dispute settlement provisions or dispute settlement chapters in free trade agreements (FTAs) with other countries in Asia and with countries in other regions. From the FTAs concluded between or among Asian countries, it is also clear that most of the FTAs negotiated in recent years have detailed dispute settlement procedures with a binding effect for the results.

In earlier times, many Asian countries favoured broad and less-detailed dispute settlement rules. For instance, the Association of Southeast Asian Nations (ASEAN) was said to have adopted the "ASEAN Way" to settle disputes through diplomatic methods, including consultation and consensus, in its early years.[2] In addition, when the ASEAN economic integration was initiated, this approach was maintained. In 1992, ASEAN countries signed the ASEAN Free Trade Agreement (AFTA), which has consultation provisions in Article 8 that serve as the basis for the settlement of disputes. Paragraph 3 of this article provides that "Any differences between the Member States concerning the interpretation or application of this Agreement or any arrangement arising therefrom shall, as far as possible, be settled amicably between the parties. If such differences cannot be settled amicably, it shall be submitted to the Council referred to in Article 7 of this Agreement, and if necessary, to the AEM [ASEAN Economic Ministers]."[3] This approach is consistent with the "ASEAN Way" of dispute settlement.

The type of broad and loosely drafted dispute settlement provisions that are being adopted could also be a result of special considerations. For instance, in 2003, China signed the Closer Economic Partnership

[1] C.L. Lim, "East Asia's Engagement with Cosmopolitan Ideals under Its Trade Treaty Dispute Provisions", *McGill L.J.*, vol. 56 (2011), 821, 845.

[2] *Ibid.*, 489.

[3] The test of the AFTA can be found at www.worldtradelaw.net/fta/agreements/afta.pdf.

Arrangements (CEPAs) with Hong Kong and Macao. From the WTO's perspective, these agreements are trade agreements concluded between separate customs territories and are of the nature of FTAs under Article XXIV of the GATT and economic integration agreements under Article V of the General Agreement on Trade in Services (GATS). However, from China's perspective, these agreements are of an intra-state nature. These parties decided to draft their dispute settlement procedures in a flexible and non-binding manner. Article 19 of both CEPAs establishes the Joint Steering Committee, which is comprised of senior representatives or officials from two sides, the functions of which include resolving disputes that may arise during the implementation of the CEPA (paragraph 3(3)). No detailed rules by which the parties could legally resolve their trade issues were included in these agreements. It seems that the reason for this decision was the Chinese political consideration not to have its disputes with its special autonomous regions (namely Hong Kong and Macao) resolved under an international binding dispute settlement mechanism.

Except for the above situations, most FTAs concluded by Asian countries in recent years include detailed dispute settlement provisions. For instance, ASEAN countries signed the Protocol on Dispute Settlement Mechanism in 1996 to establish more detailed rules for resolving trade disputes that arise from their FTAs. In 2004, those countries further used a WTO DSU model to formulate their rules and signed the ASEAN Protocol on Enhanced Dispute Settlement Mechanism (hereafter the 2004 Protocol) to replace the 1996 Protocol.[4] The adoption of the 2004 Protocol occurred due to the excessively bureaucratic and ineffective nature of the 1996 Protocol, which was not invoked until the 2004 Protocol was concluded.[5] The 2004 Protocol designates that ASEAN's Senior Economic Officials Meeting (SEOM) will administer the protocol and the consultation and dispute settlement provisions of the covered agreements. The authority of SEOM includes the establishment of panels, the adoption of panel and Appellate Body reports, the maintenance of surveillance of the implementation of findings and recommendations, and the authorization of the suspension of concessions and other

[4] The text of the 2004 Protocol can be found at www.asean.org/news/item/asean-protocol-on-enhanced-dispute-settlement-mechanism.

[5] Weidong Zhu, *The Dispute Settlement Mechanism of ASEAN Free Trade Area (AFTA) and Its Implications for SADC* (2008), 2. The paper is available at www.tipmoz.com/library/resources/Oldsite1/Dispute_Settlement_Mechanism_ASEAN.pdf.

obligations.[6] The 2004 Protocol encourages its member states to settle their disputes through an amicable consultation process.[7] The 2004 Protocol also has good offices and conciliation or mediation, panel and appellate review procedures that allow disputing parties to resolve their cases in a more legalistic manner.[8] Panel and Appellate Body reports are adopted by the SEOM by negative consensus. In other words, the reports shall be adopted unless the SEOM decides by consensus not to adopt them.[9] Under the design, the dispute settlement findings and recommendations will be respected and implemented, and no specific country will be able to prevent the adoption of the panel or Appellate Body reports. This requirement is the key element that ensures adherence to the obligations of the member states. The elements and procedures of the 2004 Protocol are highly similar to those provided in the DSU under the WTO.

In addition to the WTO dispute settlement model, which is adopted by many FTAs concluded between Asian countries, many FTAs concluded between Asian countries and the United States adopt the NAFTA model (i.e., the model adopted by the North American Free Trade Agreement) for their dispute settlement mechanisms. This model has only the panel procedure (instead of two "instances"), gives strong legal force to the panel reports, and very importantly, emphasizes prompt implementation of unilateral retaliation, monetary settlements and numerical limits for special disputes that typically concern labour and the environment.[10] For instance, the US–Singapore FTA[11] establishes consultations and additional dispute settlement procedures to deal with measures that are inconsistent with obligations or to deal with the failure to carry out obligations through consultation. If the FTA forum is selected by the parties, a dispute settlement panel will be established to hear the case, to issue its report and to make recommendations for the resolution of the dispute.[12] There is no appellate review procedure in the US–Singapore FTA. However, the panel report has a determinative effect. On receipt of the final report of a panel, the parties shall agree on the resolution of the dispute, which shall normally conform to the determinations and

[6] 2004 Protocol, Article 2. [7] *Ibid.*, Article 3. [8] *Ibid.*, Articles 4, 5, 12.

[9] *Ibid.*, Articles 9.1, 12.12.

[10] Dukgeun Ahn, "Dispute Settlement Systems in Asian FTAs: Issues and Problems", *Asian Journal of WTO & Int' L. Pol'y*, vol. 8 (2013), 413.

[11] The text of the US–Singapore FTA can be found at www.ustr.gov/sites/default/files/uploads/agreements/fta/singapore/asset_upload_file708_4036.pdf.

[12] US–Singapore FTA, Articles 20.1, 20.2.

recommendations of the panel. If the panel determines that a party has not conformed to its obligations under the FTA, the resolution shall be to eliminate the non-conformity.[13] In addition, a very important feature of the US–Singapore FTA, which is different from the WTO dispute settlement model, is the approach to non-implementation. The US–Singapore FTA allows the suspension of benefits by the complaining party and an annual monetary assessment to be paid by the party complained against.[14] The unilateral suspension of benefits and monetary compensation are effective measures for ensuring that panel reports will be fully implemented.

It also should be noted that under the WTO dispute settlement model, good offices, mediation and conciliation are key components of the rules, but in the NAFTA model, such amicable procedures are not necessarily included. For instance, in the US–Singapore FTA, the procedures of good offices, conciliation and mediation are only available for labour issues[15] and environment issues.[16] These procedures are not explicitly provided for other disputes that arise from the FTA.

Although it has been suggested that Asian FTAs should not adopt "Western-style" dispute settlement mechanisms, as such mechanisms might not be suitable for the region,[17] Asian countries do not have a general attitude of rejecting or opposing the inclusion of detailed and binding dispute settlement procedures in their FTAs.

III Asian countries' lack of enthusiasm about engaging in detailed rule-based dispute settlement procedures

Certainly, Asian countries are increasingly using the dispute settlement mechanism under the WTO. More specifically, a limited number of Asian countries are currently using WTO dispute resolution procedures more frequently.

For instance, China has been gradually becoming a major player in dispute settlement procedures, both initiating complaints and engaging in responses.[18] However, compared with the absolute and relative

[13] *Ibid.*, Article 20.5. [14] *Ibid.*, Article 20.6. [15] *Ibid.*, Article 17.6.

[16] *Ibid.*, Article 18.7.

[17] Songling Yang, "The Contribution of East and Southeast Asia Legal Culture on the Improvement of DSMs in Newly Created FTAs in this Region", *I.J.P.L. & P.*, vol. 2 (2) (2012), 105–128.

[18] Matthew Kennedy, "China's Role in WTO Dispute Settlement", *World T.R.*, vol. 11 (4) (2012), 555, 58–59.

numbers of times the WTO mechanism has been used by countries in other regions, Asian countries definitely cannot be considered to be enthusiastic about relying on detailed rule-based procedures to settle their cases under the multilateral regime, despite the fact that they do not reject detailed dispute settlement rules, as explained above.

There are three ways to observe the general attitude of a country concerning the utilization of dispute settlement mechanisms. One approach is to look at the number of cases in which the countries engage in real disputes as one of the disputing parties, either on the complaining side or on the responding side. Even if a country is the responding party, such engagements still show the country's intention to resolve the dispute through a formal procedure, instead of voluntarily removing or modifying the challenged measure. Another approach is to look only at the complaining side to determine whether a country decides to initiate the dispute settlement procedure. This approach provides a more precise understanding of the general attitude of a disputing country. As a complaining party, a country would have to make a more difficult decision about bringing the dispute to a formal procedure. It is that country's sole decision to initiate the legal proceeding. Such a decision more correctly reflects the country's general attitude about utilizing the mechanism. In contrast, as a responding party, the country only passively responds to the complaint. In many cases, it is not important whether the responding party intends to engage in the procedure. It is very likely that the country does not have an option to avoid being brought into the procedure.

An even more focused approach is to look at both the complaining and the responding sides to observe their interactions. This approach reflects both the decision to initiate the proceedings by the complaining side and the decision not to settle the case before a formal proceeding is initiated. This chapter uses the last approach to observe this phenomenon. The author chose this approach because although there are many more cases in which Asian countries were the complaining parties against non-Asian countries or were the responding parties in cases that were initiated by non-Asian countries,[19] focusing on Asian countries as complaining parties and their Asian trading partners as responding parties under the DSU of the WTO would more precisely reflect the attitude of Asian countries.

[19] For instance, China, Japan, India and Korea were "frequent targets" in quite some WTO cases.

From this perspective, although a very large portion of WTO members are from Asia, their reliance on the WTO dispute settlement procedure is limited. Based on statistics, it is apparent that Asian countries are relatively hesitant to resort to formal dispute settlement procedures to settle trade disputes among themselves. A total of 466 complaints were initiated under the WTO. However, only fourteen complaints were brought by an Asian WTO member against another Asian WTO member.

Certainly, if we include the disputes settlement cases in which only one of the parties was an Asian WTO member, the number is far higher. However, in comparison with the total number of WTO cases, this number is still relatively small. Slightly more than one hundred complaints were initiated by Asian countries in total.

The disputes that involved two Asian WTO members as the complaining and responding parties are listed below:

(1) Bangladesh against India
- (i) India – Antidumping Measure on Batteries from Bangladesh (DS306)

(2) Japan against China
- (ii) China – Measures Related to the Exportation of Rare Earths, Tungsten and Molybdenum (DS433)
- (iii) China – Measures Imposing Antidumping Duties on High-Performance Stainless Steel Seamless Tubes ("HP-SSST") from Japan (DS454)

(3) Taiwan against India
- (iv) India – Antidumping Measures on Certain Products from the Separate Customs Territory of Taiwan, Penghu, Kinmen and Matsu (DS318)

(4) India against Turkey
- (v) Turkey – Restrictions on Imports of Textile and Clothing Products (DS34)
- (vi) Turkey – Safeguard Measures on Imports of Cotton Yarn (Other Than Sewing Thread) (DS428)

(5) Indonesia against Korea
- (vii) Korea – Antidumping Duties on Imports of Certain Paper from Indonesia (DS312)

(6) Japan against Indonesia
- (viii) Indonesia – Certain Measures Affecting the Automobile Industry (DS55)

(ix) Indonesia – Certain Measures Affecting the Automobile Industry (DS64)

(7) Korea against Japan

(x) Japan – Import Quotas on Dried Laver and Seasoned Laver (DS323)

(xi) Japan – Countervailing Duties on Dynamic Random Access Memories from Korea (DS336)

(8) Korea against the Philippines

(xii) Philippines – Antidumping Measures Regarding Polypropylene Resins from Korea (DS215)

(9) Singapore against Malaysia

(xiii) Malaysia – Prohibition of Imports of Polyethylene and Polypropylene (DS1)

(10) Philippines against Thailand

(xiv) Thailand – Customs and Fiscal Measures on Cigarettes from the Philippines (DS371)

Trade disputes definitely arise from FTAs concluded between Asian countries. However, no statistics are available for an assessment. In addition, these types of disputes are not widely reported, with only limited exceptions. It is a reasonable assumption that disputes that arose from Asian FTAs and were settled under dispute settlement rules are very limited.

IV Factors affecting the lack of enthusiasm about formal rule-based dispute settlement procedures

1 Trade volume cannot explain the lack of enthusiasm

In theory, more international transactions could result in more frequent disputes between traders and hence more disputes between the respective countries. Thus, one logical interpretation of the fact that few disputes were initiated between Asian countries could be a low volume of trade among Asian countries. However, this is not the case. Asian countries engage vigorously in international trade not only with countries in other regions but also with countries within Asia.

Using trade between China and ASEAN countries as an example, it is reported that China has surpassed the United States and become the largest trading partner for ASEAN countries, "going from being an inconsequential trading partner in the region as recently as the late

1990s to a two-way trade volume of $293 billion in 2010".[20] In addition, many Asian economies, such as China, Hong Kong, Indonesia, Malaysia, Singapore, Korea, Taiwan, Thailand and Vietnam, are commonly identified as rapid-growth markets, which are predicted to dominate world trade over the next ten years and to collectively account for a quarter of global consumption by 2020.[21]

These facts show that Asian countries are generally economically active and that intra-Asia trade is vigorous. The fact that there were few dispute cases between Asian countries that were resolved at the multilateral and regional levels must not be the result of a low volume of trade among the countries in this region.

2 No general favouritism for power-oriented regimes exists, so power orientation is not the reason

The fact that few intra-Asia trade disputes were settled by the WTO or by FTAs might also be explained by a general attitude among Asian countries to not prefer rule-oriented dispute settlement proceedings. This statement was partly true in earlier times. For instance, the above-mentioned previous practice by ASEAN countries reflected the preference for diplomatic solutions. However, this is not true today because when the WTO was established and the dispute settlement rules were transformed from power-oriented approach into more rule-oriented approach, Asian countries were in favour of that change. Actually, in addition to the developed countries that proposed the detailed rules, developing countries, including Asian developing countries, were all in favour of a rule-oriented dispute settlement system, rather than a power-oriented or diplomacy-oriented dispute settlement system.[22] In addition, as mentioned above, recent Asian FTAs almost always contain detailed dispute settlement rules.

[20] See Jane Perlez, "For Clinton, an Effort to Rechannel the Rivalry with China", *New York Times*, 8 July 2012, a7; cited from Flynt Leverett and Hillary Mann Leverett, "The Balance of Power, Public Goods, and the Lost Art of Grand Strategy: American Policy toward the Person Gulf and Rising Asia in the 21st Century", *Penn S.J.L.Int'l Affairs*, vol. 1, 202, 233, footnote 64.

[21] "Asia-Pacific's Trade Flows to Experience Exponential Growth in the Next Decade", 28 November 2012. www.ey.com/GL/en/Newsroom/News-releases/News_Asia-Pacific-trade-flows-to-experience-exponential-growth-in-the-next-decade.

[22] Lucas Eduardo F.A. Spadano, "Cross-agreement Retaliation in the WTO Dispute Settlement System: An Important Enforcement Mechanism for Developing Countries?", *World T.R.*, vol. 7 (3) (2008), 511, 512.

Thus, the fact that there were few dispute settlement cases is not the result of Asian countries' general preference for power-oriented regimes.

3 *A general non-litigious philosophy and pragmatism exist*

It is a general perception that less contentious settlement of disputes, such as mediation/conciliation, is the preferred method of dispute settlement in most Asian jurisdictions.[23]

It might be argued that East Asian countries' attitude was affected by the Confucius philosophy.[24] Confucius (551–497 BC) was a Chinese thinker and educator, who founded the *Ru* School of thought and whose teachings in the form of short and concise statements were preserved in the *Analects*.[25] A large portion of this work is still taught in schools in some countries, including Taiwan and China. Under this philosophy, harmonious solutions for differences and avoiding litigious and confrontational situations are preferred because litigation always leads to an adverse result. In addition, for many Asian people, confrontational proceedings, such as litigation, mean that the disputing parties are ready to rupture their relationship. Such proceedings are an emotionally serious matter. This philosophy has influenced not only Taiwan and

[23] Lucas Eduardo F.A. Spadano, "Cross-agreement Retaliation in the WTO Dispute Settlement System: An Important Enforcement Mechanism for Developing Countries?", *World T.R.*, vol. 7 (3) (2008), 511, 512. A paper provides possible explanations for Asian countries' lower participation in WTO dispute settlement procedures. These explanations include (1) the legal capacity of the states concerned, (2) the traditional culture of non-litigation, (3) the cost of WTO actions, (4) levels of democracy, (5) political considerations, (6) trading stakes and (7) the use of Asian production networks. Michael Ewing-Chow, Alex W.S. Goh and Akshay Kolse, "Are Asian WTO members Using the WTO DSU 'Effectively'?", *J.I.E.L.*, vol. 16 (3), (2013), 669–705. I agree with some of these reasons, including capacity, culture, and cost, but I do not necessarily agree with the others. A.F.M. Maniruzzaman, "The Problems and Challenges Facing Settlement of International Energy Disputes by ADR Methods in Asia: The Way Forward", *I.E.L.T.R.*, vol. 6 (2003), 193, 194.

[24] Confucianism, which was developed from the teachings of Confucius and his disciples, is concerned with the "principles of good conduct, practical wisdom, and proper social relationships". It "has influenced the Chinese attitude toward life, set the patterns of living and standards of social value, and provided the background for Chinese political theories and institutions. It has spread from China to Korea, Japan, and Vietnam." *Philosophy of Religion*, www.qcc.cuny.edu/socialsciences/ppecorino/phil_of_religion_text/CHAPTER_2_RELIGIONS/Confucianism.htm.

[25] See www.chinaeducenter.com/en/chistory.php.

China but also other East Asian and some Southeast Asian countries, including Korea, Japan, Vietnam and, to some extent, Singapore.[26] For instance, in Japan, Confucian thought played an important role in the development of ethical and political philosophies in earlier ages.[27] This influence still affects the general practice of the Japanese people. General comments have been made concerning the Japanese as non-litigious because of deep-rooted cultural preferences.[28]

It must be said that more and more Asian people are learning "litigious ways" of protecting their business interests in domestic court proceedings and in arbitrations,[29] especially in some fields, such as "derivative action" (lawsuits brought by a shareholder on behalf of the company to enforce or defend a legal right or claim), in which the Japanese have become quite litigious.[30] This change is partly influenced by the western legal culture and the practice of resorting to an effective dispute resolution mechanism and partially reflects the nature of modern society, in which business competition is fierce and the involved economic interests could be enormous. The increasing use of international arbitration is also a reflection of this phenomenon. This change is also partly due to the increasing acceptance of foreign arbitration by domestic legislators and courts in Asia and the promotion of international arbitration in Asia by some administering institutions (including those in Hong Kong and Singapore).[31] However, the litigious attitude has not become so prevalent or overwhelming in all fields in East Asia so as to totally override the general preference for the harmonious resolution of disputes.

Although it is not clear whether and to what extent this philosophy has an effect on the attitudes of countries in Southeast Asia, the general situation in these regions has revealed the similarities in their attitudes. For instance, some studies focused on the tradition that Indonesian society is somewhat "non-litigious" and that the Indonesian people are

[26] See www.ibiblio.org/chinesehistory/contents/02cul/c04s04.html.

[27] See www.onmarkproductions.com/html/japanese-confucianism.html.

[28] John Owen Haley, "The Myth of the Reluctant Litigant", *J. Japanese Stud.*, vol. 4 (1978), 359.

[29] See www.linkedin.com/groups/Yet-Another-Sign-Japan-is-1848408.S.5822299243070640128.

[30] Dan W. Puchniak, "The Derivative Action in Asia: A Complex Reality", *Berkeley Bus. L.J.*, vol. 9 (1) (2012), 4.

[31] Kent Phillips and Roger Milburn, "Arbitration Builds on Progress in Asia", www.scmp.m/business/companies/article/1274205/arbitration-builds-progress-asia.

thought to prefer amicable dispute settlement through negotiation and to value greatly the preservation of commercial relationships.[32]

From the WTO's perspective, Asian countries' non-litigious attitude is also "evidenced by the increasing tendency to participate as co-complainants or third parties and the substantial number of disputes being resolved through consultations".[33] To elaborate a little further, some Asian countries have a lower extent of psychological difficulty concerning becoming co-complainants and avoiding the confrontational situation in which they are the sole challengers against the disputed measures of their trading partners. Many countries participated in the WTO dispute settlement procedure as third parties with the hope that their participation would help correct the challenged measures that also affect their trade interests, without the need to confront the complained party. More importantly, the preference for settling cases at the consultation stage also reflects the general tendency of Asian countries to deal with international disputes in a less confrontational manner.

4 *Capacity, experiences and resources also affect attitude*

There is also a possible argument that Asian countries have a lower capacity for legal and language skills. WTO dispute settlement procedures are highly complicated and technical. These procedures require sophisticated legal representatives to handle the cases in an effective manner. Many Asian countries do not possess a sufficient legal capacity and the necessary staff to effectively engage in such proceedings. These countries are also generally less experienced in effectively conducting rule-based dispute settlement proceedings at international fora. Many Asian countries have relatively limited resources to effectively engage in WTO litigations.

In addition, most parts of Asia are non-English-speaking countries. Language is definitely an important barrier that these countries must overcome to effectively engage in international litigation. If these countries are to hire experienced law firms from the United States or Europe to conduct the proceedings for them, the costs might be beyond their

[32] Noah Rubins, "The Enforcement and Annulment of International Arbitration Awards in Indonesia", *Am. U. Int'l L. Rev.*, vol. 20 (2005), 359, 364.

[33] Chulsu Kim, "East Asia in the WTO Dispute Settlement Mechanism" in Yasuhei Taniguchi, Alan Yanovich and Jan Bohanes (eds.), *The WTO in the Twenty-First Century: Dispute Settlement, Negotiations, and Regionalism in Asia* (Cambridge: Cambridge University Press, 2007), 261, 264.

financial capability. Of course, for some Asian countries, such as Singapore, the Philippines and India, language is not a problem. Other factors, such as the general attitude towards litigation and the needed resources, might play more important roles for these countries.

The problems of low expertise, financial resources and language skills are solved to a large extent by the availability of the assistance that has been provided by the Advisory Centre on WTO Law since 2001.[34] In addition, after being exposed to WTO legal proceedings for an extended period of time and gaining experience from litigations with WTO members from other regions, Asian countries are not that inexperienced. Thus, the lack of legal and language capacity, experience and resources plays a smaller role in the decision by Asian countries to enter into detailed rule-based dispute settlement procedures under multilateral and regional regimes.

5 *Strategic considerations are sometimes but not always the reason*

Self-restraint concerning initiating detailed rule-based dispute settlement proceedings could also be caused by strategic considerations. For instance, China has used the WTO dispute settlement procedure more frequently and initiated some complaints against the United States and Europe. However, interestingly, China has not initiated a complaint against a developing country member, even though the relevant measures adopted by the developing countries were similar to those that were adopted by the United States and the European Union and challenged by China under the WTO. One example is Turkey's textile safeguards against imports from China.[35] There is no clear evidence concerning the reason for this differentiation. A possible interpretation could be China's strategic consideration to avoid bringing complaints against other developing countries so as to maintain its leadership role in the developing world.

It must be said, however, that although such strategic considerations may play a role in China's decision to initiate complaints against other Asian countries, such considerations play a minor role in other Asian countries' decisions about initiating complaints under the multilateral trade regime.

[34] See www.acwl.ch/e/index.html.

[35] Kennedy, "China's Role in WTO Dispute Settlement", 555, 564.

V The creation of permanent regional good offices for trade disputes in Asia

1 Efficient, professional and neutral dispute settlement mechanisms are still needed

Asian countries appear to be happy with the inclusion of detailed rules in trade agreements for possible use. Such detailed rules are definitely not for declarative purposes because such rules can function when a complaint is initiated and because such rules deter possible violations of the respective trade provisions.

The fact that these countries do not use these rules very often does not mean that they have not had and will not have any trade disputes among themselves. Although real disputes under the detailed dispute settlement procedures are few, trade disputes will definitely need to be resolved. These trade disputes could be complicated and economically important and will need to be resolved in an efficient, professional and neutral manner.

Apparently, if there is a mechanism to assist Asian countries to resolve their differences without resorting to litigious proceedings and if such a mechanism possesses high expertise and efficiency, it is possible that countries will be more interested in considering such a mechanism. In the opinion of the author, some kind of permanent regional good offices could be established to meet the efficiency, professionalism and neutrality requirements and expectations.

2 The mechanisms must be non-contentious and pragmatic with a lower extent of legality to maintain amicable relationships and flexibility

It has long been a practice for Europe to have a standing judicial body to resolve relevant disputes between European countries, such as the Court of Justice of European Union, which decides matters of EC law, and the European Court of Human Rights, which hears allegations of violations of the European Convention on Human Rights. However, the author of this chapter argues that this approach does not automatically apply to the Asian setting.

Although Asian countries are increasingly capable of effectively engaging in detailed rule-based settlement procedures to resolve trade disputes with their trading partners, the general attitude of Asian countries remains similar to their previous practice, mainly due to their preferences or philosophical attitudes. Hence, it might be too ambitious or unrealistic to expect that a permanent court or tribunal will be created in Asia to decide trade disputes in a very legalistic manner.

However, this does not mean that the non-litigious philosophy smooths things by blurring the line between right and wrong or confusing rights and obligations. The essence of the non-litigious approach is to find a "mutually acceptable solution" in a non-contentious manner to maintain friendly relations. In other words, it is still important to resolve possibly complex trade issues in an effective and professional manner. From these perspectives, it might be worthwhile to consider establishing some kind of permanent regional good offices for the settlement of trade disputes in Asia, with the fundamental elements of neutrality, lower resource demands and less legality to help Asian countries manage their trade relations and maintain their preference for non-contentious and pragmatic solutions to trade disputes.

3 *The mechanism must also be low-cost and less resource-intensive*

In litigation, a large portion of the costs are spent on recruiting capable legal counsels. If the dispute is resolved in a non-litigious manner, it could significantly reduce the costs. This is particularly important for developing countries. The remaining important costs of having standing good offices for Asian countries as proposed by the author are the costs associated with the establishment of such organizations.

The author is not very concerned about this issue because the costs are borne by the countries that are interested in utilizing the facilities. In addition, a design that differentiates the financial capability to decide the burden could vastly resolve the cost issue from the perspective of developing countries.

4 *Permanent regional offices can be designed to complement and supplement Asian FTAs*

Permanent good offices are established so that countries can select such facilities for trade disputes that arise from their FTAs and for disputes that do not arise from their FTAs.

As explained above, many Asian FTAs use the WTO model to design their dispute settlement procedures, which include good offices, mediation and conciliation. If permanent good offices are established for Asian countries to decide whether to utilize the mechanism, countries whose disputes arise from FTAs that adopt the WTO dispute settlement model would not have a legal problem with using the suggested permanent good offices. This is because good offices, mediation and conciliation have already been options for countries to resolve disputes that arise from such FTAs. The permanent good offices are to assist the FTA parties in implementing the dispute settlement procedures. Thus, permanent good offices and the WTO type of dispute settlement mechanisms are mutually supportive.

For those FTAs that do not have provisions for good offices as an alternative for dispute settlement procedures, permanent good offices can still be chosen through a separate mutual agreement between the disputing parties for the settlement of their trade issues. In other words, the suggested permanent good offices should be compatible with all FTAs, whether or not they have provisions stating that good offices, conciliation and mediation are alternatives for their dispute resolution mechanism.

VI Conclusion

This chapter starts with the explanation that a stable environment for business activities is essential for Asian countries. Although in practice, few trade disputes have occurred between Asian countries, potential disputes might arise from their trade agreements. It is desirable to have an effective but acceptable dispute settlement mechanism for the region to ensure a stable trade environment.

In practice, Asian countries have accepted and adopted detailed rule-based dispute settlement mechanisms under trade agreements. However, Asian countries do not use such detailed rules to resolve their disputes very often. This does not mean that no disputes arose from trade agreements between those countries. Neither does it mean that there will not be important trade disputes between Asian countries. The author holds the view that there should be a proper balance between detailed rules and practical approaches, such as a forum or facility like permanent good offices, for future trade disputes.

Such a facility would not change Asian countries' general non-litigious attitude or practices towards the settlement of trade disputes. However, such a facility could provide efficient and professional solutions for intra-Asia trade disputes. This chapter considers that some essential elements should be included in such a facility in addition to the requirements for efficiency and professionalism. These elements include neutrality, lower resource demands and less legality. This chapter holds the view that permanent regional good offices that are created to provide efficient but non-contentious and pragmatic solutions for trade disputes should be a desirable option for Asian countries.

3

African regional judiciaries and their jurisprudence in trade law matters

AMOS SAUROMBE

Introduction

Several trade "courts" have been set up in Africa. These courts attempt to balance the interests of the member states' private citizens, the national interests of the member states and the supranational interests of the region. This chapter attempts to explain the rationale behind the setup of these courts. In doing so, it is important to investigate the success or lack of success of these courts and to understand which ideas, policies, events and people drove the development of these courts. Economic integration in Africa is inundated with challenges and failures. Most of Africa's attempts at economic integration have ended with dismal outcomes. The economic conditions that are prevalent in Africa do not seem to be conducive to economic integration, as will be shown in this chapter.[1] The non-implementation of treaty obligations, such as the elimination of trade barriers by signatories of Regional Economic Communities (RECs),[2] is often cited as a major hindrance to the progression of regional integration.[3] Africa is home to some thirty regional trade arrangements, many of which are part of broader initiatives to achieve intra-regional cooperation. Africa's RECs are making progress in certain areas, but the integration process still faces numerous challenges.[4] This is a common phenomenon in the East African

[1] See generally A. Saurombe, "An Analysis of Economic Integration in Africa with Specific Reference to the African Union and the African Economic Community", *SA Public Law*, vol. 27 (2012), 192–314.

[2] Hereinafter "RECs".

[3] N. Meyer et al., "Bilateral and Regional Trade Agreements and Technical Barriers to Trade: An African Perspective", OECD Trade Policy Working Papers No. 96 (OECD Publishing, 2010), accessed 20 November 2013, doi: 10.1787/5kmdbgfrgnbv-en.

[4] *Ibid.*

Community (EAC), the Common Market for Eastern and Southern Africa (COMESA) and the Southern African Development Community (SADC). These RECs form part of what is now recognised as "new regionalism" in Sub-Saharan Africa.[5] Under the treaties that established these RECs, member states made attempts to implement treaty obligations in various areas of cooperation, such as trade, to promote the development of the region and enhance the welfare of the general public. Most of these RECs have created tribunals that are empowered to act as trade courts in cases in which trade rules have been breached. This chapter will analyse how the tribunals of SADC, COMESA and EAC have attempted to implement judicial authority when dealing with trade law. It is the finding of this chapter that most member states fail to bring their domestic policies in line with their binding international treaties. These states are unwilling to put regional interests ahead of domestic interests[6] or to give regional institutions the necessary authority to push forward the regional agenda.[7] This issue is particularly related to the function of the tribunals. Monitoring and enforcement mechanisms are also absent with respect to the treaty obligations. Thus, judicial institutions play a marginal role, causing the African continent to be perceived as having no litigation culture.[8] These courts exist, but they do not always function in the intended way. The basic reason for this disconnect is that most African trade organisations make decisions on the basis of consensus. Thus, one must ask whether the member states are committed to honouring their obligations under the treaties they sign. Some findings have suggested that African tribunals were never intended to exercise jurisdiction in trade matters. That conclusion might be true, but this issue raises familiar debates about the careful drafting of legal instruments.

[5] See generally B. Hettne, "The New Regionalism: A Prologue" in B. Hettne et al. (eds.), *National Perspectives on the New Regionalism in the South* (Basingstoke, New York: Palgrave Macmillan 2000), 64.

[6] This is a direct product of nationalism, which, in this context, poses a major constraint to regional integration, as regional schemes are only relevant and used to the extent that they further domestic interests.

[7] W.P. Hannun "Economic Integration in Africa", 2, accessed 24 May 2015, www.valt.helsinki.fi/kmi/english/HannunWP.pdf.

[8] E. Tino, "The Role of Regional Judiciaries in Eastern and Southern Africa" in Andrè du Pisani et al. (eds.), *Monitoring Regional Integration in Southern Africa: Yearbook 2012* (Stellenbosch, Tralac Law Centre, 2013), 140.

Scope of the chapter

Due to the limited scope of this chapter, only three trade law courts that operate on the continent of Africa will be discussed. These courts are the SADC Tribunal, the East Africa Court of Justice (EACJ) and the COMESA Court of Justice. These tribunals represent a new era of the "judicialisation process".[9] These courts can also be defined as the heartbeat of the regional organisations to which they belong.[10] All of these courts have a wider mandate to resolve other disputes; trade law disputes are only some of the disputes that the courts resolve. Article 28(1) of the EAC Treaty and Article 24(1) of the COMESA Treaty provide that:

> A Partner State which considers that another Partner State or an organ or institution of the Community has failed to fulfill an obligation under this Treaty or has infringed a provision of this Treaty, may refer the matter to the Court for adjudication.

Because trade issues remain at the periphery of integration in Africa, it is no surprise that trade cases are limited. However, this chapter will refer to at least one trade-related case from each of the three subregional courts that has jurisdiction to deal with trade disputes. The three treaties that established SADC, EAC and COMESA have legal instruments that promote trade. Thus, the effective enforcement of negotiated commitments is one of the preconditions for a successful trading system. In addition, these RTAs make provisions for dispute settlement through the establishment of regional courts and give these courts jurisdiction to determine disputes between member states with respect to the breach of treaty obligations, among other things. The processes of dispute settlement in RECs require legal certainty, uniformity in interpretation and the application of the law of the organisation, as well as homogeneity in the protection of different interests.[11]

The EACJ has been in existence for ten years, the COMESA Court has been in existence for fifteen years and the SADC Tribunal was operational for ten years before it was suspended by the SADC Summit in 2012. There have been few references by the courts with respect to breaches of treaty obligations in the area of trade cooperation. The lack of utilisation

[9] G. Erasmus, "Is the SADC Trade Regime a Rule Based System?" *SADC Law Journal*, vol. 1 (2011), 17–34.

[10] See generally COMESA Treaty Article 7, EAC Treaty Article 9 and the SADC Treaty Article 9.

[11] Tino, "Regional Judiciaries", 141.

of the courts for the settlement of disputes among member states could mean one of two things: that disputes related to regional trade obligations do not arise between states or that all disputes are resolved peacefully. The first presumption is very unlikely because as stated earlier, the non-implementation of treaty obligations is one of the major hindrances to the deepening of regional integration. In some instances, member states have acted blatantly in breach of their treaty obligations, but the regional courts have not been called upon to exercise their adjudicative functions. Thus, this chapter will briefly account for a very few cases to enhance the discussion.

The SADC tribunal

SADC came into existence in 1992, following the dissolution of the Southern African Development Coordination Conference (SADCC). In 2001, the SADC Treaty was amended, and a further commitment was made by Member States to proceed in accordance with principles that include human rights, democracy and the rule of law.[12] SADC was formed as an international regional organisation and was established in terms of a treaty and declaration that is referred to as the "Treaty of Southern African Development Community". This treaty was signed by the heads of state and governments of the signatory Member States.[13] This treaty has supranational powers over Member States, but the full extent of this power has not been fully realised. SADC's origins lie in the frontline states,[14] which are a group of eminent Southern African countries who fought to obtain independence from colonial rule. The aim of these countries was to help liberate the whole region from colonial rule. In the 1960s and 1970s, these newly independent states supported national liberation movements in the region by coordinating their

[12] See Article 4(c) SADC Treaty as amended. The members of SADC are: Angola, Botswana, Democratic Republic of Congo, Lesotho, Malawi, Mozambique, Namibia, South Africa, Swaziland, Seychelles, Mauritius, Madagascar, Tanzania, Zambia and Zimbabwe

[13] The SADC Treaty was signed at Windhoek, Namibia on 17 August 1992, entering into force on 30 September 1993. The treaty was amended at Blantyre, Malawi, in August 2001. A consolidated version of the treaty and all its amendments can be accessed on the SADC official website, accessed 20 May November 2015, www.sadc.int.

[14] M. Clough and J. Ravenhill, "Regionalism in Southern Africa: The SADCC" in Michael Clough (ed.)*Political Change in Southern Africa* (Berkeley: Institute of International Studies, University of California, 1982), 67. See also C.B. Thompson, *Challenge to Imperialism: The Frontline States in the Liberation of Zimbabwe* (Harare: Zimbabwe Publishing House, 1984), 743.

political, diplomatic and military struggles to bring an end to colonial and white minority rule. This commitment was shown by subsequent conferences that were held in Arusha, Tanzania, in July 1979, where the economic ministers of the frontline states drafted the broad lines of the declaration and the programme of action. The heads of state also met in Dar es Salaam, Tanzania, in November 1979.[15] The declared aim of the southern nine was to form an alliance that would pursue an economic strategy that would reduce the economic dependence of the countries on South Africa.[16] The idea was to secure international cooperation for economic liberation and collective self-reliance.[17] At that time, according to the late president of Botswana, Sir Seretse Khama, "economic dependence had in many ways made political independence somewhat meaningless".[18] Additional efforts were made under former president Kaunda of Zambia to establish a transcontinental belt of independent and economically powerful nations, from Dar-Es-Salaam and Maputo on the Indian Ocean to Luanda on the Atlantic Ocean.[19] In this context, the SADCC[20] was the forerunner of the social-economic cooperation leg of the current Southern African Development Community.

The SADC Treaty provides the legal framework of the organisation by setting out the status,[21] the principles and objectives[22], the obligations of the member states,[23] membership,[24] the institutions,[25] procedural

[15] A.J. Nsekela (ed.), *Southern Africa: Towards Economic Liberation* (London: Rex Colling, 1981), 41.

[16] G.H. Oosthuizen, *The Southern African Development Community: The Organisation, Its Policies and Prospects* (Johannesburg: Institute for Global Dialogue, 2006), 11. See also L. Abegunrin, "The Southern African Development Coordination Conference: Politics of Dependence" in R.I. Onwuka and A. Sesay (eds.),*The Future of Regionalism in Africa* (Nairobi: Academy of Science Publishers, 1990), 36. See also "Southern Africa: Union of the Southern Nine" in Africa No. 105 (London, 1980), 45. Reginald Green argued during the first year of SADCC that "At one extreme Lesotho would find a total break with South Africa either impossible or economically suicidal." See R.H. Green "First Steps towards Economic Integration" in A.J. Nsekela (ed.) *Southern Africa: Towards Economic Liberation* (Rex Collins: London, 1981).

[17] Y. Tsikata "Southern Africa: Trade, Liberalisation and Implications for a Free Trade Area", Paper presented at the 1999 *Annual Trade and Industrial Policy Secretarial Forum*, Muldersdrift, 1999.

[18] *Africa Research Bulletin*, 15 June–14 July 1979, 5155.

[19] *An Address by President Kaunda of Zambia to the Lusaka Economic Summit of the Southern African Development Coordination Conference* (SADCC), Lusaka, 1 April 1980, 3–4.

[20] Hereinafter "SADCC". [21] *SADC Treaty*, Article 14.

[22] *Ibid.*, Chapter 3, Articles 4 and 5. [23] *Ibid.*, Article 6.

[24] *Ibid.*, Chapter 4, Articles 37 and 8. [25] *Ibid.*, Chapter 5, Articles 9 and 16A.

matters relating to areas of cooperation among member states,[26] cooperation with other international organizations,[27] financial issues[28], dispute settlement[29] and sanctions, withdrawal and dissolution.[30] The SADC Treaty contains provisions for the formulation of subsidiary legal instruments, such as protocols that give specific mandates to various SADC institutions. A total of twenty-four protocols have been formulated to date.[31]

Article 15(1) of the SADC Protocol on the tribunal provides that:

> The Tribunal shall have jurisdiction over disputes between States, and between natural or legal persons and States.

And Article 17 goes on to provide that:

> Subject to the provisions of Article 14 of this Protocol, the Tribunal shall have exclusive jurisdiction over all disputes between the States and the Community. Such disputes may be referred to the Tribunal either by the State concerned or by the competent institution or organ of the Community.

The tribunal was established in 1992 under Article 9 of the SADC and became operational in 2005. As the Supreme Policy Institution of the SADC (Article 4(4)) Protocol on the tribunal, the Summit of Heads of State appointed the members of the tribunal during its Summit of Heads of State and Government, which was held in Gaborone, Botswana, in August 2005. The community's members approved the protocol that was required to set up the tribunal in the year 2000. Finally, the protocol entered into force with the signing of the Agreement Amending the Treaty of SADC in August 2001. This amendment marked renewed energy towards the integration of the community, making the protocol on the tribunal an integral part of the treaty and thus automatically applicable to all member states.

However, the SADC Tribunal is currently not functioning, as the summit closed it down in 2012 in protest of a judgement that went against Zimbabwe's land reform programme. On 28 November 2008, the SADC Tribunal ruled that seventy-eight white Zimbabwean farmers could keep their farms because the Zimbabwean land reform programme

26 *Ibid.*, Article 21. 27 *Ibid.*, Article 24.

28 *Ibid.*, Chapter 9, Articles 25–27; chapter 10, Articles 28–30. 29 *Ibid.*, Article 32.

30 *Ibid.*, Chapter 13, Articles 33–35.

31 See list of protocols available on SADC official website, accessed 11 November 2013, www.sadc.int.

had discriminated against them.[32] The Zimbabwean government rejected this ruling, challenging its legality, and lobbied the summit to suspend the tribunal. The tribunal was suspended in August 2010 pending an independent six-month review of its "role, functions and terms of reference". However, after the review was completed, SADC justice ministers and attorney generals questioned anew its fundamental elements and then initiated a new partisan review. The June 2011 summit then suspended all work for the tribunal, going so far as to stop the tribunal from hearing new cases that are not related to the Campbell case. The summit also decided not to reappoint or replace the tribunal's 10 judges, rendering the tribunal inoperative until at least August of the following year. At the time, the remaining four judges[33] of the SADC Tribunal described this move as amounting to the total dissolution of the tribunal. This action is contrary to the findings of the review process, which actually commended the tribunal ruling as legitimate and suggested a need for its further strengthening. The tribunal had acted within its mandate when it made a decision in accordance with Article 32(5) of the Protocol on the tribunal to make a report of non-compliance to the summit of SADC. However, this procedure shows the handicap of international judicial institutions in terms of their ability to enforce their own decisions. This outcome also demonstrates that political organs of international institutions are vital for the creation of a culture of compliance.[34] The actions of the summit are actually illegal because without amending the SADC Treaty and protocol on the tribunal, the summit has no power to restrict the tribunal's jurisdiction or to overrule the protocol.

Thus, the tribunal would be unable to accept new cases because it did not comply with tribunal composition requirements as prescribed by Article 3 of the SADC Tribunal Protocol.[35] Notwithstanding the current status of this judicial forum, the rationale for this discussion is to demonstrate the legal mandate given to the tribunal by the SADC Treaty and

[32] S. Ebobrah, "Human Rights Developments in Sub Regional Courts in Africa during 2008", *African Human Rights Law Journal*, (2009), 329; SADC (T) Case 2/2007; see also *Campbell & Others* v *Zimbabwean Government*, www.newzimbabwe.com/pages/farm75.19086.html; SADC Trade Agenda, 693.

[33] These judges include the tribunal president, Mauritius chief justice Ariranga Pillay and justices Rigoberto Kambovo, Onkemetse Tshosa and Frederick Chomba.

[34] By the organisational structure of SADC, the Summit of Heads of State and Government is the highest authority of SADC.

[35] Scholtz, "Review of the Role, Functions and Terms of Reference of the SADC Tribunal", *SADC Law Journal* (2011), 197–201.

the way in which that mandate relates to regional integration. The tribunal of SADC is provided for under Article 16 of the Declaration and Treaty Establishing SADC of 1992. Before this happened, the regional expectations for a well-functioning tribunal were high. The expectation was that the tribunal would improve on the rule of law and human rights in the region. The tribunal provided a legal basis for all SADC institutions and, most importantly, played an oversight role during the implementation stages of the integration agenda. The decisions of the tribunal are final and binding.[36] If SADC is truly rule-based, its rulings will be binding for the parties involved.[37]

The SADC Tribunal was expected to serve as a key institution in the SADC legal and institutional integration process. The cases of the tribunal were expected to build precedents, just as the experience of the European Union has demonstrated that such dispute settlement bodies can indeed play a significant role in regional integration. However, to develop the current SADC dispute settlement system into an ideal model, improvements may have to be considered.[38] The tribunal was constituted to ensure adherence to the proper interpretation of the provisions of the SADC Treaty and subsidiary instruments and to adjudicate any disputes that may be referred to the tribunal.[39] The tribunal is also authorised to determine, inter alia, any disputes regarding the interpretation and application of the treaty and its protocols that cannot be settled amicably.[40] This provision is reiterated in Article 14 of the Protocol of the tribunal.[41] If the interpretation of the SADC Treaty becomes an issue, the SADC Tribunal should act as an independent forum to rule on the correct interpretation or application of the legal instruments at stake.[42] Persistent failure to fulfil obligations under the treaty can result in the imposition of sanctions on the defaulting member.[43] However, such sanctions can only be imposed by the summit.[44] Accordingly, sanctions can be imposed on a member state that persistently, without

[36] SADC Treaty, Article 16.5. [37] Erasmus, "SADC Trade Regime".
[38] Ruppel and Bangamwabo, "The SADC Tribunal: A Legal Analysis of Its Mandate and Role in Regional Integration", accessed 20 November 2013, tralac.org/wp-content/blogs.dir/12/files/2011/uploads/MRI2008Chapter8Ruppel.pdf.
[39] SADC Treaty, Article 16.1. [40] *Ibid.*, Article 3.
[41] According to Article 16.2 of the SADC Treaty, the composition, powers, functions, procedures and other related matters governing the tribunal shall be prescribed in a protocol, which shall, notwithstanding the provisions of Article 22 of this treaty, form an integral part of this treaty, adopted by the summit.
[42] Erasmus, "SADC Trade Regime", 17–34. [43] SADC Treaty, Article 33.
[44] *Ibid.*, Article 33.2.

good reason, fails to fulfil obligations assumed under the SADC Treaty.[45] However, in view of the summit's consensus-based nature, resorting to such drastic measures is not contemplated because the defaulting member would have to support the sanction resolutions.[46] It is very unfortunate that no sanctions have been imposed on Member States who fail to fulfil obligations prescribed by the treaty.

The tribunal is critical for trade and integration processes for SADC, as it provides a legal basis for all SADC institutions and, most importantly, can play an oversight role during the implementation stages of the integration agenda, as well as in resolving trade disputes. Member states and their private citizens have jurisdiction to bring cases before the SADC Tribunal. The theme of this chapter emphasises on the main function of the tribunal is to ensure adherence to the proper interpretation of the provisions of the SADC Treaty and subsidiary instruments and to adjudicate any disputes that may be referred to the tribunal.[47] This tribunal is also authorised to determine, inter alia, any disputes regarding the interpretation and application of the treaty and its protocols that cannot be settled amicably.[48] This provision is reiterated in Article 14 of the Protocol of the tribunal.[49] If the interpretation of the SADC Treaty becomes an issue, the SADC Tribunal should act as an independent forum to rule on the correct interpretation or application of the legal instruments at stake.[50] Persistent failure to fulfil obligations under the treaty can result in the imposition of sanctions on the defaulting member.

Campbell and another v. Republic of Zimbabwe

However, the discussion of the SADC Tribunal will point to its apparent weaknesses and, most importantly, to its failure to sanction its judgment in the Campbell case.[51] On 28 November 2008, the SADC Tribunal ruled that seventy-eight white Zimbabwean farmers could keep their farms

[45] *Ibid.*, Article 33.1. [46] Tribunal Protocol, Article 10(8). [47] *Ibid.*, Article 16.1.

[48] SADC Treaty, Article 3.

[49] According to Article 16.2: the composition, powers, functions, procedures and other related matters governing the tribunal shall be prescribed in a protocol, which shall, notwithstanding the provisions of Article 22 of this treaty, form an integral part of this treaty, adopted by the summit.

[50] Erasmus, "SADC Trade Regime", 19.

[51] *Campbell & Another* v Zimbabwe SADC (T) Case 2/2007, ruling of 13 December 2007. See also SADC (T) Case 2/2007 in which judgement was delivered on 28 November 2008.

because the Zimbabwean land reform programme had discriminated against them.[52] The Zimbabwean government rejected this ruling, challenging its legality, and lobbied the summit to suspend the tribunal. The tribunal was suspended in August 2010, pending an independent six-month review of its "role, functions and terms of reference".[53] The review process was required to address inter alia, the jurisdiction of the tribunal; the interface between community law and national laws in SADC; the mandate of the existing appeals chamber of the tribunal; the recognition, enforcement and execution of the tribunal's decisions; the lack of clarity in some provisions of the SADC Treaty and the Tribunal Protocol; the tendency of member states to give primacy to domestic laws or jurisdiction over SADC law; and the reluctance of member states to relinquish some aspects of their sovereignty to SADC.[54] However, after the review was completed, SADC justice ministers and attorney generals questioned anew the fundamental elements of the tribunal and then initiated a new partisan review. This process led the June 2011 summit to suspend all work for the tribunal, going so far as to stop the tribunal from hearing new cases unrelated to the Campbell case.

The decision not to reappoint or replace the tribunal's ten judges rendered the tribunal inoperative. The remaining four judges[55] of the SADC Tribunal described this move as amounting to the total dissolution of the tribunal. This outcome is contrary to the findings of the review process, which had recommended that the tribunal ruling was legitimate and suggested a need for further strengthening of the tribunal. The tribunal had acted within its mandate when it made a decision in accordance with Article 32(5) of the Protocol on the tribunal to make a report of non-compliance to the Summit of SADC. However, this procedure shows the handicap of international judicial institutions in terms of their ability to enforce their own decisions. The SADC Tribunal does not have its own judgement enforcement mechanism; thus, the tribunal relies on member states to enforce its decisions.[56] Article 32(1) of the Protocol on the tribunal requires the decisions of the tribunal to be registered and enforced by member states as foreign

[52] S. Ebobrah, "Human Rights Developments in Sub-regional Courts in Africa during 2008", *Afr Human Rights Law Journal* (2009), 312–335.

[53] Scholtz, "Review". [54] *Ibid.*

[55] These judges include the tribunal president, Mauritius chief justice Ariranga Pillay and justices Rigoberto Kambovo, Onkemetse Tshosa and Frederick Chomba.

[56] Scholtz, "Review".

judgements.[57] This setup creates a gap in the enforcement of the tribunal's decisions because it subjects the enforcement of the tribunal's decisions to domestic laws that govern the enforcement of foreign judgements in member states.[58] This provision is an example of a matter on which the SADC instruments are unclear and deserves urgent attention and clarification.[59]

The weakness of the above mechanism played itself out when in the case *of Gramara (Pvt) Ltd. and Another v. The Government of Zimbabwe* (2009), the Zimbabwe High Court refused to register and enforce a judgement of the tribunal on the grounds that the decision of the tribunal was contrary to public policy in the Republic of Zimbabwe. Zimbabwe's action is contrary to the spirit of regional integration and sends the wrong message, namely that member states can undermine regional jurisprudence or fail to honour their obligations under the relevant regional instruments.[60] Accordingly, if regional integration is to be firmly rooted within SADC, the SADC Tribunal must be allowed to develop the jurisprudence of SADC law, as was the case for the European Court of Justice in the formative years of the European Union.[61] This change would in effect allow the tribunal to develop jurisprudence that has both direct effects on supranational powers and a positive effect on deeper integration and trade.

This discussion demonstrates that political organs of international institutions are vital for the creation of a culture of compliance.[62] The actions of the summit are actually illegal because without amending the SADC Treaty and Protocol on the tribunal, the summit has no power to restrict the tribunal's jurisdiction or to overrule the protocol. The suspension of the tribunal due to a member state's dissatisfaction with the decisions of the tribunal casts doubt on the acceptability of decisions of supranational institutions among SADC member states.

Assuming that the tribunal is reinstated, its influence and credibility have already been eroded. Many scholars and politicians have lost hope

[57] A. Afadameh-Adeyemi and E. Kalula, "SADC at 30: Re-examining the Legal and Institutional Anatomy of the Southern African Development Community" in *Monitoring Regional Integration in Southern Africa: Yearbook 2010* (Stellenbosch, Tralac Law Centre, 2010), 5–22.

[58] *Ibid.* [59] Scholtz, "Review". [60] Afadameh-Adeyemi and Kalula, "SADC at 30".

[61] A. Arnull, *The European Union and its Court of Justice* (New York: Oxford University Press, 1999).

[62] By the organisational structure of SADC, the summit is made up of heads of states and governments and is the highest authority of SADC.

that the tribunal will be reinstated.[63] If it is envisaged that the tribunal will be called upon in the near future to decide on issues relating to regional integration and if the Zimbabwean experience is used as a precedent, member states may avoid being sanctioned after a breach of their obligations under the SADC Treaty. This is a dangerous precedent for an institution that is entrusted with developing the jurisprudence of the region.[64] The summit can, at will, decide to make decisions that directly impact the path of regional integration in the SADC. Several regional integration breaches are already happening in the region, especially to citizens of the region. One example is the charging of high tariffs on intra-SADC imports. This state of affairs was supposed to end by the time of the establishment of the FTA in 2008. The FTA covers 85 per cent of all goods except motor vehicles and parts, as well as clothing material. However, high tariffs on virtually all goods are still being reported in the region. The tribunal is the most relevant forum to address these issues because the court has jurisdiction to hear matters affecting private citizens.[65]

The tribunal is empowered by the treaty to apply SADC law without fear or favour and to pave the way for the harmonisation of business law to the extent that these laws can also be applied by the tribunal.[66] The harmonisation of policies or the adoption of similar policies is a signal that a regional arrangement is seeking to achieve a high degree of economic integration. The drastic action taken to dissolve the tribunal has sent the worst possible signal to the SADC region, to potential investors and to the whole international community, reflecting SADC's poor stance on human rights, democracy and the rule of law.[67]

[63] G. Erasmus, "Does It Matter whether SADC Has a Tribunal", www.tralac.org/2013/06/12/does-it-matter-whether-sadc-has-a-tribunal/; see also O.C. Ruppel and F.X. Bangamwabo, "The SADC Tribunal: A legal Analysis of Its Mandate and Role in Regional Integration" in *Monitoring Regional Integration in Southern Africa: Year Book 2008* (Stellenbosch, Tralac Law Centre, 2008), 5.

[64] Afadameh-Adeyemi and Kalula, "SADC at 30".

[65] See *Mondlane* v *SADC Secretariat* SADC (T) No. 7/2009 (5 February 2010); *Kanyama* v *SADC Secretariat* SADC (T) 5/2009 (29 January 2010).

[66] The tribunal will be discussed further in Chapter 8 under the legality of SADC Treaty: Compliance and compatibility with legal instruments.

[67] G. Erasmus, *What Has Happened to the Protection of Rights in SADC?* (Stellenbosch: Tralac Law Centre, 2012).

The COMESA court of justice

The Common Market of Eastern and Southern African States (COMESA) was established by treaty in 1982.[68] This treaty then established the court in 1994 upon the adoption of the current COMESA Treaty, and the court assumed the overall jurisdiction of the previous judicial bodies that existed under the Preferential Trade Area of the Common Market for Eastern and Southern Africa (PTA).[69] The judicial organs under PTA were as follows. The function of the PTA tribunal was to ensure the proper interpretation of the provisions of the treaty, as well as to adjudicate all disputes between member states that arose from the interpretation and application of the PTA Treaty. The COMESA Treaty provides that the council shall give directions to all other subordinate organs of COMESA other than the court in the exercise of its jurisdiction.[70] This provision ensures that the court is independent.

In addition, the jurisdiction of the PTA Administrative Appeals Board was to adjudicate disputes between the PTA and its staff that arose from the interpretation and application of the PTA Treaty, Staff Rules and Regulations and Terms and Conditions of Contracts of Employment of Staff. Lastly, the PTA Centre for Commercial Arbitration was responsible for facilitating international arbitration and conciliation of private commercial disputes. The centre was based in Djibouti and operated under the auspices of the PTA Federation of Chambers of Commerce and Industry.

The court operates as an independent organ of the common market and is comprised of two divisions: the Appellate Division, which is headed by the president, and the First Instance Division, which is headed by the principal judge. The day-to-day operations of the court are handled by the Registrar of the Court under the supervision of the judge president, with assistance from other registry and administrative staff. These characteristics are some of the similarities that this tribunal shares with the ECJ.

In COMESA, there has been a long-standing dispute between various COMESA member states and Egypt. Egypt refuses to amend its legislation to comply with the COMESA Protocol on Rules of Origin, which

[68] Treaty Establishing the Common Market of Eastern and Southern Africa (adopted 21 December 1981, came into force 30 September 1982), Article 7(1)(c).

[69] The members of COMESA are Burundi, Comoros, Democratic Republic of Congo, Djibouti, Egypt, Eritrea, Ethiopia, Kenya, Libya, Seychelles, Swaziland, Madagascar, Malawi, Mauritius, Rwanda, Sudan, Uganda, Zambia and Zimbabwe.

[70] COMESA Treaty, Article 9(2)(c).

provides for a 35 per cent value added threshold on COMESA exports that were originally imported into the region to quality for duty-free importation into a COMESA member state. Egypt had maintained a 45 per cent requirement of value addition on a product imported into Egypt from a COMESA state for exemption from import duty in accordance with the COMESA Protocol on Rules of Origin. In defence of this action, Egypt insisted that it was under an obligation to apply terms negotiated with the EU and the Pan Arab Free Trade Area. In many instances, this argument has been proved to be illegal and illegitimate. The existence of non-tariff barriers continues to negatively impact intra-regional trade in COMESA, EAC and SADC by increasing costs due to delays incurred at border posts and other administrative delays during customs clearance of goods traded in the three regions. This scenario will now be demonstrated in the following case.

Polytol paints and Adhesives Manufacturers Co. Ltd. v. *The Republic of Mauritius* (2012)

This case is a landmark case in which the COMESA Court of Justice decided that by imposing a customs duty on imports of a product (car paint) from Egypt, the Government of Mauritius acted contrary to Article 46 of the COMESA Treaty, which required that Member States eliminate by the year 2000 all customs duties and other charges of equivalent effect on goods that originate from the member states in the COMESA Free Trade Area.[71] In addition, the court ruled that an agreement between two or more Member States to reinstate customs duties on trade among themselves, in this case between Egypt and Mauritius, is contrary to the object and purpose of the treaty and in breach of the treaty; instead, Member States can use Article 61 of the treaty, which provides the possibility to take safeguard measures against import surges for one year after informing the secretary general and for additional years if approved by the council of ministers.

According to the COMESA Treaty, the court again cited Article 26 of the treaty and held that "the content of this rule shows the extent the signatories of the COMESA Treaty have committed themselves to give some space in the COMESA territory not only to the Member States but

[71] See generally G. Erasmus, *The COMESA Court of Justice: Regional Agreements Do Protect Private Parties* (Stellenbosch: Tralac Law Centre, 2013), accessed 25 May 2015, www.tralac.org/files/2013/10/S13TB092013-Erasmus-COMESA-Court-of-Justice-Legal-agreements-protect-private-parties-20131015-fin.pdf.

also to individuals". By giving the residents of any member state the right to challenge the acts thereof on the grounds of unlawfulness or infringement of the treaty, the member states have in some areas limited their sovereignty. Guided by proportionality, the court ruled that the proper functioning of the common market is therefore not only a concern of the member states but also a concern of the residents. The treaty is more than an agreement that merely creates obligations between member states. The treaty also gives enforceable rights to citizens who reside in the member states. Furthermore, the court made reference to Article 55 of the treaty, which prohibits any practice that negates the objective of free and liberalised trade. The agreement between Egypt and Mauritius hampered the process of trade liberalisation within the COMESA territory and could not relieve the respondent from its obligations to uphold the principles of the treaty.

The Court had to deal with a number of issues that were raised by both the applicant and the respondent. First, the company was challenged based on claims that it had no basis for challenging the failure of the Government of Mauritius to implement some treaty obligations into its national law. This challenge was based on the question of whether the company could sue the government for failing to implement some obligations under the COMESA Treaty or whether only the secretary general or a member state could sue another member state for failing to fulfil its obligations, under Article 24 of the treaty. At the same time, the court cited Article 26 of the treaty, which says that "any person who is resident in a Member State may refer for determination by the Court the legality of any act, regulation, directive or decision of the Council or of a Member State on the grounds that such act, directive, decision or regulation is unlawful or an infringement of the provisions of this Treaty". The court therefore held that "a legal or natural person is only permitted to bring to Court matters relating to conduct or measures that are unlawful or an infringement of the Treaty but not the non-fulfilment of a Treaty obligation by a Member State. The responsibility of bringing a matter relating to non-fulfilment of obligations under the Treaty is reserved for Member States and the Secretary General."

The court then proceeded to the question of whether or not the Government of Mauritius acted consistently with the treaty when it introduced a customs duty on imports of car paints from Egypt. The government argued that obligations under the COMESA Treaty are to be implemented progressively, "irrespective of the Treaty time-frame", because only some member states joined the COMESA FTA and also because the COMESA council of ministers recently extended the transition period for the Customs Union. The COMESA Court rejected both of these arguments. After citing Article 31 of the Vienna Convention on the Law of Treaties, which provides that "a treaty shall be interpreted in good faith in accordance with the ordinary meaning to be given to the terms of the treaty in their context and in light of the its object and purpose", the court held that "Article 46 is clear and unambiguous and its terms must be interpreted with their ordinary meaning in the context of the purpose and objective of the treaty to achieve free trade with the COMESA area" and that "Mauritius infringed Article 46 by reintroducing duties on Egyptian products including Kapci paints even if it was for the protection of its industries". After all, Mauritius had the option of using safeguard measures, as prescribed by the treaty.

On the question of whether or not individuals who reside in the member states have an enforceable right under the COMESA Treaty, the court again cited Article 26 of the treaty and held that

> the content of this rule shows the extent the signatories of the COMESA Treaty have committed themselves to give some space in the COMESA territory not only to the Member States but also to individuals. By giving the residents of any Member State the right to challenge the acts thereof on grounds of unlawfulness or infringement of the Treaty, the Member States have in some areas limited their sovereignty. The proper functioning of the Common Market is, therefore, not only a concern of the Member States but also that of the residents. The Treaty is more than an agreement which merely creates obligations between Member States. It also gives enforceable rights to citizens residing in the Member States.

This interpretation of the treaty was also informed by proportionality.

The government attempted to argue that the COMESA Treaty was not enforceable in Mauritius, as the government had not taken measures to domesticate the treaty. The Zimbabwean government tried to use the same argument without success in the Campbell case. The court made it a point to explain at length that the government's actions had breached the treaty and caused prejudice to the company in breach of the rights provided by the COMESA Treaty and that the government could not use its own internal laws as an explanation or a defence for not implementing the COMESA Treaty. Likewise, the SADC Tribunal ruled in the Campbell case that the Zimbabwean government could not renege on its international obligations by invoking a domestic law. The court said, "In the case at hand, the Respondent has imposed a customs tariff that is in breach of the Treaty. If the Respondent's Customs Tariff and Regulations were consistent with the rules of the Treaty, the Applicant would have paid no customs duty on the Kapci products imported from Egypt during the relevant time."

The applicant was therefore clearly prejudiced because the regulations of the respondent were in breach of the treaty. The argument of the respondent's counsel that the treaty is not directly enforceable in some jurisdictions, including Mauritius, and that therefore, individuals cannot have rights emanating from the treaty is misconceived. It is important to acknowledge that there are differences among legal systems with respect to their positions on the domestication of international law. In some member states, treaties become directly applicable; in others, treaties require another domestic legal instrument for their incorporation. Notwithstanding the differences among domestic legal systems, the treaty objectives can be achieved when all member states fulfil their obligations under the treaty. Therefore, any member state that acts contrary to the treaty cannot plead the nature of its legal system as a defence when citizens or residents of that state are prejudiced by its acts. This finding is clearly stipulated in Article 27 of the Vienna Convention on the Law of Treaties, 1969 which provides that "[a] party may not invoke the provision of its internal law as justification for its failure to perform a treaty".

Comparison with ECJ

The COMESA Court drew upon the previous decision of the European Court of Justice on a similar issue. The European Court of Justice held that the community constitutes a new legal order of international law for the benefit of which the states have limited their sovereign rights, albeit within limited fields, and the subjects of which comprise not only member states but also their nationals. Independently of the legislation of member states, community law therefore not only imposes obligations on individuals but is also intended to confer upon them rights, which become part of their legal heritage. These rights arise not only where they are expressly granted by the treaty but also by reason of obligations, which the treaty imposes in a clearly defined way upon individuals, as well as upon the member states and upon the institutions of the community ... according to the spirit, the general scheme and the wording of the treaty, Article 12 must be interpreted as producing direct effects and creating individual rights, which national courts must protect.

This important realisation draws directly on the direct effect of EU law on member states.

Another important issue on which the COMESA Court decided was whether or not the bilateral agreement between Egypt and Mauritius could be relied upon by the Government of Mauritius, under which it was agreed to impose customs duties on imports from Egypt contrary to the COMESA rules, which required that no customs duties or charges of equivalent effect should be imposed on imports that originate from other member states. The COMESA Court again went at length to explain that bilateral agreements between member states should aim to promote the achievement of the objectives of the COMESA Treaty and that by instead seeking to reverse the rules under the COMESA FTA, the bilateral agreement could not stand. The court explained that Article 61 of the treaty provides for the possibility of a safeguard measure that can be used by a member state facing import surges, rather than seeking bilateral agreements that are inconsistent with the object and purpose of the treaty. The court explained that the treaty allows member states to enter into bilateral agreements with each other or with third party states. However, this provision should not be construed as giving the member states a right to enter into agreements that defeat the main purpose of the treaty that they have undertaken to respect. In this context, Article 56(3) states that

> Nothing in this Treaty shall prevent two Member States from entering into new preferential agreements among themselves which aim at achieving the objectives of the Common Market, provided that any preferential treatment accorded under such agreements is extended to the other Member States on a reciprocal and non-discriminatory basis.

Article 56(3) of the treaty allows member states to enter into agreements among themselves only if some basic requirements are met. First, whatever agreement the member states enter into must contribute to the achievement of the objectives of the common market. Second, the agreement should relate to preferential treatment. Third, such preferential treatment should be extended to all of the other member states, provided that the other member states reciprocate. That there was communication between the states of Mauritius and Egypt on this matter is admitted by the applicant's counsel. The argument is that even if there was such an agreement, it was contrary to the requirements of the treaty.

The court also examined the nature of the communication that preceded the imposition of the duties and the impact of the regulations in light of Article 56(3) of the treaty. The regulation that was issued in 2001 by Mauritius imposed a 40 per cent duty on Kapci products imported from Egypt. Therefore, the purpose of the negotiations was not to give preferential treatment to products from Egypt, as envisaged by Article 56, but to levy additional duty on the same products. Article 56(3) envisages a situation in which member states give additional benefits to products, in addition to the minimum protection given to them under the treaty. The agreement between Egypt and Mauritius had in effect raised the duty from zero, which is the rule under the treaty, to 40 per cent. This bilateral act clearly went against the basic objectives of the treaty, which include the elimination of customs duties and other non-tariff barriers within the time limit provided by the treaty.

Under Article 55 of the treaty, any practice that negates the objective of free and liberalised trade shall be prohibited. The agreement between Egypt and Mauritius hampered the process of trade liberalisation within the COMESA territory and could not relieve the respondent from its obligations to uphold the principles of the treaty. The court then went on to cite Articles 18 and 41 of the Vienna Convention on the Law of Treaties, which provide that any such bilateral agreement can be entered by member states if it is not prohibited by the treaty and if the bilateral agreement does not create a derogation that is incompatible with the effective executive of the object and purpose of the COMESA Treaty as a whole.

In conclusion, the COMESA Court issued an order that the Government of Mauritius should refund to the company the customs duties paid for the period from 1 April 2005, when the company first sent a letter formally complaining about the customs duties, to 20 November 2010, when the law was removed, with interest at the rate applied by the courts in Mauritius, and pay 70 per cent of the costs the company incurred in pursuing the case.

East African court of justice

The EAC was initially founded by Kenya, Tanzania and Uganda in 1967 but was dissolved in 1977 following disputes between the partner states.[72] Various reasons have been advanced for the collapse of the old EAC.

[72] See generally S. Ebobrah and A. Tanoh (eds.), *Compendium of African Sub-regional Human Rights Documents* (Pretoria: Pretoria University Law Press, 2010), 37.

These reasons have included political differences, especially between Uganda and Tanzania. The actual collapse of the old EAC was occasioned by different levels of economic development, which meant Kenya received the lion's share of the EAC benefits, with the rest of the partner states only importing from Kenya. This sense of *primus inter pares* made Kenyan officials question the relevance of the East African railways and harbours being headquartered in Dar es Salaam and the East African posts and telecommunications being headquartered in Kampala, while substantive ministries in Kenya were in charge of these sectors. One other crucial factor that seems to be better left buried is the Kampala Agreement. This agreement sought to establish an even distribution of industries across the region, as a means of ensuring balanced development and mutual benefits in the Community. Each partner state is attempting to protect its own turf.[73]

With the new wave of regionalism that was partly prompted by reactions to globalisation, the EAC was revived with the adoption of a new founding treaty in 1999.[74] This treaty was amended first in 2006 and later in 2007. With the accession of Burundi and Rwanda to the treaty of the EAC, the community has now increased in number to five. The EACJ became operational on November 30, 2001. The East EACJ was established under the Treaty Establishing the East African Community. This court is mandated to ensure adherence to the law in the interpretation and application of and compliance with the EAC Treaty. The EAC Treaty gives the EACJ

> jurisdiction over the interpretation and application of [the EAC] Treaty . . . [as well as] such other original, appellate, human rights and other jurisdiction as . . . determined by the Council . . . [in] a protocol . . .. Before the amendments of 2006 decisions of the EACJ were final, binding and conclusive and not open to appeal . . . and [a]ny dispute concerning the interpretation or application of [the EAC] Treaty . . . shall not be subjected to any method of settlement other than those provided for in [the EAC] Treaty.

The Treaty provides that the judges on the EACJ are to be appointed based on recommendations by the partner states. Before the 2006 amendments, the EAC Treaty provided that the EACJ would consist of no more than six judges, with no more than two judges from each of the original

[73] Peter Twagira, "Why the First EAC Collapsed", *Daily Monitor*, 30 December 2012, accessed 25 May 2015, www.monitor.co.ug/OpEd/Letters/Why-the-first-EA-Community-collapsed-/-/806314/1653726/-/oipj5n/-/index.html

[74] *Ibid.*

three partner states. The amended EAC Treaty split the EAC into a First Instance Division and an Appellate Division and provided that the court shall be composed of a maximum of fifteen judges, with a maximum of ten judges for the First Instance Division and five judges for the Appellate Division. No more than two judges from each of the five partner states can be appointed to the First Instance Division, and no more than one judge from each partner state can be appointed to the Appellate Division.

The court did not receive its first case until 2005. This delay led to much criticism from leading scholars, who pointed out that the court had suffered a still birth due its failure to decide any cases and due to the court's restricted jurisdiction.[75] However, a number of cases have now been heard by this court. For the purposes of this chapter, the following case that is related to trade will be discussed.

Modern Holdings (E.A.) Limited v. *Kenya Ports Authority*

Morden Holdings (applicant) sued the Kenya Port Authority (respondent) for losses amounting to US$24 million for the value of beverages that were imported from the United Arab Emirates through the Mombasa Port and were not delivered.[76] A total of twenty-one containers with a range of beverages that the applicant imported via Mombasa Port could not be cleared in time by officials. This failure led the applicant to incur a loss of US$24 million. This consignment was meant for the Kenya, Tanzania, Uganda, Rwanda, Burundi and Southern Sudan markets. At first, the initial delays were attributed to postelection violence that rocked various parts of Kenya in the aftermath of the country's 27 December 2007, general election. However, it was established that the disruption caused by the political violence lasted only for a few days. The applicant argued that all of his efforts to have his cargo released did not succeed.

The applicant blames Kenya Ports Authority management for transferring his consignment to a third party (Makupa Transit Shade), which is a container terminal at Mombasa Port. The applicant claimed that this

[75] Joe-Oloka Onyango, "Who Owns the East African Community", *Occasional HURIPEC Paper*, 2005, accessed 15 November 2013, www.huripec.mak.ac.ug/Occasional_series_1.pdf.

[76] See *Nyongo* v. *Attorney-General of Kenya & Others* (2007) EACJ 6; *Modern Holdings* v. *Kenya Ports Authority* (Reference 1 of 2008) ruling delivered on 12 February 2009, accessed 10 May 2015, www.eacj.org/docs/final%20%20MODERN%20HOLDINGSVS%20KENYA%20PORTS%20AUTHORITY%202.pdf.

third party could be operating under suspect circumstances. According to the applicant, all efforts were made to have the containers released; at one time, the applicant sought the intervention of the Kenyan minister for transport, Ali Chirau Makwere, and even written waivers from KPA senior officials to Makupa terminal to have the containers released were turned down, leading to the expiry of his goods.

The EACJ dismissed the applicant's case on a technicality. The court ruled that the Kenya Ports Authority was created by the Republic of Kenya and not by the summit and that the mere fact that the Kenya Ports Authority rendered services to East African partner states and their citizens did not ipso facto make it an institution. The applicant failed to satisfy the EAC Article 28 provision that deals with the determination of the legality of an institution's action. According to this provision, if a claimant (applicant) considers that an institution has failed to fulfil its obligation under the treaty, he may refer the matter to the court for adjudication. Thus, in this case, the Kenya Ports Authority is not an institution created by the EAC Treaty.

Conclusion

The peaceful settlement of disputes is always desirable when a dispute arises, and states usually rely on diplomatic means as a way of settling their differences. However, when breaches of treaty obligations have a negative impact on regional trade, as in some of the cases discussed, invoking the regional courts is one way to hold member states accountable for these breaches. This approach is also a peaceful way to settle disputes in comparison to unilateral retaliation and armed conflict. Furthermore, member states willingly entered into these trade agreements and set rules and procedures to be followed in instances of breaches of treaty obligations.

Gathii thus opines that African RTAs should be regarded as

> establishing flexible regimes of cooperation as opposed to containing rules requiring scrupulous and rigorous adherence [...] and that flexibility is not necessarily incompatible with assuming legally binding commitments. Often these obligations are assumed on the understanding that compliance will not be stringently enforced because the commitments are balanced against a variety of safety valves, such as the principles of variable geometry a as well as differences in timelines to comply with commitments that are based on the varying economic capabilities of their members."

This opinion is very relevant if put in the context of the approach of most African countries to international legal obligations. However, where there are clear rules and obligations to which member states can adhere without incurring economic losses, these rules and obligations should be enforced effectively. Supranational authority requires that parties compromise in their dealings with issues of mutual benefits. Based on the above discussion and analysis, these African courts and tribunals have not fully assumed supranational powers. This change will have to be made for regional courts to have a clearly defined role and to ensure that disputes are determined in accordance with treaty provisions.

Other scholars have asked questions, such as, "Could the lack of the utilisation of the dispute settlement mechanism be a sign that the role of regional courts is not recognised by member states?" This question was mostly raised in the Campbell case. The SADC Tribunal was clear in its finding that member states are the signatories to the treaty and therefore are, or should be, aware of the role that they gave to the court. While the pronouncements made by the court may not immediately change approaches to treaty obligation implementation, the possibility of having a case of a breach of treaty obligation come before a regional court may make states more cautious regarding the need to align their policies with the treaties that govern their trade relations. The courts have a duty to make member states' governments aware that the tribunals are there to safeguard the rights of all parties, as prescribed by the treaty. The tribunals do not exist as institutions that protect only the interest of the governments of the REC members. Regional courts or tribunals are an indication of the existence of political will by member states to uphold their treaty obligations. Allowing the tribunals to function without fear or favour is a step in the right direction. Member states, their citizens and other legal persons should utilise the options that are already available in the RECs, such as the role that regional courts have been given to ensure adherence to treaty obligations. Ultimately, the major challenge facing the African Trade tribunals is making law and rights relevant to Africa's social experience of massive poverty and inequality, rather than merely existing in the liberal sense of protecting individual civil and political rights and securing property rights. This challenge is daunting but can be accomplished.

4

Coordinated actions in international economic law as illustrated by investment treaty arbitration and World Trade Organization disputes

GREG TEREPOSKY AND LAURA NIELSEN

1 The interaction between different areas of international economic law

This chapter examines the interaction between different areas of international economic law as illustrated by the interaction between the law of investment treaties and the law of the World Trade Organization (WTO). This interaction must be viewed from the perspective of the parties invoking international economic law as well as from the perspective of the dispute settlement bodies that interpret and apply international economic law.

The proliferation of value chains and cross-border investment has increased the level of integration in global commerce. Combined with the increased sophistication of the commercial entities making up that commerce, international commercial problems are increasingly being resolved by invoking in a coordinated manner one or more elements of the multilayered environment that makes up international economic law. This environment comprises public international law reflected in multilateral, plurilateral and bilateral trade and investment treaties as well as private international commercial law. This environment is, itself, becoming more complex with the negotiation of new trade and investment agreements that cover broader subject matter in greater detail than in the past.

In the commercial world, different areas of international economic law are not viewed as independent silos but, rather, they are viewed cumulatively because they offer different opportunities to resolve commercial problems. Depending on the circumstances and the interests of the affected commercial entities, one or more different areas of international economic law may be invoked by or at the behest of the affected commercial entities to resolve a particular economic problem. This reality is illustrated by entities, through their governments, invoking in parallel the dispute settlement procedures in regional trade agreements and the WTO as well as by entities in their private capacity initiating investor-state claims and, through their governments, parallel WTO disputes. This chapter focuses on the latter.[1]

The complex nature of international economic law and its staged development from the multilateral model of the General Agreement on Tariffs and Trade 1947 (GATT 1947), through to the negotiation of the WTO Agreements, and the more recent proliferation of regional trade agreements and bilateral investment treaties, have naturally led to the cross-fertilization of principles and concepts between these different areas of international economic law. Not surprisingly, given their earlier development and rich body of jurisprudence, concepts and principles developed in the GATT 1947 and the WTO agreements have been particularly influential.

The two foregoing perspectives are strongly reflected in the interaction between the law of investment treaties and the law of the WTO.

First, the different substantive obligations, dispute settlement mechanisms and remedies available under the two regimes can and have been invoked in *parallel* against certain government measures that adversely affect both investment and trade. Where parallel investor-state/WTO challenges are initiated, the interaction between the two regimes is not

[1] The former is aptly illustrated in the context of North American trade remedy issues whereby parallel challenges have been initiated under Chapter 19 of the *North American Free Trade Agreement* (NAFTA) and under the WTO *Understanding on Rules and Procedures Governing the Settlement of Disputes* (DSU).

* Greg Tereposky is the principal author of this chapter. He is a partner of Borden Ladner Gervais LLP. He is a member of the firm's International Trade and Arbitration Group and has appeared as counsel before investor-state tribunals, WTO panels, and the Appellate Body. He is the founder and editor of TradeLawGuide (www.tradelawguide.com), the leading research database for WTO law. He is cofounder and adviser of InvestorStateLawGuide (www.investorstatelawguide.com), the leading research database for investment treaty law. The views expressed in this chapter are those of the author and are not necessarily those of the clients of Borden Ladner Gervais LLP.

The content of this chapter is based, in part, on Greg Tereposky and Morgan Maguire, "Utilizing WTO Law in Investor-State Dispute Settlement" in Arthur Rovine (ed.), *Contemporary Issues in International Arbitration and Mediation: The Fordham Papers 2010* (Leiden, Martinus Nijhoff Publishers, 2011).

** Laura Nielsen is the secondary author and is responsible only for rewriting parts of the chapter so that it addresses more squarely the conference theme.

limited to how they complement each other. Litigation tactics and rulings under one regime can affect litigation tactics and rulings under the other. Moreover, a successful challenge under one regime may resolve or partially resolve claims brought under the other regime. Examples of parallel proceedings are set out in Section 2 of this chapter.

Second, claimants, respondents, interveners, tribunals and individual arbitrators in investor-state arbitrations often *refer to WTO law for guidance*. This is not surprising given that WTO and investor-state law share many similar concepts and that the rich body of WTO jurisprudence provides helpful insights into the interpretation and application of such concepts in different contexts. Examples and analyses of this type of interpretive and result-oriented interaction, including the litigation strategies associated with this possibility, are set out in Section 3 of this chapter.

The above observations naturally give rise to broader theoretical questions going straight to the core of the founding principles of *jus gentium*. *If* the two systems indeed interact in specific *in casu* situations (*i.e.*, in instances concerning the same "case"), it may at first glance seem like the most optimal and pragmatic solution is to have the tribunals adhere to each other's conclusions – because it ensures that the systems do not render opposing decisions. In this manner, "fragmentation of international law" is thus avoided in the specific case. However, transcending beyond the *in casu* situations and looking at the situation *in abstracto* (*i.e.*, when viewing case law as an emerging body and whether different tribunals render opposing decisions), it becomes apparent that fragmentation is inevitable because even if two cases have been coordinated across the tribunals, there will be other cases that can proceed in opposing directions and thereby contribute to the creation of an inconsistent body of law. These issues are discussed further in Section 4.

2 Coordinated proceedings and litigation tactics

At the outset, it is interesting to observe that it seems to be the desire of most governments to include some type of investment protection in the portfolio of treaties that they conclude. It should not be forgotten or underestimated that from a respondent's perspective (*i.e.*, the state in the role as the respondent in both an investor-state proceeding and a WTO case), the cumulative application of the two regimes increases the exposure of government measures to challenge and increases the risk that a government will be subject to monetary liability. Conversely, having solid investment protection secures a predictable investment climate and – supposedly – leads to increased foreign direct investment (FDI). Lately, the Transatlantic Trade and Investment Partnership between the European Union and the United States and Comprehensive Economic and Trade Agreement between the European Union and Canada have reinvigorated the debate about whether investment protection ought to be included in trade negotiations and, if it is, whether this should include recourse to investor-state arbitration rather than addressing the issues through state-to-state dispute settlement and/or in national courts. From a claimant's/complainant's perspective, having two different tribunals with two different sets of rules provides for additional opportunities, grounds and arguments for challenging a measure. It also provides additional remedies. It goes without saying that this very aspect contributes to an investment climate that gives foreign investors increased confidence that their investments are secure even where there is a risk that a foreign government could act in a manner that would undermine their investments or parts thereof.

When focusing solely on the two parallel proceedings which a complaining party can bring (here noting that the complaining party indeed is a private company in the investor-state proceeding whereas in the WTO proceeding the private party has to convince its government to initiate a state-to-state proceeding), the two systems seem to complement each other in several ways.

The key differences that create the complementarities are:

- Investor-state arbitration concerns alleged violations of obligations relating to investment in a host state, a subject matter that is currently not covered by the WTO agreements except in limited circumstances.[2]
- Investor-state arbitration is initiated by an investor against a host state without the involvement of the investor's home government as would be required in state-to-state WTO dispute settlement. As such, an investor has more flexibility when making claims and arguments because it is not constrained by broader government policy considerations that can limit claims and arguments in WTO dispute settlement.
- The primary remedy provided by investor-state arbitration is an award of monetary damages against the host state in favour of the investor,

[2] Certain government measures affecting investment in a WTO member can be challenged in a limited manner under, inter alia, the *Agreement on Trade-Related Investment Measures* (TRIMS Agreement) and the *General Agreement on Trade in Services* (GATS), in particular in relation to the "commercial presence" mode of supply of services.

whereas the primary remedy provided by WTO dispute settlement is the obligation to bring the challenged measure into compliance with a member's obligations under the WTO agreements backed by the right of the complainant member to impose countermeasures.

- Finally, investor-state arbitration lacks the common institutional infrastructure of the WTO as well as a permanent review body akin to the Appellate Body. Most investment treaties accord claimants a choice of forum (e.g., institutional arbitration administered by the ICSID or ad hoc arbitration under the UNCITRAL Arbitration Rules). Arbitral tribunals are not bound by precedent and the grounds for review are limited for the most part to questions of jurisdiction. As a consequence, there can be considerable variability in the interpretation and application of similar obligations between treaties and also of the same obligations within the same treaty by different tribunals. Investor-state claims that may be viewed as border line or even rejected by some tribunals may succeed under others. This variability introduces an additional element of uncertainty into investor-state arbitration compared to WTO dispute settlement.

3 An example of coordinated proceedings

The parallel application of investor-state arbitration and WTO dispute settlement is most illustrated in the recent challenges of Australia's tobacco plain packaging requirements.[3] However, these proceedings are currently under way and final decisions have not yet been issued. Final decisions were issued in three investor-state arbitrations: *ADM & Tate & Lyle* v. *Mexico, Cargill* v. *Mexico* and *CPI* v. *Mexico* and in the WTO dispute *Mexico – Taxes on Soft Drinks*.[4] These proceedings concerned tax

[3] Investor-state arbitration: *Philip Morris Asia Limited* v. *Commonwealth of Australia*, PCA Case No. 2012-12 (UNCITRAL Rules); WTO disputes: *Australia – Certain Measures Concerning Trademarks and Other Plain Packaging Requirements Applicable to Tobacco Products and Packaging; Australia – Certain Measures Concerning Trademarks, Geographical Indications and Other Plain Packaging Requirements Applicable to Tobacco Products and Packaging* (DS434, DS435, DS441, DS458, DS467).

[4] *Archer Daniels Midland Company and Tate & Lyle Ingredients Americas, Inc.* v. *United Mexican* States, ICSID Case No. ARB(AF)/04/5 (NAFTA); *Cargill, Incorporated* v. *United Mexican States*, ICSID Case No. ARB(AF)/05/2 (NAFTA); *Corn Products International, Inc.* v. *United Mexican States*, ICSID Case No. ARB(AF)/04/1 (NAFTA); *Mexico – Tax Measures on Soft Drinks and Other Beverages*, DS308. Although these three arbitrations concerned the same Mexican measures, they were dealt with in three separate arbitrations because of differences in some of the claims and because the competitive situation between

measures imposed by the Mexican Congress on soft drinks and other beverages that used any sweetener other than cane sugar, in particular beet sugar and high-fructose corn syrup (HFCS).[5]

a The Mexican Soft Drink Tax

The tax measures at issue included: (1) a 20 per cent tax on the transfer or, as applicable, the importation of soft drinks and other beverages that use any sweetener other than cane sugar; (2) a 20 per cent tax on specific services (commission, mediation, agency, representation, brokerage, consignment and distribution), when provided for the purpose of transferring products such as soft drinks and other beverages that use any sweetener other than cane sugar; and (3) a number of requirements imposed on taxpayers subject to the soft drink tax and to the distribution tax.[6] For simplicity, this chapter refers to these measures collectively as the "Soft Drink Tax". It had the effect of imposing what amounted to a 20 per cent additional tax on soft drinks sweetened with HFCS whether produced by US investors in Mexico or imported from the United States.

In December 2001, the Mexican Congress introduced the Soft Drink Tax as a consequence of a dispute between Mexico and the United States over sweetener bilateral trade. It was introduced after all other efforts had failed to resolve the dispute. Specifically, it was a response to: (1) the US refusal to address Mexico's repeatedly stated concern that the United States had breached its NAFTA market access commitments regarding trade in sugar while HFCS continued to enjoy preferential access to the Mexican market, severely affecting the sugar sector in Mexico; (2) the continued refusal of the United States to submit to NAFTA dispute

the claimants made it difficult to address confidentiality issues in a single consolidated tribunal. See *Archer Daniels Midland Company and Tate & Lyle Ingredients Americas, Inc.* v. *United Mexican States*, ICSID Case No. ARB(AF)/04/5, Order of the Consolidation Tribunal, 20 May 2005.

[5] Panel Report, *Mexico – Tax Measures on Soft Drinks and Other Beverages*, WT/DS308/R (adopted 7 October 2005) [hereinafter *Mexico – Taxes on Soft Drinks* Panel Report], paras. 2.1, 2.6. HFCS is a corn-based liquid sweetener made using a multistage production process. HFCS exists in the following three grades: HFCS-55 is the primary grade of HFCS used in soft drink production. HFCS-42, while used in soft drink and juice production, is also used in the production of bakery products, canned goods, dairy products and other foods. HFCS-90 is typically blended with HFCS-42 to make HFCS-55, but it is also used as a sweetener in juices, candies, bakeries and food processing.

[6] *Ibid.*, para. 2.2.

settlement to resolve the dispute; and (3) the ineffectiveness of bilateral negotiations that the parties had conducted over several years.[7]

The Mexican government and the Mexican Congress disagreed over the application of the tax. In March 2002, the government exempted, inter alia, all imports and transfers of soft drinks and syrups (and not only those of soft drinks and syrups sweetened with cane sugar) from payment of the Soft Drink Tax.[8] The Congress successfully challenged this action in the Mexican Supreme Court of Justice, and the exemption was annulled and the Soft Drink Tax was reapplied.[9] This was followed by the initiation of the three investor-state arbitrations and a parallel WTO dispute.

b The three investor-state arbitrations

On 14 October 2003, ADM and Tate & Lyle served Mexico with a Notice of Intent to Submit a Claim to Arbitration.[10] The claim sought approximately $200 million in damages.[11] The claimants submitted that the Soft Drink Tax had a direct impact on their investments in HFCS production and distribution facilities in Mexico, causing substantial loss or damage in violation of NAFTA Articles 1102 (National Treatment), 1106 (Performance Requirements) and 1110 (Expropriation).[12] Mexico countered that the Soft Drink Tax amounted to a legitimate countermeasure, in accordance with customary international law, because the United States had breached its NAFTA obligations regarding: (1) US market

[7] *Ibid.*, paras. 4.72, 4.432. [8] *Ibid.*, paras. 8.92–8.94. [9] *Ibid.*

[10] *Archer Daniels Midland Company and Tate & Lyle Ingredients Americas, Inc.* v. *United Mexican States*, ICSID Case No. ARB(AF)/04/5, Award, 21 November 2007 [hereinafter "ADM Award"], para. 13.

[11] The Notice of Intent indicated damages "in excess" of $100 million were being sought (see *Request for the Institution of Arbitration Proceedings Submitted Pursuant to Chapter 11 of the* NAFTA, 31 December 2003. See also "ADM Files Notice of Intent to Submit Claim against Government of Mexico for Violations of the Investment Provisions of the North American Free Trade Agreement", *PR Newswire*, 14 October 2003). The *IA Reporter* reported that "[a]lthough details about the amounts claimed are redacted in the ICSID award, information gleaned from a subsequent filing made by ADM & TLIA in the Canadian courts indicates that the two firms sought some $200 Million (US) in damages from Mexico" (see Luce Eric Peterson, "Award in Archer Daniels Midland & Tate and Lyle Ingredients America v. Mexico is Released in Redacted Form; Following Partial Arbitration Victory, US Agriculture Giants Continue to Seek Further Damages from Mexico", *The IA Reporter*, 16 July 2008, www.iareporter.com).

[12] ADM Award, para. 3.

access commitments for Mexican sugar exports; and (2) the state-to-state dispute settlement provisions of the NAFTA by blocking the appointment of panellists under Chapter 20.[13] Mexico further countered that it did not breach any of Articles 1102, 1106, or 1110 of the NAFTA.[14] Procedural issues delayed the constitution of the Arbitral Tribunal hearing the claim until 14 June 2005.[15]

On 28 January 2003, Corn Products International (CPI) filed a Request for Institution of Arbitration Proceedings.[16] The claim sought damages in excess of $325 million.[17] CPI claimed that the Soft Drink Tax violated Articles 1102, 1106 and 1110 of the NAFTA.[18] Mexico denied that the claims had any merit, and, in the event they did, the Soft Drink Tax amounted to a legitimate countermeasure.[19] The Arbitral Tribunal was constituted on 13 July 2004.[20]

On 30 September 2004, Cargill served Mexico with a Notice of Intent to Submit a Claim to Arbitration.[21] The claim sought damages in excess of $100 million.[22] Cargill claimed that the Soft Drink Tax violated Articles 1102, 1103 (MFN Treatment), 1105 (Minimum Standard of Treatment), 1106 and 1110 of the NAFTA.[23] Mexico responded that the tribunal did not have jurisdiction to hear the dispute, and, if it decided it had jurisdiction, the measure did not violate the NAFTA and, even if it did, the measures amounted to a legitimate countermeasure in accordance with international law.[24] The Arbitral Tribunal was constituted on 11 May 2006.[25]

Thus, three separate arbitrations were initiated claiming violations of five different NAFTA provisions and seeking damages in excess of half a billion US dollars. The ADM and Tate & Lyle, CPI and Cargill Tribunals issued their awards on 21 November 2007, 15 January 2008 and 18 September 2009, respectively. All three found that Mexico had

[13] *Ibid.*, para. 4. [14] *Ibid.*, para. 5. [15] *Ibid.*, para. 23.

[16] *Corn Products International Inc.* v. *United Mexican States*, ICSID Case No. ARB(AF)/04/1, Decision on Responsibility, Award, 15 January 2008 [hereinafter "CPI Award"], para. 15.

[17] *Request for the Institution of Arbitration Proceedings Submitted Pursuant to Chapter 11 of the NAFTA*, 21 October 2003.

[18] CPI Award, para. 50. [19] *Ibid.*, paras. 59–71. [20] *Ibid.*, para. 16.

[21] *Cargill, Incorporated* v. *United Mexican States*, ICSID Case No. ARB(AF)/05/2, Award, 18 September 2009 [hereinafter "Cargill Award"], para. 12.

[22] *Request for the Institution of Arbitration Proceedings Submitted Pursuant to Chapter 11 of the NAFTA*, 29 December 2004.

[23] *Ibid.*, para. 10. [24] *Ibid.*, para. 11. [25] *Ibid.*, para. 21.

violated its obligations under Chapter 11 (Investment) of the NAFTA and awarded damages.[26]

c The WTO challenge

On 16 March 2004, before any of the arbitral tribunals were constituted, the United States requested WTO consultations with Mexico concerning the Soft Drinks Tax and its alleged violation of Articles III:2 and III:4 of the GATT 1994.[27] The parties were unable to resolve the matter during the consultations, and a panel was constituted on 18 August 2004.[28] During the proceedings, Mexico either did not respond or substantially limited its response to the discrimination claims of the United States under Articles III:2 and III:4.[29] Its defence was limited to three arguments: (1) the panel should decline to exercise its jurisdiction in respect of a dispute on the basis that it was a NAFTA dispute that should be subject to NAFTA dispute settlement; (2) the measure had a legitimate objective and was not intended to afford protection to domestic production within the meaning of Article III of GATT 1994; and (3) in the event of any inconsistency, the measure was justifiable as a countermeasure under Article XX(d) of GATT 1994.[30]

The panel rejected Mexico's request that it decline to exercise its jurisdiction in favour of the NAFTA. It found that the Soft Drinks Tax was inconsistent with Articles III.2 and III.4 of GATT 1994 and could not be justified as a countermeasure under Article XX(d) of GATT 1994. The Appellate Body upheld the panel's findings.

As a result of these rulings, the Soft Drinks Tax was abolished in December 2006, almost one year before the first NAFTA arbitral

[26] See ADM Award, Cargill Award, and CPI Award. The Cargill Tribunal awarded $77 million in damages. At the time of writing this chapter, the decisions on damages for ADM and CPI had not been made public. The *IA Reporter* reported that "the ICSID tribunal awarded $33.5 Million" (see Peterson, "Award in Archer Daniels Midland"). It also reported that the CPI award was $58 million (see Luke Eric Peterson, "Corn Products Asks Tribunal to Correct Award so as to Take Account of Likely Taxation of Award in Mexico", *The IA Reporter*, 14 October 2009, www.iareporter.com).

[27] *Mexico – Taxes on Soft Drinks*, WT/DS308/1, G/L/674, Request for Consultations by the United States, 18 March 2004.

[28] *Mexico – Taxes on Soft Drinks*, WT/DS308/5, Constitution of the Panel Established at the Request of the United States – Note by the Secretariat, 20 August 2004.

[29] *Ibid.*, paras. 4.115, 8.23, 8.62, 8.99, 8.127, 8.160.

[30] *Ibid.*, paras. 4.102–4.138.

tribunal issued its award and almost three years before the final tribunal issued its award.[31]

d *Interaction between the arbitrations and the WTO challenge*

Given their overlap, it is not surprising that the various proceedings interacted with each other. Most of the interaction flowed from the WTO dispute settlement to the arbitration proceedings. In part, this was most likely because the WTO panel and Appellate Body reports were issued during the course of the arbitration proceedings, allowing them to be referenced by the parties and by the tribunals. One can only speculate whether a WTO panel or the Appellate Body would have paid similar attention to the arbitration awards had they been issued before or during the WTO proceedings. This aspect will be discussed further in Section 4.

i The concern expressed by Mexico to the WTO panel

Aside from references to the arbitrations in the parties' arguments, the principal interaction between the arbitration and the WTO proceedings was the concern expressed by Mexico about the implications of the WTO panel's rulings on the three arbitrations. Mexico's argument was as follows:

> Mexico cannot jeopardize its litigating position through speculation about the various ways in which the WTO proceedings could interact with Chapter Eleven proceedings and influence the tribunals concerned. Evidently, the claimants in these cases would use any finding that this Panel might make in connection with a violation of Article III as evidence that Mexico denied national treatment in breach of NAFTA Article 301 (since it incorporates GATT Article III) and would probably argue that Mexico also denied national treatment to United States investors producing HFCS for sale in the Mexican market. Mexico will have a great deal to say about the interaction between Articles 301 and 1102. However, should this Panel find a violation of Article III that is not justifiable under Article XX, the claimants will clearly demand that the Chapter Eleven tribunals base their findings on those made by the Panel.
>
> For prudential reasons, Mexico will not go into further detail on these cases but would draw the Panel's attention to a recent instance in which it was insisted before a Chapter Eleven tribunal that a WTO ruling makes a *prima facie* case of breach of one or more obligations under this chapter of NAFTA. In *Canfor Corporation v. United States of America*, the

[31] *Mexico – Taxes on Soft Drinks*, WT/DS308/16, Status Report by Mexico, 12 January 2007.

> claimant argues *inter alia* that the United States, in refusing to implement the DSB decision in the well-known Byrd Amendment case (formally entitled *United States – Continued Dumping and Subsidy Offset Act of 2000*), has breached NAFTA Chapter Eleven.[32]

This argument was in addition to Mexico's unsuccessful jurisdictional argument that *NAFTA* Chapter 20 was the appropriate forum for the dispute.[33] Mexico argued that, if the panel exercised its jurisdiction, "it should refrain from making certain findings that could jeopardize Mexico's ability to mount a proper defence in international proceedings that are taking place in other fora".[34] Mexico further requested that "the Panel recommend that the parties (Mexico and the United States) take steps to resolve their sweeteners trade dispute within the *NAFTA* framework".[35] Finally, Mexico requested "the Panel to employ particular care in terms of how it formulates its findings and recommendations, making clear that its findings apply solely to the parties' respective rights and obligations under the WTO agreements and cannot be taken to prejudge legal rights under other rules of international law".[36]

The panel rejected the argument to refrain from making findings on the basis that there was nothing to suggest that panels have the discretion not to issue rulings and recommendations in disputes where they have found measures to be inconsistent with WTO obligations.[37] The panel also made the following statement:

> Both parties acknowledge that there is a dispute between them concerning the United States' commitments under the NAFTA regarding the access of Mexican sugar to the United States market. However, that is a separate dispute from the one that has been brought before this Panel. First, it is a dispute regarding obligations under a different international agreement, the NAFTA. Second, the DSU and the terms of reference approved by the DSB define the limits of the matter that is before of this Panel. Article 3.10 of the DSU states that WTO Members understand that "complaints and counter-complaints in regard to distinct matters should not be linked". Consequently, even if, *arguendo*, the dispute between Mexico and the United States regarding access of Mexican sugar in the United States market were a matter under the WTO covered agreements, a Panel could not link the complaints and counter-complaints related to distinct matters in one single case.[38]

[32] Mexico's Response to Question 36 of the Panel, *Mexico – Taxes on Soft Drinks* Panel Report, Page C-17.

[33] *Ibid.*, paras. 7.4–7.18. [34] *Ibid.*, para. 8.205. [35] *Ibid.* [36] *Ibid.*

[37] *Ibid.*, paras. 8.218–8.230. [38] *Ibid.*, para. 8.232.

As it is made clear in the following discussion, Mexico was justified in its concern that the WTO rulings could spill over into the three arbitration proceedings.

ii Acknowledgement of the WTO reports by the arbitral tribunals

All three arbitration tribunals acknowledged the existence of the WTO Panel and Appellate Body reports and referred to them in their awards.

iii The countermeasure argument

In response to arguments of the parties, two of the arbitration tribunals ruled on whether the findings of the WTO panel and Appellate Body precluded Mexico from raising the countermeasures defence. Both tribunals ruled in the negative.

The ADM and Tate & Lyle Tribunal observed that the panel dismissed the countermeasure defence, not because the measure was in itself contrary to international law, but because Mexico could not resort in the WTO proceedings to a countermeasures defence in relation to the alleged breach by the United States of a non-WTO treaty, such as the NAFTA.[39]

The CPI Tribunal did not accept that Mexico was precluded from raising the defence of countermeasures as a result of the WTO rulings.[40]

The Cargill Tribunal did not consider the WTO rulings when addressing the countermeasures defence.

iv "Like circumstances", "like product" and "directly competitive or substitutable products"

Turning to the question of whether the claimant investors and the Mexican HFCS producers were in "like circumstances" within the meaning of Article 1102 (National Treatment), the CPI Tribunal took note of the fact that the WTO panel and Appellate Body held that HFCS and sugar were "like products" for the purposes of Article III of *GATT 1994*.[41] The tribunal considered that the fact that HFCS and sugar were like products for the purposes of the GATT 1994 was "highly relevant" to the application of the test for "like circumstances".[42]

On the same question, the Cargill Tribunal stated that the fact that the WTO panel in *Mexico – Tax Measures on Soft Drinks and Other*

[39] ADM Award, para. 130. [40] CPI Award, paras. 154, 157. [41] *Ibid.*, para. 121.
[42] *Ibid.*, para. 122.

Beverages concluded that cane sugar and HFCS are "directly competitive or substitutable products" was relevant but not determinative of whether the producers of these products were in "like circumstances" for the purposes of Article 1102.[43]

v Discrimination

The WTO rulings appear to have carried the most weight in the ADM and Tate & Lyle Tribunal's ruling that the Soft Drink Tax denied national treatment to the claimants and their investment in violation of Article 1102 of NAFTA.[44] The tribunal stated:

> The evidence on the record shows the Tax discriminated between sugar and HFCS; designed to afford protection to the production of cane sugar, which is in line with the measures taken by Mexico before the imposition of the Tax. The WTO Panel and Appellate Body Report held that:
>
> Dissimilar taxation imposed on directly competitive or substitutable imports (HFCS) and domestic products (cane sugar) is applied in a way that affords protection to domestic production, and that the tax measures are therefore inconsistent with Article III:2, second sentence, of the GATT 1994 (WTO Panel Report, p. 132, para. 8.96).
>
> In the present case, the Tribunal also finds that the IEPS Amendment imposed dissimilar taxation on directly competitive products (HFCS and cane sugar) which is discriminatory and contrary to the national treatment principle under Article 1102. The Tax was applied in a way that afforded protection to the domestic cane sugar industry, targeting the HFCS industry, which is largely owned by foreign U.S. investors, including the Claimants.[45]

4 Potential applications of WTO law in investor-state arbitration

WTO law has been referred to frequently in investor-state arbitrations in various contexts with varying degrees of success. Tribunals have explicitly found that WTO law is relevant to investor-state arbitration. For example, in *Methanex Corporation* v. *United States of America*, the tribunal stated:

> [T]he Tribunal may derive guidance from the way in which a similar phrase in the GATT has been interpreted in the past. Whilst such interpretations cannot be treated by this Tribunal as binding precedents, the

[43] Cargill Award, para. 194. [44] ADM Award, para. 213. [45] *Ibid.*, para. 212.

> Tribunal may remain open to persuasion based on legal reasoning developed in GATT and WTO jurisprudence, if relevant.[46]

Although reference to WTO law in investor-state arbitration can be helpful, it can also be problematic where the differences between WTO and investor-state law are not recognized and accounted for or where the nuances of WTO law are misunderstood and the law misapplied. This difference in the scope of application of WTO law and investor-state treaties must be taken into account when interpreting and applying WTO legal concepts in investor-state arbitrations.

Some aspects of WTO law, such as the law elaborating upon the rules of treaty interpretation, are directly applicable to investor-state arbitration. Other aspects of WTO law may provide guidance on the interpretation and application of similar terms and concepts in investment treaties or simply offer a different perspective from which to identify and analyse issues. Reference to WTO law may be particularly useful in borderline cases where it is unclear whether the facts demonstrate a violation of a provision of an investment treaty.

a Treaty interpretation

Both WTO dispute settlement and investor-state arbitration are treaty-based, and, therefore, the rules of treaty interpretation in the Vienna Convention on the Law of Treaties (Vienna Convention) play an important role in determining the meaning of applicable provisions.

Section 3 of Part III of the *Vienna Convention*, which governs the interpretation of treaties and comprises Articles 31 (General Rule of Interpretation), 32 (Supplementary Means of Interpretation) and 33 (Interpretation of Treaties Authenticated in Two or More Languages), has been elaborated upon in a considerable body of WTO jurisprudence. For example, over 100 WTO reports, awards and decisions have substantively cited Article 31.

Since the same rules of treaty interpretation apply in both the WTO and investor-state contexts, the rich body of WTO jurisprudence elaborating upon the rules of treaty interpretation can be used in investor-state arbitration. A review of the WTO jurisprudence in the area of treaty interpretation shows a highly sophisticated and nuanced appreciation of the *Vienna Convention*. It compares favourably to the often

[46] *Methanex Corporation* v. *United States of America*, Final Award of the Tribunal on Jurisdiction and Merits, 3 August 2005 [hereinafter *Methanex*, Final Award], para. 6.

pro forma references to the *Vienna Convention* in investor-state arbitral awards.

b National treatment

Similar to WTO agreements, investment treaties typically (but not always) contain national treatment provisions. However, even where there are apparent commonalities in drafting, depending on the specific investment treaty and WTO provision at issue, their language and context can differ considerably.

The national treatment provisions in investment treaties use varying language.[47] For example, the phrase "no less favourable" or "less favourable" is common to the national treatment provisions. It is notable that the qualifying language "like circumstances" and "like situations" is absent from some of the provisions.

In the WTO, the national treatment provisions are found in a number of WTO agreements and instruments.[48] Most of these national treatment provisions include the phrase "no less favourable". The qualifying term "like" is used in most but not all of these examples. In one instance, the qualifier "where identical or similar conditions prevail" is used. With one exception, the terms "like circumstances" and "like situations" which are used in national treatment provisions in investment treaties are not used in any of the WTO national treatment provisions.[49]

Thus, there are both commonalities in investment treaty and WTO law (*e.g.*, less favourable treatment) and differences (*e.g.*, like circumstances). These provisions must be interpreted within their context which includes their surrounding treaty text. Of critical importance is that many of these provisions have additional obligations, qualifications and exceptions which are not shown in the extracts and which may further distinguish them from other provisions which, on their face, may seem similar.

[47] See e.g., NAFTA, Article 1102(1); Argentina-United Kingdom BIT (1990), Article 3(1); Argentina-United States BIT (1991), Article II(1); Energy Charter Treaty, Article 10(3); Netherlands-Bolivia BIT (1992), Article 4; Canada-Ecuador BIT (1996), Article IV(1); ASEAN Comprehensive Investment Agreement, Article 5(1).

[48] See e.g., GATT 1994, Articles III:2, III:4; GATS, Article XVII:1; SPS Agreement, Article 2.3; TBT Agreement, Article 2.1; TBT Agreement, Article 5.1.1; TRIPS Agreement, Article 3.1; Agreement on Government Procurement, Article III:1.

[49] The term "like circumstances" is used in a national treatment provision in the *GATS Annex on Telecommunications*, fn. 15. The term "comparable situation" is used in *TBT Agreement*, Article 5.1.1.

WTO law concerning national treatment has been referred to in numerous investor-state arbitrations, including *Pope & Talbot* v. *Canada, Feldman* v. *Mexico, Occidental* v. *Ecuador, Methanex* v. *US, UPS* v. *Canada, ADM* v. *Mexico, CPI* v. *Mexico, Cargill* v. *Mexico* and *Merrill* v. *Canada.*[50]

c *Most-favoured-nation treatment*

Most-favoured-nation (MFN) provisions are found in both investment treaties and WTO agreements. The general purpose of MFN provisions is to ensure that the parties to a particular treaty treat each other no less favourably than they treat other parties or third parties. Similar to national treatment provisions, there are some commonalities in the drafting of MFN provisions; however, differences in language, qualifications and context create a variance in the scope of such provisions.

As in the case of national treatment provisions, the MFN provisions in investment treaties use varying language.[51] Many treaties combine national and MFN treatment into the same provision, and thus, the phrase "no less favourable" or "less favourable" is common in MFN provisions as it is in national treatment provision. Qualifying language, such as "like circumstances" and "like situations", is found in some treaties and absent in others.

In the WTO, MFN provisions are found in a number of WTO agreements and instruments.[52] Some of the MFN provisions include the phrases "no less favourable"; others provide that a party shall be accorded "any advantage, favour, privilege or immunity" granted to a third party. In two examples, MFN treatment is only applicable to treatment accorded to "other Members" or "any other Party".[53] Such provisions

[50] An interesting analysis of the use of WTO law as guidance when interpreting national treatment obligations in investment treaties is presented in Jürgen Kurtz, "The Use and Abuse of WTO Law in Investor-State Arbitration: Competition and Its Discontents", *European Journal of International Law*, 20 (3) (2009), 749.

[51] See e.g., Argentina-United Kingdom BIT (1990), Article 3(1); Argentina-Spain BIT (1991), Article IV(2); Argentina-United States BIT (1991), Article II(1); NAFTA, Article 1103(1); Energy Charter Treaty, Article 10(3); Netherlands-Bolivia BIT (1992), Article 4; Canada-Ecuador BIT (1996), Article III(1); ASEAN Comprehensive Investment Agreement, Article 6(1).

[52] See e.g., GATT 1994, Article I:1; GATS, Article II:1; SPS Agreement, Article 2.3; TBT Agreement, Article 5.1.1; TRIPS Agreement, Article 3.1; Agreement on Government Procurement, Article III:1.

[53] *SPS Agreement*, Article 2.3; *Agreement on Government Procurement*, Article III:1.

do not incorporate treatment that is accorded to non-parties of a particular agreement or a defined group of states. Qualifying "like" phrases are also found in some of the provisions.

d Other

WTO law has been referred to in investor-state arbitrations in other contexts including performance requirements,[54] "legitimate expectations" in the context of fair and equitable treatment,[55] the interpretation of the term "relating to",[56] the treatment of different provisions as cumulative and complementary except in cases of conflict,[57] the application of the doctrine of judicial economy,[58] the power to accept *amicus curiae* submissions from a third party,[59] the burden of proof in international law,[60] and the general principal of good faith in international law.[61]

5 Broader theoretical perspectives and conclusion

There are many reasons why it might be attractive for counsel in investor-state arbitrations to cite WTO jurisprudence. This includes the availability of a rich body of case law that addresses similar complex concepts

[54] In *S.D. Myers*, the tribunal considered WTO law to support the finding that in determining whether a performance requirement has been imposed, a tribunal must look at the substance of the measure, not only its form, *S.D. Myers, Inc.* v. *Government of Canada*, Partial Award, 13 November 2000 [hereinafter *SD Myers*, Partial Award], paras. 273–275.

[55] *International Thunderbird Gaming Corporation* v. *United Mexican States*, Separate Opinion, Thomas Wälde, 31 December 2005, para. 29.

[56] *Methanex*, Partial Award, 7 August 2002, paras. 144–147; *S.D. Myers*, Separate Opinion, 13 November 2000, paras. 51–64.

[57] *S.D. Myers*, Partial Award, paras. 291–294.

[58] *Canfor Corporation* v. *United States of America* and *Tembec et al* v. *United States of America* and *Terminal Forest Products Ltd.* v. *United States of America*, Order of the Consolidation Tribunal, 7 September 2005 [hereinafter *Canfor*, Order on Consolidation], paras. 182–183.

[59] *Methanex*, Decision of the Tribunal on Petitions from Third Persons to Intervene as "Amici Curiae", 15 January 2001, para. 33; *United Parcel Service of America Inc.* v. *Government of Canada*, Decision of the Tribunal on Petitions for Intervention and Participation as "Amici Curiae", 17 October 2001, para. 64. See also *Suez, Sociedad General de Aguas de Barcelona S.A. and Vivendi Universal S.A* v. *Argentine Republic*, ICSID Case No. ARB/03/19, Order in Response to a Petition for Transparency and Participation as Amicus Curiae, 19 May 2005, para. 15.

[60] *Canfor*, Order on Consolidation, para. 93; *Canfor*, Decision on Preliminary Question, para. 176; *Feldman*, para. 177.

[61] *Mobil Corporation and others* v. *Bolivarian Republic of Venezuela*, ICSID Case No. ARB/07/27, Decision on Jurisdiction, 10 June 2010, paras. 169–175.

in many different factual scenarios. The attractiveness of WTO jurisprudence may also be enhanced by its predictability and consistency, which results from its development by panels with the support of a strong WTO Secretariat and an independent Appellate Body, both of which rely heavily on de facto *stare decisis*. This is in contrast to the ad hoc nature of investor-state tribunal decisions which are made without a strong secretariat and without the possibility of appeal.

Recognizing that there are differences in the scope and content of the provisions of investment treaties and the WTO agreements, to the extent that these provisions address similar concepts, it also appears to be attractive and the optimal pragmatic solution to have investor-state tribunals interpreting and applying such provisions in a manner that is consistent with the interpretation and application of similar WTO provisions both *in casu* and *in abstracto*. In this way, potential problems associated with two systems rendering opposing interpretations in the same case could be minimized. Moreover, it would help to facilitate the development of a predictable hard-law-based international economic law and avoid the fragmentation that could render the international economic legal regime void and unpredictable.

Given the advanced development of the WTO dispute settlement system, one wonders whether there is merit in extending the scope of that dispute settlement system into subject matter beyond the WTO Agreements, including investment disputes and possibly disputes under regional trade agreements. This might be possible through Article 25 of the DSU, which provides for special arbitrations, or through the creation of a new plurilateral agreement providing for private parties to participate directly in investor-state cases as suggested by Jemielniak and Nielsen in Chapter 10. Alternatively, one wonders whether other trade and investment dispute settlement mechanisms could and/or should be modified to reflect more closely the WTO model. The above-noted Mexican Soft Drink dispute clearly illustrates the deficiencies in the dispute settlement mechanism that governs the trade provisions of the NAFTA, a sophisticated regional trade agreement. The high variability and lack of consistency in the rulings of investment tribunals illustrate the deficiencies in ad hoc arbitration.

If one subscribes to the WTO Appellate Body extending its scope into other areas of international economic law and issuing decisions which have the effect of being not only persuasive but having some form of de facto precedential value, it would essentially become the world economic law court. This is not entirely unproblematic. First, under this model the

Appellate Body will start applying non-WTO law. This will give rise to issues relating to the de facto precedential value of such cases in relation to cases concerning only WTO law. Second, dispute settlement in areas such as investor-state and international commercial arbitration, which involve the direct participation of private parties, is inherently different than state-to-state dispute resolution. Third, the differences between trade and investment law outlined above may be extremely difficult for the Appellate Body to deal with as the Appellate Body is born out of the WTO system and perhaps not geared to creating a new body of case law interpreting (*e.g.*, national treatment as to mean something slightly different than what it used to mean). This may mean that the Appellate Body would have to be severed from the WTO and function as the world economic court being able to interpret and apply all economically related treaties. Finally, extending the scope of the WTO dispute settlement mechanism into new areas would require that additional capacity be added to the Secretariats, panels and the Appellate Body. The WTO mechanism is already being pushed to capacity with the existing case load.

PART II

The development and usage of precedents in international economic law

5

Minority rules: precedent and participation before the WTO Appellate Body

JOOST PAUWELYN

I Introduction and main findings

Like most international tribunals, states created the World Trade Organization (WTO) Appellate Body *without* a system of binding legal precedent.[1] In fact, to a greater degree than other tribunals, WTO members carefully detailed that panel and Appellate Body reports were *not* to create rights or obligations for anyone but the disputing parties. WTO members explicitly retained "the exclusive authority to adopt interpretations"[2] of WTO agreements. Although an "Appellate Body report shall be ... unconditionally accepted by the parties to the dispute"[3] and could thus be said to be legally binding for the disputing parties, the Dispute Settlement Understanding (DSU) explicitly provides that panel and Appellate Body findings "cannot add to or diminish the rights and obligations provided in the covered agreements."[4] This is

I am enormously grateful to Wolfgang Alschner, Aksel Erbahar, Enric Garcia Torrents, and Weiwei Zhang for their tireless help in collecting and sorting the data and running it through network analysis tools. Our discussions have once again confirmed the need, in my mind, for multidisciplinary cooperation. I would also like to thank iCourts – Centre of Excellence for International Courts in Copenhagen for funding part of this project.

[1] The only international tribunal to date that was set up with a binding rule of precedent (*stare decisis*) is the Caribbean Court of Justice. See Revised Treaty of Chaguarames, Article 221, entitled "Judgment of the Court to Constitute Stare Decisis": "Judgments of the Court shall constitute legally binding precedents for parties in proceedings before the Court unless such judgments have been revised in accordance with Article 219."

[2] Article IX: 2 of the Agreement Establishing the WTO. See also DSU Article 3.9: "The provisions of this Understanding are without prejudice to the rights of Members to seek authoritative interpretation of provisions of a covered agreement." (WTO Understanding on Rules and Procedures Governing the Settlement of Disputes or Dispute Settlement Understanding, Marrakesh Agreement Establishing the World Trade Organization, 1867 U.N.T.S. 154.)

[3] DSU Article 17.14. [4] DSU Articles 19.2 and 3.2.

hardly surprising. Governments and their domestic audiences are reluctant to delegate lawmaking power to "unelected judges," all the more so to international tribunals which are not subject to the same legislative oversight that is known in domestic legal systems (in practice, for the Appellate Body to be reversed, a consensus decision by all WTO members is needed).

At the same time, the WTO Appellate Body is one of only a handful of international appeal bodies. Its task is to review the legal interpretations developed by first instance panels and to "uphold, modify or reverse the legal findings and conclusions of the panel."[5] In addition, WTO members explicitly stated that the two-tiered WTO dispute settlement system is "a central element in providing security and predictability to the multilateral trading system."[6] As an appeals court enforcing a multilateral treaty binding on 159 parties (as of 2013), can the Appellate Body not be expected to seek a level of consistency across disputes, if only to guide first instance panels and offer some predictability and neutrality to WTO members?

In the eighteen years since its creation (1996–2013), how has the Appellate Body dealt with these two somewhat contradictory signals? Has the Appellate Body developed a practice of de facto rule of precedent? If so, when did this occur? And over time, is it influenced more or less by earlier reports? Have some Appellate Body reports been more influential than others? Conversely, do some Appellate Body reports rely more extensively on earlier decisions than others do?

This contribution uses data in the 108 Appellate Body reports issued up through the end of 2013 to tackle these questions. It focuses on explicit cross-references between Appellate Body reports and uses tools developed in network analysis.[7] As we cannot look into the minds of Appellate Body members, we instead use the number of explicit cross-references from one Appellate Body report to another. Every reference is counted as one "tie" between the two reports. We consider cross-references in the entire Appellate Body report, not just the legal findings sections, as a proxy for the extent to which earlier Appellate Body reports weigh on the outcome in future Appellate Body decisions. Admittedly, explicit cross-references between Appellate Body reports are a limited proxy to measure the degree to which precedent influences decisions. A cross-reference may

[5] DSU Article 17.13. [6] DSU Article 3.2.

[7] See Mark Newman, *Networks: An Introduction* (New York: Oxford University Press, 2010).

be dropped sincerely because it genuinely guided the Appellate Body or merely opportunistically as it happens to support an outcome that the Appellate Body would have reached regardless. Conversely, the Appellate Body may have been influenced heavily by an earlier decision but, for whatever reason, decide not to drop an explicit cross-reference.[8] In addition, cross-references between Appellate Body reports may be an indication of the way in which outcomes are influenced by past decisions. As such, cross-references would say little, if anything, about the content or scope of these past decisions. For example, they would not provide evidence of the Appellate Body making law or adding rights or obligations not included in WTO agreements.

Subject to these caveats, using the proxy of cross-references between the first 108 Appellate Body reports, it is safe to conclude that

(1) From its creation, the Appellate Body has opted for a strong de facto rule of precedent: in 108 reports, the Appellate Body has dropped a total of 2,957 cross-references to earlier reports for an average of 27.4 cross-references per report and an average number of 0.3 cross-references per page (indeed, this trend began with the second report, which cross-referenced the first report four times);
(2) this strong de facto rule of precedent has continued unabated over time and, if anything, an upward trend can be detected as demonstrated by the rise over time in the total number of cross-references per report (although this is partially due to longer reports and more reports in existence as time passes, also the number of cross-references per page does show a slight upward trend over time);
(3) the network of cross-references between Appellate Body reports is surprisingly dense, as all reports have been referred to in subsequent cases, except for the last two; 83 of the 108 Appellate Body reports have been referred to more than ten times; if every report would refer back to each and every preexisting report, a total number of 5,778 ties is theoretically possible, and the data show the Appellate Body made 2,044 of all possible ties (i.e., an impressive 35.4 percent of possible ties);
(4) at the same time, although the distribution of the total number of citations per report is spread out relatively equally, especially considering time and subject matter factors (i.e., 24 reports are referred to less than 10 times; 32 between 10 and 19 times; 18 between 20 and 29; 14 between 30 and 39; 7 between and 49; 13 have been cited more than

[8] See K. Pelc, "The Politics of Precedent in International Law: A Social Network Application," *American Political Science Review*, vol. 108 (2014), 1–18, 1.

49 times), some Appellate Body reports stand out (although older reports obviously have greater opportunity to be cited): the absolute champion is *Zeroing (EC)* (DS294) which has been cited no less than 232 times; only two other reports have attracted more than 100 citations: *Bananas* (DS27) (147 citations) and *Zeroing (Japan)* (DS322) (132 citations), while the average is 27.4 citations per report and the mean 19; if we count multiple (inward) references to the same report as one (in network terms referred to as "indegree centrality"), the winner is *Hormones* (cited by no less than 70 reports), with *Japan – Alcohol* as runner-up (cited by 57 reports);

(5) similarly, all but the very first Appellate Body report cite earlier reports; here as well, the distribution of the number of outward citations is spread out relatively equally (24 reports include less than 10 cross-references; 26 between 10 and 19; 26 between 20 and 29; 15 between 30 and 39; only 17 have 40 or more outward cites); only 3 reports have more than 100 references to other Appellate Body reports: *Zeroing (EC) 21.5* (DS294) with 267 outward citations; *Zeroing (Japan) 21.5* (DS322) with 161; and *US – AD & CVD (China)* with 111; the average is 27.4 outward citations per report and the mean 20; if we count multiple (outward) references to the same report as one (in network terms "outdegree centrality"), the winner is *US – AD & CVD China* (citing no less than seventy-six different reports), with *US – Tyres* as the runner up (citing sixty-six reports).

These results confirm the importance of previous Appellate Body reports for future WTO litigation. No one can successfully engage in WTO dispute settlement without knowing prior Appellate Body case law. In addition, it is not enough to know only the main or a handful of Appellate Body reports; given the density of the network of cross-references between Appellate Body reports, litigants must potentially be aware of all 108 reports. Even where an Appellate Body report does not add to or fill gaps in the WTO treaty, it clarifies existing rules and provides guidance for how the Appellate Body is likely to interpret these rules in the future. For all practical purposes, the Appellate Body has thereby added to the legal texture of the WTO treaty, through clarification, interpretation, and application of WTO agreements in what are now more than 100 disputes. Whether or not it has thereby crossed the line between law application and lawmaking is a notoriously difficult question and one that is left open in this contribution. As elaborated below, the Appellate Body itself has stated that its reports become "part and parcel of the *acquis* of the WTO dispute settlement system" and that "absent cogent reasons, an adjudicatory body will resolve the same legal question in the same way in a subsequent case."[9]

This raises the second set of questions that this contribution seeks to answer. If the Appellate Body is effectively engaged in rule refinement, if not rule-making, with legal ramifications for all WTO members and not just the disputing parties, which WTO members shape this rule development? Are some WTO members more active in Appellate Body litigation than others? Are other WTO members completely outside of this norm-development process, with no input as to their interests, even though at the end of the day (and "absent cogent reasons") Appellate Body interpretations may also affect them?

Here, we use data on country participation in all 108 Appellate Body proceedings to date (1996–2013). Instead of examining the network of cross-references between Appellate Body reports, we examine the network of WTO members involved in Appellate Body litigation. Our assumption is that if a WTO member does not participate as either party or third-party participant in an Appellate Body proceeding, then the Appellate Body case law is developed without weighing that member's input, arguments, or preferences. On this basis, it is safe to conclude that

(1) only a small minority of WTO members are shaping Appellate Body case law or the so-called WTO *acquis*: if we count the 28 European Union (EU) nations as one member, only 29 out of 131 WTO members have ever been involved as a main party (i.e., complainant or defendant; appellant or appellee) before the Appellate Body; and only 72 WTO members have been involved as third participant in at least one proceeding;
(2) within the already small group of WTO members involved in Appellate Body proceedings, a select subgroup of WTO members take center stage: of the 29 WTO members who have been main party to an Appellate Body proceeding, 10 have only been party once; another four have only been party twice; yet, seven WTO members have been a party before the Appellate Body 10 or more times: the United States (64), EU (39), Canada (20), Japan (12), Brazil (11), Mexico (11), and India (10)); of the 72 WTO members who have been third participants, 24 have been third participant only once,

[9] APPELLATE BODY Report, *United States – Final Anti-Dumping Measures on Stainless Steel from Mexico*, WT/DS344/AB/R (adopted April 30, 2008) [hereinafter *US – Stainless Steel (Mexico)* Appellate Body Report], para. 160.

another 12 only twice; yet, 18 WTO members have been a third participant 10 or more times;

(3) the network of participants in Appellate Body proceedings is small and sparsely connected, with two major hubs (the United States and the EU); with 131 WTO members, 8,515 ties are theoretically possible, yet only 67 ties have actually been made, representing a density of only 0.8 percent; in network analysis terms, this network is a scale-free network with a power law distribution or "long tail," meaning that a large majority of WTO members were involved as main party in zero or only a few Appellate Body proceedings and just a couple of WTO members are involved in or attract most of the "ties" or Appellate Body action (the so-called "rich get richer" phenomenon).

Section II summarizes the current state of affairs in WTO jurisprudence with regard to precedent. Section III elaborates on data collection and methodology. Section IV details the network of Appellate Body cross-references. Section V analyzes the network of WTO member participation in Appellate Body litigation. Section VI offers concluding remarks.

II Precedent in WTO jurisprudence

Even after eighteen years of operation, the WTO's position on precedent remains somewhat tortured. On the one hand, "it is well settled that Appellate Body reports are not binding, except with respect to resolving the particular dispute between the parties."[10] As one recent WTO panel put it, "there is not a system of precedent within the WTO dispute settlement system."[11] Indeed, to this day, the practice remains that whenever the Appellate Body tackles a legal issue, regardless of how many times the issue may have been addressed already, the Appellate Body will start with the relevant treaty text, interpret it according to the Vienna Convention rules, and only at the very end will it refer to prior Appellate Body reports. The United States in particular (and somewhat ironically, as *stare decisis* is engrained in its own legal system) is adamant about rejecting a rule of precedent in the WTO:

[10] *Ibid.*, para. 158.

[11] Panel Report, *United States – Use of Zeroing in Anti-Dumping Measures Involving Products from Korea*, WT/DS402/R (adopted January 18, 2011) [hereinafter *US – Zeroing (Korea)*], para. 7.31.

> The United States considers that a concern over consistency with a prior report adopted by the DSB should not and cannot override [DSU] provisions [in particular, DSU Article 11 directing a panel to make an objective examination of the matter before it] which do not direct a panel to apply or defer to previously adopted reports.[12]

At most, the United States "recognizes that prior adopted panel and Appellate Body reports may be taken into account by a panel."[13] In one recent panel hearing, the United States went as far as to say that:

> Appellate Body reports adopted by the DSB do not have an elevated status above adopted or even unadopted panel reports. The relevant question is whether the Panel finds the reasoning in any given report persuasive and useful for its own application of the customary rules of interpretation.[14]

On the other hand, the Appellate Body has explicitly stated that "the legal interpretation embodied in adopted panel and Appellate Body reports becomes part and parcel of the *acquis* of the WTO dispute settlement system," and that "absent cogent reasons, an adjudicatory body will resolve the same legal question in the same way in a subsequent case."[15] In other words, "absent cogent reasons," we can expect the Appellate Body to follow prior Appellate Body interpretations. Therefore, for a panel to contradict a prior Appellate Body interpretation is most likely to be fruitless since "absent cogent reasons," the Appellate Body will stick to its prior findings. Indeed, in the one case where a panel openly defied the Appellate Body, the latter came back with a vengeance. It did not go as far as finding, as Mexico had claimed, that the panel violated its DSU Article 11 obligation by failing "to assist the DSB in discharging its responsibilities" under the DSU. Yet, the Appellate Body did state that the panel's "failure to follow previously adopted Appellate Body reports addressing the same issues undermines the development of a coherent and predictable body of jurisprudence."[16] It added that Appellate Body members "are deeply

12 Panel Report, *United States – Anti-Dumping Measures on Certain Shrimp and Diamond/Sawblades from China*, WT/DS422/R (adopted June 8, 2012), para. 6.7.

13 *Ibid.*, para. 7.30.

14 US Opening Statement, Second Substantive Meeting, July, 2013, in *US – Countervailing Duties Measures on Certain Products from China*, DS437, para. 7.

15 *US – Stainless Steel (Mexico)* Appellate Body Report, para. 160. Somewhat strangely, in support of this theory, the Appellate Body (in footnote 313) relied, inter alia, on an International Centre for Settlement of Investment Disputes (ICSID) arbitration tribunal award along the same lines, even though most ICSID tribunals are notorious for not feeling bound by prior (often contradictory) awards.

16 *Ibid.*, para. 161.

concerned about the Panel's decision to depart from well-established Appellate Body jurisprudence," an approach that, in its view, "has serious implications for the proper functioning of the WTO dispute settlement system."[17] The Appellate Body reversed the decision of the recalcitrant panel but, after the lashing out, left it at that.

Thus far, the Appellate Body has never explicitly deviated from any of its prior interpretations (then again, it has only been in place for eighteen years). It remains debated whether only the Appellate Body or also panels can offer "cogent reasons" to change a prior Appellate Body interpretation.[18] The European Union in particular (and somewhat ironically, given the absence of *stare decisis* in most of the legal systems of EU member states) has been one of the strongest supporters of legal precedent in the WTO. Contrary to the United States, the European Union is on the record as supporting the Appellate Body approach of following precedent absent cogent reasons "without reservation," adding that, in its view, "only the Appellate Body [and not panels] can invoke 'cogent reasons' in order to depart from previous Appellate Body findings."[19] The EU would therefore support the creation of a formal legal hierarchy between panels and the Appellate Body, where the former is legally bound to follow the interpretations of the latter.

One incidence of note, however, was when a panelist in one of the zeroing disputes, which had found that certain types of zeroing were permissible under the Anti-Dumping Agreement,[20] was elected to the Appellate Body. Rather than insisting on his prior views as a panelist, he issued a concurring opinion as an Appellate Body member noting that, with regard to zeroing:

> The interpretative endeavour has ranged far and wide ... There is little point in further rehearsing the fine points of these interpretations. In my view, there is every reason to survey this debate with humility. There are arguments of substance made on both sides; but one issue is unavoidable.

[17] *Ibid.*, para. 162.

[18] See Appellate Body Report, *United States – Continued Existence and Application of Zeroing Methodology*, WT/DS350/AB/R (adopted February 4, 2009) [hereinafter *US – Continued Zeroing* Appellate Body Report], paras. 362–365 (where, at para. 363, the European Union took the view that "a panel may invoke 'cogent reasons' in order to depart from previous panel findings; but only the Appellate Body can invoke 'cogent reasons' in order to depart from previous Appellate Body findings").

[19] *Ibid.*, para. 363.

[20] See Panel Report, *United States – Measures Relating to Zeroing and Sunset Reviews*, WT/DS322/R (adopted September 20, 2006) [hereinafter *US – Zeroing (Japan)*], reversed on appeal.

> In matters of adjudication, there must be an end to every great debate. The Appellate Body exists to clarify the meaning of the covered agreements. On the question of zeroing it has spoken definitively . . . For these reasons, I concur in the decision reached [finding against zeroing].[21]

This is probably the strongest evidence of precedent in the WTO: absent earlier decisions by the Appellate Body, this Appellate Body member would have decided otherwise, and indeed he did decide otherwise when he was a panelist.

The above normative debate of what is or should be the weight of a prior panel or Appellate Body report remains open and contested. This contribution now takes an empirical turn and will examine the actual weight given by the Appellate Body to prior Appellate Body reports, using cross-references between Appellate Body reports as a proxy measurement. A recent empirical analysis by Pelc confirms the importance of precedent in the WTO. He not only finds consistent cross-references between reports (he limits his analysis to panel reports that cite other panel or Appellate Body reports and excludes cross-references between Appellate Body reports, which are the subject of this contribution). More importantly, Pelc shows that WTO members strategically file (costly) disputes or "test cases," even though little commercial value is at stake, to achieve a "rule gain" and subsequently use the precedent in commercially more important disputes and against more powerful opponents.[22] If prior decisions held no sway over the future, it would make little sense for countries to invest in commercially unimportant test or systemic cases. Even if WTO members insist that prior decisions are not formally binding, when one looks at the disputes they choose to file, it becomes apparent that they behave as if prior decisions do indeed set a legal precedent.

III Data and methodology

To collect data on the cross-references, page numbers, and the number of footnotes in Appellate Body reports, we used the actual text of Appellate

[21] Appellate Body Report, *United States – Laws, Regulations and Methodology for Calculating Dumping Margins ("Zeroing")*, WT/DS294/AB/R (adopted April 18, 2006) [hereinafter *US – Continued Zeroing (EC)*], paras. 311–313.

[22] Pelc, "Politics of Precedent," 13 ("disputes' commercial value is negatively related to their subsequent precedential value, offering support for the article's main hypothesis: countries appear to strategically file low commercial value disputes which go on to build favorable precedent for subsequent cases").

Body reports and double-checked our data with cross-references that are identified on www.tradelawguide.com. At this stage, we counted all instances where the title and reference of an Appellate Body report was mentioned in any part of the Appellate Body report including both the summary of the parties' arguments and the legal findings sections (a future iteration could count only the cross-references in the legal findings sections). This may be somewhat overinclusive as it includes cross-references in the summary of the parties' arguments (although this number was low when compared to the legal findings sections). At the same time, in order to gauge the impact of prior Appellate Body reports, the weight given to a report by the parties also has its importance. We counted both the "total" number of references (i.e., one report may be referred to several times and each reference contributed to the total count) and the "unique" number of references (i.e., counting only the number of prior reports that were cross-referenced). For Appellate Body reports in (DSU Article 21.5) compliance procedures, we did not include cross-references to the original Appellate Body report in the same case, since these cross-references between Appellate Body reports remain within the same dispute and thus cannot be seen as evidence of precedential value of one case/report for another dispute.

For the assessment of WTO member participation in Appellate Body litigation, we used the WTO dispute settlement website, as well as data gathered on www.worldtradelaw.net. We counted the 28 EU member states as one WTO member (the EU), as all cases that have appeared before the Appellate Body thus far that have either involved an EU member state or the EU itself were either filed by or against the EU and not against individual member states of the EU.[23] This left a total of 131 (instead of 159) WTO members. By reducing the number of WTO member states we may have actually over-estimated member participation in Appellate Body litigation. The EU is invariably represented by the EU Commission, which has one of the most sophisticated and knowledgeable WTO litigation teams in-house. The question remains, however, how much legal capacity individual WTO member states have as a result of this centralization within the EU. In other words, by counting the EU-28 as one and portraying the EU (and its twenty-eight member

[23] One peculiarity is *Thailand – Anti-Dumping Duties on Angles, Shapes and Sections of Iron or Non-Alloy, Steel and H-Beams from Poland*, Panel Report, WT/DS122/R (adopted September 28, 2000) (*Thailand – H-Beams*) where Poland participated in the Appellate Body proceeding as complainant before its accession to the EU. We counted this retroactively as an EU participation.

states) as the second most active and knowledgeable in Appellate Body litigation, we may attribute legal capacity to the EU-28 that, in practical terms, may only rests with the EU Commission.

We used the open-source software Visone for all of the network analysis results and visualizations, available at http://visone.info.

IV The network of Appellate Body cross-references

Using the 30,288 majority opinions written by the US Supreme Court and the cases they cited (220,500 cross-citations) between 1754 and 2002, Fowler and Jeon quantitatively tracked the use of precedent by the US Supreme Court. Using this data, they demonstrated that "[p]rior to the 19th century, both inward and outward citations were rare. This reflects the fact that during this period there was no 'firm doctrine of *stare decisis*'."[24] In the nineteenth century, they showed that "the average number of outward citations slowly rises as the norm [of *stare decisis*] takes hold." Indeed, "hardly any 18th Century cases cited at least one precedent, but starting in about 1800 there is a slow and steady increase in the practice. This increase levels off by 1900, when about 90% of the cases are citing precedent."[25] In the twentieth century, "the average number of inward and outward citations continued to rise." However, between 1953 and 1969 something remarkable happened: "a sharp decrease in average number of outward citations and the portion of cases that do not cite any precedents." This periodic reduction in use of precedent, Fowler and Jeon argue, coincided with the activist Warren Court, which "not only overruled more precedents than any other court ... but revolutionized Constitutional law ... Since the process of creating new law frequently involves breaking with existing precedent, it is no surprise that the Warren Court cited fewer cases in their opinions and handed down a greater number of cases without any citations."[26]

It is particularly instructive to contrast this U.S. Supreme Court story (i.e., little precedent in the eighteenth century, a slow rise in precedent in the nineteenth century, and a temporary dip in precedent in the mid-twentieth century) to the use of precedent by the Appellate Body. Although we are considering a much shorter period (1996–2013), the Appellate Body has, from its creation (i.e., starting with its second report, which cross-referenced

[24] James H. Fowler and Sangick Jeon, "The Authority of Supreme Court Precedent," *Soc. Networks*, vol. 30 (16) (2008), 16–30, 18.

[25] *Ibid.*, 19. [26] *Ibid.*

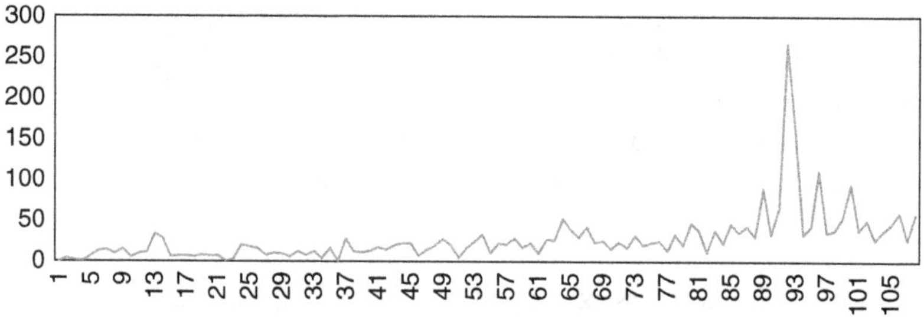

Figure 5.1 Total number of cross-references for Each AB report (1996–2013)

the first report four times), opted for a strong de facto rule of precedent. The Appellate Body did not go through a test period before cross-referencing earlier reports. It immediately opted for a de facto rule of precedent. In the 108 Appellate Body reports to date, the Appellate Body has dropped a total of 2,957 cross-references to earlier reports; on average 27.4 cross-references were dropped per report. Indeed, all but the very first Appellate Body report contains citations to earlier reports. Contrast this to the International Court of Justice (ICJ), where Ginburg finds that "only" 26 percent of cases decided between 1948 and 2002 invoke past ICJ rulings (however, one explanation may be that the ICJ deals with a much wider variety of subject-matter disputes than the Appellate Body, such that for any given case there may be fewer relevant precedents available to the ICJ).[27]

This strong de facto rule of precedent has continued unabated over time and remains surprisingly stable. If anything, a slow upward trend can be detected. There is a clear upward trend (with a number of peaks) in the total number of cross-references per report (Figures 5.1 and 5.2). However, this is partially because Appellate Body reports have increased in length and contain many more footnotes over time (Figures 5.3 and 5.4; again, note that there are a number of peaks), and also due to the fact that the stock of Appellate Body reports has increased over time. Nonetheless, the number of cross-references per page also shows a slight upward trend (Figures 5.5 and 5.6; again, note that there are a number of peaks).

We can now put these cross-references between Appellate Body (AB) reports in a matrix and use network visualization tools. Every AB report is a "node." When one AB report refers to another, a "tie" is formed between the two "nodes" in question. Should one report refer multiple times to another report, then more than one cross-reference or "tie" will

[27] Tom Ginsburg, "International Judicial Lawmaking," *University of Illinois Legal Working Paper Series (2005)*, 5.

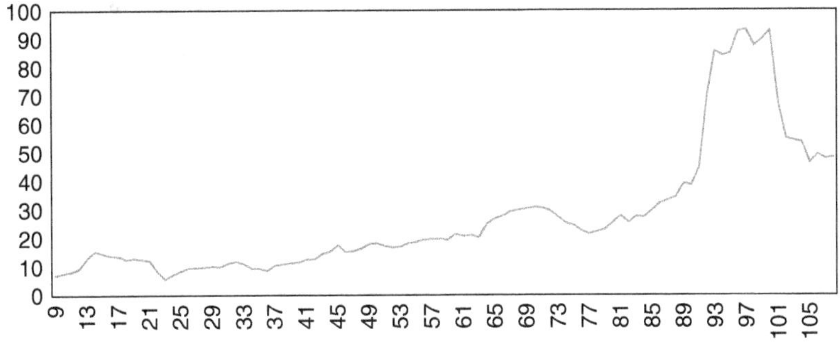

Figure 5.2 Total number of cross-references for each AB report (1996–2013) – total-simple moving average

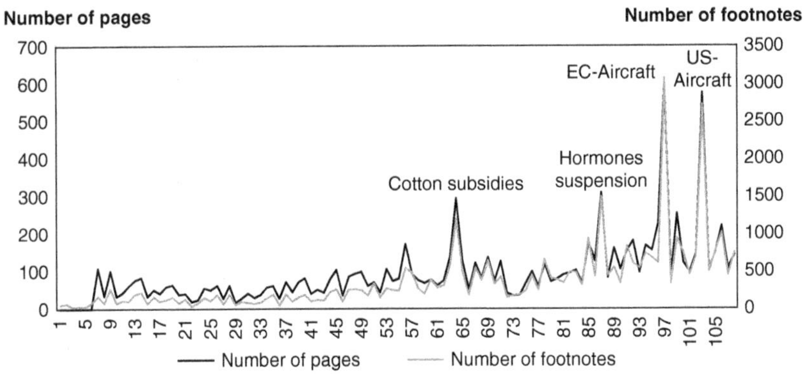

Figure 5.3 AB report pages and footnotes (total)

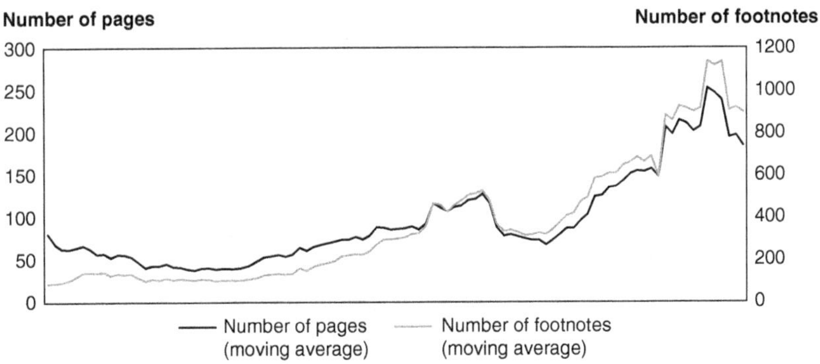

Figure 5.4 AB report pages and footnotes (moving average)

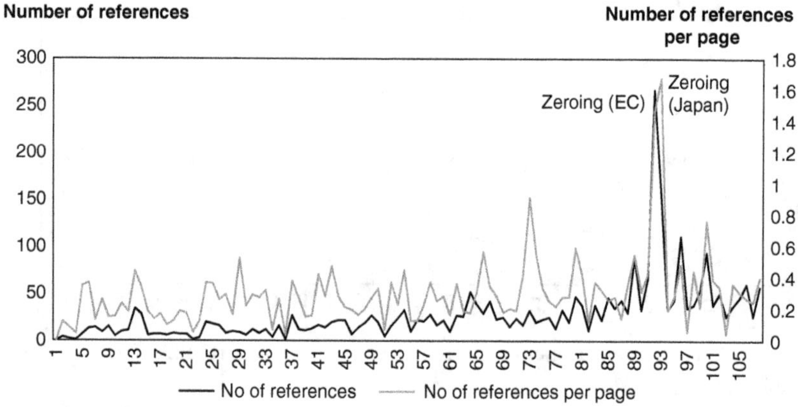

Figure 5.5 AB cross-references (total and per page)

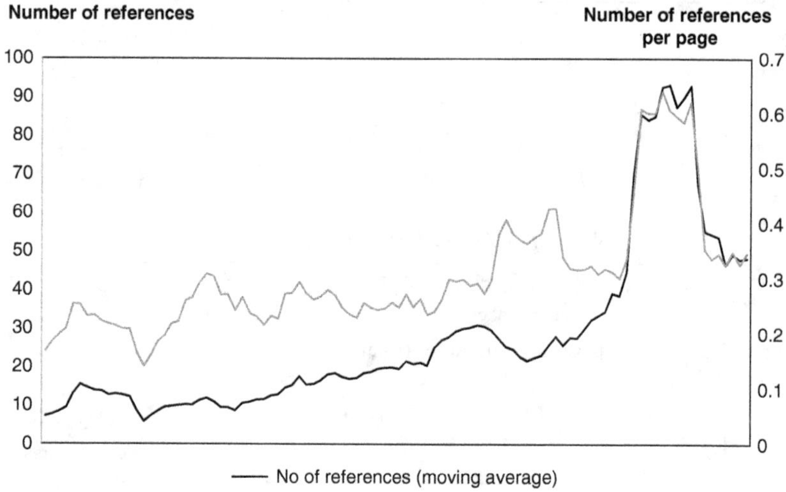

Figure 5.6 AB cross-references (moving average)

exist between these two reports. The more "ties" in place, the thicker the line between the two "nodes." Ties in this kind of network are unidirectional, as earlier reports cannot refer to later ones. The more ties a particular node has, the more centrally placed and larger the node becomes. Figure 5.7 demonstrates the results of network visualization between five randomly selected AB reports.

If we now put all 108 reports into this structure, Figure 5.8 is the result.

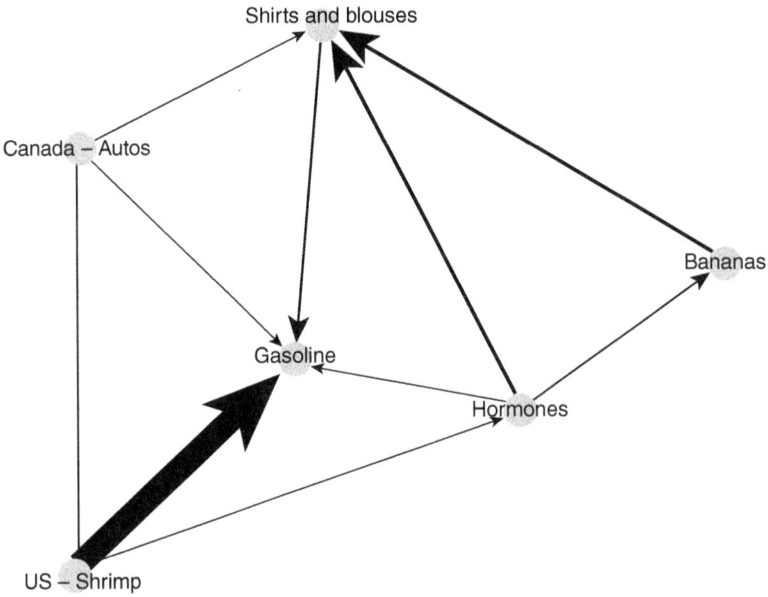

Figure 5.7 Cross-reference visualization between five AB reports

The network of cross-references between AB reports is surprisingly dense. With the exception of the last two AB reports, all other reports have been referred to in subsequent cases. An impressive 83 of the total 108 AB reports have even been referred to more than ten times. If every report referred back to each and every preexisting report, a total number of 5,778 ties would be made. In reality, the AB made 2,044 of all possible ties, or 35.4 percent.

As noted earlier, the AB, unlike the US Supreme Court, did not wait to cross-reference its earlier case law. It did so from the beginning. This is confirmed in the network analysis of AB cross-references, when considered over time. Figures 5.9–5.11 depict the eighteen years of AB jurisprudence during three periods (1996–2000, 1996–2004, and 1996–2008; please see Figure 5.8 for results from the full period, 1996–2013). From the visualizations below, it is clear that the network was already very dense and centralized in the first period (Figure 5.9, 1996–2000), with many reports connected to earlier reports and all notes linked into the network. Note also that a certain number of ties are particularly thick/extensive for obvious subject-matter reasons, for example *Australia – Salmon* (the second case under the WTO Agreement on Sanitary and Phytosanitary Measures (SPS)) extensively cross-references *EC –*

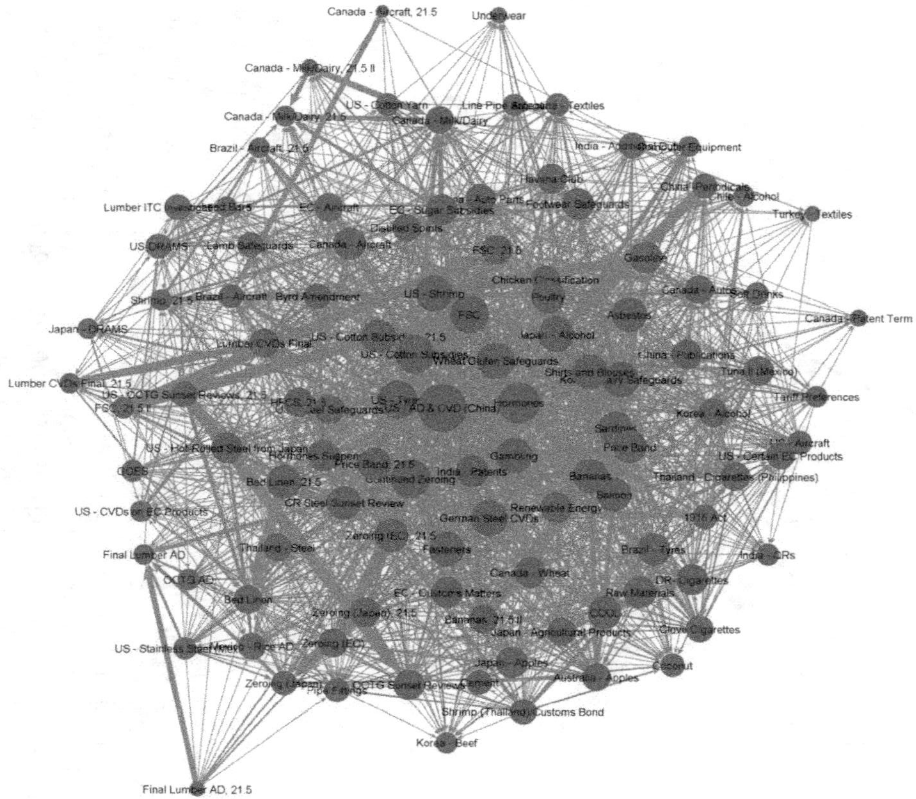

Figure 5.8 The network of AB reports (1996–2013)

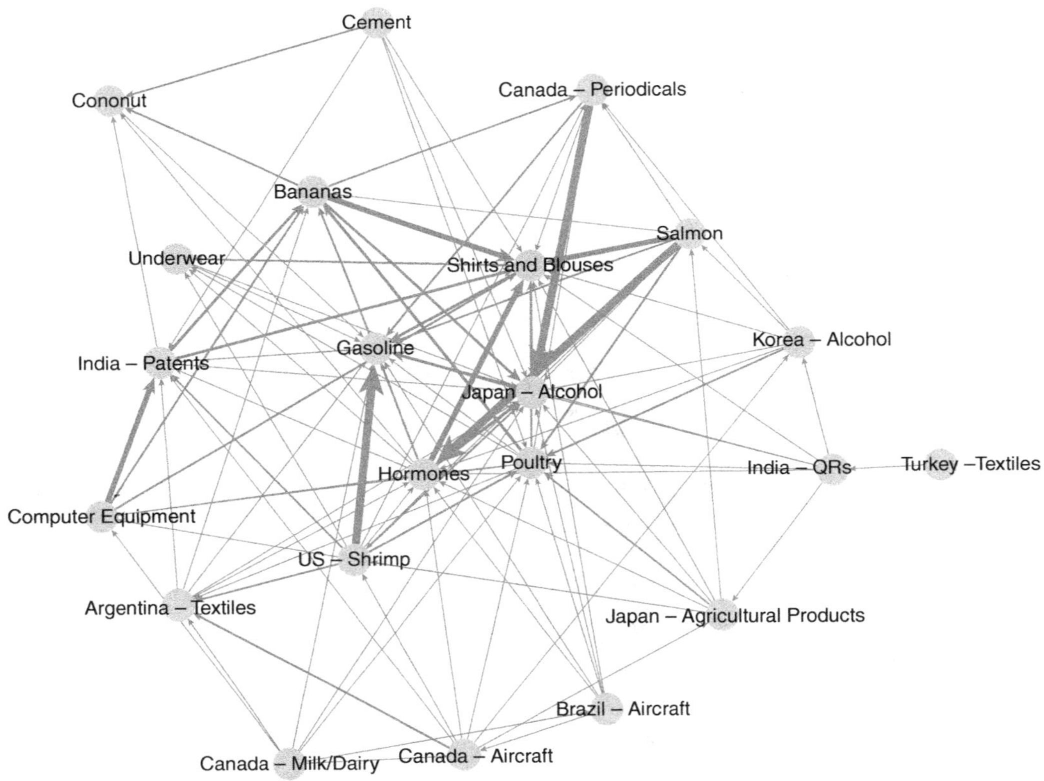

Figure 5.9 AB citation network, 1996–2000

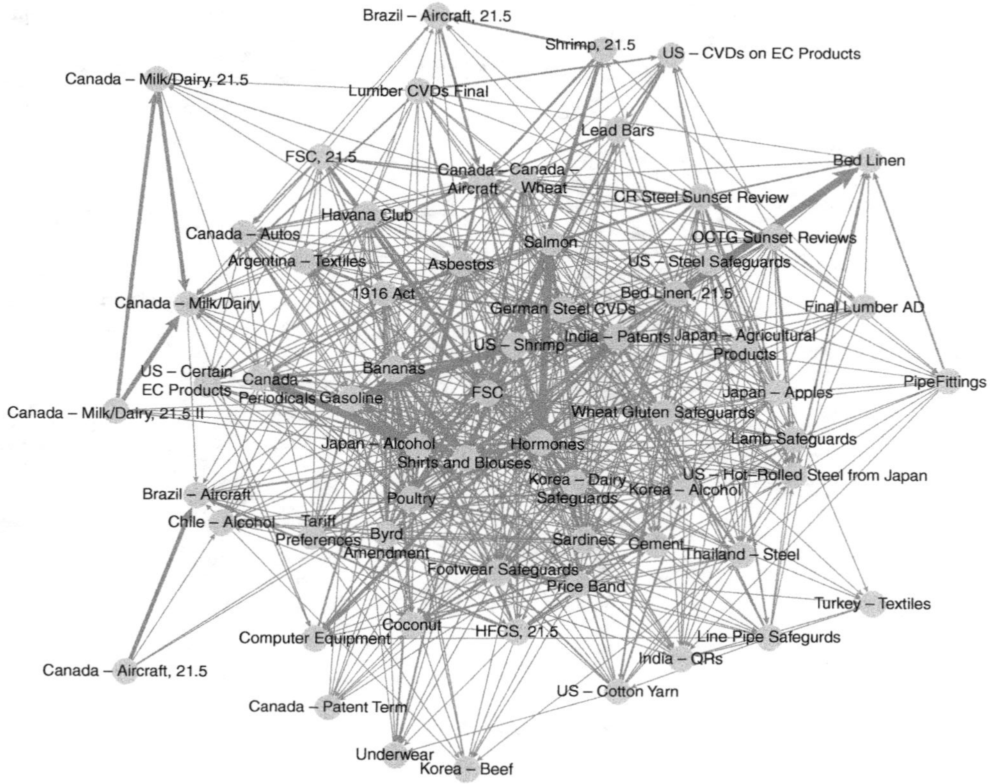

Figure 5.10 AB citation network, 1996–2004

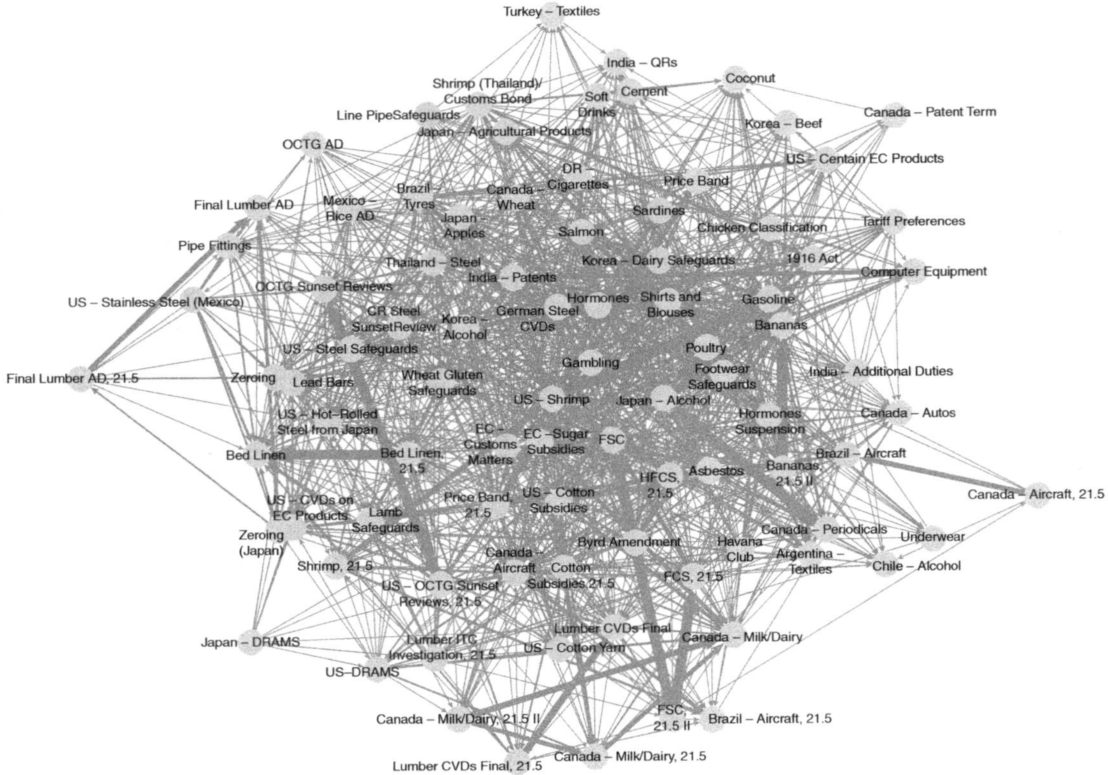

Figure 5.11 AB citation network, 1996–2008

Table 5.1 *Most cited AB reports*

No.	*Dispute name (short)*	DS No.	Number of times cited
1	Zeroing (EC)	294	232
2	Bananas	27	147
3	Zeroing (Japan)	322	132
4	Hormones	26,48	88
5	FSC	108	80
6	Gasoline	2	78
7	Japan – Alcohol	8,10,11	77
8	Shirts and Blouses	33	73
9	US – Shrimp	58	67
10	Canada – Aircraft	70	58

Hormones (the first SPS case), *Canada – Periodicals* cross-references *Japan – Alcohol* and *US – Shrimp* cross-references *US – Gasoline.*

We can now also rank the importance of individual AB reports. If we only consider the number of "ties" or citations that each AB report received in subsequent reports (i.e., if one report refers five times to another report, we count this as five citations), Table 5.1 lists the top 10 "Most Cited AB Reports." As Fowler and Jeon stated in the context of the US Supreme Court, "each citation is a latent judgment by the justice who authors it about which cases are most important for resolving questions that face the Court."[28] Note that we have not neutralized the time factor, thus older reports have greater chance of being cited than more recent reports.

It is possible to create a different ranking that considers not the number of (inward) citations that a report has attracted, but instead the number of (outward) citations that a report makes to other reports. The results of this ranking are available in Table 5.2. Once again, even if one report refers to another report five times, we count this as five outward citations.

Barring a few outliers, the distribution of total number of cites per report is spread out relatively equally (Figures 5.12 and 5.13), especially considering time and subject matter factors. Twenty-four reports are referenced less than ten times; thirty-two between ten and nineteen times; eighteen between twenty and twenty-nine; fourteen between thirteen and thirty-nine; seven between forty and forty-nine; thirteen have

[28] Fowler and Jeon, "The Authority of Supreme Court Precedent," 18.

Table 5.2 *AB reports that include the most cross-references*

No.	***Dispute name***	DS No.	Total number of cross-references (outward/citing)
1	Zeroing (EC), 21.5	294	267
2	Zeroing (Japan), 21.5	322	161
3	US – AD & CVD (China)	379	111
4	US – tyres	399	94
5	Bananas, 21.5 II	27	89
6	Continued zeroing	350	66
7	COOL	384,386	60
8	Renewable energy	412,426	57
9	Fasteners	397	54
10	US – cotton subsidies	267	52

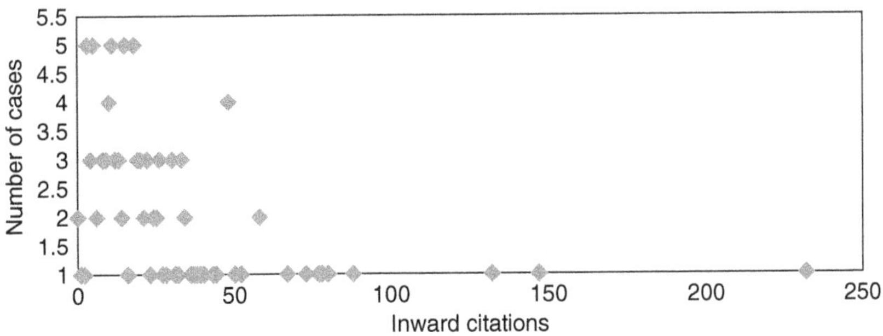

Figure 5.12 Distribution of number of cites attracted by each of the 108 AB reports

been cited more than forty-nine times. At the same time, some AB reports stand out (Table 5.1); the absolute champion is *Zeroing (EC)* (DS294), which has been cited no less than 232 times. Only two other reports also attracted more than 100 citations: *Bananas* (DS27; 147 citations) and *Zeroing (Japan)* (DS322; 132 citations). The average is 27.4 citations per report and the mean is 19.

Turning to "outward citations," (i.e., the number of times an AB report refers to other AB reports), all but the very first AB report cite earlier reports. Barring a few outliers, the distribution of number of outward cites is spread out relatively equally (Figures 5.14 and 5.15). Twenty-four reports include less than ten cross-references; twenty-six between ten and

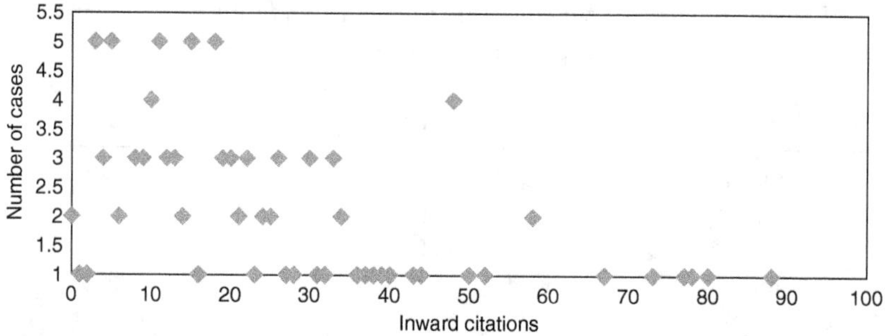

Figure 5.13 Distribution of number of cites attracted by each AB report excluding three outliers zeroing (EC), bananas, zeroing (Japan)

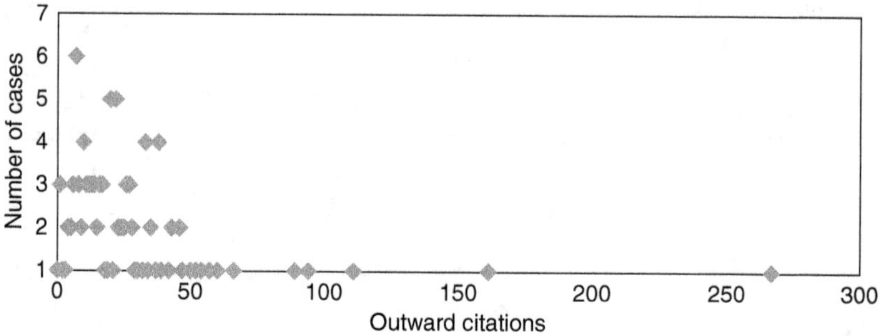

Figure 5.14 Distribution of number of outward citations (all 108 AB reports)

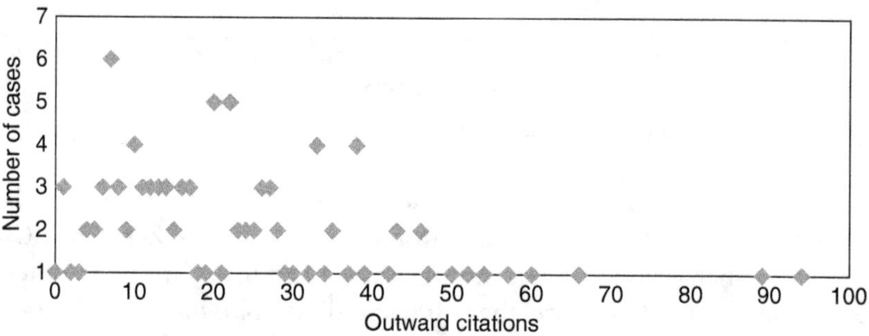

Figure 5.15 Distribution of number of outward citations excluding three outliers zeroing (EC) 21.5, zeroing (Japan) 21.5, US – AD & CVD

nineteen; twenty-six between twenty and twenty-nine; fifteen between thirty and thirty-nine; only seventeen have forty or more outward citations. Only three reports have more than 100 outward citations: *Zeroing (EC) 21.5* (DS294) with 267 outward citations, *Zeroing (Japan) 21.5*

(DS322) with 161, and *US – AD & CVD (China)* with 111. The average is 27.4 outward citations per report and the mean is 20.

Using additional tools taken from network analysis, we can also calculate different measures of "centrality." First, we can rank AB reports based on the number of ties that they have with other reports. Here, as for all other centrality measures below, we only consider whether or not one report refers to another report. If it does, then there is a tie; if it does not, then there is none. Should a report refer several times to another report, this still counts as just one tie. "Indegree" centrality counts the number of AB reports that cite a given report. For example, *Hormones* is referred to by no less than 70 of the 108 reports, and is thus ranked first in "indegree centrality." Seventy is an amazingly high number, given that *Hormones* was the ninth AB report issued, which means that 70 out of a possible total of 99 AB reports refer to *Hormones*.

"Outdegree" centrality counts the number of AB reports a given report cross-references. For example, *US – AD & CVD (China)* is the 96th AB report (chronologically), is cross-referenced by no less than 76 other AB reports (out of a total of 95), and is thus ranked first in "outdegree centrality." Table 5.3 provides the top 15 "most central reports," as measured according to these criteria.

Table 5.4 translates the "indegree centrality" ranking for AB reports to an "indegree centrality" ranking of AB members. In other words, for each AB member appointed between 1995 and 2013 (a total of twenty-three) we added up all the references made in AB reports to AB reports authored by that particular AB member (although the AB is composed of seven members; only three AB members sit on a division deciding a particular dispute). This ranking gives an indication of AB members that have, to date, been most influential in terms of influencing AB jurisprudence. Obviously, this type of ranking makes it easier for AB members who were on the AB earlier, or for a longer period, to obtain a higher score. Yet, if we want to gauge the influence of particular AB members on the network of AB cross-references, we do want to include this "bias" in favor of early and/or longer-term appointees.

A second centrality measure identifies a report's "authority score." Here, we consider not only the number of reports that cite the report in question but also the quality (i.e., relative importance) of the cases that cite to it. In contrast to the "top 10 rankings" in Tables 5.1 and 5.2 (above), for this measure when a report cites another report several times we only count one "tie." The top-ranking AB reports in terms of "authority" are listed in Table 5.4.

Table 5.3 *Indegree and outdegree centrality (top 15 reports)*

Rank	Dispute name	Indegree (cited)	Dispute name	Outdegree (citing)
1	Hormones	70	US – AD & CVD (China)	76
2	Japan – alcohol	57	US – tyres	66
3	Shirts and blouses	53	Continued zeroing	54
4	US –shrimp	51	COOL	49
5	Bananas	50	Fasteners	46
6	FSC	48	Renewable energy	45
7	Gasoline	48	Raw materials	44
8	Salmon	46	Zeroing (EC), 21.5	43
9	Wheat gluten	44	US – cotton subsidies	42
10	Korea – dairy safeguards	43	Tuna II (Mexico)	38
11	Poultry	43	Gambling	36
12	Canada – aircraft	41	US – cotton, 21.5	36
13	India – patents	41	Hormones suspension	35
14	German steel CVDs	40	Distilled spirits	34
15	Bed linen	37	Price band, 21.5	34

A third centrality measure identifies a report's "hub score." The hub score depends on both the number of other reports that it cites *and* the quality (i.e., relative importance) of the reports cited. Again, when a report cites another report several times, we only count one "tie." The top ranking AB reports in terms of "hub" score are also listed in Table 5.5. As Fowler and Jeon said of the US Supreme Court, authority scores indicate "the degree to which a case is thought to be important for resolving other important issues that come before the Court." In contrast, "hub scores indicate the degree to which a case is well-grounded in previous important rulings."[29]

[29] *Ibid.*, 17. Authority centrality is proportional to the sum of the hub centralities of the nodes that point to it and vice versa. Hub centrality is proportional to the sum of the authority centralities of the nodes that a given node points to. In laymen terms, the authority centrality of an AB report depends on how many AB reports point to it and to how important they are. If an AB report is cited by an AB report that contains only few references, this will do less to increase its authority than if it is cited by an AB report that

Table 5.4 *AB members with the most cross-references*

No.	Appellate body member name	Appointment period	Number of cases decided	Total number of cross-references
1	Bacchus	1995–2003	27	741
2	Feliciano	1995–2001	21	667
3	Lacarte-Muro	1995–2001	22	581
4	Ehlermann	1995–2001	21	509
5	Matsushita	1995–2000	13	410
6	Taniguchi	2000–2007	22	399
7	Abi-Saab	2000–2008	27	362
8	Ganesan	2000–2008	24	354
9	El-Naggar	1995–2000	12	327
10	Baptista	2001–2009	20	322
11	Beeby	1995–2000	10	306
12	Sacerdoti	2001–2009	23	284
13	Lockhart	2001–2006	11	203
14	Unterhalter	2006–2013	12	119
15	Janow	2003–2007	10	111

One infamous question that is often posed to AB candidates in interviews with WTO members is "Which AB report do you consider the most important?" For most candidates this is a terrifying question, as it risks unearthing their personal or ideological preferences. The above analysis offers objective ways to answer the question. As Fowler and Jeon state:

> We can use authority scores to classify the importance of every case in the network with a fraction of the time and effort and without the ideological bias that might be present in expert surveys . . . why rely on third parties to evaluate which cases are most important when the network contains the evaluations of the justices themselves?[30]

V The network of participation in Appellate Body litigation

The above results confirm the importance of prior AB reports for future WTO litigation. No one can successfully engage in WTO dispute settlement without knowing prior AB case law. In addition, it is not enough to

contains many references to other AB reports. This introduces a weighting mechanism for citations, as only those reports that are cited consistently throughout the network will achieve a high authority score.

30 *Ibid.*, 17 and 20.

Table 5.5 *Authority and hub score of AB reports (top 15)*

Rank	Dispute name	Authority score	Dispute name	Hub score
1	Hormones	2.86	US – AD & CVD (China)	3.08
2	Salmon	2.26	US – tyres	2.81
3	US – shrimp	2.18	Continued zeroing	2.40
4	FSC	2.17	US – cotton subsidies	2.14
5	Wheat gluten safeguards	2.16	Fasteners	2.04
6	Bananas	2.10	Raw materials	2.02
7	German steel CVDs	2.08	COOL	1.97
8	Korea – dairy safeguards	2.08	Gambling	1.89
9	Shirts and blouses	2.07	Zeroing (EC), 21.5	1.82
10	Japan – alcohol	2.04	Renewable energy	1.78
11	Asbestos	1.86	Price band, 21.5	1.70
12	Gasoline	1.81	Tuna II (Mexico)	1.69
13	Price band	1.80	EC – sugar subsidies	1.68
14	Sardines	1.70	US – cotton, 21.5	1.67
15	Bed linen	1.69	Hormones suspension	1.61

only know the main or a handful of AB reports; given the density of the network of cross-references between AB reports, litigants potentially need to be aware of all 108 reports. For all practical purposes, the AB has thereby added to the legal texture of the WTO treaty.

This raises the second set of questions that this contribution seeks to answer: if the AB is effectively engaged in rule refinement, if not rule-making, with legal implications for all WTO members and not just the disputing parties, then which WTO members shape this rule development? Are some WTO members more active in AB litigation than others? Are other WTO members completely outside of this norm-development process, with no input as to their interests, even though, at the end of the day (and "absent cogent reasons"), AB interpretations also affect them?

Our assumption is that if a WTO member does not participate as either party or third participant in an AB proceeding, AB case law is developed without weighing that member's input, arguments, or preferences.

Table 5.6 *WTO members participating as main party*

No.	Member	No. of cases involved	No.	Member	No. of cases Involved
1	United States	64	16	Guatemala	2
2	European Union	39	17	Honduras	2
3	Canada	20	18	Indonesia	2
4	Japan	12	19	Pakistan	2
5	Brazil	11	20	Antigua and Barbuda	1
6	Mexico	11	21	Costa Rica	1
7	India	10	22	Dominican Republic	1
8	Korea, Republic of	8	23	Ecuador	1
9	China	7	24	Malaysia	1
10	Thailand	7	25	Norway	1
11	Australia	6	26	Peru	1
12	Argentina	4	27	Switzerland	1
13	New Zealand	4	28	Turkey	1
14	Chile	3	29	Venezuela	1
15	Philippines	3			

Only a small minority of WTO members shape AB case law or the so-called WTO *acquis.* Counting the EU-28 as one member, only 29 out of 131 WTO members have ever been involved as a main party (i.e., complainant or defendant; appellant or appellee) before the AB (Table 5.6).

Seventy-two WTO members have been involved as third participants in at least one proceeding. Even if the EU-28 are counted as one member, 102 WTO members have never participated as a main party in any of the 108 AB proceedings. Fifty-nine have even never been a third participant.

Within the already small group of WTO members involved in AB proceedings, a select subgroup of WTO members take center stage. Of the twenty-nine WTO members who have been main party to an AB proceeding, ten have only been party once, four have only been party twice, but seven WTO members have been a party before the AB ten or more times: the United States (64), EU (39), Canada (20), Japan (12),

Brazil (11), Mexico (11), and India (10). Of the seventy-two WTO members who have been third participants, twenty-four have been third participant only once, another twelve only twice, but eighteen WTO members have been a third-party participant ten or more times.

The network of main parties in AB proceedings (Figure 5.16) is small and sparsely connected, with two major hubs (the United States and the EU). Each WTO member involved in this network represents a "node." When two members or "nodes" are involved in an AB proceeding as main parties, a "tie" or line between the nodes is established. The more cases that exist between two WTO members, the thicker the line. The visualization in Figure 5.8 also indicates the direction of the tie (i.e., who is suing who) and if a tie is established in both directions, through use of arrows to indicate directionality. Ties between WTO members that go in both directions are represented with colored lines.

Figure 5.17 represents the same network as Figure 5.16 but adds all of the WTO members (102) who have never been a main party before the AB to date.

Among 131 WTO members, 8,515 ties are possible. Yet only sixty-seven ties have actually been made, representing a density of only 0.8 percent. In network analysis terms, this network is a scale-free network with a power law distribution or "long tail" (Figure 5.18), meaning that a large majority of WTO members were involved as main party in zero or only a few AB proceedings and just a couple of WTO members are involved in, or attract, most of the "ties" or AB action (the so-called rich get richer phenomenon).

VI Conclusion

The network of cross-references between AB reports is both large and dense (35.4 percent), with multiple cross-references between many of the 108 reports to date. In contrast, the network of participants before the AB is small and sparse (0.8 percent), where two WTO members act as central hubs or feeders of WTO AB jurisprudence, leaving all other WTO members well behind. Combining these two phenomena, one can speak of rule development steered by a (small) minority of WTO members; minority rules.

This brings to the forefront one of the core, and often forgotten, arguments against too strong a rule of precedent: if few stakeholders are actually involved in shaping the precedent, then precedent risks becoming rule by minority. After all, few shape precedent yet precedent

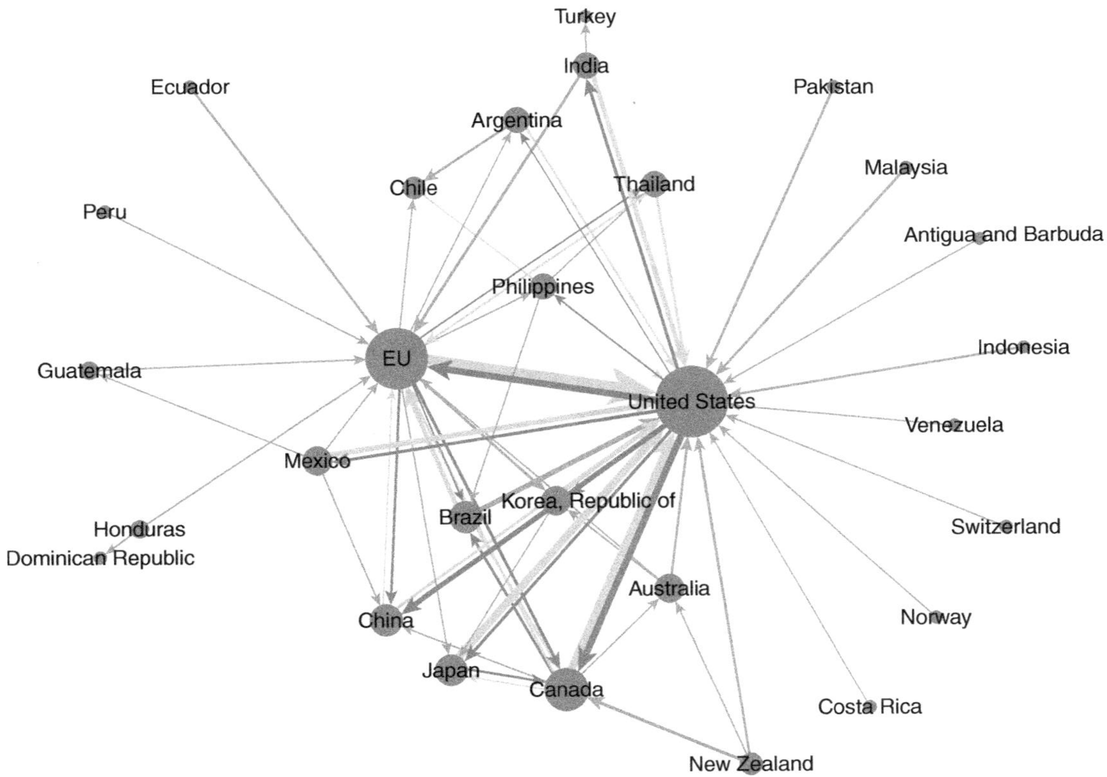

Figure 5.16 The network of main parties in AB proceedings

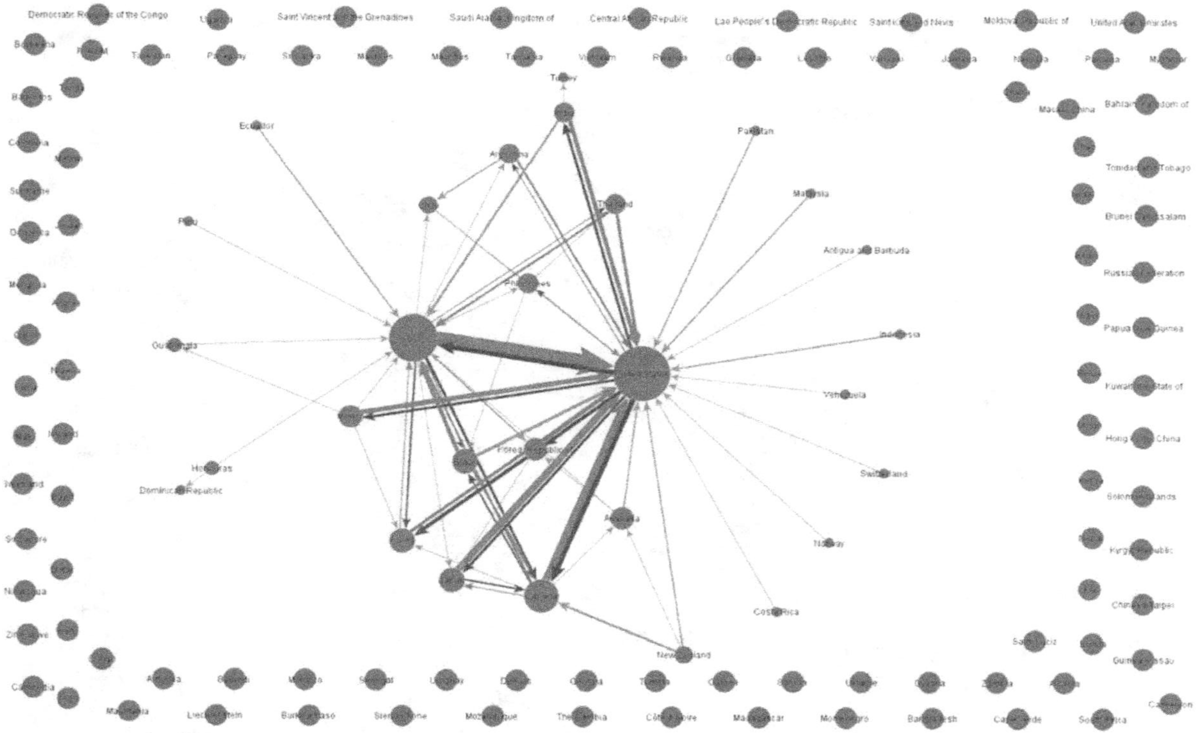

Figure 5.17 The network of main parties in AB proceedings, including outsiders

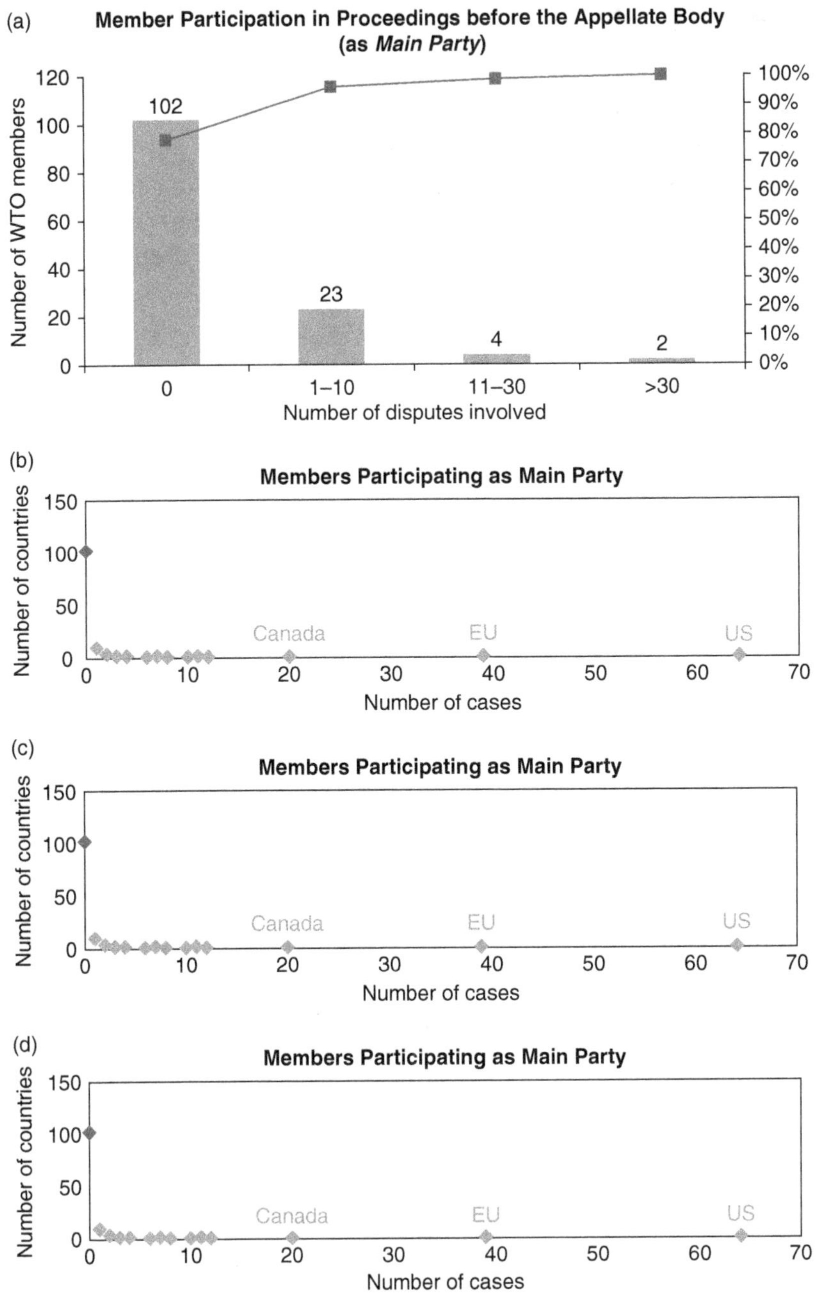

Figure 5.18 The distribution of WTO member participation in AB proceedings

affects the rights and obligations of all. This does not necessarily mean that precedent or prior decisions should not play a role in WTO litigation. Instead, the best strategy moving forward is to (1) realize the risks and limits of too strong a rule of precedent before international tribunals and (2) enhance the legal capacity, involvement, and active input of all WTO members in developing the case law of the AB, in particular via participation as third parties. As Pelc said, "if some countries are sufficiently farsighted to invest in precedent on low-salience disputes, others should be able to recognize and contest these efforts, if the resulting precedent would be unfavorable to them."[31]

[31] Pelc, "Politics of Precedent," 2.

6

The welfare implications of precedent in international law

KRZYSZTOF J. PELC

Introduction

There is no formally binding precedent in international law. The rest is in dispute. Legal scholars have long suspected that despite the widely agreed-upon fact that international law denies the formal authority of precedent, something akin to *de facto stare decisis* or effectively binding precedent operates nonetheless. International trade law is no exception: legal texts and judicial opinions explicitly deny that past decisions have precedential authority, yet there is a growing sense that the significance of precedent has steadily risen with the trade regime's increased legalization, as marked by the passage from the General Agreement on Tariffs and Trade (GATT) to the World Trade Organization (WTO), and the introduction of the Appellate Body.

After reviewing this debate, this chapter proposes some empirical strategies to assess the claim that precedent in international law is effectively binding. The common premise behind these approaches is that if precedent is binding on courts, then this should be reflected in other actors' behaviour. I show how recent findings that use the entire universe of WTO disputes and the legal citations between them suggest that WTO member governments systematically invest in precedent. Countries thus behave *as if* precedent were binding; specifically, they appear to file some disputes for precedential rather than for commercial gains. Such "test cases", which tend to involve small stakes, then become highly likely to be cited, especially by the country who initiated the first dispute.[1] In other words, governments strategically bet that courts will be swayed by past precedent, even as the formal rules explicitly deny their

[1] Krzysztof J. Pelc, "The Politics of Precedent in International Law: A Social Network Application", *American Political Science Review*, vol. 108 (3) (2014), 547–564.

authority. One can perform a similar exercise by looking at financial markets to assess whether or not markets make links between disputes: specifically, do financial markets update their beliefs about the likely outcome of one dispute when another dispute produces an unexpected ruling? The answer appears to be yes: firms that benefit from measures shown to be in violation in another country see their market valuation negatively affected.[2] This occurs even as there is no formal legal link between the ruling and the foreign firms under observation. From this review of recent findings, the chapter's first section concludes that although binding precedent may be, legally speaking, a fiction, it is a fiction that countries allow themselves to be bound by.

The second section of the chapter interrogates this first conclusion. Namely why would countries tolerate the informal rise in authority of precedent? After all, there is good reason for the widespread denial of the binding force of precedent in international law. To put it bluntly, countries fear judicial activism. Domestic audiences are skittish at the notion of countries delegating enforcement power to unelected international institutions, let alone delegating rule-*making* power to those institutions. Allowing for binding precedent constitutes a politically untenable concession to institutions "taking on a life of their own". A foreign judge who rules on a dispute that a country may not even be party to can suddenly modify the meaning of the rules that its government has committed to. Moreover, binding precedent falls prey to condemnations of undemocratic decision-making, since unelected individuals can potential changing the system's balance of rights and obligations.[3]

Given the expected political reticence to delegate such power to international courts, why do we observe a tacit acceptance of the rising authority of precedent among governments? I suggest that allowing for de facto binding precedent may constitute a strategic response by states to the weakness of international courts. Allowing judges to invoke the authority of past decisions limits the otherwise significant risk that international courts will yield to political pressure. Countries that join international institutions make binding commitments to one another and to their domestic audiences; they appoint third-party enforcement mechanisms to ensure that they and their partners keep these commitments. The problem that inevitably arises is that international courts

[2] Jeffrey Kucik and Krzysztof J. Pelc, "Can International Legal Rulings Deter? Financial Markets Say Yes", Working Paper (2014).

[3] Richard Steinberg, "Judicial Lawmaking at the WTO: Discursive, Constitutional, and Political Constraints", *International Organization*, vol. 98 (2) (2004), 247–275.

have even less power than their domestic counterparts.[4] We know from anecdotal evidence from courts as varied as the European Court of Justice (ECJ) and the North American Free Trade Agreement (NAFTA) that judges are often wary of rendering rulings that are unfavourable to governments, especially to those states who are at the origin of the institution. Paradoxically, this judicial deference to political power may come at the expense of governments themselves, if their international commitments lack credibility as a result. Indeed, if courts can be pushed around, then the commitments that countries make, and which rely on those same courts for enforcement, lose much of their meaning.

This view also explains an otherwise puzzling fact. It may account for how major powers traditionally appear most wary of binding precedent. Indeed, scholars have remarked that the reticence of major powers like the United States towards legal precedent is puzzling, given that they are also the ones best able to manipulate precedent to suit their interests.[5] In this line of reasoning, major powers should view binding precedent as an opportunity to use litigation to obtain what they were unable to get through negotiation. There are numerous examples of the United States and the European Union doing just that in the WTO context. Why, then, should these members be associated with the hardest stance against *stare decisis*? One implication of the argument presented here is that in the short-term perspective major powers stand to lose the most political influence within the litigation process from binding precedent. Although binding precedent likely serves these members in the long term by imbuing the litigation process with greater credibility, in the short term it reduces their unique political influence over the judicial process. The empowerment of judges that binding precedent allows for is likely to be especially felt by great powers.

Does precedent change minds, and how might we know?

The difficulty of assessing the impact of a norm is well established. We know for a fact that courts invoke precedent; we can count their citations, and indeed these are a constant feature of both panel and Appellate Body reports at the WTO (e.g., the average case now cites

[4] Political theory from the *Federalist Papers* onwards expresses the view that the judicial branch is invariably the weakest of the three branches of government.

[5] Ginsburg, "Judicial Lawmaking", 2005. See also the accompanying chapter by Pauwelyn. For examples of such suspicion against binding precedent on the part of US legal scholars, see Ragosta et al., "WTO Dispute Settlement" (2003).

nearly twenty other disputes). This does not necessarily mean that judges are swayed by past cases. In this way, Ginsburg (2005) notes that while a quarter of International Court of Justice (ICJ) cases cite past ICJ rulings, this does not mean that ICJ judges are truly constrained by these past rulings, nor does it mean that past rulings serve as focal points for current cases. Courts may invoke precedent for *ex post* legitimation or for rhetorical flourish. They may simply choose among precedents that bolster their position after the fact, and ignore those precedents that invalidate their position.[6] If this is the case, then precedent may have no real effect on either the reasoning or the content of rulings.[7] In Chapter 5, Pauwelyn demonstrates the tightness of the WTO citation network, highlighting the degree to which WTO judges rely on past cases to inform their reasoning. Yet this still leaves open the question of whether these citations have an effect, or whether they are epiphenomena, occurring after a decision has already been made.

The test for precedent-as-constraint can be stated succinctly: does the existence of precedent change minds? Specifically, are there instances where international courts would rule differently due to a past ruling than they would have in its absence? Whether or not precedent matters must be judged by whether or not it is counterfactually valid; courts must have behaved differently as a result of it. This is not to say that breaking with precedent invalidates its authority. As opposed to physical phenomena, violations of norms need not nullify their existence.[8] Norms are not deterministic; they acquire importance through their ability to help actors discern right from wrong. We might instead expect, for instance, that for those instances where past precedent *was* broken, judges expended considerable resources attempting to justify the decision to do so. Failure to pass the counterfactual test as worded here would thus not be sufficient to claim that precedent does not matter; yet it would be enough to question whether it affects behaviour in a meaningful way.

One thing is certain. Precedent lacks formal authority in international law. Legal scholars habitually point to Article 59 of the ICJ Statute to support the view that an international legal ruling has no implications

[6] Even here, precedent would serve a limiting function, if those rulings that would find no precedent for rhetorical flourish were less likely to be arrived at.

[7] Jack Knight and Lee Epstein, "The Norm of Stare Decisis", *American Journal of Political Science* (1996), 1018–1035; Ginsburg, "Judicial Lawmaking".

[8] F.V. Kratochwil, *Rules, Norms, and Decisions: On the Conditions of Practical and Legal Reasoning in International Relations and Domestic Affairs* (Cambridge: Cambridge University Press, 1989).

past the confines of the case and the parties at hand. The WTO is faithful to this perspective. Article 3.2 of the Dispute Settlement Understanding (DSU) reads, "Recommendations and rulings of the DSB cannot add to or diminish the rights and obligations provided in the covered agreements." Though scholars have remarked on the odd nature of this provision,[9] its intent is relatively unambiguous: judicial decisions should not affect the meaning of countries' obligations beyond the ratification of an agreement. More creative interpretations by panels that aim to institutionalize a de facto form of *stare decisis* have also been forcefully rejected by the Appellate Body (AB). The panel in *Japan – Alcoholic Beverages II* famously claimed that past rulings comprised "subsequent practice" within the meaning of the Vienna Convention on the Law of Treaties (VCLT), thus past rulings should become a source of law. The AB disagreed. Hewing to the formal consensus, it countered that the treaty's designers did not intend for panels' rulings to become definite interpretations of the rules.

In spite of this, students of trade law have long argued that for all intents and purposes, the WTO has gradually developed a form of *de facto stare decisis*.[10] This view is supported by such developments as the GATT and WTO Analytical Indexes which the institution itself provides to trace the lineage of decisions through time, and by anecdotal evidence. The judicial views themselves express some ambiguity. As one example, the same AB that forcefully denied that WTO rulings were "subsequent practice" under the VCLT also noted in *US – Zeroing* that "adopted reports create legitimate expectations among WTO Members and . . . 'following the Appellate Body's conclusions in earlier disputes is not only appropriate, but is what would be expected from panels' ".[11] Yet even when judges admit to the importance of precedent, they are quick to qualify their claims. "The basis by which panels and the Appellate Body decide cases is substantially formulated on precedents [. . .] although there is no formal 'stare decisis' doctrine."[12] What remains is an ambiguous overall picture.

[9] See e.g., Ingo Venzke, *How Interpretation Makes International Law: On Semantic Change and Normative Twists* (Oxford: Oxford University Press, 2012).

[10] Raj Bhala, "Myth about Stare Decisis and International Trade Law (Part One of a Trilogy)", *Am. U. Int'l L. Rev.*, vol. 14 (1998), 845.

[11] Panel's own citation: Appellate Body Report, US–Oil Country Tubular Goods Sunset Reviews, para. 188. in *United States – Use of* Zeroing *in Anti-Dumping Measures Involving Products from Korea*, Panel Report, WT/DS402/R (adopted 18 January 2011), para. 7.31.

[12] Former AB judge. Cited in: David Palmeter and Petros C. Mavroidis, *Dispute Settlement in the World Trade Organization: Practice and Procedure* (Cambridge: Cambridge University Press (2004), 56 (emphasis added).

How are we to know, then? How might one determine the weight of past disputes on subsequent disputes when the text claims this influence to be nil, yet practice suggests otherwise? One method is to ask whether actors whose interests depend on the answer to this question behave in accordance with one view over the other. Do the actors affected by precedent act *as if* precedent were binding, or does their behaviour instead concord with a view of legal disputes as independent events? Regardless of its legal status, if actors are observably vested in one stance over the other, this may be reason enough to elect it as the valid stance for the purpose of analysis. One can observe the behaviour of two sets of actors in this regard: governments and financial markets. The question is, does the behaviour of these actors conform to one view of precedent over the other? Strategic governments would care little for rhetorical flourish unless it also affected their subsequent interests, for example by empowering some domestic groups over others, or adding legal merit to some claims while subtracting merit from others. Similarly, since trade disputes ultimately impact real firms, we can look to financial markets to see whether firms affected by a precedent in a case against a foreign country see a corresponding dip in their market valuation. In other words, do markets bet that disputes will have spillover effects across borders?

The first approach examines the cases countries choose to file. As it turns out, there exists a puzzling class of trade disputes that concern markets of little or no commercial value. Conventional wisdom states that disputes are costly to file, and governments would primarily file these disputes to enforce their WTO rights to open unfairly restricted markets for their exporters,[13] thus all disputes would be expected to cross some threshold commercial value, as filing would otherwise be a losing proposition.[14] Indeed, even if most disputes do not make it to litigation, complainants have to be willing to go to litigation in case negotiations during consultations break down.[15] Yet many disputes concern trivial markets. Why are these cases filed?

[13] Christina Davis, *Why Adjudicate? Enforcing Trade Rules* (Princeton: Princeton Press, 2011).

[14] H. Horn, P.C. Mavroidis and H. Nordström, "Is the Use of the WTO Dispute Settlement System Biased?" CERP Discussion Papers, No. 2340 (1999).

[15] The cost of all disputes is not the same. Disputes that are settled early naturally cost less than disputes that proceed to litigation and appeal. Yet since filing and backing off would negatively affect both a country's reputation for resolve and its odds of obtaining concessions during consultations in subsequent disputes, the relevant cost in such calculations should allow for the possibility of escalation. Indeed, as with all instances of bargaining, the threat to escalate has to be credible for states to get what they want.

One component of the answer to this question can be gleaned from the data on the entire network of citations between WTO cases. As Pauwelyn points out, not all cases are cited with the same frequency. To try and account for this variation, one can regress citation rates on the dispute characteristics we might expect to play a role. Strikingly, controlling for such factors, low commercial value disputes – the very disputes that fall short of the expected "filing threshold" – get cited disproportionately *more* often.[16] Moreover, the complainant who files the initial low-stakes case is most likely to be the one reaping the precedential benefits, citing this precedent to its advantage in subsequent cases. These often have far higher commercial stakes. This results in chains of cases filed by the same complainant that begin with low-stakes and proceed to high-stakes cases.

The reasoning underlying this strategic behaviour is that that low commercial stakes leave complainants with more latitude to tailor their legal arguments and obtain the language they seek from a ruling. Defendants commit fewer resources to defending the case, and the complainant's affected domestic groups are less insistent on dictating specific arguments. In sum, low commercial stakes cases allow complainants to take a tangible loss in exchange of a *rule gain*.[17]

The series of safeguard disputes filed in rapid order by the European Union over a period of four years serves as an apt illustration. The disputes began in 1997 with *Korea – Dairy* and *Argentina – Footwear*, two nearly value-less commercial markets, where the European Union obtained AB rulings that made safeguards more difficult to use. The European Union then went on to file against the United States in two high-stakes steel cases, *US – Steel Safeguards* and *US – Line Pipe*, in a way that rested heavily on the initial safeguards cases against Korea and Argentina. The striking finding, however, is that this relationship appears to hold *on average*: lower commercial stakes cases have disproportional subsequent influence, especially from the point of view of the initial complainant.[18] The final related finding is that some countries appear better able to file these series of cases of increasing commercial importance than other nations. This may not seem surprising. To use Galanter's term, the United States and European Union are "repeat players" in the trade

[16] Pelc, "Politics of Precedent".

[17] Amelia Porges, "Settling WTO Disputes: What Do Litigation Models Tell Us?", *Ohio State Journal on Dispute Resolution*, vol. 19 (2003), 141–184.

[18] Pelc, "Politics of Precedent".

system.[19] This comes across in econometric findings, where these two members are significantly better able than other countries to set precedents that they then build upon in subsequent litigation.

A similar exercise can be performed by looking at financial markets. This approach proceeds from the same premise as above; much like countries, markets have an interest in knowing whether precedent is a true constraint on judicial behaviour, insofar as it allows them to anticipate the likely outcome of subsequent cases. One can then examine whether rulings have spillover effects beyond a given case. When a ruling strikes down a measure that benefits other countries, do financial markets update their beliefs about the viability of these foreign measures and the ability of the relevant firms to continue benefiting from them?

In a recent case, the European Union filed against Canada to challenge Ontario's feed-in-tariff, a subsidy program for a nascent solar energy industry.[20] India happens to have a nearly identical program that features similar domestic content requirements. Both Canada and India have long defended the WTO legality of their policies. The AB ruled against Ontario's program, making it possible to measure whether financial markets reacted by updating their beliefs about Indian firms. The analysis relied on an event study of the stock market valuation of all publicly traded Indian solar firms.[21] The findings suggest that markets take precedent to heart. Indian firms' stock prices, normalised against the stock index, registered significant negative abnormal returns in the week following the AB announcement. This effect is observed even though, as Davis puts it, "WTO members are not obligated to change policies in light of new information from a ruling against another country."[22] In sum, binding precedent may be, legally speaking, a fiction, yet it is one that both governments and financial markets are willing to bet on.

In sum, far from blocking the rise in authority of binding precedent, for example by protesting against invocations of past rulings by panellists, governments appear to have tacitly accepted it. What is more, countries appear to have internalized the weight of precedent in their litigation strategies, investing in low-stakes cases to build favourable

[19] Marc Galanter, "Why the 'Haves' Come Out Ahead: Speculations on the Limits of Legal Change", *Law and Society Review* (1974), 95–160.

[20] See *Canada – Certain Measures Affecting the Renewable Energy Generation Sector*, DS412.

[21] Kucik and Pelc, "Can International Legal Rulings Deter".

[22] Christina Davis, "WTO Adjudication as a Tool for Conflict Management", Working Paper, Princeton University (2012).

precedent for subsequent, higher-stakes cases. This leads to a theoretical puzzle, which I examine next.

Why do states tolerate the rising authority of precedent?

Both governments and their domestic audiences are traditionally wary of delegating power to international institutions. The danger of a "democratic deficit" is frequently invoked, alleging that the negotiations that form international rules are insufficiently responsive to the public's demands. In this context, the possibility of binding precedent represents a considerable additional threat. If the mere act of committing to shared rules comes at a political cost, then the notion that the meaning of those rules, and the precise balance of rights and obligations they represent, might be further affected through litigation would seem politically unpalatable.[23] The prospect of judicial activism and rule-making by international courts is invariably discussed in negative terms.[24] If this is the case, then why have WTO members tacitly accepted the rise of de facto binding precedent?

Different scholarly perspectives offer different answers. A common explanation among legal scholars is that judges value continuity in reasoning, no matter whether it is formally prescribed or not. Respecting precedent is also viewed as respecting the rule of law; to follow past decisions is to steer clear of judicial bias. It increases predictability and legal certainty,[25] which are stated goals of the WTO dispute settlement system.[26] Scholars have also claimed that binding precedent increases adjudicatory harmonization and fairness.[27]

On the other hand, an interpretivist view has claimed that the norm of arguing by precedent is intrinsic to the legal setting.[28] From this perspective, the very question of why precedent would operate in international law may appear ill conceived. Precedential reasoning is not an institution to be accepted or rejected; it is inseparable from the practice of lawyers

[23] Observers already complain that the DSB might adopt judicial activism and abuse its binding nature to create WTO "common law", to which the members never agreed (Ragosta et al., "WTO Dispute Settlement")

[24] *Ibid.*

[25] Felix David (2009), Knight and Epstein, "Stare Decisis": "To the extent that the members of a community base their future expectations on the belief that others in that community will follow existing laws, the Court has an interest in minimizing the disruptive effects of overturning existing rules of behaviour."

[26] Article 3.5 speaks of "stability and predictability". [27] Bhala, "Stare Decisis".

[28] Kratochwil, *Rules, Norms, and Decisions*.

arguing over the validity of a measure. Law is seen as the act of reasoning and arguing by seeking support from past decisions to buttress one's own case. Precedent is not a causal factor whose force can be isolated and measured, but instead it is an intrinsic part of the legal environment that limits what constitutes an acceptable argument.

The notion that reasoning through precedent is an inherent part of law is especially true of common law systems, but less so of civil law systems. Some have claimed that it is precisely the existence of both systems, and their difference in this respect, that keeps *stare decisis* from operating in international law.[29] Reasoning by precedent nonetheless remains a pervasive norm in the legal sphere. Yet the same can be said of the norm against judicial activism. Since the latter is backed by the strong political interests described above, the interpretivist perspective offers little means of deciding in which cases the practice of reasoning by precedent should trump the norm against judicial activism. In fact, even as states themselves may have internalized precedential reasoning in their legal arguments, we also observe states openly challenging the invocation of precedent. In other words, the practice of citing precedent is not so internalized that states are unable to distinguish it as such. In cases where the practice disadvantages them, they appear able to contest it. In the salient example of *US – Civil Aircraft*, the United States made the following demand:

> The United States requests that the first sentence of paragraph 7.248 of the Interim Report be modified to remove any suggestion that reports of the Appellate Body are binding except with respect to resolving the particular dispute between the parties to that dispute.[30]

Yet such challenges are remarkably rare, which leads to the puzzle that this chapter attempts to elucidate. The final challenge to explanations of *de facto stare decisis* in international trade law that hinge on the pervasiveness of the juristic practice of reasoning by precedent is that these explanations merely defer the question. The question becomes, why is law so inherently tied up with precedential reasoning? And why do countries not avail themselves more often of formal rules that would trump such a legal practice, no matter how long its tradition?

[29] Steinberg, "Judicial Lawmaking": "*stare decisis* is not followed formally by international tribunals, partly because many civil law systems do not adhere to this principle."

[30] Panel Report, *European Communities and Certain Member States – Measures Affecting Trade in Large Civil Aircraft*, WT/DS316/R (adopted 30 June 2010), para. 6.26.

One rationalist response might argue that a tacit acceptance of binding precedent is what one would expect of far-sighted strategic states. This vein of argument is based on the premise that courts fill in the optimal ambiguity produced by the legislative process when consensus over sensitive questions is difficult to obtain. In this reading, legislators are aware of and knowingly defer to the way in which the functionalist domain of the law is removed from politics, knowing that a court decision will sufficiently defuse political conflict to achieve the very outcome that would have been difficult to obtain through legislative means.[31] In the case of international trade law, however, such cross-purpose use of courts may strain credulity. While states may tolerate some gap-filling by courts when it happens to suit their interests, it may be a step too far to argue that countries weave in such judicial gap-filling into the design of the institution. I suggest that a simpler explanation is that binding precedent is a means of empowering otherwise weak international courts. In other words, the value of de facto binding precedent from the point of view of countries lies not in the interstitial legislating it allows courts, but in the way it empowers courts to rule against actual violations by states, in accordance with their institutional design.

Binding precedent empowers weak international courts

This chapter argues that despite the political costs associated with the perception that they have delegated decision-making power to courts, states may nonetheless gain by doing so. Binding precedent serves as an antidote against the incentives courts have to defer to political power. This, in turn, favours governments themselves in the long run. Indeed, countries create international institutions because they are better off by committing to a set of shared rules. In the case of the trade regime, countries' commitments lower the risk that trade partners will erect unfair barriers, and it provides governments with a potent bargaining tool vis-à-vis import-competing groups who demand distortionary protection.[32] Yet sovereign states have difficulty making credible promises, as there is nothing to prevent them from simply breaking their commitments. To address this problem, states create third-party

[31] Anne-Marie Burley and Walter Mattli, "Europe before the Court: A Political Theory of Legal Integration", *International Organization*, vol. 47 (1993), 41–41.

[32] Mansfield, Milner and Rosendorff (2002); Pelc (2013).

enforcement bodies such as courts that are set up to provide an unambiguous condemnation of policies that flout agreed-upon rules.[33]

Here, too, the power of states gets the better of them. Courts themselves are inevitably prone to political pressure. The European context is instructive in this respect. A large part of the political science literature that studies the ECJ suggests that the court must be politically savvy: "the judges of the ECJ realize that their power is ultimately contingent on the acquiescence of member states and hence are reticent to make decisions of which governments disapprove."[34] The interests of member states like France and Germany are perceived to weigh particularly heavily in the calculations of judges. Moreover, political pressure need not be actualized to have a strong impact. As long as judges anticipate the likely reactions of governments (e.g., defiance of rulings, wilful noncompliance, renegotiation of the rules themselves), they may let those expectations colour the content of their rulings. Others have pointed out that the ECJ must walk a fine line in this respect, as its power not only relies on not provoking the ire of member governments, but also relies on not appearing overly motivated by political concerns.[35] In sum, the court's power relies on walking the fine line between awareness of political constraints and excessive deference to political interests.[36] Similar concerns exist for the North American Free Trade Agreement (NAFTA) and its investor-state mechanism. Analysts point to instances such as the *Loewen* case, where NAFTA arbitrators are believed to have caved to anti-NAFTA sentiment in the US Congress out of fear that a finding against the United States might lead Congress to do away with Chapter 11 altogether.

Power undermines promises. The power that states hold over courts impedes their ability to tie their own hands through institutions. In this respect, states face a similar dilemma to that of dictators who are unable to bind themselves through a central bank – which would never be viewed as truly independent – and whose monetary policy suffers as a result.[37] Governments have a short-term incentive to exert pressure over courts to rule in their favour, but this works against their long-term

[33] Mansfield, Milner and Rosendorff (2002).

[34] Geoffrey Garrett, R. Daniel Kelemen and Heiner Schulz, "The European Court of Justice, National Governments, and Legal Integration in the European Union", *International Organization*, vol. 52 (1998), 149–176.

[35] Burley and Mattli, "Europe before the Court". [36] Steinberg, "Judicial Lawmaking".

[37] Lawrence Broz, "Political System Transparency and Monetary Commitment Regimes", *International Organization*, vol. 56 (4) (2002), 861–887.

incentive to have unbiased courts that will render politically unbiased, predictable verdicts.

The same literature on political bias in the ECJ yields another claim. When judges have precedents to rely on, this decreases the likelihood of bias, as "the greater the clarity of ECJ case law precedent, the lesser the likelihood that the Court will tailor its decisions to the anticipated reactions of member governments".[38] In other words, the more legal discretion judges have in a given case, the more likely they cede to political pressure, and vice versa.

Binding precedent may thus serve a blame-shifting function. The underlying mechanism is the same as when governments motion to international institutions when denying demands for trade protection from import-competing interest groups. In this case, however, it is judges who use this means against governments, by claiming that prior verdicts dictate their opinion in a given instance. By limiting judges' apparent agency, clear precedent thus limits political backlash. The reduced fear of backlash means that judges may be less vulnerable to pressure when they can rely on a past ruling.

Strategic governments who realize this may have an incentive to allow for such precedents to take hold. If precedential reasoning increases judicial independence and such independence strengthens the credibility of state commitments, then tacitly allowing precedent may be welfare enhancing. Of course, precedents may work against governments in particular instances. The same can be said of the rules themselves, yet countries continue to support these. The greater point is that a tacit acceptance of precedent increases judicial independence, because it allows countries to shift the blame in politically sensitive rulings. This, in turn, increases the credibility of enforcement, and with it, countries' willingness to exchange reciprocal commitments in the first place.

Finally, why is the equilibrium outcome that of "tacit allowance" rather than outright, formal *stare decisis*, as Bhala, among others, has called for?[39] Despite its potential welfare-enhancing qualities, formal binding precedent remains a politically unpalatable solution. Domestic audiences in countries such as the United States are unlikely to accept it.[40] Informal acceptance may be the best governments can do to empower international courts while assuaging the fears of their domestic audiences.

[38] Kelemen et al., "Legal Integration". [39] Bhala, "Stare Decisis".

[40] To wit, see the views of observers such as Ragosta et al., "WTO Dispute Settlement".

Explaining US reticence

The account presented here may also help account for the heretofore puzzling stance of major countries on the question of binding precedent. Indeed, of all the WTO members, major powers such as the United States have been most vocal about resisting anything approaching *stare decisis*. The aforementioned demand of the United States in *US – Civil Aircraft* is a case in point. The United States is also said to screen AB judges by first asking about their view on precedent. This stance is puzzling insofar as we would expect major powers to be the ones best able to exploit the implications of binding precedent. Indeed, this is one of the concerns of scholars like Pauwelyn: precedent may reinsert power politics into the equation, insofar as major powers with high legal capacity are uniquely placed to take advantage of precedent. The empirical findings cited above provide some support for these concerns.[41] Major powers who are able to file series of precedent-building disputes may then use precedent as a means of obtaining through litigation what they were unable to secure through negotiations. Why, then, have these members been the most reticent to accept anything approaching binding precedent? Ginsburg (2005) notes this apparent paradox:

> There is no small irony that many of the criticisms of international tribunals emanate from American scholars. Powerful states like the United States, and groups of less powerful states, retain means of controlling and cajoling international judges.

The argument presented here may account for this apparent irony. Insofar as binding precedent increases courts' judicial independence, it achieves the greatest increase in independence from member states like the United States. These are the states whose political clout within the institution allows them to exert the most pressure over the court, much like France and Germany in the case of the ECJ. Although these members may still achieve long-term gains from the resulting increase of the system's credibility, they are also the ones who stand to lose the most from a short-term loss of political influence over judges, since they have the most influence to lose.

Conclusion

In international trade law, the effective authority of precedent lies somewhere between its denial under formal rules and its standing in domestic

[41] See Pelc, "Politics of Precedent".

common law systems.[42] One way to approach the question is to ask whether or not actors such as governments and financial markets, who have a vested interest in the answer, behave in a manner consistent with a view of precedent as binding. I describe two findings that support an answer to the affirmative. The status of precedent in international trade law appears considerably closer to its authority in common law systems than what the formal rules would lead us to believe.

The second section of the chapter addressed the implications of these findings. There is good reason for the formal denial of precedent's authority in international law, as domestic audiences are likely to be wary of the sheer delegation of power to international courts that is entailed by binding precedent. Yet if binding precedent is politically unpalatable yet also exists in practice, why have we not seen more attempts by states to block its rising authority?

After reviewing possible answers from the literature, I propose that the tacit acceptance of binding precedent empowers otherwise weak courts. Building on findings that describe how courts are less likely to cede to political pressure when they have precedent to rely upon when ruling against a powerful party, I claim that precedent plays a blame-shifting function. It reduces the apparent agency of courts and allows judges to rule against powerful governments in a way that avoids political backlash, thus increasing judicial independence. This, in turn, increases the credibility of the commitments that countries make to one another in the first place. Legally speaking, binding precedent in international trade law remains a fiction. Yet it is a fiction that countries may find welfare enhancing, insofar as it strengthens the courts that they have created to keep themselves and their partners in check.

[42] Where considerable literature has nonetheless also thrown doubt on the actual effect of precedent. See e.g., Knight and Epstein, "Stare Decisis".

7

Features of trade law adjudication and their impact on the development of legal concepts and precedents

ANTON K. SCHNYDER AND STEFANIE PFISTERER

A Introduction

Trade law adjudication, specifically the use of trade relations, investment arbitration, and commercial arbitration, has taken on increasing importance. Over time, the adjudicating bodies, which for the purposes of this chapter are hereafter called trade "courts," have developed legal concepts.[1]

The ongoing development of legal concepts in trade law raises the question if trade law adjudication can create law. There is substantial debate on the definition on the rule of law.[2] A detailed discussion of this topic lies outside the scope of this chapter, as the aim of this chapter is to show whether certain features of trade law adjudication promote or impede the development of a rule of law and whether trade law adjudication can create precedents. In order to develop a working understanding of the rule of law, this chapter refers to the legal philosopher Lon L. Fuller, whose account of rule of law has been highly influential and can be seen as a natural starting point for discussion.[3] According to Fuller, the essential function of law and the one that a norms system must fulfill in order to count as law, is to "subject [...] people's conduct to the guidance of general rules by which they may themselves orient their

[1] David W. Rivkin, "The Impact of International Arbitration on the Rule of Law: The 2012 Clayton Utz/University of Sydney International Arbitration Lecture," *Arb. Int'l.*, vol. 29 (2013), 327, 328.

[2] For a detailed study, see Hague Institute for the Internationalisation of Law (HiiL), *Rule of Law Inventory Report Academic Part, Discussion Paper for the High Level Expert Meeting on the Rule of Law of 20th April 2007*; Brian Z. Tamanaha, *On the Rule of Law: History, Politics, Theory* (Cambridge: Cambridge University Press, 2004).

[3] See Colleen Murphy, "Lon Fuller and the Moral Value of the Rule of Law," *Law and Philosophy*, vol. 24 (3) (2005), 239, 240.

behaviour."[4] Following this premise, Fuller identified eight procedural principles that a system of rules must comply with in order to be considered law.[5] Four of Fuller's principles are particularly relevant for trade adjudication and its ability to generate law. These four principles are governance by general norms, public ascertainability, prospectivity, and steadiness over time.[6] None of these four principles is straightforwardly fulfilled in trade dispute resolution.[7] In particular, certain features examined in this chapter collide with these four principles, or at least they appear to. These features thus interrelate to the ability of trade adjudication to create both law and legal precedents.

As trade law adjudication has become increasingly popular, certain aspects of its decision-making process have been criticized.[8] For example, it is often said that trade law adjudication, particularly arbitration, lacks formal legal mechanisms for ensuring that arbitrators reach consistent decisions such as an appellate mechanism,[9] and that arbitrators need not follow the law and may instead resolve disputes in whatever fashion they deem just.[10] Other criticisms highlight the fact that proceedings and awards are kept private,[11] or that trade law awards are not

4 Lon L. Fuller, "A Reply to Professors Cohen and Dworkin," *Vill. L. Rev.*, vol. 10 (1965), 655, 657.

5 These eight constitutive elements of legality are: (1) governance by general norms (i.e., the generality of expression and application of the rules that are part of the system); (2) public ascertainability (i.e., the public promulgation of the rules of the system); (3) prospectivity (i.e., the nonretroactivity of the rules of the systems; (4) perspicuity (i.e., the formulation of the mandates provided by the legal system in lucid language); (5) noncontradictoriness (i.e., the normative coherence of legal system); (6) compliability (i.e., near absence of unsatisfiable behests); (7) steadiness over time (i.e., limits in the pace and scale of the transformations of the sundry norms in a legal system); and (8) congruence between formulation and implementation (i.e., publicly promulgated rules are actually applied and are applied impartially). See Matthew H. Kramer, *Objectivity and the Rule of Law* (Cambridge: Cambridge University Press, 2007), 102, 103–86. It is generally agreed upon that Fuller's principles of legality capture the essence of the rule of law; see Murphy, "Lon Fuller," 240; Kramer, *Objectivity*, 103–04.

6 Thomas Schultz, "The Concept of Law in Transnational Arbitral Legal Orders and Some of Its Consequences," *J Int'l Disp. Settlement*, vol. 2 (2011), 59, 72.

7 *Ibid.*

8 Stavros Brekoulakis, "Systemic Bias and the Institution of International Arbitration: A New Approach to Arbitral Decision-Making," *J Int'l Disp. Settlement*, vol. 4 (2013), 553, 554; W. Mark C. Weidemaier, "Toward A Theory of Precedent in Arbitration," *Wm. & Mary L. Rev.*, vol. 51 (2010), 1895, 1904.

9 Christopher R. Drahozal, "Is Arbitration Lawless?," *Loy. L. Rev.*, vol. 40 (2006), 187, 208.

10 Edward Brunet, "Arbitration and Constitutional Rights," *N.C. L. Rev.*, vol. 71 (1992), 81, 85.

11 Anthony DePalma, "NAFTA's Powerful Little Secret: Obscure Tribunals Settle Disputes, but Go Too Far, Critics Say," *New York Times*, March 11, 2001 ("Their meetings are

reasoned.[12] These critical voices raise legitimate questions about these individuals who act as trade law adjudicators and whether they should have the power to make decisions on issues that impact national public policy and sovereignty.[13] The criticisms reveal a subliminal fear that trade law adjudication creates a rule of law, and they target specific trade law adjudication characteristics. This chapter focuses on these disputed characteristics.

In the following sections, the chapter explores specific features of trade law adjudication and their influence on the development of legal concepts and precedents. These characteristics are both crucial to the ability of trade law adjudication to create law, and are also the elements that are most criticized within trade law adjudication.

B Features of trade law adjudication and their impact on the development of legal concepts and precedents

I General remarks

Having assessed the relevance of trade law adjudication characteristics, these features deserve closer attention. Given the topic of this conference, particular weight will be given to the assessment of whether these characteristics are equally present in the different bodies of trade law adjudication, the trade "courts." The first set of characteristics to be analyzed stem from the design of trade "courts" (*see* Subsection II below). The analysis then covers the role of the adjudicators themselves (*see* Subsection III below), certain procedural characteristics (*see* Subsection IV below), and the nature and substance of trade disputes (*see* Subsection V below). Finally, attention turns to the orientation of legal interpretation in trade law adjudication (*see* Subsection VI below).

secret. Their members are generally unknown. The decisions they reach need not be fully disclosed. Yet the way a small number of international tribunals handles disputes between investors and foreign governments has led to national laws being revoked, justice systems questioned and environmental regulations challenged."); Richard M. Alderman, "Consumer Arbitration: The Destruction of the Common Law," *J. Am. Arb.*, vol. 2 (2003), 1, 11.

12 Alan S. Rau, "The Culture of American Arbitration and the Lessons of ADR," *Tex. Int'l L.J.*, vol. 40 (2005), 449, 512–14.

13 Brekoulakis, "Systemic Bias," 554.

II Design of international trade "courts"

1 Selection of the members of trade "courts"

Critics often cite the selection of the members of the trade "courts" as a potential source of systemic bias.[14] The selection of their members differs considerably among the various trade "courts."

The European Court of Justice (*hereinafter* ECJ), the only "formal" trade court, takes up a special position. The court consists of twenty-eight judges who are appointed by common accord of the governments of the member states[15] and who sit as a full court, in a grand chamber of fifteen judges, or in chambers of three or five judges.[16] Unlike the other bodies of trade law adjudication under consideration, in the ECJ there is no party autonomy. In proceedings within the World Trade Organization (*hereinafter* WTO) framework, parties to the dispute are free to agree upon the members of the three-person panel based on a previously agreed-upon list.[17] The WTO Appellate Body (a feature introduced after the Uruguay Round[18]) consists of seven permanent members, and appeals are heard by three members.[19] Party autonomy exists at the first stage but not for the appeals stage.

In international arbitration, whether commercial or investment arbitration, there is typically no central authority who is entrusted with collectively selecting and appointing the members of the tribunals.[20]

14 *Ibid.*, 577.

15 Article 253(1) of the Consolidated Version of the Treaty on the Functioning of the European Union, 2008 O.J. C 115/47.

16 Articles 3 and 16 of the Protocol (No 3) on the Statute of the Court of Justice of the European Union, annexed to the Treaties, as amended by the Regulation (EU, Euratom) No 741/2012 of the European Parliament and of the Council, O.J. L 228 (Statute of the Court of Justice of the European Union).

17 Article 8 of the WTO Understanding on Rules and Procedures Governing the Settlement of Disputes or Dispute Settlement Understanding, Marrakesh Agreement Establishing the World Trade Organization, 1867 U.N.T.S. 154 (hereinafter WTO DSU). If the parties are unable to agree (e.g., in case of a conflict of interest), the WTO's director general or someone replacing him selects the panel.

18 Following the Uruguay Round of multilateral trade negotiations, WTO members agreed on the Dispute Settlement Understanding (WTO DSU). The WTO DSU introduced a clearly structured procedure for dispute settlement. The DSU also created an appeals system.

19 WTO DSU, Article 17(1)–(3).

20 Brekoulakis, "Systemic Bias," 577. E.g., it is the parties in an ICSID arbitration that select the tribunal. As envisioned in Article 12 of the ICSID Convention on the Settlement of Investment Disputes between States and Nationals of Other State (1964), 17 U.S.T. 1270 (hereinafter ICSID Convention), ICSID maintains a panel of arbitrators. The panel is not exclusive and the parties are not obliged to appoint arbitrators from this panel. In NAFTA cases, the disputing parties may select any arbitrator they wish; Article 1123 of the NAFTA

The multilateral and fluid processes for selecting arbitrators underpin the pluralistic, diverse, and democratic potential of international arbitration.[21] Nevertheless, a close examination is required to determine whether international arbitration actually operates as a pluralistic institution.[22] Some studies have investigated the institutional aspects of international arbitration, suggesting for example that there is both a limited pool of arbitrators and limited cultural diversity within that pool.[23] Indeed, a common criticism is that arbitrators are drawn from an elite group who all have backgrounds in commercial law. This is perceived to be particularly problematic when arbitrators face public interests involved in investment disputes.[24] Not surprisingly, there have been proposals to abolish the party-appointed system in arbitration.[25] Other proposals suggested that the model of multilateral selection of investment treaty tribunals should be replaced by a new international investment court with tenured judges who operate under the supervision of national courts or an appellate body.[26] If such proposals are adopted, there is a danger that the pluralistic, diverse, and democratic potential of international arbitration will be undermined. Adopting the procedural design of national and international judiciaries may create systemic biases.[27]

does not provide a roster arbitrators, *cf.* Meg N. Kinnear et al., *Investment Disputes under NAFTA: An Annotated Guide to NAFTA Chapter 11* (2006/2008 suppl.), 1123–24.

21 Brekoulakis, "Systemic Bias," 578. 22 *Ibid.*, 579.

23 Daphna Kapeliuk, "The Repeat Appointment Factor: Exploring Decision Patterns of Elite Investment Arbitrators," *Cornell L. Rev.*, vol. 96 (2010), 47, 78 found of the arbitrators appointed in ICSID cases, there existed an elite group of arbitrators; one arbitrator was appointed 11 times, three were appointed 10 times, four arbitrators were appointed 9 times, one arbitrator was appointed 8 times, two were appointed 7 times, four arbitrators were appointed 6 times, three were appointed 5 times, and eight arbitrators were appointed 4 times. Of all concluded cases 80.2 percent included at least one elite arbitrator, which clearly signifies that a solid group of elite arbitrators receive repeated appointments to ICSID tribunals.

24 Rivkin, "Impact of International Arbitration," 355.

25 Jan Paulsson, "Moral Hazard in International Dispute Resolution," *ICSID Rev.*, vol. 25 (2010), 339, 339; Albert J. van den Berg, "Dissenting Opinions by Party-Appointed Arbitrators in Investment Arbitration" in M. Arsanjani et al. (eds.), *Looking to the Future: Essays on International Law in Honor of W. Michael Reisman* (Leiden: Koninklijke Brill, 2011), 821. See also Brekoulakis, "Systemic Bias," 582.

26 See e.g., Gus Van Harten, *A Case for an International Investment Court*, Working Paper No. 22/08 for the Society of International Economic Law Inaugural Conference, Geneva, July 15–17, 2008, 30; Alec Stone Sweet and Florian Grisel, "Transnational Investment Arbitration: From Delegation to Constitutionalization?" in P.M. Dupuy et al. (eds.), *Human Rights in International Investment Law and Arbitration* (Oxford: Oxford University Press, 2009), 135, 118–36.

27 Brekoulakis, "Systemic Bias," 582.

In sum, party autonomy is not always present when selecting the members of the trade "courts." Even when tribunals are selected by the parties, there is no guarantee of a pluralistic and democratic adjudication. However, any change to the system has the potential to create new, systemic biases.

2 Absence of an appeal system

Another feature of trade law adjudication is the absence of an appeal system. As mentioned above, one of Fuller's requirements for law is steadiness over time. In a rules system composed of scattered individualized decisions, there is no guarantee of consistency.[28]

Until recently, appellate review rarely happened in international trade law adjudication. It was only in 1994 that the WTO Dispute Settlement Understanding that was created after the Uruguay Round introduced an Appellate Body to hear appeals from panel cases. This innovative feature in international trade law was created to support one of the main goals of the WTO dispute settlement system, to provide "security and predictability to the multilateral trading system."[29] In investment arbitration, awards issued within the framework of the International Centre for Settlement of Investment Disputes (*hereinafter* ICSID) can be appealed, but the grounds are limited and mostly procedural.[30] Because of the relatively narrow scope of the annulment grounds, consistent outcomes on the merits are unlikely.[31] The introduction of an appellate mechanism for investment arbitration was intensely discussed,[32] and it faced serious difficulties. Since Article 53(1) of the ICSID Convention provides that ICSID awards "shall not be subject to any appeal,"[33] the introduction of

[28] Schultz, "Concept of Law," 75. [29] WTO DSU, Article 3(2).

[30] ICSID Convention, Article 52(1)(a)–(e).

[31] Anders Nilsson and Oscar Englesson, "Inconsistent Awards in Investment Treaty Arbitration: Is an Appeals Court Needed?," *J Int'l Arb.*, vol. 30 (2013), 561, 575; Gabrielle Kaufmann-Kohler, "Arbitral Precedent: Dream, Necessity or Excuse?," *Arb. Int'l*, vol. 23 (2007), 357, 377.

[32] August Reinisch, "The Proliferation of International Dispute Settlement Mechanisms: The Threat of Fragmentation vs. the Promise of a More Effective System? Some Reflections from the Perspective of Investment Arbitration" in J. Crawford et al. (eds.), *International Law between Universalism and Fragmentation, Festschrift in Honour of Gerhard Hafner* (Leiden and Boston: Brill, 2008), 107, 119. See also Nilsson and Englesson, "Inconsistent Awards," 573. In 2004, ICSID published a working paper describing the idea of a new "Appeals Facility," *cf.* ICSID Secretariat, *Possible Improvements of the Framework for ICSID Arbitration* 14–16 (October 22, 2004), icsid.worldbank.org/ICSID/FrontServlet?requestType=ICSIDPublicationsRH&actionVal=ViewAnnouncePDF&AnnouncementType=archive&AnnounceNo=14_1.pdf.

[33] ICSID Convention, Article 53(1).

an appellate system would need a treaty amendment, which was hardly feasible. It was also doubtful that appellate bodies established under different bilateral treaties would lead to coherent case law. Harmonization could only be achieved if the same mechanism was applied to all or at least the majority of the treaties.[34] In addition, an appeal before a panel selected from a pool of dozens of arbitrators would not guarantee uniformity of decisions.[35] For these reasons, the plan was not pursued.[36]

Similarly, in international arbitration, there is no appeals system that provides the ability to appeal an award on the merits.[37] As party autonomy prevails on the appeals issue,[38] parties could agree on an internal appeal mechanism.[39] Nevertheless, a study conducted in 2006 revealed that only 9 percent of users would welcome the ability to appeal awards.[40]

[34] Christoph Schreuer and Matthew Weiniger, "Conversations across Cases – Is There a Doctrine of Precedent in Investment Arbitration?" in P. Muchlinski et al. (eds.), *The Oxford Handbook on International Investment Law* 15 (Oxford: Oxford University Press, 2008), www.univie.ac.at/intlaw/conv_across_90.pdf; L. Yves Fortier, *Investment Protection and the Rule of Law: Change or Decline?*, Lecture given at the British Institute of International and Comparative Law, 50th Anniversary Event Series, London, UK, March 17, 2009, 1; Mark B. Feldman, "The Annulment Proceedings and the Finality of ICSID Arbitral Awards," *ICSID Rev.*, vol. 85 (1987), 105.

[35] Schreuer and Weiniger, "Conversations across Cases," 17.

[36] Reinisch, "Proliferation of International Dispute Settlement," 120.

[37] Article 34 of the UNCITRAL Model Law on International Commercial Arbitration (hereinafter UNCITRAL Model Law); §10 of the U.S. Federal Arbitration Act, 9 U.S.C. (U.S. FAA); Article 1502 of the French Code of Civil Procedure; Article 190(2) of the Swiss Law on Private International Law. However, §69(1) of the English Arbitration Act 1996 provides the right to appeal an award on a question of English law to an English court. In international arbitration, sports arbitration takes a special position: the Appeals Division in Court of Arbitration for Sport (hereinafter CAS) may count as an exception, as the CAS Appeals Division is entitled to review the facts and the law of a first-instance decision on a *de novo* basis, Article R57 of the CAS Code of Sports-related Arbitration. *Cf.* William McAuliffe and Antonio Rigozzi, "*Sports Arbitration*" in *The European & Middle Eastern Arbitration Review 2012.*

[38] Rowan Platt, "The Appeal of Appeal Mechanisms in International Arbitration: Fairness over Finality?," *J Int'l Arb.*, vol. 30 (2013), 531, 560.

[39] The American Arbitration Association (hereinafter AAA) recently introduced its newly revised set of Optional Appellate Arbitration Rules, effective as of November 1, 2013, go .adr.org/AppellateRules. The new rules provide parties with a streamlined and standardized appellate arbitration procedure that allows for high-level review of arbitral awards. Parties may use these rules only when there is an agreement within the parties, either by contract or by stipulation.

[40] Queen Mary School of International Arbitration, University of London and PricewaterhouseCoopers, *International Arbitration: Corporate Attitudes and Practices* (2006), 15.

In sum, while international courts and tribunals in other sectors, in particular criminal law,[41] increasingly provide for appellate review, the WTO Appellate Body remains the exception in trade law adjudication. One must acknowledge that in the context of criminal law, there is a compelling rationale for appellate review, namely the fundamental right of individuals to have their convictions reviewed by a higher tribunal.[42] There is no such corollary rationale in trade law; nonetheless, the absence of an appeal system creates a coherence and consistency issue. Furthermore, "the concept [. . .] that an arbitrator is a super-judge, that an arbitral tribunal can operate above any international law with a discretion not given to state courts, a lack of accountability for its conduct and an absence of transparency not afforded to any other comparable professional activity in the world, except, possibly, secret policemen,"[43] creates a legitimacy and accountability issue. The absence of an appeals system also means that there is typically no hierarchy of awards in trade law adjudication.[44] Hence, it is often hard to ascertain whether an award rendered in a comparable case does in fact represent a "leading case." The precedential weight of an award may still be ascertained due to the reputation and eminence of the members of the trade "court," but the member composition is not always discernible from the award.[45] As a consequence, awards ought to have less precedential weight than state court judgments, because state court judgments have presumptively received greater attention and scrutiny. Nonetheless, this is merely one factor affecting an award's precedential weight.[46] On the other hand, an appellate body would have a negative influence on the overall speed and efficiency of the proceedings and would

41 E.g., the Appeals Division of the International Criminal Court for review of judgments of the trial chambers.

42 See Article 14(5) of the International Covenant on Civil and Political Rights, 999 U.N.T.S. 171 ("Everyone convicted of a crime shall have the right to his conviction and sentence being reviewed by a higher tribunal according to law"). See Reinisch, "Proliferation of International Dispute Settlement," 119.

43 Johnny Veeder, *Due Process – Balancing Fairness and Efficiency – The Harmonising Chord*, Transcript of the IBA 12th International Arbitration Day, Due Process in International Arbitration, 27, www.ibanet.org; see also Rivkin, "Impact of International Arbitration," 359.

44 *SGS Société Gén. de Surveillance SA* v. *Republic of the Philippines, Decision on Jurisdiction*, ICSID Case No. ARB/02/6 (January 29, 2004); *ICSID Rep.* 8 (2004), 515, 545.

45 Klaus Peter Berger, "The International Arbitrators' Application of Precedents," *J Int'l Arb*, vol. 9 (1992), 5, 20.

46 Gary B. Born, *International Commercial Arbitration* (The Hague: Kluwer Law International, 2009), 2969.

undercut the finality of awards, and private parties would be more reluctant to use the dispute settlement system which would ultimately undermine the legitimacy of the system.[47] Instead of establishing an appellate body, other mechanisms could be implemented to minimize the risk of inconsistent decisions.[48]

III Role of adjudicators

In its early stages, trade "courts" and arbitration in particular were sought for the expertise of their adjudicators.[49] The adjudicators possessed specialized knowledge, thus there was no need for additional experts.[50] These days, however, arbitrators, like court judges, tend to be generalists in substantive legal knowledge but specialists in legal procedure. International arbitrators are ordinarily lawyers or academics (i.e., arbitration specialists) rather than persons engaged in the same business as the parties to the arbitration.[51] This has a great influence on the role of arbitrators in generating precedents. Repeat-play arbitrators will be more familiar with past awards and thus more likely to cite them. On the other hand, because established arbitrators are sought for their judgment and not for their knowledge of what other arbitrators have done they may also be less likely to cite prior awards.[52]

Members of a trade "court" often also hail from different legal systems, have different experiences, and use different methods for determining disputes.[53] This has significant consequences for the decision-making process, as international lawyers can manage different sets of procedural rules and are not necessarily attached to the national law of the country in which they practice. Rule-making in international trade law is thus presumably transnational and applicable against the background of multiple national laws.

The increase of trade law adjudication has proffered scholarship to examine the decision-making process. Scholars embarked on empirical studies of the judicial behavior of arbitrators and departed from the

[47] Nilsson and Englesson, "Inconsistent Awards," 577. [48] *Ibid.*, 578.

[49] Born, *Commercial Arbitration*, 64.

[50] Jacques Werner, "The Trade Explosion and Some Likely Effects on International Arbitration," *June J Int'l Arb.*, vol. 14 (1997), 10.

[51] Christopher R. Drahozal, "Commercial Norms, Commercial Codes, and International Commercial Arbitration," *Vand. J. Transnat'l L.*, vol. 33 (2000), 97, 96.

[52] Weidemaier, "Theory of Precedent," 1953.

[53] Rivkin, "Impact of International Arbitration," 358.

assumption that decision-making is driven almost exclusively by extra-legal factors.[54] For example, studies have amassed the personal background information of hundreds of arbitrators, including nationality, gender, education, career, legal expertise, and cultural background.[55] Other studies have centered their analysis on awards rather than on arbitrators.[56] The studies have revealed conflicting findings on whether the arbitrators' personal background influences their judicial attitude.[57] This is not surprising, as these studies exhibit clear limitations and fail to account for the complexities of decision-making.[58] It is necessary to look into the wider institution behind the individual and examine how institutional structures guide and constrain individuals in decision-making.[59] The multilateral and fluid processes for selecting the members of trade "courts," as well as the lack of an appeals mechanism both underpin the pluralistic, diverse, and democratic potential of trade law adjudication.[60] Nevertheless, decision-makers who are institutionally embedded are bound by legal precedent and text but tend to decide on the basis of what they believe to be the most authentic interpretation and representation of law in light of the dominant values of the institutional context within which they decide.[61]

In sum, this section reveals that present-day trade law adjudicators are institutionally embedded repeat-players with international backgrounds, and are thus likely to feel bound by legal precedent and presumably create transnational rules applicable against the background of multiple national laws.

IV Procedural characteristics

1 Requirement of awards to be reasoned

Let us now shift our attention to another feature that also affects the ability of trade law decisions to create law: the principle of perspicuity. "How can anybody follow a rule that nobody can understand?"[62]

[54] Brekoulakis, "Systemic Bias," 556.

[55] See e.g., the forthcoming study of Michael Waibel and Yanhui Wu, *Are Arbitrators Political?* (working draft), 22, www.wipol.uni-bonn.de/lehrveranstaltungen-1/lawecon-workshop/archive/dateien/waibelwinter11-12.

[56] Susan D. Franck, "The Legitimacy Crisis in Investment Treaty Arbitration: Privatizing Public International Law through Inconsistent Decisions," *Fordham L Rev.*, vol. 73 (2005), 1521.

[57] Brekoulakis, "Systemic Bias," 569. [58] *Ibid.*, 571. [59] *Ibid.*, 572. [60] *Ibid.*, 584.

[61] *Ibid.*, 573. [62] Lon L. Fuller, *The Morality of Law* (Yale University Press, 1964), 33, 36.

Unreasoned decisions, or decisions accompanied by only extremely succinct reasons, do not create an informative exposition of a rule.[63] To allow for inference from a rule that has a perspicuous meaning, the individual decisions that form the rule must be supplemented with sufficiently detailed reasons.[64] Indeed, scholars suggest that the use of reasoned awards is a necessary precondition for the evolution of precedents.[65]

While ECJ judgments,[66] WTO reports (panel and Appellate Body reports),[67] ICSID awards,[68] and awards issued under the North American Free Trade Agreement (*hereinafter* NAFTA)[69] need to be reasoned, a different regime can apply to commercial arbitration. Although some authors have claimed that many arbitration systems do not require that arbitrators write reasoned awards,[70] it is now a nearly universal principle that international arbitral awards must set forth the

[63] Schultz, "Concept of Law," 80. [64] *Ibid.*, 80.

[65] Drahozal, "Is Arbitration Lawless?," 214 ("[T]he available evidence suggests that some system of precedent is likely to develop when arbitration awards are published"); Fabien Gélinas, "Investment Tribunals and the Commercial Arbitration Model: Mixed Procedures and Creeping Institutionalisation" in M. Gehring et al. (eds.) *Sustainable Developments in World Trade Law* (The Hague: Kluwer Law International, 2005), 577, 585.

[66] Article 36 of the Statute of the Court of Justice of the European Union ("Judgments shall state the reasons on which they are based. They shall contain the names of the Judges who took part in the deliberations").

[67] WTO DSU, Article 12(7).

[68] Article 47(1) of the ICSID Rules of Procedure for Arbitration Proceedings (Arbitration Rules) provides that the award shall be in writing and shall contain, inter alia, a statement of the facts as found by the tribunal (letter *g*) and the decision of the tribunal on every question submitted to it, together with the reasons upon which the decision is based (letter *i*).

[69] The applicable arbitration rules for NAFTA cases establish formal requirements for awards. The formal requirements under all sets of applicable rules provide for the award to be reasoned, *cf.* Article 32(3) of the UNCITRAL Arbitration Rules (as revised in 2010) ("The arbitral tribunal shall state the reasons upon which the award is based, unless the parties have agreed that no reasons are to be given"); Rules 52 and 53 of the ICSID Arbitration (Additional Facility) Rules ("Additional Facility Arbitration Rules") ("The award shall be made in writing and shall contain, inter alia, a statement of the facts as found by the Tribunal (letter g) and the decision of the Tribunal on every question submitted to it, together with the reasons upon which the decision is based (letter i)"); Rule 47(1) of the Rules of Procedure for Arbitration Proceedings ("ICSID Arbitration Rules") ("The award shall be made in writing and shall contain, inter alia, a statement of the facts as found by the Tribunal (letter g) and the decision of the Tribunal on every question submitted to it, together with the reasons upon which the decision is based (letter i)").

[70] Weidemaier, "Theory of Precedent," 1914.

reasons for the tribunal's decision.[71] Nevertheless, the tribunal's duty to state reason might not fully prevent the existence of unreasoned awards, as the mere fact that an award is unreasoned does not make it susceptible to an annulment,[72] nor will the recognition of unreasoned awards be denied, even in states that require reasoned awards for arbitrations that occur within their territory.[73] In any event, this is an academic problem as in practice there are multiple interests that guarantee that awards are reasoned. For parties, reasoned decisions provide an explanation that can be used to guide future conduct and give a sense that the dispute resolution process was a deliberate and fair one, which is particularly important to the losing party.[74] Reasoned awards may also facilitate judicial review of the award; despite the limited statutory grounds for vacatur, a petition to vacate the award would be virtually impossible without a reasoned award.[75] Adjudicators themselves may also benefit from reasoned decisions, for these may confer prestige with lawyers, future disputants, other adjudicators, and the public at large.[76]

In sum, it is clear that reasoned awards will be a relatively common, if not ubiquitous, feature of trade law adjudication.[77]

2 Publication of awards

"If the international community of merchants aspires to give itself an autonomous system of law, this law has to be made known to all those

[71] Born, *Commercial Arbitration*, 2450–51. E.g., modern arbitration legislation in most developed jurisdictions except for the United States has superseded the common law rule and expressly requires that arbitrators give reasons for awards that are made within national territory, unless otherwise agreed by the parties. See, e.g., Article 31(2) of the UNCITRAL Model Law; §52(4) of the English Arbitration Act 1996. See generally Albert J. van den Berg, *The New York Arbitration Convention of 1958. Towards a Uniform Judicial Interpretation* (The Hague: T.M.C. Asser Institute, 1981), 380–81; Thomas Carbonneau, "Rendering Arbitral Awards with Reasons: The Elaboration of a Common Law of International Transactions," *Colum. J. Transnat'l L.*, vol. 23 (1984–1985), 579.

[72] Judgment of the Federal Supreme Court dated August 21, 1990, BGE 116 II 373, 375 (Switzerland); Stephen Berti and Anton K. Schnyder, "Article 190" in S. Berti et al. (eds.), *International Arbitration in Switzerland Art. 190* (The Hague: Kluwer Law International, 2000), para. 77.

[73] Judgment of the Rotterdam Rechtbank dated November 24, 1994, XXI Y.B. Comm. Arb. 635 (1996) (Netherlands); Judgment of the Brussels Tribunal de Première Instance dated January 25, 1996, *Inter-Arab Inv. Guarantee Corp.* v. *Banque Arabe et Internationale d'Investissements*, XXII Y.B. Comm. Arb. 643, 651–52 (1997), aff'd, Judgment of the Brussels Cour d'Appel dated January 24, 1997, 655 (1997) (Belgium).

[74] Weidemaier, "Theory of Precedent," 1919. [75] *Ibid.*, 1917. [76] *Ibid.*, 1917.

[77] *Ibid.*, 1919.

who have an interest in it."[78] Rules must be promulgated in order to count as law.[79] Public ascertainability is another one of Fuller's principle.

WTO reports (both panel and Appellate body) are published, circulated, and available as a public document.[80] In the past, investment arbitration decisions were not consistently published; however, the transparency initiatives of the last decades have included efforts to open up the arbitral process to the public through various mechanisms, such as the participation of third parties or amici curiae, the holding of open hearings, and the publication of awards.[81] The new ICSID Arbitration Rules, which entered into effect in 2006, are an excellent example of this progress.[82] These revisions made it mandatory for the center to promptly publish excerpts of the legal reasoning of an award,[83] and as a result ICSID awards are now virtually always published.[84] For NAFTA awards, while the rules are not entirely consistent,[85] in practice all three NAFTA

[78] Philippe Fouchard, *L'arbitrage Commercial International* (Paris: Dalloz, 1965), 451.

[79] Fuller, *Morality of Law*, 35.

[80] The panel should submit its final report to the parties involved in the dispute within two weeks of the conclusion of the interim review. Once the report is translated into all official WTO languages, it is circulated to all WTO members and becomes a public WT/DS document.

[81] Fortier, *Investment Protection*, 1; *cf.* Kinnear, *Investment Disputes*, 1120–28c.

[82] The increasing use of investor-state arbitration under the auspices of ICSID has prompted discussions. Because of the impact of investor-state arbitration on public interests, criticism has arisen regarding certain aspects of ICSID arbitration. The ICSID's amended arbitration rules took effect April 10, 2006; these amended rules can be found in its Arbitration (Additional Facility) Rules (hereinafter "Additional Facility Arbitration Rules"), as well as its Administrative and Financial Regulations. The amendments address the ability of nonparties to intervene in arbitration proceedings and attend hearings, the public disclosure of ICSID awards, the independence of arbitrators and the fees arbitrators can charge, and the ability to use fast-track procedures to both obtain interim relief and have groundless claims dismissed.

[83] This modification was the result of various changes proposed by the ICSID Secretariat in May 2005 to enhance the transparency of the ICSID rules.

[84] Article 48(5) of the ICSID Convention authorizes the center to publish an award or decision only with the consent of both parties. Parties themselves may publish awards and decisions unilaterally, and most invariably do. Today, virtually all ICSID decisions are available online, both on the ICSID website and on arbitration websites such as Investment Treaty Arbitration, see ita.law.uvic.ca; and for Investment Claims, see www.investmentclaims.com, *cf.* Lucy Reed et al., *Guide to ICSID Arbitration* (2nd edn., 2010), 153. Under the 2006 amendments, Rule 48(4) of the Arbitration Rules now requires the center to promptly include excerpts of the legal reasoning of tribunals in its publications.

[85] Chapter 11 of the NAFTA has few provisions addressing arbitration confidentiality. Article 1137(4) and Annex 1137.4 state that where Canada or the United States is the disputing party, either disputing party may make an award public. The applicable arbitration rules govern publication of an award when Mexico is the disputing party. The applicable arbitration rules for NAFTA cases establish that awards are confidential,

countries maintain extensive award databases,[86] as do a number of private persons.[87] Nevertheless, a number of other investment arbitration awards do still remain unpublished.[88]

Arbitral awards, on the other hand, are generally not accessible to the public or even to system users other than the disputants and their counsel.[89] In fact, a survey found that only six out of hundred awards cited other awards.[90] This may not have mattered much when the market for international commercial arbitrators and lawyers was highly concentrated. At least until recently, international commercial arbitration was dominated by an elite, relatively homogenous group of lawyers and arbitrators,[91] which means that these repeat players accumulated knowledge of past arbitrations and "knew how to research and present arguments," even when awards were not published.[92] This suggests that arbitral precedents may evolve more readily in systems in which relatively few arbitrators capture a large share of the arbitration business.[93] Even then, problems may arise if arbitrators refer to unpublished awards

cf. Article 32(5) of the UNCITRAL Arbitration Rules (the award may be made public only with the consent of both parties); Rule 48(4) of the ICSID Arbitration Rules ("The Centre shall not publish the award without the consent of the parties. The Centre shall, however, promptly include in its publications excerpts of the legal reasoning of the Tribunal"); Rule 53(3) of the ICSID Additional Facility Arbitration Rules ("Except to the extent required for any registration or filing of the award by the Secretary-General under paragraph (1) of this Article, the Secretariat shall not publish the award without the consent of the parties. The Secretariat shall, however, promptly include in the publications of the Centre excerpts of the legal reasoning of the Tribunal").

86 For the U.S. Department of State, see www.state.gov/s/l/c3439.htm; for International Trade Canada, see www.international.gc.ca/trade-agreements-accords-commerciaux/topics-domaines/disp-diff/nafta.aspx; for Mexico's Ministry of the Economy, see www.economia.gob.mx/en.

87 Investment Treaty Arbitration Resource Website, italaw.com; NAFTA Claims, naftaclaims.com.

88 Franck, "Legitimacy Crisis," 1542.

89 Weidemaier, "Theory of Precedent," 1914; see also Stacie I. Strong, "Research in International Commercial Arbitration: Special Skills, Special Sources," *Am. Rev. Int'l Arb.*, vol. 20 (2009), 119, 127.

90 Kaufmann-Kohler, "Arbitral Precedent," 362.

91 Yves Dezalay and Bryant G. Garth, *Dealing in Virtue: International Commercial Arbitration and the Construction of a Transnational Legal Order* (Chicago: University of Chicago Press, 1996), 18–29, 34–62; Alan S. Rau, "The Arbitrator and 'Mandatory Rules of Law'," *Am. Rev. Int'l Arb.*, vol. 18 (2007), 51, 88.

92 Strong, "Research in Commercial Arbitration," 127; Gélinas, "Investment Tribunals," 585 n.24.

93 Weidemaier, "Theory of Precedent," 1921, citing Carbonneau, "Rendering Arbitral Awards," 607–08; Catherine A. Rogers, "Transparency in International Commercial Arbitration," *U. Kan. L. Rev.*, vol. 54 (2006), 1301, 1319.

without making the unpublished arbitral awards available to the parties prior to rendering their award.[94] Although the Paris Cour d'Appel decided that arbitral due process does not require international arbitrators to make unpublished arbitral awards accessible to the parties prior to rendering their award,[95] this type of procedure is still not satisfying. Gradually, however, the market for international arbitration and legal services will expand to the point that many participants will be unaware of the vast majority of potentially relevant awards.[96] Under such circumstances, the lack of widespread awards may hinder the development of precedents.[97] Potentially useful awards from which relevant knowledge and experience could be drawn will be unavailable to participants in other arbitral proceedings.[98] From a jurisprudential perspective, individualized decisions that are largely kept confidential cannot count as a legal regime.[99] This is detrimental to the development of the law itself.

As a result, there is substantial debate today about whether commercial arbitration awards should be published more often, with appropriate redactions to keep the parties private. There are strong voices for the desirability of arbitral awards to be published in excerpted and redacted form.[100] There are also voices that claim that the drawbacks of greater publication outweigh its potential advantages. Opponents of greater publication worry that if the publications include the names of the arbitrators, the arbitrators will feel compelled to write awards that do more than resolve the commercial dispute; they will feel motivated to demonstrate their abilities as an arbitrator to future appointers.[101] Unlike investment treaty arbitration where public awards are necessary to create standards of conduct and to interpret treaties with standard provisions, there is no such compelling need in international commercial arbitration where usually a national law applies and where there are other sources to consult. Thus, there are fewer benefits available to outweigh the potential disadvantages of publication.[102]

In sum, while the publication of awards is common for more institutionalized trade "courts" such as WTO panels, ICSID, and NAFTA

[94] Berger, "Application of Precedents," 21.

[95] Judgment of the Cour d'Appel de Paris dated February 14, 1989, *Société Ofer Brothers* v. *The Tokyo Marine and Fire Insurance Co. Ltd. et al.*, RdA 695, 697 (1989) (France).

[96] Strong, "Research in Commercial Arbitration," 129.

[97] Weidemaier, "Theory of Precedent," 1923.

[98] Rivkin, "Impact of International Arbitration," 340.

[99] Schultz, "Concept of Law," 79.

[100] Born, *Commercial Arbitration*, 2968.

[101] Rivkin, "Impact of International Arbitration," 340.

[102] *Ibid.*, 340–41.

tribunals this is not the case for commercial arbitral tribunals. Their awards will have less precedential force, but it is questionable whether precedential weight is needed at all, thus there is substantial resistance to the systematic publication of arbitral awards.

V Nature and substance of trade disputes

The resolution of international commercial disputes raises particular challenges because the parties in conflict frequently come from different legal systems. The multilingual and multicultural environment typically present in international trade disputes affects the interpretation and application of the law in the sense that established concepts are recontextualized and adapted to international settings. The multilingual and multicultural environment has led to the development of the *lex mercatoria* as a set of rules created by users of international trade and observed globally. To an even greater extent, the multilingual and multicultural environment has also created a new conceptualization not only of the substantive law to be applied, but also of trade law adjudication itself. Emmanuel Gaillard proposed that there are currently three dominant conceptualizations of international arbitration: perception of arbitration as merely an emanation and therefore part of a domestic legal system; a multilocal representation where an award is based on all potentially involved legal systems; and a theory of arbitration as an autonomous legal order.[103] It is this last, transnational representation that is particularly connected to the multicultural environment. Several scholars, all based in Dijon, launched the idea of a transnational legal system that cannot be reduced to a public national legal system.[104] This concept of a "law beyond the state" was heavily criticized.[105] Hence, the prevailing view is that, in spite of the multicultural and multilingual environment of trade disputes, the ensuing principles are still rooted in (multi-)national law.

Trade disputes often entail another characteristic that is also closely connected to the ability of trade law adjudication to create rules of law. Governance by general norms is an essential principle for a system to perform the essential function of law. If "every issue [is] decided on an *ad hoc* basis," this prevents the system from being jural.[106] Hence, a normative system that is not primarily composed of general rules

[103] Emmanuel Gaillard, *Aspects philosophiques du droit de l'arbitrage international* (Leiden: Martinus Nijhoff Publishers, 2008).

[104] Schultz, "Concept of Law," 61.

[105] See, e.g., *ibid.*, 62–66, with many references.

[106] Fuller, *Morality of Law*, 38 (emphasis added).

would not be functional as law.[107] This seems to be at odds with the characteristics of some trade disputes.

Trade disputes that go to commercial arbitration are usually centered on contract interpretation and are therefore individualized. A regulatory regime built on arbitral awards runs the risk that it will be marked by *ad hoc*ness.[108] In addition, because most arbitration is governed by state-supplied law, arbitral precedent serves little function. In such cases, parties are not likely to research past awards themselves or to appreciate arbitrators who invoke such awards in the face of ample judicial or other authority. Moreover, participants in some arbitration systems may view public rather than private actors as the primary, and perhaps the only, legitimate producers of law.[109]

This situation differs from other aspects of trade law adjudication. Most bilateral investment treaties (*hereinafter* BITs) share similar, often identical, substantive and procedural protections such as national treatment, most-favored nation, and fair and equitable treatment.[110] While there is no doctrine of *stare decisis* or binding precedents in international law, the development of an investment treaty case law is unmistakable.[111]

In sum, as a result of the multilingual and multicultural environment within trade disputes, legal concepts are adapted to international settings that are nevertheless rooted in (multi-)national law. However, as commercial arbitrations are usually centered on contract interpretation and governed by state-supplied law, arbitral precedent serves little function, in contrast to investment arbitration. This leads directly to the next section and last feature examined, namely the orientation of legal interpretation.

VI Orientation of legal interpretation in trade law adjudication

1 General remarks

The final feature to be examined is the orientation of legal interpretation. Depending on the nature of the legal interpretation performed by trade "courts," their decision-making resembles either commercial services performed from case to case (i.e., *a casu ad casum*) or the

107 Schultz, "Concept of Law," 73. 108 *Ibid.*, 75.

109 Weidemaier, "Theory of Precedent," 1952.

110 Rivkin, "Impact of International Arbitration," 344.

111 Kaufmann-Kohler, "Arbitral Precedent," 368; Jeffery P. Commission, "Precedent in Investment Treaty Arbitration," *J Int'l Arb.*, vol. 24 (2007), 129.

administration of justice. The appropriate nature of legal interpretation is highly debated in legal doctrine[112] and simultaneously relevant for Fuller's notion of law. The principle of prospectivity requires the majority of rules in a system to be prospective and not retrospective, which means that rules should be created before the events to which they pertain occur.[113] As stated above, most international dispute settlement rules expressly or implicitly disavow any binding force of precedent.[114] Nevertheless, as a practical matter, most trade "courts" have developed a *de facto* case law whereby they tend to follow earlier decisions.[115] The ECJ is notorious for closely following its earlier judgments, almost exclusively citing its own precedent and rarely overruling itself.[116] In the same manner, WTO panels and the WTO Appellate Body have developed a consistent body of international trade law by *de facto stare decisis.*[117]

The last couple decades have seen similar developments in investment arbitration. ICSID tribunals frequently cite and engage with awards issued by investment or other international tribunals. A survey analyzing ICSID awards issued between 1990 and 2006 found that nearly 80 percent of the time, tribunals cited awards rendered by other ICSID panels.[118] Tribunals thus have "a duty to seek to contribute to the harmonious development of investment law and thereby to meet the legitimate expectations of the community of States and investors towards certainty of the rule of law."[119] There is a "moral obligation to follow precedents so as to foster a normative environment that is predictable."[120] In these areas of trade law adjudication, the absence of a *stare decisis* does not prevent trade law adjudication from serving as an administration of justice. The situation is less clear in commercial arbitration, which is examined more closely in the next section.

[112] Emmanuel Gaillard, *Legal Theory of international Arbitration* (Leiden: Martinus Nijhoff Publishers, 2010), 35.

[113] Schultz, "Concept of Law," 75.

[114] Reinisch, "Proliferation of International Dispute Settlement," 122.

[115] *Ibid.*, 123.

[116] Robert Jennings, "The Judiciary, International and National, and the Development of International Law," *Int'l & Comp. L.Q.*, vol. 45 (1996), 1, 9.

[117] Raj Bhala, "The Precedent Setters: De Facto Stare Decisis in WTO Adjudication," *J. Transnat'l L. & Pol'y*, vol. 9 (1999), 1.

[118] Commission, "Precedent," 149–50.

[119] *Saipem S.A.* v. *Bangladesh*, ICSID Case No. ARB/05/07, Decision on Jurisdiction and Recommendation on Provisional Measures (March 21, 2007), para. 67.

[120] Kaufmann-Kohler, "Arbitral Precedent," 374.

2 A spotlight on the orientation of decision-making in commercial arbitration

As the practice of commercial arbitration grows and arbitral case law increases in volume, the ideas and concepts contained within them are regarded as valuable knowledge by other arbitrators.[121] Arbitration is gradually developing into a self-contained judicial system in which awards hold significance beyond the individual case.[122] Arbitral awards have played significant roles in the development of fundamental aspects of the international arbitral process.[123] Although arbitral awards do not often serve as precedent on matters of substantive law (e.g., offer and acceptance or adequacy of contractual performance), this is because there are other valid sources of precedent such as national court decisions, and not because arbitral awards cannot serve as precedent.[124] Also, as mentioned earlier, because international arbitrations are focused on issues of contract interpretation, they frequently do not have the occasion to deal repeatedly with the same issues of substantive law.[125] Many awards also remain confidential and thus are unavailable as precedent. In addition, a judge's decision is always subject to correction on appeal. International commercial arbitration is different. An arbitral tribunal is freer than a state court to deal with the actual case in front of it, as the tribunal is established to deal with a particular case. Once it has pronounced its decision, its function is over. There is more scope for tailoring the award to the particular nature of the dispute.[126] Generally, arbitral tribunals are thus more susceptible to the specific needs of international trade in a specific case.[127] There is also less need to be concerned with consistency of decisions, as there is generally no court of appeal to ensure uniformity of arbitral decision.[128] Though accurate to a degree, this abovementioned portrait of arbitration is quite stylized and offers a vision of "folklore

[121] Berger, "Application of Precedents," 19. [122] *Ibid.*

[123] Born, *Commercial Arbitration*, 2966–67, e.g., the separability presumption and the competence-competence doctrine. Equally, arbitral practices relating to matters such as disclosure or use of written witness statements have developed.

[124] *Ibid.*, 2967. [125] *Ibid.*

[126] Allan Redfern, "International Commercial Arbitration: Winning the Battle" in The Southwestern Legal Foundation (ed.), *Private Investors Abroad* (Dallas, 1989), 11–1, 11–12.

[127] Berger, "Application of Precedents," 12.

[128] Redfern, "International Commercial Arbitration," 11–12. See also Karl-Heinz Böckstiegel, "The Future: What Will Change? Round Table Discussion" in A. J. van den Berg (ed.), *Arbitration: The Next Fifty Years*, ICCA Congress Series No 16 (2012), 181, 201.

arbitration."[129] There are strong voices that these "stylized" views are incompatible with the adjudicative function and mandate of international arbitrators,[130] but even these voices accept that an arbitral tribunal may properly conclude that a particular national judicial precedent was not intended to, nor would it be applied to, international transactions, or a particular type of international transaction.[131] Hence, awards in international commercial arbitration have gained significance beyond the individual case for procedural issues, but less so for substantive issues.[132]

3 Do we need or want decision-making to be administration of justice?

When arbitrators apply a national law in commercial arbitration, that law is usually sufficiently developed so as to be predictable, and the arbitrators' role does not involve developing rules. After all, developing rules is the role of national legislators. On the other hand, when arbitrators apply a body of rules that are less developed, their role with respect to the establishment of predictable rules becomes much more important.[133] This is particularly true in present-day investment law.[134] As investment disputes are predominantly adjudicated by international trade "courts," the development of legal concepts in investment cannot emanate other than by the consistent case law of trade "courts." In investment arbitration, the development of consistent rules through arbitral awards is therefore more necessary than in commercial arbitration.[135] In addition, as mentioned above, disputes in commercial arbitration are most often fact- and contract-driven. The outcome revolves around a unique set of facts and depends upon the interpretation of a unique contract that was negotiated between private actors to fit their specific needs.[136] Unsurprisingly, given this context awards are only published sporadically, as opposed to investment arbitration where publication has become the rule.[137]

129 Weidemaier, "Theory of Precedent," 1905. 130 Born, *Commercial Arbitration*, 2964.
131 *Ibid.*
132 In this regard, sports and investment arbitration take up a special position. While this chapter analyzes investment arbitration, in sports arbitration there is a strong evolution toward reliance on other sports law cases and a focus on administration of justice. Although there is no principle of binding precedent, a panel of the Court of Arbitration for Sport (hereinafter CAS) will attempt to come to the same conclusion on matters of law as a previous CAS panel, *cf.* Rivkin, "Impact of International Arbitration," 351. Indeed, a survey shows that ever since 2003 nearly every award contains references to earlier CAS awards, *cf.* Kaufmann-Kohler, "Arbitral Precedent," 364.
133 Kaufmann-Kohler, "Arbitral Precedent," 374. 134 *Ibid.* 135 *Ibid.*, 376.
136 *Ibid.*, 375–76. 137 *Ibid.*, 376.

In sum, Fuller's notion of law requires that decision-making is prospective. While this is the case for the more institutionalized trade "courts" such as the ECJ and WTO panels, and is also true for investment tribunals, the situation is different for commercial arbitration. However, due to the fact that cases in commercial arbitration are individualized and rooted in more or less clearly established national law, there seems to be less need for arbitral tribunals to prospectively create law and precedents.

C Role of international arbitration in trade law adjudication

I General remarks

Based on the findings of the prior sections, this section analyzes the role of international arbitration in trade disputes and explains the circumstances under which international arbitration becomes a desirable alternative for other public dispute resolution mechanisms.[138]

II The Softwood Lumber Dispute

The Softwood Lumber Dispute is a series of disputes between the United States and Canada that pertains to the import of softwood lumber from Canada to the United States. At the heart of the dispute is the US allegation that the Canadian lumber industry unfairly subsidizes Canadian lumber production. The controversy is the largest forest-products trade dispute in the world and the longest-lasting trade dispute between the two states.[139] The dispute also sets a record for the number of dispute resolution mechanisms involved in the settlement of a single controversy.[140] For the purpose of this chapter, interest lies in the last phase of the dispute because it involves a state-to-state dispute adjudicated under the auspices of the London Court of International Arbitration (*hereinafter* LCIA), which is more commonly used for commercial arbitration.

On September 12, 2006, Canada and the United States concluded a Softwood Lumber Agreement (*hereinafter* SLA) about timber pricing policies. Only months after the conclusion of the SLA, the United States initiated arbitration proceedings. The dispute resolution provision contained in the SLA is over four pages long and highly complex.[141]

[138] *Ibid.*, 374.
[139] Leonila Guglya, "The Interplay of International Dispute Resolution Mechanisms: the Softwood Lumber Controversy," *J Int'l Disp. Settlement*, vol. 2 (2011), 175, 176–77.
[140] *Ibid.*, 175. [141] SLA, Article XIV.

In essence, it provides for a two-step process that requires consultations as the first step, and if these are unsuccessful then either party may "refer the matter to arbitration by delivering a written Request for Arbitration to the Registrar of the LCIA Court. The arbitration shall be conducted under the LCIA Arbitration Rules in effect on the date the SLA 2006 was signed. [. . .] The legal place of arbitration shall be London, United Kingdom." The dispute resolution provision is significant as this is likely the first time in history that two states have agreed to arbitrate their differences using the arbitration rules of the LCIA. Softwood Lumber is thus a public international arbitration dispute that used a private dispute settlement mechanism.

III Use of international arbitration for trade disputes

The characterization of international trade disputes defines the roles and responsibilities of all participants in the system.[142] If a dispute is viewed as a public investor-state matter, then the dispute goes beyond private business interests and implicates the host state's public policies and the rights of its domestic constituencies.[143] The subject matter of investment disputes already highlights its public law aspects.[144] In addition, the increasing size of damages awards show that the public purse of the host state is often involved.[145] On the other hand, if a dispute is viewed as a private contractual matter between two parties, there is a strong case for the tribunal to narrow its focus to the interests of the two parties in the dispute.[146] Awards usually cannot be appealed and are rarely published, which creates less pressure for tribunals to adequately and consistently apply the law and instead adequately resolve the dispute before them.

The negotiation history that led Canada and the United States to opt for LCIA arbitration remains unknown, and we can only guess what brought the parties to that state. The findings of this chapter would suggest that the commercial interests underlying the SLA played a significant role, as those interests would be comfortable with private commercial dispute resolution mechanisms. However, reality is often more complex than pure theory; in the Softwood Lumber dispute, the

[142] Rivkin, "Impact of International Arbitration," 352.

[143] Ernst-Ulrich Petersmann, "International Rule of Law and Constitutional Justice in International Investment Law and Arbitration," *Ind. J. Global Legal Stud.*, vol. 16 (2009), 513, 524–25.

[144] Rivkin, "Impact of International Arbitration," 352–53.

[145] *Ibid.*, 352–53.

[146] *Ibid.*, 352.

reason for choosing LCIA arbitration might have instead been that the parties did not want to go back to any dispute resolution mechanism they had already used (recall that the dispute was both lengthy and had already involved multiple resolution mechanisms). Having exhausted all available institutions of public international law, they had to resort to commercial arbitration.

D Conclusion

This chapter shed light on several features of trade law adjudication that are both crucial elements for the ability of trade law adjudication to create law and legal precedents, and also the source of criticisms lobbied against trade law adjudication.

The first set of features that were analyzed stem from the design of trade "courts." The more institutionalized trade "courts" are enclosed in firm rules that govern their composition and the availability of an appeal mechanism, whereas arbitrations are more pluralistic and diverse yet less likely to create consistent case law. The examination of the role that trade law adjudicators play revealed that they are often institutionally embedded repeat-players with an international background and are thus likely to feel bound by legal precedent, and they thus presumably create transnational legal concepts. A procedural characteristic of trade law adjudication is that most trade dispute awards are reasoned, although this requirement is not always stipulated by the procedural rules. On the other hand, the publication of awards is only common for the more institutionalized trade "courts" but not for commercial arbitral tribunals. The multilingual and multicultural environment present in international trade disputes ultimately means that legal concepts are adapted to international settings, which are nevertheless rooted in (multi-)national law. At the same time, commercial arbitrations are usually centered on contract interpretation and are governed by state-supplied law so that arbitral precedent serves little function, whereas the opposite is true for investment arbitration. Due to the combination of all of these features, particularly those features that differ between the various trade "courts," the more institutionalized bodies can well serve as administrators of justice while others are better seen as commercial services that are performed on a case-by-case basis.

The different features of international trade disputes examined in this chapter are not equally present in all trade dispute resolution mechanisms and therefore impact the ability of the different trade "courts" to create law and precedents. The selection of the most appropriate dispute resolution mechanism should bear in mind the different background and interests underlying the given dispute, the different precedential weight of the decisions going forward, and the desirability of such precedential weight.

PART III

Legitimating decisions in international economic law

8

Judicial ethics in international economic law: what standards of independence and impartiality apply to arbitrators and panellists?

KRISTA NADAKAVUKAREN SCHEFER*

Introduction

Much has been written about the dispute settlement mechanisms of international economic law (IEL) institutions. Indeed, the attention of academia to IEL institutions seems to be largely driven by the dispute settlement mechanisms that those institutions establish. This situation should not surprise us; as scholars trained in the study of rule-application, we are drawn to legal analyses by those with the competence to interpret legal texts. Thus, the World Trade Organization (WTO) dispute settlement mechanism has received attention and awe due to its untypically "courtroom-like" procedures and binding awards. International arbitration tribunals, with their increasingly formalised procedures and sophisticated legal opinions, have nearly overshadowed the substantive law they apply. Their emergence in the public eye as "courts" signals their increasing acceptance as global decision-makers, even as individual opinions are often criticised.

One of the key issues for investigation has been that of the legitimacy of dispute settlement mechanisms. With their competence to issue decisions that often result in a demand for changes to national legislation, the international IEL tribunals must strive to maintain states' acceptance of their authority to issue such judgments, even where adherence to a decision is viewed as an infraction on sovereignty. Equating "adjudication" with legitimacy, IEL tribunals have increasingly adopted courtroom-like practices, even while denying that they have established "courts" or that their members are "judges". One example of such

* I would like to acknowledge the excellent research assistance of Dimitrij Euler, Jasmin Haecker and Julian Powell. My thanks also extend to Thomas Cottier, Christian Haeberli, and Gabrielle Marceau for their insights into the WTO dispute settlement processes. All mistakes remain my own.

practices is the development of more formalised procedural rules and practices that have characterised the move of IELs from diplomatic dispute resolution toward adjudicatory methods. Another example of the adjudication of IEL dispute settlement that fosters legitimacy is an insistence on tribunals' sole reliance on the law as the basis for its reasoning. This insistence should eliminate any "political" rulings, which would likely be seen as an impermissible intrusion into the state party's policymaking. A third method of enhancing the legitimacy of a tribunal ruling is requiring a written decision to be issued to the parties. The decision document assists the parties in ensuring that their arguments were considered and that the final result was reasonable and considered, given the relevant legal framework and the facts of the particular case.

However, the legitimacy of courts relies not only on the formalisation of the rules that guide the proceedings. That legitimacy also relies on the perceived legitimacy of the decision-makers who are responsible for ensuring that the procedural rules are followed and the substantive rules are applied appropriately. In other words, the tribunal members *as individuals* are an integral factor in the legitimacy of international dispute settlement as an institution.[1] The legitimacy of these decision-makers depends on a certain standard of decision-maker ethics.

While the details concerning precisely what standard of ethics should apply to decision-makers in different contexts are contested, the idea that there must be adherence to *some* standard is firmly established in principle in both domestic legal systems and international law. How well do IEL dispute settlement systems fare when it comes to this aspect of legitimacy?

This chapter investigates the norms of judicial independence that are applied in international law and compares those norms to the standards of investment arbitration tribunals and the WTO's dispute settlement panellists. Because the expressed standards are practically the same across all international fora, the following work considers that how these standards are discussed by tribunals and scholars is as interesting as the definition of the standard itself.

Section II of this chapter will establish the general international law standards for judicial independence that stem from the right to a fair trial

[1] Daniel Terris, Cesare P.R. Romano and Leigh Swigart, *The International Judge: An Introduction to the Men and Women Who Decide the World's Cases* (Oxford: Oxford University Press, 2007), 227 (noting that "judges themselves have contributed at times to the fragility of their institutions, through all-too-human weaknesses that have exposed their courts to ridicule, criticism, and vitriol").

and the need for legitimacy in the system. Section III will then take up a review of the discussion of arbitrator ethics that is ongoing in the context of investor-state dispute settlements. In Section IV, I turn to the WTO to compare its approach to panellist ethics to both the international law norms and the practice of investment tribunals. Section V summarises and concludes.

Why dispute settlement systems need judicial independence

Right to fair trial

The legal discussion of judicial independence often centres on the necessity of judicial independence to secure the right of every individual to a fair trial. The International Covenant on Civil and Political Rights (ICCPR) declares, in paragraph 1 of Article 14, the content of the right to fair trial as follows:

> All persons shall be equal before the courts and tribunals. In the determination of any criminal charge against him, or of his rights and obligations in a suit at law, everyone shall be entitled to a fair and public hearing by a competent, independent and impartial tribunal established by law.

Clearly, the right to a fair trial extends beyond judicial independence – there is also a (qualified) requirement for publicity – but just as clearly, the right to a "competent, independent and impartial tribunal established by law" is central. The benefits of publicity, as indicated by the text, can be outweighed by other considerations (morals, national order or security, or to protect parties' privacy). However, no interests can override the need for an independent judiciary,[2] for the competence, independence and impartiality of the tribunal directly serve the interest of ensuring that each party is "equal before the courts and tribunals". It does this by fostering the ideal of decision-making based solely on the given law and the facts of the case at hand. Itself supporting the general norm of protecting equality, judicial independence can therefore be viewed as integral to the system of human rights protections in both its broad and narrow senses.

The essential protection of judicial independence for ensuring the principle of equality before the law and the individual's right to fair trial is only a part of the value of independence of the judiciary and judges. The equally significant role that is played by judicial

[2] See ICCPR, Comment 32, para. 19 (calling the right to a competent, independent and impartial tribunal "an absolute right that is not subject to any exception").

independence is applicable beyond human rights to the entire dispute settlement context in general. Briefly stated, judicial independence forms the foundation of the legitimacy of third-party settlement of disputes.

Legitimacy of the decision

Judicial independence is a value that has been recognised and set forth in nearly every national law system, as well as in non–human rights regimes of international law. This universality is caused by the fact that the principle of independence of courts and judges is implicit to the use of third-party decision-makers in dispute settlement and is thus a part of the overall maintenance of peace within and between communities.[3] As Kiener explains, the submission of a dispute to resolution by a non-party (whether in the form of a go-between, a mediator, an arbitrator or a judge) is only acceptable by each of the parties – and therefore will only motivate the loser to adhere to the decision – if the decision-maker can be assumed to be assessing the specific facts of the conflict on the basis of accepted rules (laws, in the case of legal resolutions).[4]

Laws, as Kiener reminds us, are norms that are intended to guide societal behaviour, and as such are necessarily general. Assuming that the laws themselves are accepted as just, as we can if they are approved of by society as a whole, behaviour in accordance with the law is just.[5] However, in any given dispute over whether a particular behaviour violated the law, decision-makers must interpret the laws in the context of that dispute. This activity assigns the decision-maker(s) as those who should ensure justice, but it opens their analysis to subjectivity. It is only by ensuring that the decision-maker is unswayed by factors external to the immediate dispute that the parties will be able to accept that justice has been done in the particular instance.[6] It is the "doing" of justice that legitimises decision-makers (i.e., mediators, arbitrators or judges), so this independence of judgment is crucial to the legitimacy of a dispute settlement system.

The elements of judicial independence

Judicial independence is composed of two aspects: the independence of the judiciary and the independence and impartiality of the judge. The

[3] Regina Kiener, *Richterliche Unabhängigkeit* (Bern: Stämpfli Verlag, 2001). [4] *Ibid.*, 6.
[5] *Ibid.*, 6–7. [6] *Ibid.*, 5.

current study is particularly interested in the latter of these aspects, but an overview of the former is helpful for gaining an insight into the broader issues of independence.

Independence of the judiciary

The independence of the judiciary is the aspect of judicial independence that focuses on the institutional, or organisational, relationship between the judiciary and other powers within the same organisation. The aim of measures to promote institutional independence is to avoid the politicisation of the judiciary.[7]

There are numerous ways to depoliticise judiciaries. For instance, within a government, judges should not be subject to or reliant on either the executive or the legislature (horizontal dependence). Nor should their decisions be subject to oversight by persons or institutions that are not themselves within the judicial system (vertical independence). In an international organisation, the dispute settlement organ should similarly have the competence to issue decisions without the approval of such opinions by other institutional organs.

To ensure such organisational independence, there must be a legal and factual separation of competences, a separation of operational organisations and a separation of personnel.[8] The separation of functions, or competences, requires that courts be the sole organs for expressing whether a violation of a law has occurred in a particular instance. The executive, in particular, should have no influence on the declaration of whether or not a law was broken. Nor should non-courts be permitted to change a court decision, even if the legislature's changing of a law in the wake of an unsatisfactory application of the law by a court is permissible.

The operational independence of a court is protected through the autonomous running of the judicial system, from the hiring of court personnel and budget making[9] to the immunity of judges from prosecution. While the legislature or administrative branches of government may well have legitimate duties to supervise the judicial branch's functioning – and may even have the opportunity to sanction judges for

[7] Ian Binnie, "Judicial Independence in Canada", 8, available at www.venice.coe.int/WCCJ/Rio/Papers/CAN_Binnie_E.pdf.

[8] See Kiener, *Unabhängigkeit*, 228.

[9] Terris, Romano and Swigart point out that the international organisation's own "fragility" – exhibited in an underfunded or uncertainly funded legal office – can be a source of judicial dependence. Terris et al., *International Judge*, 226.

misbehaviour – within an independent judiciary, such oversight must stay within the bounds of controlling for behaviour and not for opinions or decisions.

Finally, institutional independence implies the separation of judicial personnel from personnel outside the court system. To ensure that the judicial system maintains institutional integrity (and the appearance of independence), court personnel should not hold positions in the executive branch or the legislature, should be minimally – if at all – engaged outside of the court in civil activities, and should have long terms of office and secured salaries.[10] Each of these considerations minimises the likelihood that judges will take extraneous factors into consideration when deciding the merits of a particular case. The Human Rights Committee has accepted the validity of these principles and has issued numerous expressions of concern[11] related to cases in which judges have been (or may be) removed from office by the executive[12] and where judges are elected for only a few years.[13] In addition, that committee has commented disapprovingly on the lack of diversity of a court's membership.[14]

International tribunals are generally subject to less stringent application of these rules than are national courts, but contemporary international law scholarship largely accepts the rules as equally beneficial at the interstate level.[15] Thus, international law

[10] The elements of secured tenure and salary originated in the need to stop kings from ousting judges who made rulings disagreeable to the monarch. Famously appearing in the United Kingdom's Act of Settlement of 1701, the command that "judges commissions be made *quamdiu se bene gesserint*, and their salaries ascertained and established" was included to underscore the independence of the judiciary from executive whim. See an act for the further limitation of the Crown and better securing the rights and liberties of the subject, 12 and 13 Will 3 c. 2, available at www.jacobite.ca/documents/1701settlement.htm

[11] See Sarah Joseph and Melissa Castan, *The International Covenant on Civil and Political Rights: Cases, Materials, and Commentary*, 3rd edn (Oxford: Oxford University Press, 2013), 450–453.

[12] E.g., *Bandaranayake* v. *Sri Lanka* (1376/05); UN doc CCPR/C/79/Add.62 (1996), para. 16.

[13] E.g., *Pastukhov* v. *Belarus* (814/98); *Busyo et al.* v. *Democratic Republic of the Congo* (933/00); Concluding Observations on the United States, UN doc CCPR/C/79/Add.50 (1995); Concluding Observations on Liechtenstein, UN doc CCPR/CO/81/LIE, (2004), para. 12; Turkmenistan, UN doc CCPR/C/TKM/CO/1/Add.1, (2012), para. 13.

[14] Concluding Observations on Sudan, UN doc CCPR/C/79/Add.85 (1997).

[15] Fabien Gélinas, "The Independence of International Arbitrators and Judges: Tampered with or Well Tempered?", *NY Int'l L. Rev.*, vol. 24:1 (2011), 1, 4; Terris et al., *International Judge*, 192. But see Eric A. Posner and John C. Yoo, "Judicial Independence in

theory[16] recognises the need to shield adjudicators and arbitrators from the influence of state pressure by offering tenured judgeships, restricting the opportunities for judges to hold other governmental offices during their time on the court, creating compulsory jurisdiction and disallowing nationals of a party from serving as decision-makers.

Independence and impartiality of the judge

While the independence of the judiciary is a structural characteristic of a legal system, the independence and impartiality of the judge is a characteristic specific to a particular decision-maker in a particular dispute settlement context. With the ultimate goal of providing for the legitimacy of the international legal system as a whole, the aim of ensuring the independence of judges is to help decision-makers stand as symbols of the legitimate system by being detached from personal interests. It is only through such detachment that the decision-makers will be able to fulfil their duty of applying the law (and only the law) to the facts of a specific case. Despite their contextual nature, the demands of independence and impartiality are crucial supplements to the independence of the judiciary in protecting the systemic legitimacy of dispute settlement, for like their institutional counterparts, the personal independence and impartiality principles safeguard the equality of the parties and, in turn, the public's appreciation of the proceedings as legitimate.[17]

International Tribunals", *California Law Review*, vol. 93:1 (2005), 1 (arguing that the effectiveness of international tribunals, unlike that of domestic courts, is unrelated to the independence of the tribunal).

16 See Gélinas, "International Arbitrators", 8–10 (describing the difference between the theory of international judicial independence and the reality of international judicial practice).

17 The symbiotic relationship between judicial independence and judge impartiality may be more complex than one of merely mutual support. Green and Roiphe assert that providing for the impartiality of the judge was a defensive move by the bar to protect the judiciary's institutional independence: "the emphasis on judicial courtesy marked a growing concern with courtroom atmospherics and the public image of the judiciary. The bar and the judiciary grew increasingly afraid that if this image was not preserved, the public through the legislature would regulate the judicial branch in such a way as to disturb its independence from the political branches. This concern grew to predominate, and by the 1970s, the bar and the judiciary responded by enforcing judicial branch regulation of individual judges." Bruce A. Green and Rebecca Roiphe, "Regulating Discourtesy on the Bench: A Study in the Evolution of Judicial Independence", New York Law School Legal Studies Research Paper Series 12/13, No. 69, available at http://ssrn.com/abstract=22438529.

Definitions

Independence Independence is often considered to be the absence of an objective interest in the outcome of a particular case. As such, a judge is independent if (s)he has neither an immediate nor a potential pecuniary interest in the result nor a personal relationship (presently or in the past) with any of the parties to the case.[18] The existence of either type of connection could conceivably change the judge's decision as to which party's arguments to support, giving the parties unequal positions before the law. Hence, the right to a fair trial and the more basic right to equality would be violated. Moreover, the losing party's acceptance of the decision would be weakened by the inequality; justice will not have been done, and the system as a whole would suffer a loss of legitimacy as a result.

The relevant community's acceptance of the decision may also be impaired by a judge's dependency on the case's outcome. If material connections to the case or the parties are known to exist, even if the connections did not in fact impact on the judge's decision-making, the legitimacy of the decision – and also of the system as a whole – may be questioned. As a result, international tribunals will insist on an objective standard of judges' independence rather than a subjective standard. What connections, personal or institutional, they ask, does the decision-maker have that would lead a reasonable person to doubt his/her independence?[19]

The concern with appearances of independence is further underlined by the rules regarding the disclosure of material relationships. Institutional rules or guidelines that apply to international decision-makers will often require the disclosure of certain types of relationships but lack a corresponding demand that the individual recuse him- or herself from hearing the case on those grounds. The disclosure of such connections – despite their potential to taint the judge's independence – suffices in itself to avoid any loss of legitimacy.[20] On the other hand, a failure to disclose such material relationships may itself be considered a

[18] See LCIA Reference No. 81224 (Decision of 15 March 2010), para. 3.7 (citing Lew, Mistelis and Kroll, *Comparative International Commercial Arbitration* (Leiden: Kluwer Law International, 2003), 261: "Independence requires that there should be no such actual or past dependent relationship between the parties and the arbitrators which may or at least may appear to affect the arbitrator's freedom of judgment").

[19] The "reasonable person" is one who is familiar with the norms of judicial independence.

[20] Of course, this is subject to the determination that the judge's independence is not actually impaired.

violation of the judge's independence, even where the relationship – had it been disclosed – would not have required recusal.[21]

Impartiality Impartiality is a mental element: the state of mind of a judge that can cause him/her to take a particular decision despite the law and facts of a case.[22] Often difficult to distinguish from independence,[23] the concept of impartiality may be considered to be a concept that focuses on emotional or impalpable influences on decision-making rather than on objectively identifiable influences. Personal prejudices (such as racism, sexism or religious antipathy) and strong political convictions come within its sphere, as do firmly stated opinions or other expressions of the judge's personality.

The idea that a judge must be impartial stems from the impulses of legal scholarship to rationalise the law and make judging a science of determining the meaning of law. While the strictly formalist view of the law has been rejected as inaccurate and unachievable, the belief in the value of impartiality has continued. Ironically, the call for judges who are unemotional, impassive, and even machine-like is just as strong among those who accept the interpretive nature of judging as those who reject it. For the former, the very fact that judges would be making laws through their decisions meant that the judges themselves should not be predisposed toward one party and that they should be impartial in their application of the facts to the legal rules.

Like independence, impartiality reinforces the belief in the ability of a dispute settlement system to afford justice to the parties. The principle of

[21] See *Commonwealth Coatings Corp.* v. *Continental Casualty Co.*, 393 US 145 (1968) (finding "evident partiality" of the arbitrator based on the fact that an arbitrator's relationship with a party was not disclosed).

[22] LCIA Reference No. 81224 (Decision of 15 March 2010), para. 3.8 (citing Lew et. al, *Commercial Arbitration*, 258 ("Impartiality requires that an arbitrator neither favours one party nor is predisposed as to the question in dispute. In so far as it is a state of mind, it is a fairly abstract and subjective standard").

[23] Note that there is no clear view among commentators on whether independence and impartiality are a single norm or two separate norms. Catherine Rogers writes that the terms are used interchangeably and suggests that there is in fact a single idea behind them. See Catherine A. Rogers, "The Ethics of International Arbitrators" in Lawrence Newman and Richard Hill (eds.), *The Leading Arbitrators Guide to International Arbitration* (Huntington, New York: Juris Publishing, 2008); Nowak (writing of "independence" as institutional considerations and "impartiality" as case-specific ones, seeming to collapse judge independence and impartiality into "impartiality"). Yet, many others write of independence and impartiality separately, implying that they are distinguishable concepts. See e.g., Kiener, *Unabhängigkeit* (referring to „Unabhängigkeit" and „Befangenheit").

equality, which is based in general international law and fundamental to human rights law, demands impartiality for any system to be accepted as legitimate. As a consequence, while impartiality is itself subjective, appearances are important. Judges must not be decision-makers in disputes in which they may appear partial to reasonable observers. Thus, statements and behaviour before or during a proceeding can be scrutinised, as can facts about the person of the judge or the circumstances of the case.[24]

Standards

Given the clear connection between the legitimacy of third-party dispute settlement and judges' independence and impartiality, it is not surprising that the principle of independent and impartial judging is also well established in international law. This principle extends beyond the rules of human rights law to the constituting documents of numerous international tribunals of every sort. The International Court of Justice, the International Criminal Court, the Tribunal for the Law of the Sea and the administrative review tribunals of multilateral development banks all contain within their statutes provisions that bar those persons who would be swayed by considerations external to the law and facts of a particular dispute from deciding whether or not the respondent violated a norm.[25]

[24] Generally, a judge's rudeness or inappropriate commenting during a case will not, on its own, be grounds for upholding a challenge of impartiality. Just how far discourteousness must go to become an appearance of partiality is a topic for future research. For an excellent historical introduction to this question as it has developed in the United States, see Bruce Green and Rebecca Roiphe, "Regulating Discourtesy on the Bench: A Study in the Evolution of Judicial Independence", available at http://ssrn.com/abstract=2243829.

[25] The different tribunals' rules contain slight variations in their wording and in their procedures for enforcing their judges' independence and impartiality. Comparing the examples of the ITLOS' Statute, ICC's Rome Statute, and ICTY's Updated Statute and Rules of Procedure, one notices that each requires actual and apparent independence and impartiality (ITLOS Arts. 2.1 and 11; ICC Art. 40; ICTY Art. 12.1 and Rule 14(A)) and calls for recusal where there are financial interests or prior connections to the particular case or parties (ITLOS Art. 8; ICC Art. 41.2; ICTY Rule 15(A)). While the ICC and ITLOS provide for challenges to be decided by a majority vote of the other judges (ITLOS Art. 8.4; ICC Art. 41.2(c)), the ICTY dictates that a panel of judges from "other Chambers" of the court will make the interlocutory decision about the challenged judge's suitability to continue (ICTY Rule 15(B)(ii)). See also Ruth Mackenzie and Philippe Sands, "International Courts and Tribunals and the Independence of the Judge", *Harvard International Law Journal*, vol. 44:1 (2003), 271, 274–276 (reviewing some of the challenges to international tribunals' decisions based on accusations of bias of a decision-maker).

The precise content of the international norm of judge independence and impartiality is difficult to pinpoint, possibly because perceptions of impartiality are culturally specific.[26] Nevertheless, certain standards have been agreed upon internationally as being applicable to national judiciaries. Among these standards, the United Nations' Basic Principles on the Independence of the Judiciary are the first to note, given their source.[27] These standards set out a series of principles that include the recognition of a state's "duty ... to respect and observe the independence of the judiciary".[28] The document backs up this claim by its reference to the Universal Declaration of Human Rights' protection of the right to a fair trial and to the UN Charter's call for states to establish "conditions under which justice can be maintained."[29] This underscores the generality of the principle's applicability in the international legal system. Independence and impartiality are norms for any tribunal, not only for those that protect individual rights.

The majority of the Bangalore principles – as indicated by the title of the document – go toward furthering the institutional independence of courts.[30] This is also applicable to impartiality, which is mentioned but defined to resemble independence:

> The judiciary shall decide matters before them impartially, on the basis of facts and in accordance with the law, without any restrictions, improper influences, inducements, pressures, threats or interferences, direct or indirect, from any quarter or for any reason.[31]

The UN guidelines are particularly notable because they apply explicitly to "lay judges" as well as professionals.[32] Thus, these guidelines would presumably be applicable to international tribunals, as well as domestic courts.

The Bangalore Principles of Judicial Conduct (BPJC), which was drafted by a number of national chief justices in the early 2000s, serves as the most detailed guide for international judges' impartiality. The

[26] *Ibid.*, 275.

[27] Adopted by the Seventh United Nations Congress on the Prevention of Crime and the Treatment of Offenders held at Milan from 26 August to 6 September 1985, and endorsed by General Assembly resolutions 40/32 of 29 November 1985, and 40/146 of 13 December 1985.

[28] UN Basic Principles, para. 1.

[29] *Ibid.*, Preamble, paras. 1–2.

[30] The principles were drafted within the UN's anti-corruption agenda. UN Office of Drugs and Crime, Commentary on the Bangalore Principles of Judicial Conduct 9 (September 2007).

[31] UN Basic Principles, para. 2.

[32] *Ibid.*, Preamble, para. 10.

Bangalore Principles list "values" and "principles", with a further explanation of their "application". Of the six values listed, several relate to impartiality, although only one is labelled as such. Under "Value 2: Impartiality", the BPJC defines "impartiality" as the absence of "favour, bias or prejudice" and asserts that impartiality should extend beyond the decision to the "process by which the decision is made".[33] BPJC values that further support judges' duties of impartiality include "integrity",[34] "propriety" in professional and private life (which includes avoiding behaviours that could appear to foster favouritism but allows for public appearances, teaching and writing about the law),[35] and "equality" (where the applications mention the need for judges to "understand diversity in society" and prohibit the expression of prejudice against persons on the basis of such differences).[36]

The value of the BPJC to international tribunals remains unclear. Because international judges face a greater challenge in establishing and maintaining the legitimacy of their courts than their brethren in national courts, further work to develop principles specifically suited to the global context will be needed.

Judicial independence and impartiality in investment arbitration

The question of "judicial" independence and impartiality has recently been the attention of fervent activity in the arbitration context. The particularities of international arbitration make the questions that surround arbitrator ethics especially challenging – the multiple sets of rules to which an individual arbitrator may be subject on account of the internationality of the arbitral proceedings, the fact that arbitrators are bound by legal ethics rules in their home jurisdiction but by potentially conflicting rules as arbitrators in the jurisdiction of arbitration, and the basic disagreement over whether the ethical rules of arbitrators should be the same as those that apply to judges.[37] These complications led the International Bar Association (IBA) to identify arbitrator ethics as a topic of study, and in 1987, the IBA Rules of Ethics for International Arbitrators appeared with the hope of providing assistance in ensuring

[33] Personal knowledge of disputed evidentiary facts and personal antipathies towards a party are indications of partiality, and any judge having either should recuse herself from sitting as a decision-maker in such case.

[34] BJPC, Value 3. [35] *Ibid.*, Value 4. [36] *Ibid.*, Value 5.

[37] See discussion in Krista Nadakavukaren Schefer, *International Investment Law: Text, Materials and Cases* (Cheltenham: Edward Elgar Publishing, 2013), 474–475.

that arbitrators fulfil the desired qualities of being "impartial, independent, competent, diligent and discreet".[38] Setting out the "fundamental rule" that "Arbitrators . . . shall be and remain free from bias,"[39] the Rules of Ethics devote substantial attention to the description of impartiality and independence (as "criteria of bias"[40]) and the role of disclosure of information "that may give rise to justifiable doubts"[41] about an arbitrator's suitability for a particular case.[42]

In May 2004, the IBA issued a further explanation of its views on independence and impartiality with the release of its Guidelines on Conflicts of Interest in International Arbitration.[43] The guidelines are designed to provide practical assistance to arbitrators who are unsure of their obligations of independence and impartiality in a particular situation. Part I contains "general standards" and explanations of these standards. Part II, on "Practical Application of the General Standards", categorises common situations in which the international arbitrator may find him-/herself according to the degree of infringement of the non-bias principle. The non-waivable red list, waivable red list, orange list and green list are not intended to be complete, but rather to lend tangible assistance to arbitrators when making decisions about whether or not to accept a mandate. Significantly, the guidelines encourage arbitrators to err on the side of caution when faced with a situation that is ambiguous: "An arbitrator shall decline to accept an appointment, or, if the arbitration has already been commenced, refuse to continue to act as an arbitrator if he or she has any doubts as to his or her ability to be impartial or independent."[44]

[38] IBA, Rules of Ethics for International Arbitrators, Introductory Note. [39] *Ibid.*, 1.
[40] *Ibid.*, 3.1. [41] *Ibid.*, 4.1.
[42] One may note that the IBA does not discuss arbitrator "neutrality" – a term referring to the combination of independence and impartiality. Used mainly in domestic commercial arbitration contexts, the relevance of arbitrator neutrality is that some processes permit parties to appoint non-neutral members to a tribunal. As the American Bar Association (ABA) points out, however, even where neutrality is not a requirement for the party-appointed arbitrators, there is the expectation that their initial bias will not prevent them from being able to uphold the "fairness and integrity of the process". American Bar Association, The Code of Ethics for Arbitrators in Commercial Disputes Effective 1 March 2004, "Note on Neutrality". To that end, any non-neutral arbitrator must fully disclose her relationships before the arbitration begins (*Ibid.*) The ABA itself presumes that any international arbitration must be composed solely of neutral arbitrators (*Ibid.*).
[43] IBA, IBA Guidelines on Conflicts of Interest in International Arbitration, approved by the Council of the IBA on 22 May 2004.
[44] *Ibid.*, (2)(b). See also *ibid.* Explanation to General Standard 2 ("(a) . . . the Working Group believes that the broad standard of 'any doubts as to an ability to be impartial and independent' should lead to the arbitrator declining the appointment").

The IBA's codification of ethical standards for international arbitrators is explicitly non-binding.[45] Accordingly, the guidelines are widely discussed and not infrequently applied, but some tribunals continue to ignore the proposed framework for determining ethical behaviour. The true added value of the guidelines, then, is not the document itself. Rather, it is that the process of composing the rules spurred wider attention to the question of what the precise expectations of parties and societies are regarding the necessary level of operational independence and impartiality of arbitrators for maintaining the perceived legitimacy of the international arbitration system. This question has since been addressed by multiple actors: professional organisations, scholars and the arbitration fora themselves.

More enlightening, however, is the search for standards revealed in the case law of the tribunals themselves – in the decisions taken to parties' challenges of arbitrators as dependent or partial. The following will capsulise the various procedures that led to the concretisation of the concept of what arbitrator independence and impartiality involve and highlight the common findings.

Challenge procedure

Challenges to arbitrators' independence may arise at a number of points during the evolution of a dispute. The precise point will depend on the applicable law that is set out in the parties' agreement but will usually include the time of the tribunal's establishment, after a decision on the merits, and at the enforcement stage.

In a typical arbitration proceeding, a party that is suspicious of an arbitrator's independence or impartiality must challenge the arbitrator at the time the tribunal is being established or at the latest, at the time that the party came to know/had reason to know of the circumstances indicating bias. If no challenge is brought at this time, the right to challenge will be presumed to be waived. If the challenge is rejected, recourse to that decision can be brought up after the final award is rendered.

If a challenge is denied in a case under the auspices of the International Centre for the Settlement of Investment Disputes (ICSID), the arbitrator remains on the tribunal, but the dissatisfied party has the possibility to raise a challenge to the final award on that basis. Article 52 of the ICSID Convention provides for annulment proceedings on a number of

[45] *Ibid.*, Introduction, para. 6, 5.

grounds, including the grounds that the tribunal was not "properly constituted" and that there was "corruption on the part of a member".[46]

In non-ICSID arbitration, if the challenge is dismissed, the dissatisfied party can request the local court to set aside the tribunal's decision on the basis of the biased tribunal. Depending on the applicable law, the standard of independence can vary. Should the set aside attempt also fail, the party can still attempt to block the enforcement of the award. Enforcement may fall under the New York Convention rules or under the rules of the jurisdiction in which the enforcement proceedings are brought. Under the former's Article 5, an award may be refused enforcement if "(d) The composition of the arbitral authority or the arbitral procedure was not in accordance with the agreement of the parties, or, failing such agreement, was not in accordance with the law of the country where the arbitration took place"[47] or if the enforcement "would be contrary to public policy".[48]

The case law

ICSID

Under the rules of the ICSID Convention, Article 14 sets out the basic rule on arbitrator characteristics:

> Persons designated to serve on the Panels shall be persons of high moral character and recognized competence in the fields of law, commerce, industry or finance, who may be relied upon to exercise independent judgment.[49]

The provisions of Article 14, which is defined to include the impartiality and the independence of arbitrators,[50] are supported by Article 57 of the Convention, which allows parties to challenge arbitrators on the basis of a "manifest lack" of any of Article 14's listed qualities.[51] The ICSID

[46] *Ibid.*, Art. 52.1(a) and (c). [47] New York Convention, Art. V.1(d).

[48] *Ibid.*, Art. V.2(b). [49] ICSID Convention, Art. 14.1.

[50] Interpreting Article 14 to include impartiality upholds the equality of legal texts (as well as the general international law adherence to the standard of subjective non-bias), given that the also-authoritative Spanish version uses the term "imparcialidad". Several tribunals have confirmed the dual meaning of "independent". See Suez, infra n. 46 at para. 28; Abaclat, infra n. 46 at para. 46; ConocoPhillips, infra n. 46 at para. 54.

[51] See ICSID Convention, Art. 57 ("A party may propose to a Commission or Tribunal the disqualification of any of its members on account of any fact indicating a manifest lack of the qualities required by paragraph (1) of Article 14.").

Convention provides that such a challenge will be heard by the remaining members of the tribunal.[52]

A number of decisions on arbitrator challenges have occupied ICSID tribunals in recent years.[53] These decisions are notable in a number of ways. First, they demonstrate an understanding of the terms "independence" and "impartiality" that is very similar to the meanings that are used in general international law and domestic law[54]: "Generally speaking," states the Suez challenge tribunal, "independence relates to the lack of relations with a party that might influence an arbitrator's decision. Impartiality, on the other hand, concerns the absence of a bias or predisposition toward one of the parties."[55]

52 *Ibid.*, Article 58.

53 E.g., *Universal Compression International Holdings* v. *The Bolivarian Republic of Venezuela*, ICSID Case No. ARB/10/9, Decision on the Proposal to Disqualify Prof. Brigitte Stern and Prof. Guido Santiago Tawil, Arbitrators, 20 May 2011; *Suez and InterAguas Servicios Integrales del Agua S.A.* v. *The Argentine Republic*, ICSID Case No. ARB/03/17 and *Suez and Vivendi Universal S.A.* v. *The Argentine Republic*, ICSID Case No. ARB/03/19, Decision on the Proposal for the Disqualification of a Member of the Arbitral Tribunal, 22 October 2007; *Tidewater Inc. et al.* v. *The Bolivarian Republic of Venezuela*, ICSID Case No. ARB/10/5, Decision on Claimants' Proposal to Disqualify Prof. Brigitte Stern, Arbitrator, 23 December 2010; *Urbaser* v. *The Argentine Republic*, Decision on Claimants' Proposal to Disqualify Professor Campbell McLachlan, Arbitrator, ICSID Case No. ARB/07/26; *ConocoPhillips Co. et al.* v. *The Bolivarian Republic of Venezuela*, ICSID Case No. ARB/07/30, Decision on the Proposal to Disqualify L. Yves Fortier, Q.C., Arbitrator (27 February 2012); *SGS Société Générale de Surveillance* v. *Pakistan*, Decision on Claimant's Proposal to Disqualify Arbitrator (19 December 2002), 8 ICSID Reports 398; *Saint Gobain Performance Plastics* v. *The Bolivarian Republic of Venezuela*, ICSID Case No. ARB/12/13. Decision on Claimant's Proposal to Disqualify Mr. Gabriel Bottini from the Tribunal under Article 57 of the ICSID Convention (27 February 2013); *Abaclat* v. *Argentina*, ICSID Case No. ARB/07/5, Recommendation Pursuant to the Request by ICSID dated 18 November 2011, on the Respondent's Proposal for the Disqualification of Professor Pierre Tercier and Professor Albert Jan van den Berg dated 15 September 2011 (19 December 2011); *Alpha Projektholding GmbH* v. *Ukraine* (ICSID Case No. ARB/07/16), Decision on Respondent's Proposal to Disqualify Arbitrator Dr. Yoram Turbowicz (19 March 2010); *PIP Sàrl* v. *The Gabonese Republic*, ICSID Case No. ARB/08/17, Decision on the Proposal to Disqualify an Arbitrator (12 November 2009); *EDF et al.* v. *Argentine Republic*, ICSID Case No. ARB/03/23, Challenge Decision Regarding Professor Gabrielle Kaufmann-Kohler (25 June 2008); *Perenco* v. *Ecuador*, PCA Case No. IR-2009/1, In the Matter of a Challenge to be Decided by the Secretary General of the Permanent Court of Arbitration Pursuant to an Agreement Concluded on 2 October 2008, in ICSID Case No. ARB/08/6 (8 December 2009).

54 The idea, as suggested in the literature, that arbitrators should be held to standards different from judges due to their nature of having been selected by the parties does not appear.

55 Suez para. 29.

Moreover, the reason for the requirement of non-bias is seen by arbitral tribunals exactly as it is for judges. While refusing to apply standards outside those of the ICSID Convention, one tribunal nevertheless declared that to fulfil Article 14.1, "[w]hat is required . . . is the ability to consider and evaluate the merits of each case without relying on factors having no relation to such merits."[56] The arbitrator's effect on the rights and obligations of the parties being the same as in a "regular" court leads to the same characteristics being necessary to ensure legitimacy.

A second characteristic of ICSID arbitration is the lax application of the rule on the appearance of conflicting interest.[57] While tribunals do refer to the need to appear independent and impartial to a reasonable observer, they seem to find it difficult to imagine any scenario in which such an appearance could exist. An arbitrator acting as opposing counsel to the challenger in another case, an arbitrator who had written about the legal questions facing him, and an arbitrator who held a position on a board of a company that held shares of the complainant company – none of these situations were found to fail the test of independence and impartiality. One reason for this relaxed view of appearance of bias is that the ICSID rule requires violations of independence and impartiality to be "manifest" before they can be successfully challenged. Under this standard, the challenged arbitrator must be obviously[58] biased (or at least be at a "real risk" of being so), and the challenging party must provide objective evidence to show this bias.[59]

Related to this issue is the role played by disclosure in the challenge determination. While the IBA Guidelines suggest the disclosure of even potentially problematic relationships and provide for possible disqualification for mere failures of disclosure, the ICSID challenge tribunals want evidence of "probable" conflicts of interest before they will accept a challenge. The respondent Venezuela's application for disqualification of the claimant's arbitrator in the ConocoPhillips case is typical. In that challenge, the claimant argued that the fact that the arbitrator (who had to leave the law firm of which he had been a long-time member upon

[56] *Urbaser* v. *The Argentine Republic*, Decision on Claimants' Proposal to Disqualify Professor Campbell McLachlan, Arbitrator, ICSID Case No. ARB/07/26 at para. 40 (12 August 2010).

[57] The information here is based on publicly available documents. There are reportedly a number of instances in which the ICSID has encouraged a challenged arbitrator to resign before a decision is taken.

[58] E.g., Alpha Projektholding para. 37; Suez, para. 34.

[59] E.g., Universal Compression para. 71; Abaclat, para. 53.

information coming out that the firm had merged with another firm that had represented several clients opposing Venezuela in past arbitrations) had not disclosed his relationship with that firm should disqualify him from being on the tribunal. The tribunal members deciding the issue referred to the IBA Guidelines[60] but emphasised that they did not bind ICSID tribunals.[61] They then continued to emphasise that the "manifest" standard places a "relatively heavy burden" on the challenger in terms of evidence and found that this burden was not fulfilled.[62]

The Suez case also took the objective appearances test lightly. There, an arbitrator's role as a director of a bank that held shares in the claimant formed the basis for a challenge of her independence and impartiality. The tribunal in this case set out four criteria for evaluating independence and impartiality for the purposes of ICSID: proximity, intensity, dependence and materiality.[63] Emphasising the indirectness of the relationship, the fact of her actual financial independence from the bank, and the arbitrator's own statement of unawareness about the challenged relationships, the other tribunal members refused to sanction her dismissal.[64]

Non-ICSID fora

Decisions made by the International Chamber of Commerce (ICC), the London Court of International Arbitration (LCIA) and the Permanent Court of Arbitration (PCA), among others, are also contributing to the discussion of arbitrator bias. Interestingly, these tribunals often have more sophisticated discussions of ethics than do the ICSID tribunals.

The LCIA offers several good examples of how an otherwise relatively intransparent arbitration forum has proven itself to be more committed to strictly applying the rules of appearance of independence and impartiality to arbitrators than does its Washington-based counterpart.[65] Applying LCIA's own rules or UNCITRAL rules and looking to the British Arbitration Act provisions and English common law, the London Court may also refer to the European Convention on Human Rights and the IBA Guidelines when interpreting the law and applying the facts of the case in front of it. Thus, the LCIA has a wide variety of

[60] ConocoPhillips, paras. 52, 58–60. [61] *Ibid.*, para. 59. [62] *Ibid.*, para. 68.
[63] Suez, second challenge, para. 35. [64] *Ibid.*, para. 40.
[65] E.g., LCIA Court Decision on Challenge to Arbitrator, LCIA Reference No. 81160, Decision rendered 28 August 2009, paras. 3.6–3.7 (noting that the IBA Guidelines are not legally binding but that they "might be seen to reflect actual practice in significant parts of the international arbitration community" and so are to be heeded).

sources available to inform its decision-making in the hazy area of arbitrator independence.

Often, the cumulative consideration of these sources leads the court to apply the rule of independence and impartiality strictly. This is particularly striking in its approach to the objective test of bias – in London, appearances seem to count more than they do in Washington. Thus, in one case in which the challenged arbitrator's refusals to make disclosures about new material relationships with one of the parties, the court noted that such failure itself could lead "a fair-minded and informed observer ... [to] reasonably have concluded that an arbitrator ... would run a real risk of exhibiting bias" and disqualifying him on that ground.[66] Another decision investigated the "real possibility of bias" standard's evolution, stressing that the new rule did indeed differ from the old one by conforming to the convention's emphasis on appearances of impartiality, as well as actual bias. Using that standard, it found that the challenged arbitrator's ex parte meetings with one party's counsel amounted to a violation and upheld the challenge, even though such meetings could possibly have been explained away.[67] It was what an informed third party might think that gave the court pause, not the arbitrator's actual state of mind.

The possible reasons for ICSID–non-ICSID differences in independence and impartiality are numerous. One such reason is the applicability of different rules to challenges: whereas ICSID requires a "manifest lack" of qualities of independence and impartiality, the LCIA, for example, speaks of "justifiable doubts" as to the arbitrator's neutrality. Moreover, tribunals' decisions may also be indirectly influenced by the fact that dissatisfied parties under non-ICSID rules have more possibilities to challenge awards than do ICSID parties. To avoid being overturned, such tribunals may be more cautious. Finally, the fact that challenges in the London system are heard by the court rather than by colleagues could play a role. In the small world of international arbitrators, disqualifying a fellow arbitrator based on "mere appearances" may not be well regarded.

This is not to say that the LCIA upholds challenges in most, or even many, cases. Yet, even when challenged members of a tribunal are allowed to continue, the contours of independence and impartiality are often investigated and explained in a way that fosters the development of

[66] LCIA Reference No. 81160, para. 4.19.

[67] LCIA Reference No. UN3490, Decision rendered 21 October 2005, and 27 December 2005, paras. 4.1–4.7, 6.8.

the law.[68] The wide number of sources – court decisions, as well as statements of other arbitration tribunals, IBA Guidelines and scholarly works – brings a depth to the discussion that ICSID tribunals often miss. The openness with which such conversations take place, which is extraordinary for a system that is often criticised as lacking transparency, is very helpful in bolstering the legitimacy of the process.

This publicly discursive approach of the arbitration system to judicial independence and impartiality stands in stark contrast to the approach of the dispute settlement system of international trade. We turn finally to this topic.

Judicial independence and impartiality in WTO dispute settlement

The WTO's dispute settlement system is the most "judicial" of all international organisations' such systems. With trial and appeals processes available, WTO parties' right to challenge their trade partner's actions is much the same as in a national court system. Called "panels", the initial instance considers factual evidence and legal arguments in a series of written and oral arguments. The panel's findings are written into a "report", which is submitted for quasi-automatic approval by the WTO members and becomes binding unless appealed.

In the nearly two decades since it went into effect, an enormous amount of activity has occurred in and around the dispute settlement organs of the WTO. With 467 cases filed since 1995, the WTO's docket is busy. In addition, scholarship surrounding the WTO's "court-like" dispute settlement system has been prolific. Articles, books, workshops and conferences have addressed nearly every aspect of the Understanding on the Rules and Procedures Governing the Settlement of Disputes (DSU) and its cases. The high level of transparency of the system fosters this attention. Disputes are publicised, decisions are published and hearings are sometimes live-streamed.

However, one issue to which very little attention has been paid is that discussed here. The independence and impartiality of the WTO decision-maker has received nearly no attention. There is, it is true, work addressing the institutional independence of WTO panels, which is an interesting topic of study, given the formal unity of legislative, executive and judicial

[68] See, e.g., (engaging in a discussion of whether an arbitrator's brusque – potentially rude – treatment of one counsel amounted to a violation of the appearance of impartiality).

authority in the hands of the members.[69] However, the behaviour and attitudes of the panellists themselves are all but missing from the radar of public awareness.[70]

Why? It is not clear, but one response that can be immediately rejected is that independence and impartiality are not relevant for WTO proceedings. Panels' exclusive jurisdiction over WTO members' trade disputes is set out in the DSU. Thus, members cannot avoid panels if they want third-party resolution of their disagreements. This lack of choice alone implicates a (higher) need for the legitimacy of the only forum available, which in turn rests on that forum's decision-makers' independence and impartiality.

Neither can one say that the members of the WTO have waived the right to dispute settlement by an unbiased tribunal. First, the WTO is incontrovertibly a part of the general international law system. As a consequence, the rules that govern the members and the organisation are those of the general international legal system, including the general principles of judicial independence and impartiality. Moreover, the members themselves demonstrated their concern with judicial bias by completing a set of rules on independence and impartiality soon after the Dispute Settlement Body (DSB) was created.[71] The Rules of Conduct, which were accepted by consensus, seek to increase "confidence in the new dispute settlement mechanism" with their "governing principle":

> Each [panellist] shall be independent and impartial, shall avoid direct or indirect conflicts of interest . . . so that through the observation of such standards of conduct the integrity and impartiality of that mechanism are preserved.[72]

The rules continue with a requirement for self-disclosure. This requirement binds each panellist to make known any information that could impinge – or could objectively be seen as impinging upon – his or her

[69] E.g., Steve Charnovitz, "Judicial Independence in the World Trade Organization", in Laurence Boisson De Chazournes, Cesare Romano, and Ruth Mackenzie (eds.), *International Organizations and Dispute Settlement: Trends and Prospects* (Ardsley, NY: Transnational Publishers, 2002), 219–240.

[70] As two exceptions, see Gabrielle Marceau, "Rules on Ethics for the New World Trade Organization Dispute Settlement Mechanism", *J. World Trade*, vol. 32:3 (1998), 57; Susan Esserman and Robert Howse, "Trade Disputes Require Fairer Arbitration", *The World Trade Rev.*, vol. 23 (2002), accessed 8 October 2013, available at www.worldtradereview.com.

[71] Rules of conduct for the understanding on rules and procedures governing the settlement of disputes, WT/DSB/RC/1 (11 December 1996).

[72] *Ibid.*, II.1.

independence or impartiality,[73] sign a statement of independence and impartiality before appointment,[74] and agree to disclose any relevant information that may emerge afterwards.[75] The "illustrative list of information to be disclosed" relates primarily to elements of independence, although "considered statements of personal opinion" are included. Like the IBA Conflict of Interest guidelines, the WTO rules emphasise the objective nature of the standard; if a reasonable person might consider a relationship to infringe on the panellist's impartiality, the relationship should be disclosed.

Another explanation for the lack of independence and impartiality of panellists could rest with the fact that disputes about conflicts of interests never arise within the system. This may actually be the most likely explanation, and it could occur due to one of three situations: (1) the standards are so clear that no panellist candidate could have a doubt as to whether (s)he is independent and impartial with respect to the case to be decided; (2) the standards of independence and impartiality are so low that no panellist candidate would ever fall below them; or (3) something else prevents disputes about independence and impartiality from rising to the level of public knowledge and debate. Let me briefly touch on the likelihood of each of these possibilities.

The first possibility is surely not the real reason. The Rules of Conduct do not define "independence" or "impartiality". There is a list of illustrative situations in which dependence or partiality can be assumed, but the list is neither exclusive nor very exhaustive. Given that the panellist candidates stem from the nearly universal WTO membership and are drawn from the diplomatic corps as well as from legal offices, it is highly improbable that each panellist will have the same view of what precisely will be considered a problematic material relationship or personal belief coming into a dispute proceeding. As one group of authors writes about the international legal system in general, this "arena presents new and unfamiliar types of ethics challenges for judges; it can be difficult even to define ethics problems, much less to resolve them".[76] That this scenario is also so in the WTO is supported by the description of the negotiations of the Rules of Conduct as "very sensitive and difficult".[77] Without more guidance on precisely what "independence" means (beyond having a nationality other than that of either party) and an assurance that the panellists all have a clear view of what standard of "reasonable person"

[73] *Ibid.*, IV.2. [74] *Ibid.*, IV.4(a). [75] *Ibid.*, IV.5.
[76] Terris et al., *International Judge*, 192. [77] Marceau, "Rules on Ethics", 57.

applies (is it one of a "fair-minded and informed" person or one who is a reasonable trade-law person?), there is little chance that panellists and parties have the same conception of what judicial independence and impartiality mean in the WTO context.

The second possibility is more plausible, although not likely to be the full story. While perhaps not so low as to prevent any panellist from falling below it, the text of the WTO standard for independence and impartiality is less stringent than that applying to arbitration (at least non-ICSID arbitration). For example, under the rules, the panellist is given substantial freedom to maintain silence over any "insignificant" matters.[78] Where the IBA Guidelines caution arbitrators to err on the side of disclosure of potentially problematic relationships, the wording of the WTO provision emphasises the "need to respect the personal privacy" of would-be panellists, as well as the desire to avoid the administrative burdens of qualifying to hear a case.[79] Given the tradition of text-based interpretation in the dispute settlement mechanism, such wording will probably lead to a limited view on panellist ethics. Nor do the rules condemn appearances of bias outside of the disclosure context and in the general principles, where panellists are "expected to" refrain from any behaviour that "could give rise to justifiable doubts" about conflicts of interest.[80]

Moreover, the rules do not explicitly tackle the repercussions of a disclosure or an alleged bias. Presumably, the DSB will not invite a candidate to be a panellist if his or her disclosure indicates a problematic relationship or belief. Yet, there is no clear discussion of this topic in the rules, and even the authority to decide such questions remains open. In one case, for example, a third party requested a ruling on a question regarding the duration of a party's waiver of the rule against permitting nationals to be panellists – an issue of the "propriety of composition" of a panel (i.e., of judicial independence). Yet, here the panel refused to rule, noting a lack of competence on the one hand to make a ruling on a third party request and on the other hand to rule on a matter "which concerns the application by the WTO Director-General of the DSU provisions regarding panel composition".[81] The latter comment was appealed, but the Appellate Body gave no response to clarify the extent of a panel's

[78] WTO Rules, IV.3. [79] *Ibid.*

[80] Marceau, "Rules on Ethics", 76; see generally *Ibid.*, 73–77.

[81] *United States – Subsidies on Upland Cotton*, Recourse to Art. 21.5 of the DSU by Brazil, WT/DS56/RW (18 December 2007), para. 8.28. In the footnote 83, to this ruling, the panel went on to reject the argument that panels are authorised to make rulings on issues

competence to determine questions relating to its own members' compliance with ethical rules.[82]

Significant, too, is the uncertainty regarding the process that is available to a party that discovers evidence of ethical misbehaviour following the close of a dispute. The rules do not address how to challenge panellists after a panel report has been affirmed by the DSB. The decision to adopt the report, being an act of the members, cannot itself be brought to a panel. Could the ICJ, perhaps, be called upon? It is unclear to this author whether any course of relief is open within the system that could address this situation.

A final possibility would be that WTO panellists' adherence to the Rules of Conduct is so exemplary that disputes over their adherence to the standards never arise. Alas, in this world of fallible humans, this is hardly probable. With the exception of the European Community's question related to a panellist's independence, which was mentioned above, the problem of panellist bias has not been brought up in the decisions of the DSB.[83] Moreover, the lack of information about such problems is itself programmed into the rules. Paragraph 20 states:

> Except to the extent strictly necessary to carry out this decision, all information concerning possible or actual material violations of these Rules shall be kept confidential.

The temporal framework of this provision is open-ended. Does it mean that there is to be confidentiality during the challenge proceedings only? Or also afterwards?

Is this the reason that so little information is publicly available? Or is the reason that the interest in the topic of judicial independence has simply not yet reached WTO scholars? Or that judicial independence scholars have not yet reached the WTO?

Whatever the reason for the stillness surrounding panellist ethics, this topic must be weighed carefully against the harm done to the acceptance of the organisation's dispute settlement system as a legitimate adjudicator of conflicts. If the WTO wants to enjoy a high regard for its ability to

important "for the smooth and equitable operation of the WTO dispute settlement system".

82 See United States – Subsidies on Upland Cotton, Recourse to Art. 21.5 of the DSU by Brazil, WT/DS267/AB/RW (2 June 2008), paras. 171–173.

83 In Thailand – *H-Beams*, Thailand raised a complaint about an alleged breach of confidentiality by another party, Appellate Body Report, *Thailand – Anti-Dumping Duties on Angles, Shapes and Sections of Iron or Non-Alloy Steel and H-Beams from Poland*, WT/DS122/AB/R (adopted 12 March 2001), paras. 62–78.

fairly consider questions of state's rights and responsibilities, those applying the law to the facts must be free from reproach and must be seen to be so by the international community. To achieve this, information is needed on how challenges to individuals' independence and impartiality are managed and resolved by the system itself.

Conclusion

As international law's adjudicatory mechanisms mature, the visibility of their legitimacy must increase. A significant aspect of judicial legitimacy rests with the clear and apparent independence and impartiality of judges. To maintain judicial authority, the public must see that justice is done, and justice will not be seen to be done where the decision-maker is suspected of favouritism.[84]

International dispute resolution fora differ in the vigour with which they enforce the various aspects of judicial ethics. While institutional independence receives substantial attention, the appearance of decision-makers' bias is not always as central in practice as it is to the theory of dispute settlement legitimacy. This is particularly so in those international economic institutions with the greatest direct impact on states' policymaking space: the ICSID and the WTO.

This chapter's suggestion to heighten the scrutiny of arbitrators and panellists in IEL dispute settlement aims to promote these systems' legitimacy in the eyes of their international publics. Unfortunately, a simple way of motivating the relevant actors to do this is not yet clear. Ultimately, the attention to ethics can only come from a deep commitment to changing the vision of international dispute settlement from one of simply resolving differences to one of supporting the legitimacy of a wider project: that of creating an international system in which everyone can believe that the pursuit of justice is the highest aim.

[84] As ICJ Judge Burgenthal wrote, "Judicial ethics are ... matters of perception ... that courts must continuously keep in mind to preserve their legitimacy ... [T]he appearance of bias ... [is] what judicial ethics are all about." Legal Consequences of the Construction of a Wall in the Occupied Palestinian Territory, Order of 30 January 2004, I.C.J. Reports 2004, p. 3, Dissenting opinion of Judge Buergenthal, p. 10.

9

Judicial authority and styles of reasoning: self-presentation between legalism and deliberation

INGO VENZKE*

I Introduction

Judicial reasoning is puzzling. International judges are often faced with cases where the law runs out or at least becomes murky. Such situations present themselves as problems because it is the image of correctly applying the given law that nurtures judges' social legitimacy. The notion of legalism suggests that judges do their utmost to present their activity as impeccable rule-following, especially when they face or anticipate critique. Legalism refers to a self-perpetuating force of narrow formalism. At the same time, it might be suggested that judges should use reasons that exceed the more narrow confines of strict formalism, particularly in those situations where the law does not readily give an answer. Such a view is supported from the perspective of discourse theory and its normative reconstruction of the separation of powers. Judicial reasoning should open up to modes of deliberation. Both claims (i.e., that legalism explains a narrow closure of the legal discourse on the one hand and that normative demands require judges to open up the legal discourse on the other hand) cannot coexist, at least not for a long period of time. In the long run, neither claim is plausible if the other holds some sway.[1]

The present contribution argues that legalism offers an appealing but ultimately inaccurate view of what drives (international) judges.

* I wish to thank Kista Nadakavukaren Shefer, the editors, and an anonymous reviewer for their helpful suggestions and comments.

1 This issue becomes especially clear in Jürgen Habermas's critique of Max Weber and his argument in favour of a conception of legitimacy, which combines descriptive and normative elements. Jürgen Habermas, 'Legitimation Problems in the Modern State' in *Communication and the Evolution of Society* (Boston, MA: Beacon Press, 1979) 178, 205.

Legalism's core propositions do not hold across different institutions and for different individual judges. It is not the case that the safe fallback position of judges is necessarily a narrow formalism. The present contribution argues that a more powerful and more nuanced answer can be developed with a closer view of judges' audiences.[2] More specifically, such a competing answer could build on the concept of self-presentation to better understand why judges reason the way that they do. Theories of self-presentation refine our understanding of what drives judges by drawing attention to social anxiety. Such anxiety arises 'when individuals are motivated to convey a particular impression – usually one that will facilitate interpersonal acceptance (or perhaps more accurately, to avoid interpersonal rejection) but doubt their ability to do so'.[3] Self-presentation manages impressions. In short, the present contribution suggests an understanding of styles of reasoning as a strategy of impression management.

The target of this discussion is not only legalism as a common explanation of judicial reasoning. This contribution also investigates the implications of viewing international judicial behaviour through the lens of judges' audiences for normative arguments. In that regard, this work focuses on the argument from a discourse-theoretical reconstruction of the separation of powers. At its core, such a normative reconstruction demands that juridical discourses be broadened 'to the extent that legal programs are in need of further specification by the courts'.[4] This contribution continues to argue that the additional legitimatory burden that arises with such a broadening of judicial discourses 'could be partly satisfied by additional obligations before an enlarged critical forum specific to the judiciary'.[5] Understanding judicial reasoning as a strategy of impression management credits the role of critical fora by suggesting that judges indeed anticipate critique. However, this approach ultimately casts doubt on the critical and potentially legitimating role that such a forum might play. Reasons are not expressed to convince or to be backed up in argument but to please an audience whose favour judges seek.

[2] This move is inspired by and draws on Lawrence Baum, *Judges and Their Audiences: A Perspective on Judicial Behavior* (Princeton University Press, 2006).

[3] Lahnna I. Catalino, R. Michael Furr, and Freida A. Bellis, 'A Multilevel Analysis of the Self-presentation Theory of Social Anxiety: Contextualized, Dispositional, and Interactive Perspectives', *Journal of Research in Personality*, vol. 46 (2012) 361, 361.

[4] Jürgen Habermas, *Between Facts and Norms: Contributions to a Discourse Theory of Law and Democracy* (MIT Press, 1996) 439–440; see also, 193.

[5] *Ibid.*, 439–440; see also *ibid.*, 193.

With this line of argument, the contribution wishes to lay further groundwork for an emerging strand of scholarship that studies the styles of reasoning of specific international courts and tribunals across different judicial institutions.[6] In contrast to some of this work – and generally, in contrast to most strands of thought about (international) judicial behaviour – I suggest that the relevant factors that come into consideration should not be limited to the legal and structural constraints of international courts and tribunals. The present contribution argues that a more social-psychological perspective must be added. This approach thrives above all on one simple proposition: 'judges, like other people, get satisfaction from perceiving that other people view them positively'.[7] Judges care about the way they are seen in the eyes of their audiences. This consideration adds to the mix of explanatory factors for judicial reasoning that cannot be reduced to the pursuit of judges' policy objectives or to the working of discursive constraints.

The argument proceeds as follows: Against the background of a brief overview of established views on judicial behaviour, I will present the dissonant perspectives on judicial reasoning as they flow from sociological accounts of legalism on the one hand and from normative accounts of deliberation on the other hand (Section III). I then introduce judges' audiences and self-presentation theory as a further angle from which to understand judicial reasoning. There are certainly a host of other factors that bear on the way in which judges act and argue. The aim here is to complement those accounts and to correct or refine the views of legalism and deliberation. The main thesis is that self-presentation theory makes a useful and at times plainly necessary addition to the framework for studying judicial reasoning (Section IV). The concluding outlook sets out a tentative programme for future research on judicial authority and

[6] For comparative studies, see Joost Pauwelyn and Manfred Elsig, 'The Politics of Treaty Interpretation: Variations and Explanations Across International Tribunals' in Jeffrey L Dunoff and Mark A Pollack (eds.), *Interdisciplinary Perspectives on International Law and International Relations: The State of the Art* (Cambridge University Press, 2013) 450–452; Armin von Bogdandy and Ingo Venzke, 'On the Functions of International Courts: An Appraisal in Light of Their Burgeoning Public Authority', *Leiden Journal of International of International Law*, vol. 26 (2013) 49–72; Benedict Kingsbury, 'International Courts: Uneven Judicialization in Global Order' in James Crawford and Martti Koskenniemi (eds.), *Cambridge Companion to International Law* (Cambridge University Press, 2012) 202–228. For an example of an audience-centred analysis of a specific decision, see André Nollkaemper, 'The Court and Its Multiple Constituencies: The Perspectives on the Kosovo Advisory Opinion', *ACIL Research Paper 2014*, 18, www.acil.uva.nl.

[7] Baum, *Judges*, 4.

styles of reasoning that is informed by core social-psychological considerations (Section V). However, first, the whole argument gains traction from a brief example of establishing judicial authority in international economic law (Section II).

II Judicial authority and styles of reasoning: an example

In a controversial and pivotal decision, a recent investment arbitral tribunal concluded that it had jurisdiction to hear the collective claim of Italian holders of Argentine bonds against the Argentine Republic.[8] The many interesting legal issues that the award touched upon included the interpretation of a so-called cooling-off period. The applicable investment treaty provided that a dispute shall only be subject to international arbitration if it continues to exist eighteen months after the commencement of domestic proceedings.[9] All three arbitrators are among the most accomplished and experienced in their field. Two of those arbitrators, Albert Jan van den Berg and Pierre Tercier, have primarily commercial law backgrounds. Among many other past and present functions, the former arbitrator is the president of the International Council for Commercial Arbitration (ICCA) and the latter arbitrator was the president of the International Chamber of Commerce (ICC). Those arbitrators are law professors at Rotterdam and Fribourg, respectively.[10] In the example at hand, van den Berg and Tercier wrote the majority opinion of the final award. They argued, among other things, that 'it would be unfair to deprive the investor of its right to resort to arbitration based on the mere disregard of the 18 months litigation requirement'.[11] They thus make an appeal to fairness that hardly squares with formalist legal reasoning. Put strongly, fairness overrides the cooling-off provision of the treaty. It is more than a platitude to say that fairness, like justice, lies in the eye of the beholder. Whether their appeal to fairness supports their delicate decision depends on the beliefs of relevant audiences. The overall context, including Argentina's persistent refusal to compensate foreign investors for violations of their rights during the upheaval that occurred in the wake of Argentina's economic crises of 1998, the truly dim prospects of domestic litigation, and possible empathy for

[8] ICSID, *Abaclat and others* v. *The Argentine Republic*, Decision on Jurisdiction and Admissibility, 4 August 2011 [hereinafter '*Abaclat*'].

[9] Art. 8(3) Argentine-Italian Bilateral Investment Treaty, quoted in claimants' unofficial English translation in *Abaclat*, para. 100.

[10] See www.arbitration-icca.org/members.html.

[11] *Abaclat*, para. 583.

ordinary Italian bondholders underpin a belief that declining to exercise jurisdiction would be unfair.

The dissenting arbitrator, Georges Abi-Saab, wrote an elaborate critique of the majority's reasoning in which he also took issue with the invocation of fairness. Just like the appointments and achievements of his co-arbitrators in the present case, those of Abi-Saab are impressive and manifold. Next to a steep academic career, he was a judge of the Appeals Chamber of the international criminal tribunals for the former Yugoslavia and for Rwanda, as well as Chairman of the Appellate Body of the WTO. Abi-Saab has a primarily public international law background. In his view, the majority in the exemplary case at hand 'strike[s] out a clear conventional requirement, on the basis of its purely subjective judgment'.[12] It is easy to see that Abi-Saab would have struck the balance differently.[13] But that is not his point. There should be no balancing at all in light of a treaty provision. A balance was struck 'at the appropriate legislative level, by the parties themselves', he argues. The balance is reflected in the treaty text that opens an avenue towards international arbitration but subjects that avenue to an eighteen-month domestic litigation requirement. Arguments of fairness or expediency were on the table when drafting the treaty text, and those arguments led to a certain outcome. The tribunal must not unravel the legislative agreement. For Abi-Saab, formalism has an appeal that it lacks for the majority. He rejects unmediated and outright references to the 'spirit' or the 'aim' of the law by referring to the Vienna Convention of the Law of Treaties, which provides the fundamental grammar of treaty interpretation, at least for public international lawyers.

III Judicial reasoning between legalism and deliberation

How should we make sense of such judicial reasoning? A whole host of factors with varying explanatory power suggest themselves. Overall – and especially in its dominant rationalist stream – scholarship sees judicial behaviour as a function of individual or institutional policy goals combined with contextual constraints. It looks at the limits of what courts and judges can possibly do in light of balances of power, institutional clout, pervasive ideas or discursive constraints.[14] Above all, the concern is with

[12] *Abaclat*, Dissenting Opinion, para. 30. [13] *Ibid.*, especially para. 33.

[14] Laurence R. Helfer and Anne-Marie Slaughter, 'Why States Create International Tribunals: A Response to Professors Posner and Yoo', *California Law Review*, vol. 93 (2005) 899–956. For a critical overview, see also Mark A. Pollack, 'Political Science and

judicial outcomes rather than reasoning, although this view is slowly changing.[15] The reasoning certainly matters, too. Actors in the field know that it does. For instance, they appeal in cases in which they had won in every practical way with the 'mere' incentive of challenging what might otherwise become a bad precedent. Adjudicators know just as well that their reasoning in the present matters for the future, and they use precedents in the gradual development of the law.[16]

The present contribution aspires to add to the groundwork of the increasing literature on judicial reasoning by arguing that studies must pay more regard to insights from social-psychological perspectives. This work will offer a view in this vein by drawing on self-presentation theory and by presenting judicial reasoning as a technique for impression management. There are a number of nascent arguments that meet this aspiration half-way. With a view to judicial reasoning, especially in the field of international investment law, an arbitrator's judicial ethos, which leans more on private or public law, has been added to the array of explanatory factors. Such an approach is already well suited to grasp some of the differences that exist, such as those between van den Berg and Tercier on one side and Abi-Saab on the other.[17] Such a move is inspired by similar work in the field of trade law, where a change in ethos from diplomats to lawyers was spotted previously.[18] Above all, these observations stem from lawyers who have a close understanding of the legal field. So far, the insights of those lawyers hardly feed into the studies of political science. I will resume such trends and suggestions for further research in the programmatic outlook on the study of international judges and their

International Courts' in Cesare Romano, Karen Alter, and Yuval Shany (eds.), *Oxford Handbook of International Adjudication* (OUP, 2016 *forthcoming*). [MR Madsen in same Handbook].

15 Recent contributions that pay more regard to judicial reasoning include Marc L Busch and Krzysztof J. Pelc, 'The Politics of Judicial Economy at the World Trade Organization', *International Organization*, vol. 64 (2010) 257–279. See also note 6.

16 Krzysztof Pelc, *The Politics of Precedent in International Law: A Social Network Application*, APSA 2013 Annual Meeting Paper (2013), SSRN: http://ssrn.com /abstract=2299638.

17 Stephan W. Schill, 'Crafting the International Economic Order: The Public Function of Investment Treaty Arbitration and Its Significance for the Role of the Arbitrator', *Leiden Journal of International Law*, vol. 23 (2010) 401.

18 Joseph H. H. Weiler, 'The Rule of Lawyers and the Ethos of Diplomats. Reflections on the Internal and External Legitimacy of WTO Dispute Settlement', *Journal of World Trade*, vol. 35 (2001) 191–207; Robert Howse, 'From Politics to Technocracy – And Back Again: The Fate of the Multilateral Trading Regime', *American Journal of International Law*, vol. 96 (2002) 94–117.

audiences. This section continues by presenting the well-received but mutually irritating views of legalism and deliberation.

A Legalism

The notion of legalism captures one of the very influential views on judicial reasoning. Typically a part of grander sociological outlooks, legalism teases out the 'belief by virtue of which persons exercising authority are lent prestige', which is 'the basis of every system of authority, and correspondingly of every kind of willingness to obey'.[19] When it comes to judicial authority, such basic belief is generally informed by a whole range of factors, including those that pertain to the person of the judge, to the scenery of the courtroom, and to the language of the law.[20] Legalism zooms in on the ethical attitude, which informs a willingness to obey, and which links up closely with the practice of the law. In Judith Shklar's seminal contribution, 'legalism' refers to 'the ethical attitude that holds moral conduct to be a matter of rule following, and moral relationships to consist of duties and rights determined by rules'.[21]

With regard to judicial authority and styles of legal reasoning, legalism suggests with a lasting legacy that, especially when their authority threatens to be disputed, judges would do their best to portray their practice as impeccable rule-following. If waters get rough, the law and the rules of legal reasoning appear to offer the best refuge. Judges tie themselves to the law not so much to resist any temptation of submitting to reasons of politics, morality, or economics but to say compellingly that their hands are tied. They speak the law, so help them God.

With additional nuances and variations, this basic ethos of legalism – and the way it turns into an appeal to formalism for judges – finds support and further explanations in many sociological studies of judicial behaviour and reasoning. Niklas Luhmanns argues in his masterful *Legitimität durch Verfahren* that the whole point of judicial procedure is to first reduce any kind of broader conflict into a specific and technical question about the law in a concrete case and to then blend out the role of the judge as actually taking a decision.[22] For Shklar, the 'aloofness from

[19] Max Weber, *Economy and Society* (University of California Press, 1978) 263.

[20] Niklar Luhmann, *Legitimität durch Verfahren* (Frankfurt am Main: Suhrkamp, 1983).

[21] Judith N. Shklar, *Legalism* (Harvard University Press, 1964) 1.

[22] Luhmann, *Legitimität*, 108. Also see Andreas Fischer-Lescano and Ralph Christensen, 'Auctoritatis Interpositio. Die Dekonstruktion des Dezisionismus durch die Systemtheorie', *Der Staat*, vol. 44 (2005) 213–242.

politics' is likewise a key ingredient of adjudicators' social legitimacy.[23] The phenomenon of legalism not only finds recognition in works with primarily sociological ambitions but likewise resonates in legal philosophical arguments. Jeremy Waldron's critique of judicial review takes off on the basis that normative disagreement is stifled in the courtroom. Meaningful differences get lost when they are reduced into differences of interpretation: 'Instead of encouraging us to confront these disagreements directly, judicial review is likely to lead to their being framed as questions of interpretation of those bland formulations'.[24] Waldron thus acknowledges the pervasive appeal of legalism and articulates a normative critique. In sum, legalism highlights the appearance of impeccable rule following, overshadowing choices, and blending out the judge as an actor.

B Deliberation

From a more decidedly legal-philosophical perspective, the sociological phenomenon of legalism can gain quite some support. Explaining this support requires a walk through venerable political philosophy at a rather high speed. This analysis will quickly reconnect to judicial authority and styles of reasoning.

At least since Kant's moral theory, it is firmly established that the practice of morality is closely, if not inextricably, intertwined with the practice of law. In all brevity: the first moral duty of man is to leave the state of nature, to enter into a civil condition, and to thereby allow that questions about what is right (what belongs to whom) are no longer based on individual judgment alone but determined by law.[25] As long as everyone follows his own inclinations, the most powerful will get their way. In Kant's famed words: 'Freedom (independence from being

[23] Shklar, *Legalism*, 11; See also Pierre Bourdieu, 'The Force of Law: Toward a Sociology of the Juridical Field', *Hastings Law Journal*, vol. 38 (1987) 814–853, 828('[t]he ritual that is designed to intensify the authority of the act of interpretation . . . adds to the collective work of sublimation designed to attest that the decision expresses not the will or the world-view of the judges but the will of the law or the legislature (*voluntas legis* or *legislatoris*)').

[24] Jeremy Waldron, 'The Core of the Case against Judicial Review,' *Yale Law Journal*, vol. 115 (2006) 1346, 1369. Nik de Boer brought this specific part of Waldron's work to my attention.

[25] Articulated as an argument about rights, this view is most clearly expressed in Immanuel Kant, Metaphysical First Principles of the Doctrine of Right, in *The Metaphysics of Morals*, [1797] (Mary Gregor trans., Cambridge University Press, 1996) 33, 44, 90.

constrained by another's choice), insofar as it can coexist with the freedom of every other in accordance with a universal law, is the only original right belonging to every man by virtue of his humanity'.[26] Both morality and freedom need law, and that law must be enforced.[27]

One problem, which has indeed received ample attention, is the difficult benchmark of a universal law.[28] Both John Rawls and Jürgen Habermas have updated Kant's truly core proposition in a way that avoids this reference. Instead, they place the notion of equal rights and liberties at the centre of their arguments. Laws must guarantee equal rights and liberties and ensure the respect of those rights and liberties.[29] Here, too, those laws must be enforced to ensure that no one's freedom is unduly constrained by that of someone else. Laws and freedom require public authority.

However, even without a reference to universal law, the question remains of how a group of people can decide what they owe to one another and when public authority is justified on the basis that it actually 'just' ensures the equal protection of rights and liberties. On the one hand, there is the private autonomy of each individual, which, by default, suggests that any authority is justified only if its subjects consent to it. On the other hand, there is the collective, or civic, autonomy that bears on the room to manoeuver of each subject so as to allow equal rights and liberties. This tension has sharpened and has been refined over the years in the eternal divide between liberalism and republicanism. To frame the tension coming from the opposite direction once more in slightly different terms: public authority must act on behalf of the collective to ensure that the exercise of freedom by one does not unduly constrain the other. However, where should one draw the line? From a liberal perspective, such authority is only justified if it can connect to the consent of each party. Because of this tension, Habermas argues persuasively that both private and civic autonomy are co-original.[30] Neither one can do without the other.

[26] Kant, *The Metaphysics of Morals*, 6:237. From the wealth of scholarly treatment of this core idea, see especially Arthur Ripstein, *Force and Freedom: Kant's Legal and Political Philosophy* (2009) 240–241.

[27] Notably and in contrast to a sociological study of legitimacy, the issue is not whether subjects are *willing* to obey (referring to internal motivation) but whether they can justifiably be forced to obey.

[28] See Ripstein, *Force and Freedom*.

[29] John Rawls, *Political Liberalism* (Columbia University Press, 1993) 261; Habermas, *Facts and Norms*, 31–32.

[30] *Ibid.*, 127.

How does that reasoning link up with (international) judicial authority and styles of reasoning? From the perspective of Habermas's deliberative theory – and in line with general ideas about the core functions of public law – the law turns into a medium that legitimises and constrains the exercise of public authority. Writing from the context of a democratic constitutional state, Habermas argues that the public sphere generates communicative power that is then absorbed by the law to legitimise the administrative power of the state. A parallel track of legitimacy leads via elections and mechanisms of representation. Both meet in parliament, where debates can use the whole spectrum of moral, ethical and pragmatic reasons to debate the law that should be adopted. The features of parliament, which connects both to the public sphere and to ideas of representation, make it the focal point for legally programming the administrative power of the state.[31]

Other institutions, administrations and courts draw on the legitimacy thus fed into the law. With reference to Jerry Meshaw, Habermas speaks of the 'transmission belt model', in which the law transports legitimacy from the public sphere and elections through the parliament into the practice of the state.[32] Habermas's discourse theoretical reconstruction of the law in democratic constitutional states certainly does not believe that the law is determinate to the extent that courts or administrations – from now on I leave aside the latter – are programmed like robotic puppets. Parties typically find themselves before the court because the law has run out. According to Habermas, what the procedure before court and, ultimately, the judicial decision need to do is complete the legislative programme. Following Ronald Dworkin, they do so in a creative and constructive fashion. However, unlike Dworkin, they are engaged in a *cooperative* enterprise in which the process of arguing, which is structured by judicial procedures, bears the burden of completing the legislative programme, rather than any ideal judge with supernatural powers.[33]

However, before court, the discourse is in principle limited to a more narrow set of possible reasons. The limits are loosely confined by the rules of interpretation.[34] What I take from the discourse-theoretical

[31] *Ibid.*, 170.

[32] *Ibid.*, 190 with reference to Jerry L. Mashaw, *Due Process in the Administrative State* (Yale University Press, 1985) 22.

[33] That is the gist of the 'theory of legal discourse' Habermas, *Facts and Norms*, 222–237.

[34] See Armin von Bogdandy and Ingo Venzke, 'In Whose Name? An Investigation of International Courts' Public Authority and Its Democratic Justification', *European Journal of International Law*, vol. 23 (2012) 7, 16.

reconstruction of the law in the democratic constitutional state is its reading of the separation of powers as a separation of types of discourses. That approach links the overall characteristics (especially procedural) of institutions with governmental functions and types of discourses. The features and setup of the parliament place it centre stage and support it to make law through *norm-justificatory* discourses. Parliament can justify the law that it makes with a whole range of moral, ethical and pragmatic reasons. Courts, conversely, are engaged in more narrow discourses of *norm-application.* Following the idea of a transmission belt: 'the judiciary must be separated from the legislature and prevented from programming itself. This explains the *principle of binding the judiciary to existing law*'.[35] At the same time, it is clear that discourses of norm-application are creative in completing the existing law or, better put, in making and changing that law.

All of this argument continues to support legalism's core propositions from a more decidedly political-philosophical angle. Norm application is the business of courts. Courts are bound by the law and should stay within the confines of formalism. For the legitimating potential of authorising the judiciary through the medium of the law to be realised at all, judges must not be allowed to simply replace the moral and ethical reasons of the legislator with their own. That issue was arguably a main concern that underpinned Georges Abi-Saab's dissent in the *Abaclat* case. Arbitrators should not unravel the agreement that was struck by negotiating parties (even if those negotiations have truly little in common with anything like parliamentary legislation). To reconsider the separation of powers as one between types of discourses already takes into account that a mechanical separation of law-making and law application is not tenable. Beyond that, Habermas keenly recognises that a number of general sociolegal trends contribute to types of law that shift ever greater chunks of law-making from the legislature to the executive and judicial branches of the state.[36] In light of this development, Habermas writes:

> to the extent that legal programs are in need of further specification by the courts . . . juristic discourses of application must be *visibly supplemented by elements taken from discourses of justification.* Naturally, these elements of a quasi-legislative opinion- and will-formation require *another kind of legitimation* than does adjudication proper. The additional burden of

[35] Habermas, *Facts and Norms*, 172.

[36] His emphasis actually falls on bureaucracies and agencies rather than on courts.

> legitimation could be *partly satisfied by additional obligations before an enlarged critical forum specific to the judiciary.*[37]

While developing his discourse-theoretical approach to the separation of powers and to adjudication, Habermas clearly has in view the democratic constitutional context of national legal orders.[38] Together with Armin von Bogdandy, I have argued elsewhere what emerges in the context of *international* adjudication.[39] Among other things, it seems to be yet more frequently the case in the context of the international legal order that legal programmes are vague. Especially where treaties set up international institutions or where they more generally delegate interpretative authority to international courts and tribunals, one might expect the terms of delegation to be precise. However, the prevailing modus of consensual rather than majority law making points in the opposite direction. Where compromises that suit everyone must be struck, precision may well be the first victim. What is more, whatever programme upon which state representatives might agree may well soon be out of touch with changing realities. The consensual modus of decision-making in political-legislative procedures largely prevents any updates. Not once have the WTO members agreed to issue an authoritative interpretation (Art. IX: 2 WTO Agreement), let alone change any of the WTO covered agreements (Art. X WTO Agreement).[40]

In the present chapter, I suggest focusing on the qualified demand that the 'juristic discourse of application must be visibly supplemented by elements taken from discourses of justification'. For one, there is a question on that same political-philosophical terrain: Would that approach actually be well justified and advisable? Would it be conducive to the legitimacy of adjudication? An answer hinges, not the least, on the additional means of legitimation, which might include lower thresholds of participation in judicial proceedings, as well as greater transparency and publicness, for instance.[41] The answer also depends, as Habermas highlights, on the role of 'an enlarged critical forum specific to the judiciary', which is supposed to contribute additional legitimacy through

[37] Habermas, *Facts and Norms* 439–440 (italics added); see also 193.

[38] More specifically, he focuses on the German constitutional order, with some detours via the US-American context.

[39] Von Bogdandy and Venzke, 'In Whose Name?', 36.

[40] Pieter Jan Kuijper, 'WTO Institutional Aspects' in Daniel L. Bethlehem et al. (eds.), *The Oxford Handbook of International Trade Law* (Oxford University Press, 2009) 79.

[41] Armin von Bogdandy and Ingo Venzke, *In Whose Name? A Public Law Theory of International Adjudication* (Oxford University Press, 2014) 171–184.

its critique of judicial reasoning. Is that at all possible, and is it advisable? There is a clear tension between this proposition and the core idea of legalism. Legalism would suggest that when the law runs out and the legal programme requires further specification, the adjudicators find themselves in a moment of crisis. The ground opens up under their feet, and they try their best to hold on to any and every branch of the law that is just within reach. They seek refuge in formalism. However, precisely in those moments, formalism is weakest. As Judith Shklar summarises: 'as denunciations of "lawmaking" multiply, the legalistic ethos is reinforced and the likelihood of judges satisfying it becomes increasingly rare'.[42]

IV Beyond legalism and deliberation: judge's audiences

To refine the discussion of both legalism and deliberation, this section introduces in further detail a third perspective from which to approach judicial reasoning, namely that of self-presentation theory and its emphasis on impression management (Subsection A). I submit that such an approach is already subtly present in Shklar's legalism. This approach must be amplified and then used to reconsider arguments about judicial reasoning from the view of social legitimacy (Subsection B). Drawing attention to judges' audiences also has implications for the possibly critical and legitimating role of an enlarged forum specific to the judiciary (Subsection C).

A Audiences

Audiences matter to judges for a variety of reasons, including because 'judges, like other people, get satisfaction from perceiving that other people view them positively'.[43] Being seen favourably can serve strategic ends, for example, if people who form part of the audience are in a position in which they might bear on the future career of a judge or on the judges' preferred policy outcome. In short, audiences can be instrumental. However, suggesting that being seen favourably gives satisfaction also endows audiences with a self-sufficient role that is not linked to further objectives. Laurence Baum, who pioneered thinking about judges and their audiences in domestic settings, maintains that 'judges care about the regard of salient audiences because they like that regard in itself, not just as a means to other ends'.[44]

[42] Shklar, *Legalism*, 13. [43] Baum, *Judges*, 3. [44] Baum, *Judges*, 4.

The argument is one of social-psychology, which can be further refined though the lens of self-presentation theory. This strand of thinking sees behaviour as an extension of the impressions that actors are trying to create in the eyes of their audiences.[45] Erving Goffman, whose work set self-perception theory on its track, draws attention to the 'arts of impression management'.[46] He sees the focus of his *The Presentation of Self in Everyday Life* to lie precisely in the 'study of impression management, of the contingencies which arise in fostering an impressions, and of the techniques for meeting these contingencies'.[47] More recently, Nezlek and Leary have argued that self-presentation is shaped by five factors: '[individuals'] self-concepts, constraints imposed by salient social roles, their desired and undesired identity images, the values of the people to whom they are impression-managing, and the current and potential nature of their public images'.[48]

The degree of self-awareness with which actors present themselves certainly differs, not the least depending on how deep-seated certain routines are. Like anyone else, judges may act in a thoroughly calculating manner based on their interests. Their interests may be shaped by previously established social relations, and their socialisation may turn their actions into unconscious knee-jerk reactions. This spectrum reflects the now generally acknowledged co-constitution of actors and social structures. With a view to the authority of international adjudicators and their choice of one rather than another style of legal reasoning, self-presentation theory and its emphasis on impression management suggests two complementary angles from which to look at judicial reasoning: anxiety and performance.

[45] Much of the work follows on the heels of Erving Goffman, *The Presentation of Self in Everyday Life*, 1956. For an overview, see Timothy J. Owens and Sarah Samblanet, 'Self and Self-Concept' in John DeLamater and Amanda Ward, *Handbook of Social Psychology*, 2nd edn (Springer, 2013), Handbooks of Sociology and Social Research 225–249, especially 234–236; Roy F. Baumeister and Debra G. Hutton, 'Self-Presentation Theory: Self-Construction and Audience Pleasing' in Brian Mullen and George R. Goethals (eds.), *Theories of Group Behavior* (Springer, 1987).

[46] Goffman, *Presentation of Self*, 132.

[47] *Ibid.*, 49. This is further worked out in B. R. Schlenker, *Impression Management: The Self-Concept, Social Identity, and Interpersonal Relations* (Brooks/Cole, 1980); M. R. Leary, *Self-Presentation: Impression Management and Interpersonal Behavior* (Westview Press, 1996).

[48] J. B. Nezlek and M. R. Leary, 'Individual Differences in Self-Presentational Motives in Daily Social Interaction', *Personality and Social Psychology Bulletin*, vol. 28 (2002) 211–223, 212. [Quoted in Owens and Samblanet, 'Self and Self-Concept' 235.]

1. Anxiety. To think of judicial reasoning from the perspective of social anxiety ties in well with legalism's idea about the self-reinforcing appeal of formalism, that is, legalism's proposition that judges attempt to present their practice as impeccable rule-following, leaving no room for discretion or choice.[49] According to self-presentation theory, social anxiety arises 'when individuals are motivated to convey a particular impression – usually one that will facilitate interpersonal acceptance (or perhaps more accurately, to avoid interpersonal rejection) but doubt their ability to do so'.[50] Social anxiety is thus a product of two components: the wish to convey a particular impression and the perceived probability of success. Social anxiety increases the more it matters to an actor to convey a particular impression and the less likely she perceives her success to be.[51]

From this angle, judicial reasoning is part of the repertoire with which judges attempt to manage their impressions.[52] Judges tackle anxieties with the art of impression management. Whether they succeed – given that they place a constant level of importance on imposing a particular impression – depends on the degree to which they master the art of impression management *and also* on the audience they are trying to impress.

2. Performance. Whereas dealing with social anxiety focuses on judges as actors, a complementary perspective looks at judges' judicial reasoning as routine performances. It is not that judges choose one style over another but rather that they get 'locked in'. Judges' anxiety is dependent on the audience they are facing. The audience is part of the cause of anxiety because it might be more or less likely to be impressed. What is more, drawing attention to routine performances highlights how the anticipation of others' reactions becomes part of the self. Baum develops this line of thinking with reference to psychologist Kristen Monroe, among others, who argues that human behaviour is driven principally by 'the actor's perceptions of self *in relations to others*'.[53] In fact, Goffman concludes that 'the very obligation and profitability of appearing always

49 *Ibid.*

50 Catalino, Furr, and Bellis, 'A Multilevel Analysis of the Self-presentation Theory of Social Anxiety: Contextualized, Dispositional, and Interactive Perspectives' at 361

51 *Ibid.*, 361–362.

52 Goffman, *Presentation of Self*, 160 ('the role of expression is conveying impressions of self').

53 Kristen Renwick Monroe, 'A Paradigm for Political Psychology' in Kristen Renwick Monroe (ed.), *Political Psychology* (Lawrence Erlbaum Associates, 2002) 399–415, 414; quoted in Baum, *Judges*, 26.

in a steady moral light, of being a socialised character, forces us to be the sort of person who is practiced in the ways of the stage'.[54] With repeat performance, actors are no longer free to choose. They are subject to constraints, and their self is constituted by those constraints. At this point, the actor no longer perceives constraints as such. In other words, individuals internalise the images that the audience draws of them.[55]

This is an important point to stress: arguing about the perceptions of others does not in and of itself suggest that judges are insincere or cynical about what they are doing. These are good reasons that all three arbitrators in the initial example were convinced that they were doing 'the right thing'. What self-presentation theory suggests is that judges also want to be seen to do the right thing, at least by those whose opinion they value. In addition, this theory suggests that the interaction with audiences influences what actors believe to be appropriate. Thus, this theory opens up a nuanced perspective for a critical understanding of the judicial reasoning of the majority by Jan van den Berg and Pierre Tercier and of George Abi-Saab's dissent.

The argument concerning how audiences matter when attempting to explain and understand judicial reasoning benefits from revisiting the main propositions of legalism, as well as the potential of deliberation. With regard to the former, self-presentation theory and its emphasis on impression management highlight the contingency of formalism: whether formalism is a valuable strategy depends on the audiences that judges are trying to impress. In fact, Judith Shklar's *Legalism* is rather amenable to such a reading. The question that concerns deliberation is whether and to what extent the dynamics of judging as self-presentation might take away from a controlling and legitimating role of a critical public.

B Reconsidering legalism's ties with formalism

The role of audiences can, in fact, already be traced in Shklar's account of legalism. She stresses societal expectations that form the core of judges' social legitimacy. Judges *generally* meet social anxiety with formalism. However, this refuge is indeed contingent: 'Professional ideology and public expectations, in fact, do mold the conduct of the judiciary and its

[54] Goffman, *Presentation of Self*, 162.

[55] Baum, *Judges*, XXX, with reference to Schlenker, *Impression Management*, 194–196; Leary, *Self-Presentation*, 167–168.

perception of its role'.[56] Formalism works as a social practice, and Shklar recognises in passing that its appeal varies. When judges face critique, '[t]he easiest resort . . . is for judges to escape into formalism *when they can*. For American judges this is frequently not possible. In England it is'.[57] Shklar's account of the appeal of formalism comes with an implicit assessment of the leaning of English judges' audiences.

What is more, her account is open to recognise the internalisation of images that audiences draw of actors. It is not so much that judges advance their policy interests in the guise of formalism, Shklar suggests. Their ideas and, by extension, their styles of legal reasoning rather correspond 'to the professional experiences and necessity of bench and bar'.[58] In much the same way, Habermas offers the sociological observation in his normative reconstruction of the rule of law in domestic democracies that standards and practices of the legal profession shape judicial reasoning and continue to strengthen the ties that bind judges to the law.[59]

Formalism is a contingent refuge. As the example already shows, it is not a destination that every judge chooses. Its appeal depends on the beliefs of a judge's audience. The practice of adjudication knows many other decisions for which formalism was not the preferred style of impression management. Adjudication in international criminal law offers many examples, but so does the law of the sea.[60] In its first case, then split into two, the majority of the International Tribunal for the Law of the Sea (ITLOS) upheld its jurisdiction by arguing inter alia that 'it would not be consistent with justice if the Tribunal were to decline to deal with the merits of the dispute'.[61] The boundaries of what is permissible in legal argument and which styles of legal reasoning in fact support judicial authority or detract from it is contingent on the predilection of relevant audiences.

C Reconsidering deliberation

What do self-presentation theory and its emphasis on the role of audiences say in relation to a normative account of the style of reasoning? The proposition here was that the additional need for legitimacy in

[56] Shklar, *Legalism*, 12. [57] *Ibid.*, 13 (italics added). [58] *Ibid.*, 12.

[59] Habermas, *Facts and Norms*, 224–225.

[60] ICTY, *Anto Furundzija* (Judgment) IT-95-17/1-T (10 December 1998), paras. 143–157.

[61] ITLOS, The M/V 'Saiga' (No. 2) Case (*Saint Vincent and the Grenadines* v. *Guinea*), Judgment, 1 July 1999, para. 73.

judicial proceedings, which arises when discourses are opened up to include discourses of norm justification (such as fairness, for instance), 'could be partly satisfied by additional obligations before an enlarged critical forum specific to the judiciary'.[62] Whether that approach works depends on the features and general quality of the respective forum.

On a first account, understanding judicial reasoning as a technique for impression management could be twisted to support the controlling and legitimating role of a critical public. Judges anticipate the reaction to their decisions and reasoning when attempting to deal with their social anxiety. This take on their practice recognises the power and influence of their onlookers. However, an overall pessimistic view prevails; the implied attitude is one of anticipation and appeasement, rather than one of good arguments that should convince.

The crucial normative question is whether the audiences, which are relevant for specific judges or for specific judicial institutions, constitute a public that has the capacity to generate supplementary legitimacy in cases in which judicial discourses are opened. Follow-up questions include: What are judges' actual audiences? Which audiences matter the most? If it at all makes sense to split up a larger and general public into more narrowly confined audiences, can those audiences exercise a controlling and possibly legitimating function?

As Nancy Fraser highlights, Habermas developed a concept of the public sphere that is ambitious in that it refers not merely to simple flows of communication but to a normatively legitimating and politically efficacious public.[63] Who participates in debates on what terms matters, as does whether public officials are at all accountable to such a public. According to Fraser, public sphere theory has overwhelmingly bought into implicit assumptions of rather hermetic nation states that align the scope of authority with a public that ties together equal members of a political community.[64] Within territorial borders, national language and media

[62] Habermas, *Facts and Norms*, 439–440 (italics added); see also, 193.

[63] Nancy Fraser, *Scales of Justice. Reimagining Political Space in a Globalizing World* (Columbia University Press, 2009) 76–77.

[64] *Ibid.*, 79–83. Fraser includes Habermas's pivotal work in this regard. She focuses on his *Structural Transformation of the Public Sphere: An Inquiry into a Category of Bourgeois Society* (Cambridge: Polity Press, 1989). Though translated and published in English only in 1989, it is an early book that was published in German in 1962 (it is Habermas's *Habilitationsschrift*, in fact). Habermas has since done much that actually chimes in well with Fraser's criticism, especially arguing that political communication needs to open up to experiences in different nation states. See only Jürgen Habermas, 'Why Europe Needs a Constitution', *New Left Review*, vol. 11 (2001) 5–26, 16–19; Jürgen Habermas, 'The Crisis

outlets nourish life in the public sphere. Finally, as citizenry, the public can be politically efficacious. There is public authority that reacts to the public. All of this of course changes in the post-national constellation, where authority, territory and rights fall apart.[65] Fraser suggests that regardless of political citizenship, those individuals must be included on an equal footing and be granted channels of influence that are 'subject[ed] to a structure of governance that set the ground rules for their interaction. For any given problem, accordingly, the relevant public should match the reach of the governance structure that regulates the relevant swath of social interaction'.[66] Of course, that is a high threshold. Not the least, massive inequality and mechanisms of exclusion stand in the way. Euphoric references to the internet as a medium that gives rise to new transnational public spaces are contrasted with the fact that the internet still only reaches less than a third of the world population (2 of roughly 7 billion people).[67] Whether such spaces at all qualify is also contested with good arguments.[68]

There are several problems in the potentially legitimating function of a 'forum specific to the judiciary'. Following Fraser and others, a persistent problem is how the relevant public should shift with the authority that it is subjected to while at the same time forming a community of sufficient quality to realise inclusive participation on par and a discourse of some density. The related and most important problem appears more clearly if considered from the perspective of judges and their audiences; there is an idea of openness embedded in the public sphere that, together with inclusiveness as to who participates, suggests that themes may not in principle be excluded or perspectives be ab initio weighted. The idea is that of generality, which is typically linked to the process of law creation in parliament. This idea demands that procedures be thematically unsettled and open to all kinds of competing perspectives.[69] The problem is that adjudication at the international level

of the European Union in the Light of a Constitutionalization of International Law', *European Journal of International Law*, vol. 23 (2012) 335–348, 346.

[65] On the shifting constellations of this trilogy see Saskia Sassen, *Territory, Authority, Rights: From Medieval to Global Assemblages* (Princeton University Press, 2006).

[66] Fraser, *Scales of Justice*, 96.

[67] This is the flipside of the upbeat 2013 Human Development Report, http://hdr.undp.org/en/.

[68] Zizi Papacharissi, 'The Virtual Sphere 2.0: The Internet, the Public Sphere, and Beyond' in Andrew Chadwich and Phillip N. Howard (eds.), *Routledge Handbook of Internet Politics* (New York: Routledge, 2009) 230–245.

[69] Bast, ‚Das Demokratiedefizit fragmentierter Internationalisierung' in H. Brunkhorst (ed.), *Demokratie in der Weltgesellschaft, Soziale Welt Sonderband*, vol. 18 (2009) 177.

is clearly thematically fragmented. Discourses are equally fragmented so that any forum that is specific to a judiciary brings specific perspectives that favour one point of view over another.[70] Such fragmentation impacts how judges deal with their social anxiety and manage their impressions. Arguments tend to be geared more towards groups that share a specific perspective. They should resonate with the interests that particular regimes of international law pursue.[71] It is in this light that the majority reasoning in the *Abaclat* can makes sense. It is one instance of the more general pattern in which the objectives of investment protection or trade liberalisation support judicial decisions in international economic law.[72]

V Outlook: a programme for studying judicial authority and audiences

The present contribution has attempted to show how thinking about judges' quest for authority and about styles of judicial reasoning gains from a closer consideration of judges' audiences. This work has challenged explanations and justifications of judicial reasoning in the forms of legalism and deliberation by drawing attention to judges' self-presentation and impression management. It has tried to give a first account of how judges' audiences matter. Granted, a number of questions remain. I hope that curiosity to explore these questions further also remains. In this concluding outlook, I wish to contrast the study of audiences with closely competing alternatives, especially those of epistemic or interpretative communities. Further, there is of course the key

Cf. Christoph Möllers, *Gewaltengliederung: Legitimation und Dogmatik im nationalen und internationalen Rechtsvergleich* (Mohr Siebeck, 2005) 31 and 223; Paulus, 'Subsidiarity, Fragmentation and Democracy: Towards the Demise of General International Law?' in T. Broude and Y. Shany (eds.), *The Shifting Allocation of Authority in International Law: Considering Sovereignty, Supremacy, and Subsidiarity* (Oxford: Hart Publishing, 2008) 193, 210.

[70] On fragmentation as a problem for the democratic legitimacy of international adjudication, see Von Bogdandy and Venzke, 'In Whose Name?' 23.

[71] For such an understanding of fragmented regimes in international law, see Andreas Fischer-Lescano and Gunther Teubner, 'Regime-Collisions: The Vain Search for Legal Unity in the Fragmentation of Global Law', *Michigan Journal of International Law*, vol. 25 (2004) 999–1045.

[72] Of course, such references may find support in the standard rule of interpretation that demands that treaties be interpreted 'in accordance with the ordinary meaning to be given to the terms of the treaty in their context and *in the light of its object and purpose*' (Art. 31 Vienna Convention on the Law of Treaties). The point is, however, that assessments of what the object and purpose is and how it should be pursued are likely to differ depending on who you ask.

question of what audiences are relevant. Moreover, differences between domestic and international contexts must be considered further.

A Audiences rather than epistemic or interpretative communities

The view of the practice of adjudication that arises from considering judges' self-presentation between legalism and deliberation might also be understood from the perspectives of the closely competing ideas of epistemic or interpretative communities. I submit that for a number of reasons, thinking about judges' audiences fares better.

The first notion – that of epistemic communities – refers to 'a network of professionals with recognised expertise and competence in a particular domain'.[73] Members of an epistemic community have 'a shared set of causal and principled (analytic and normative) beliefs, a consensual knowledge base and a common policy enterprise (common interests) that distinguishes epistemic communities from various other groups'.[74] The notion is highly ambitious and demanding, as it includes members that share all of these things. To argue that audiences matter, it is not necessary to buy into all or even any of these elements. Self-presentation theory is both less demanding and more nuanced. It allows for a whole range of sincere and also cynical motivations.[75]

The notion of interpretative communities is also less demanding. This notion comes close to thinking about judicial reasoning in light of audiences, in that it takes communicative practices to lie at the heart of a community.[76] In their practice, interpretative communities uphold beliefs about what is a correct interpretation and, above all, uphold standards concerning how to argue about what is a correct interpretation.[77] In Stanley Fish's strong view, it is precisely how one

[73] Peter M. Haas, 'Epistemic Communities and International Policy Coordination', *International Organization*, vol. 46 (1992) 1–35, 3.

[74] *Ibid.*, 18.

[75] On cynical self-performance, see Goffman, *Presentation of Self*, 10–13; see more generally, Alexis T. Franzese, '*Motivation, Motives, and Individual Agency*', in DeLamater and Ward, *Handbook of Social Psychology*, 286.

[76] Stanley Fish, *Doing What Comes Naturally. Change, Rhetoric, and the Practice of Theory in Literature and Legal Studies* (Duke University Press, 1989) 141–160.

[77] The notion of communities of practice is set up along similar lines; see P. Eckert, 'Communities of Practice' in Keith Brown (ed.), *Encyclopedia of Language and Linguistics* (Elsevier, 2006).

should look at a text that makes the text.[78] This way of looking at interpretative practice is complementary to that of considering audiences. However, the latter approach has the additional advantage of zooming in on the perspective of the actor. It is thus able to contribute to explaining the stabilising dynamics of an interpretative community by highlighting the varying motives of the interpreter. The interpreter wants to be seen as being a good member of a community – she wants to please her audience.

B *The power of audiences at the international level*

The key question is of course: Which are the relevant audiences for international judges? Writing for the domestic setting, Baum sets up a whole range of possibilities, each with varying plausibility for different specific contexts but all with some sway. Ranging from the microcosmic personal context via the immediate workplace to broader political audiences, Baum zooms in on colleagues at the court, other branches of government and social and professional groups, such as Bar Associations, as well as policy groups and the news media. With regard to the latter, he revisits arguments as to how the reception of Supreme Court judges' reasoning in the *New York Times*, especially the reception of reporter Linda Greenhouse, has arguably given rise to a 'Greenhouse effect' on judicial behaviour.[79] The audiences differ for judges at different courts. For instance, Baum draws attention to how two rivalling conservative judges at the federal appeals court with aspirations to be appointed for the Supreme Court went to great lengths in their judgments to win the favour of the future president's closer circle in the lead-up to presidential elections.

Some observations may be made as to which audiences are relevant for international judges. I have already highlighted that at least in some contrast to the domestic setting, adjudication is much more fragmented along thematic lines. Second, it only happens rarely – though increasingly – that international adjudication is taken up in the public media. Relevant audiences are likely to be rather limited to professionals, more specifically, legal professionals in a specific field of law. All of this questions the possibly legitimating role that audiences could play. To the

[78] Stanley Fish, 'What Makes an Interpretation Acceptable' in *Is There a Text in This Class? The Authority of Interpretative Communities* (Harvard University Press, 1980).

[79] Baum, *Judges*, 138–144.

contrary, drawing attention to the role of judges' audiences in the construction of their authority and their styles of reasoning may even highlight and explain how international law is pushed in directions that follow the interests and inclinations of specific regimes. The question then is whether inclusive publics emerge that contest those moves. Evidence suggests that they do.[80]

For instance, in trade law, jurisprudence and styles of reasoning have shifted visibly and significantly in reaction to widespread criticism to decisions that seemingly categorically rule out the possibility that unilateral trade-restrictive measures could be justified by the environmental objectives they pursued.[81] Public contestation played its role in changing that view. This factor points to shifts in adjudicators' strategic space. A change in adjudicators – with the new Appellate Body and its general public international lawyers – also came with a shift in the audiences that mattered. The pivotal and programmatic decisions clearly speak a different language that is geared towards different interlocutors.[82] While much is currently in flux in the field of investment arbitration, it is safe to say that public contestation has drawn the field out into the open, where the argumentative space has already shifted.

[80] Michael Zürn, 'The Politicization of World Politics and Its Effects: Eight Propositions', *European Political Science Review*, vol. 6 (2014) 47–71.

[81] GATT Panel Report, *United States – Restrictions on Imports of Tuna*, DS21/R (3 September 1991) unadopted, BISD 39S/155, see especially para. 5.27.

[82] Appellate Body Report, *United States – Standards for Reformulated and Conventional Gasoline*, WT/DS2/AB/R (adopted 29 April 1996) especially at p. 16; Appellate Body Report, *United States – Import Prohibition of Certain Shrimp and Shrimp Products*, WB/DS58/AB/R (adopted 12 October 1998) especially at paras. 152–154.

10

'Global Citizens' in international commercial arbitration and WTO dispute resolution

JOANNA JEMIELNIAK AND LAURA NIELSEN

1 Introduction

1.1 Abstract

The notion of 'global citizens' has two different meanings in the international commercial arbitration (ICA) and World Trade Organization[1] (WTO) contexts. These two systems of dispute resolution appear to embody different (though in each case, conceptually well-established) ideals of citizenship: a civic and participatory ideal versus a liberal and individualistic ideal.

In this chapter, we argue that there is an interplay between the two ideals; if one pushes the 'inclusive' understanding of the 'global citizens' agenda too far at the WTO, governments will respond by moving their dispute settlement to international commercial arbitration, where the notion of 'global citizens' appears to have the opposite meaning. We also examine the possible effects of such tendencies; in particular, we aim to unveil the often-overlooked participatory potential of arbitration and to explore the possible opening of this model to broader inclusiveness.

1.2 Object and scope of analysis

The legitimacy of the WTO depends not only on the degree of state participation but also on non-state participation. This dependence is evidenced by the numerous discussions related to the democratic deficit

[1] The World Trade Organization was established in 1995 by the founding act – Final Act Embodying the Results of the Uruguay Round of Multilateral Trade Negotiations, 15 April 1994, 1967 U.N.T.S. 14 (1994). The WTO Agreement establishes the WTO, and all other agreements are annexed to this agreement. See the Marrakesh Agreement Establishing the World Trade Organization, 15 April 1994, 1967 U.N.T.S. 14 (1994), into force 1 January 1995 [hereinafter the WTO Agreement].

of the organisation and the public interest in disputes. To this end, it is important to note that while a strict understanding of legal formalism or positivism might make it possible to dismiss the entire notion of non-state participation in the WTO simply on the grounds that the WTO is an *intergovernmental organisation* (IGO) and not a public democracy organisation,[2] the opposite has happened in real life. Analogously, legal scholarship also advances the idea of broader participation in shaping international law.[3] In fact, after Seattle was left resembling a civil war area during the WTO Ministerial Conference in 1999, the massive focus on 'democratic deficit' and lack of 'openness' probably paved the way for the openness that currently exists in the WTO. In the words of the former director general Mike Moore:

> So how should we respond to civil society's demand for greater engagement in the overwhelming issues of the day? I believe we need to welcome and open up to the globalisation debate, not try to resist it. Organisations like the UN, the ILO, the WTO, the IMF and the World Bank do important work. And the decisions they take increasingly affect the lives of ordinary men and women. It is good that people want more information and control, greater accountability and greater ownership. International organizations should welcome this scrutiny. It makes them stronger, less distant, more legitimate.[4]

Singling out the WTO dispute settlement (DS) system, the same concern arises as a natural consequence of the fact that the results of WTO cases affect people all over the world, and the effect is even stronger when one includes the influence on government decisions that is caused by the precedential effect of the cases. The same can be argued to be

[2] However, see Steve Charnovitz, 'Transparency and Participation in the World Trade Organization', *The George Washington University Law School Public Law and Legal Theory Paper*, No. 142 (also published in Rutgers Law Review) (2005), which discusses transparency in relation to good governance at the national level, as well as the development of transparency norms within the WTO. However, he states clearly that he is unaware of the emergence of any international norms of transparency and citizen participation.

[3] See e.g., Jean D'Aspremont (ed.), *Participants in the International Legal System – Multiple Perspectives on Non-State Actors in International Law* (London: Routledge, 2011); Steve Charnovitz, 'Nongovernmental Organizations and International Law', *AM. J. Int'L L.*, vol. 100 (2006), 348; Peter Van den Bossche, 'NGO Involvement in the WTO: A Comparative Perspective', *J. Int'l Econ. L.*, vol. 11 (2008), 717; Steve Charnovitz, 'Opening the WTO to Non-Governmental Interests', *Fordham Int'l L. J.*, vol. 24 (2000), 173.

[4] Mike Moore, *A World without Walls* (Cambridge: Cambridge University Press, 2003), 194–195.

happening to international commercial arbitration, as not only do international commercial cases exist in which public interest considerations are present but also the states themselves resort to that type of arbitration, and the results of those cases thus also affect a great number of non-party actors. Moreover, the recently growing recourse to arbitral mechanisms when addressing trade disputes calls for a relevant interpretation. This recourse has taken several different forms, from the inclusion of an embedded (and generally unused) arbitration mechanism into the WTO DS system through Article 25 of the Dispute Settlement Understanding (DSU)[5] to the well-established practice of allocating the powers to resolve disputes to ad hoc arbitral panels, as provided by numerous preferential trade agreements (PTAs). Another highly interesting development is the privatisation and outsourcing of the process of dispute resolution by seeking the services of a commercial arbitral centre, as was the case of two arbitral awards (issued in 2008 and 2009) in the Canada–United States *Softwood Lumber* dispute, which was resolved under the auspices of the London Court of International Arbitration.

As we framed the research questions concerning public interests and non-party participation in such types of cases, we realised that when we used the term 'global citizens', we spoke of two different concepts. The popular understanding of the term 'global citizens' is probably described most comprehensively by Ron Israel as meaning inter alia:

> Global citizen is someone who identifies with being part of an emerging world community and whose actions contribute to building this community's values and practices.
>
> ... values that ... include human rights, environmental protection, religious pluralism, gender equity, sustainable worldwide economic growth, poverty alleviation, prevention of conflicts between countries, elimination of weapons of mass destruction, humanitarian assistance and preservation of cultural diversity.[6]

It is this meaning that most people would attach to 'global citizens' in the WTO context (i.e., a participatory inclusive understanding of non-state participation). Conversely, in international commercial arbitration, this term may have nearly the opposite meaning when used to describe the global elite of lawyers, who are capable of fluently handling and

[5] See Understanding on Rules and Procedures Governing the Settlement of Disputes, 15 April 1994, WTO Agreement Annex 2, Legal Instruments – Results of the Uruguay Round, 33 I.L.M. 1125 (1994).

[6] Ron Israel, 'What Does It Mean to Be a Global Citizen', *Kosmos Journal*, vol. 79 (Spring, 2012), www.kosmosjournal.org/articles/what-does-it-mean-to-be-a-global-citizen.

participating in arbitration proceedings organised under different sets of rules and standards and adopting a transnational approach to the application of laws that are frequently foreign to them. The institutional and procedural network of arbitration – this hugely successful version of the processes of the transnationalisation of law – supports the development of this new 'elite' class of global citizens. However, it should be noted that these two approaches are not completely divergent; a highly professional class of global citizens also exists amongst WTO lawyers. Similarly, the issue of global citizens as non-party actors in dispute resolution can also be discussed in relation to international commercial arbitration.

However, it is evident that the interest in world, global, universal, cosmopolitan or transnational versions of citizenship has grown remarkably in recent years.[7] A comparison of the two concepts of global citizenship discussed above suggests that the usual understanding in the WTO, related to opening the system to external parties, seems to rely on the Aristotelian and republican ideal of civic and political participation as a key virtue, whereas the understanding in international commercial arbitration, which is a private means of dispute resolution based on agreement, fulfils the liberal ideal of citizenship as primarily a sphere of freedom.[8] In this chapter, we explore the interplay between these two models, as well as the consequences of employing the arbitral mechanisms of dispute resolution in fully public (non-investment) cases. We find it relevant to analyse the issue of non-state participation/non-party participation and the legitimacy of the two systems together, as we note that there is an interplay between the WTO system and international commercial arbitration when discussing global citizens in the WTO. We predict that the effects of a push for increased transparency in the WTO may have a possible backlash, with the states seeking recourse to less participatory and less transparent mechanisms, such as arbitration. This potential move to change the venue to international commercial arbitration brings about the question of whether arbitration has a self-transformation potential so that such cases could have increased participatory involvement. Playing further on the terminology of the article, we thus seek to answer whether at the conceptual level of global citizenship

[7] Peter Kivisto and Thomas Faist, *Citizenship: Discourse, Theory, and Transnational Prospects* (Malden, MA: Wiley-Blackwell, 2009), 2; Keith Faulks, *Citizenship: Key Ideas* (London: Routledge, 2000), 132 ff.

[8] Adrin Oldfield, 'Citizenship: An Unnatural Practice?' in Bryan Stanley Turner and Peter Hamilton (eds.) *Citizenship: Critical Concepts* (London and New York: Routledge, 1994).

there can be a shift from the negative 'liberty from' (the unnecessary intervention of the state) towards the positive 'freedom to' type of involvement in common, public undertakings.[9]

1.3 The argument and structure of this chapter

The argument in this chapter (i.e., that the two different meanings of 'global citizens' in the two systems remain in an interplay) will be illustrated by holding an analysis of the WTO system up against an analysis of international commercial arbitration.

In Section 2, the current situation is described in both the WTO and international commercial arbitration. In Section 3, the analytical approach is set out in regard to both systems. The WTO analysis commences by questioning and putting into a legal context the trend towards increased public access to the WTO DSM and international courts in general. Thereafter, we question whether the evolution has gone so far that it in effect requires a formal codification of the practices, as well as the feasibility of such a change and its potential consequences. This analysis is further developed in a discussion of international commercial arbitration, which highlights its consolidating, autonomous status. The issue of transparency in international commercial arbitration is discussed in the context of its possible openness to public interest considerations. This discussion further serves as a basis for exploring the concept of global citizenship in ICA, which is arguably currently realised by a highly skilled, cosmopolitan group of professionals, who are able to overcome the limitations of domestic legal systems. However, this concept can also be expanded through a recontextualisation of arbitral mechanisms in the resolution of trade disputes. Possible interpretations of the current move towards arbitration in trade DS are further considered.

2 The current situation: a diagnosis

2.1 The WTO

'Global citizens', when understood as a group of actors, can simply be defined as groups (whether formal NGOs or not) that are not represented by a government or any other governmental structure.

[9] Isaiah Berlin, 'Two Concepts of Liberty' in Henry Herdy (ed.) *Liberty: Incorporating Four Essays on Liberty* (New York: Oxford University Press, 2002), 166 ff.

In many instances, these groups protect values across borders or irrespective of borders, although they can also include, for example, indigenous groups that focus solely on an issue within one country. These groups are generally understood as promoting 'positive' and 'sympathetic' causes, although certain anti-globalisation movements may not generally fit that description. However, if one singles out the more obvious 'positively' loaded policies, it is generally thought to be 'positive' and attractive that these groups are heard; thus, broader access to the expression of opinions and interests in the WTO would ensure that some kind of 'democratic deficit' was countered. In a sense, the European Parliament represents a formalised version of 'global citizens' or 'European citizens' who act as one and transcend borders in an international organisation, although this organisation is of a supranational nature. The reality of having a European Parliament (and that this body has attained more powers over the years) may have even legitimised the idea of 'global citizens' having broader access in other international organisations.

Focusing solely on the DSM of the WTO, it can safely be argued that 'global citizens' seem to have increasingly acquired a position of being actual stakeholders in WTO cases, most notably by virtue of the ability to submit amicus curiae briefs and participate in open hearings. Whilst private parties were also previously the actual stakeholders because the state effectively brought the case on behalf of important stakeholders (such as aircraft manufacturers or banana distributors), the notion of the access of 'global citizens' to the DS mechanism of the WTO goes beyond that idea.

The WTO DSM is likely to have received an increased amount of attention, not only concerning participation, because it holds the unique position of being the only mandatory, binding and enforceable DSM of its scale in the world. This standing has also, perhaps more in the early days, made the WTO DSM an object of discussions amongst other international legal subareas, such as the international environmental law community's lengthy discussion of whether environmental issues could be addressed in this 'world trade court'. Whilst the answer is obviously 'no', given that cases at the WTO can only be brought concerning the 'covered agreements' of the WTO, the discussions all tend to point in the same direction: while case law is building, it seems to attract increasing attention because it also affects more and more people. This observation also serves to explain how the system legitimises itself by opening itself to participation by others, as well as by broadening its transparency.

2.1.1 Amicus curiae briefs

Today, it is unsurprising when a WTO case attracts amicus curiae submissions from non-state actors. Conversely, the Appellate Body's authorisation of solicited and unsolicited amicus curiae submissions in *US – Shrimp*[10] in 1998 and in *US – Carbon Steel*[11] in 1999 generated quite extensive scholarly discussion and debate amongst members.[12] The real turning point probably came when a WTO member provided an amicus curiae brief –Morocco submitted such a brief in the *EC – Sardines* case.[13] This action illustrated the multitude of options through which WTO members can participate in WTO disputes: as actual parties to the dispute, as third parties, and by submitting amicus curiae briefs. Today, the perceived threat by some members of having a province or territory that longs for independence submit an amicus curiae brief is probably numbed by the sensational fact that the Kingdom of Denmark recently gave its consent to the Faroe Islands to bring a case against the European Union (also counting Denmark as an EU member, whilst Denmark is also one of the three parts of the Danish Kingdom, which includes Denmark, Greenland and the Faroe Islands).[14] In that light, it seems quite harmless that private persons and NGOs may submit an amicus curiae brief from time to time.

2.1.2 Open hearings

In August 2005, the chairman of the panel in the *US – Continued Suspension* and *Canada – Continued Suspension* cases for the first time authorised the usage of 'open hearings' at the request of the parties to the dispute.[15] 'Open hearings' function so that the registered audience sits in a room next to the actual proceedings and watches the proceedings on a closed circuit transmission. Following this decision, several proceedings have been opened in a similar manner.

[10] See Appellate Body Report, *United States – Import Prohibition of Certain Shrimp and Shrimp Products*, WT/DS58/AB/R (adopted 12 October 1998).

[11] See Appellate Body Report, *United States – Imposition of Countervailing Duties on Certain Hot-Rolled Lead and Bismuth Carbon Steel Products Originating in the United Kingdom*, WT/DS138/AB/R, (adopted 10 May 2000).

[12] See e.g. Steve Charnovitz, 'Opening the WTO', 7–9, for an account of the developments around that time.

[13] See Appellate Body Report, *European Communities – Trade Description of Sardines*, WT/DS231/AB/R (adopted 26 September 2002), para. 165.

[14] See *European Union – Measures on Atlanto-Scandian Herring*, Request for Consultations by Denmark in respect of the Faroe Islands, WT/DS469/1 (adopted 7 November 2013).

[15] See WT/DS320/8, WT/DS321/8, 2 August 2005.

2.1.3 Derestricting documents

In May 2002, the General Council adopted new rules for how quickly the WTO documents could be derestricted,[16] reducing the average time from eight months to forty-five days.[17]

2.2 International commercial arbitration

2.2.1 The ubiquitous ICA

The growing recourse to arbitral mechanisms in international trade law DS raises a question concerning how the participatory aspect and openness to new categories of actors are handled in this form of dispute resolution. A further issue is that of the consequences that the selection of such forms of dispute resolution might bring to the public sphere of trade law and how the originally intrinsically private character of this form of dispute resolution may potentially augment or weaken the positions of specific stakeholders. The trend, as further discussed infra, is not only one of reaching to the experience of investment arbitration as an arguably private-public buffer zone between ICA and trade DS but also one of adopting procedural solutions that were originally developed in the field of commercial arbitration, or even seeking recourse to ICA institutions directly. An analysis of the procedural and institutional framework of ICA, which determines the level of its participatory openness, is thus needed to uncover what concept of global citizenship the ICA might be supporting.

As a private mechanism of DS, which was devised for commercial actors and triggered by their agreement, commercial arbitration is based on the original common intent and on the direct participation of the actual stakeholders. One of the key components of arbitration (i.e., the fact that it is handled privately and with minimal substantial intervention from the domestic courts) has been traditionally accounted as one of the reasons for its success[18] (allowing for the avoidance of domestic litigation, which is deemed to be time-consuming, not sufficiently neutral and lacking specialised expertise).

According to the widely cited data that were offered by Ana Lopez Rodriguez, as many as 95 per cent of contracts in international commerce

[16] See WT/L/452, 16 May 2002.

[17] See www.wto.org/english/forums_e/ngo_e/derestr_explane_e.htm

[18] Artur von Mehren and Eduardo Jiménez de Aréchaga, 'Final Report on Arbitration between States and Foreign Enterprises', *Annuaire de Institut de Droit International*, vol. 63 (1989).

include an arbitration clause.[19] The dominance of ICA and its evolution from a (possible) method to 'the' method of dispute resolution in this field is undisputed. Thus, it might seem to be less of a paradox that a private DS mechanism, which has effectively led to a large extent to the exclusion of a state from the process of administration of justice, is now being chosen by the states themselves to supplement – and in some cases substitute – public international law tracks.

Described by many commentators as 'anational', 'floating' or 'drifting'[20] due to the minimal national court intervention into the substance of the dispute, arbitration, under the New York Convention regime, cannot be characterised as completely delocalised (mostly due to concerns about the recognition and enforcement of awards). The existing limitations on judicial review, as well as the spectacular global popularity of ICA in recent decades, have nevertheless certainly contributed to the emergence of the doctrine (and as has been argued, growing self-consciousness) of arbitration as an autonomous legal order.[21] The existing, far-reaching institutional and procedural independence of arbitration from the constraints of domestic legal systems has been supplemented by notable autonomy in the determination of substantive rules that govern the disputes. The increasing number of instances in which arbitral tribunals based their reasoning on a recourse to public transnational order can be interpreted as indicative of growing confidence in rules and standards that represent a global rather than a domestic perspective.

Moreover, the decisive role of arbitration in the formulation and development of the new *lex mercatoria* rules is well known. Originally defined as usages and customs of *societas mercatorum* (the global community of merchants),[22] it gained significance and began to be expressed and clarified as a body of transnational principles largely due to the activity of arbitral tribunals. The re-emergence of the medieval concept of a set of supranational standards that are observed by the participants of

[19] Ana M. López Rodríguez, *Lex Mercatoria and Harmonization of Contract Law in the EU* (Copenhagen: DJOF Publishing, 2003), 67

[20] William W. Park, 'The Lex Loci Arbitri and International Commercial Arbitration', *The International and Comparative Law Quarterly*, vol. 32 (1983), Filip De Ly, *International Business Law and Lex Mercatoria* (Amsterdam: North-Holland, 1992).

[21] Emmanuel Gaillard, *Legal Theory of International Arbitration* (Leiden: Martinus Nijhoff Publishers, 2010).

[22] Berthold Goldman, 'The Applicable Law: General Principles of Law—The Lex Mercatoria' in J.D.M Lew (ed.), *Contemporary Problems in International Arbitration* (Dordrecht: Martinus Nijhoff Publishers, 1987).

global commercial exchange, who come from diverse legal systems, was announced by Berthold Goldman in the 1950s.[23] The concept of such a 'common core' of various legal systems began to be implemented in practice in arbitral awards in a series of oil cases in the 1950s and 1960s.[24] Further consolidation of this substantive area of transnational rules, including restatement-type codification efforts, since the 1980s (such as the UNIDROIT Principles of International Commercial Contracts and the CENTRAL database), has been possible thanks to the accumulation of an arbitral case law body,[25] which referred to such principles as supplementing, and in some cases replacing, domestic law governing the case.

Another factor that determines the specific function of commercial arbitration is its multiplicity of globally dispersed, rivalling, private fora. This institutional dispersion and the accompanying competition of different procedural orders that affect the processes of forum selection (and shopping) by the parties can be seen as an expression of the needs of the global commercial community, which is not willing to be bound by the constraints of domestic litigation but is interested in retaining a range of dispute resolution options. Indeed, competition ('between the arbitration sites, between the arbitral institutions, between counsel, between arbitrators, and even between the periodicals on international arbitration',[26] as well as 'regulatory competition'[27]) has long been indicated as a defining characteristic of ICA. Operating in this way, commercial arbitration might be perceived as a highly successful yet specific instance of the transnationalisation of law that is achieved largely by private means. In addition, while commercial arbitration does not necessarily lead to the creation of a uniform, harmonised legal system, this approach nevertheless efficiently overcomes the constraints of legal parochialisms.

All of these trends can be perceived as symptomatic of what Gaillard describes as the concept of arbitration as an autonomous transnational

[23] cf. {Goldman, 1964 #88}.

[24] cf. e.g. *Petroleum Development Ltd v. Sheikh of Abu Dhabi* Ad Hoc Award, *International Law Reports*, vol. 18 (1951); *Sapphire International Petroleums* v. *NIOC*, *International Law Reports*, vol. 35 (1967).

[25] cf. Klaus Peter Berger, *The Creeping Codification of the New Lex Mercatoria* (Alpen aan den Rijn: Kluwer Law International, 2010).

[26] Jacques Werner, 'Competition within the Arbitration Industry', *Journal for International Arbitration* (June 1985), 5.

[27] Yves Dezalay and Bryant Garth, 'Merchants of Law as Moral Entrepreneurs: Constructing International Justice from the Competition for Transnational Business Disputes', *Law and Society Review*, vol. 29 (1995), 30.

system, the functions of which transgress the pragmatic yet minimalistic logic of the *a casu ad casum* resolution of isolated commercial disputes. When approached as a procedural and institutional model for DS in other fields, especially those involving public parties and public interest, arbitration appears to be worth careful consideration. In particular, its famously opaque nature should be taken into account.

2.2.2 Confidentiality and privacy in arbitration

The discreet nature of arbitral proceedings, combined with the limited and selective availability of awards, can be at the same time perceived as a major advantage of ICA (having attracted over decades multiple commercial parties, which are arguably not interested in the publicity of litigation), as well as a potential threat in those contexts where the need for transparency is increased. The two procedural aspects (i.e., confidentiality *sensu stricto* (an obligation concerning the non-disclosure of information about arbitration to outsiders) and privacy (excluding third parties from the arbitral proceedings)[28]) of ICA, even if long disputed in legal doctrine, have been nevertheless largely maintained in practice.[29] Moreover, as Kyriaki Noussia remarks, the originally sharp distinction between confidentiality and privacy has become more blurred in recent years.[30]

A number of reasons have been offered to explain this well-established trend, ranging from the parties' will to avoid publicising specific types of allegations (such as bad faith or misrepresentation) with which they are faced, through reluctance to exposing the loss to the general public, to the protection of trade secrets and confidential business information concerns.[31] While the confidentiality of the proceedings as a presumed component of arbitration is sometimes treated as axiomatic,[32] the

[28] cf. Alexis C. Brown, 'Presumption Meets Reality: An Exploration of the Confidentiality Obligation in International Commercial Arbitration', *Am. U. Int'l L. Rev.*, vol. 16 (2001).

[29] Catherine A. Rogers, 'Secrecy and Transparency in Dispute Resolution: Transparency in International Commercial Arbitration', *Kan. L. Rev.*, vol. 54 (2006).

[30] Kyriaki Noussia, *Confidentiality in International Commercial Arbitration: A Comparative Analysis of the Position under English, US, German and French Law* (Berlin: Springer, 2010), 1–2.

[31] Cindy G. Buys, 'The Tensions between Confidentiality and Transparency in International Arbitration', *Am. Rev. Int'l Arb.*, vol. 14 (2003), 123.

[32] cf. Patrick Neill, 'Confidentiality in Arbitration', *Arbitration International*, vol. 12 (1996); Christina Knahr and August Reinisch, 'Transparency versus Confidentiality in International Investment Arbitration – The Biwater Gauff Compromise', *Law & Prac. Int'l Cts. & Tribunals*, vol. 6 (2007).

opinions on this issue among commentators are actually divided.[33] Similarly, the views on the practical significance of the confidentiality of arbitration have ranged from the opinion that it is 'perhaps one of the fundamental, if not the most compelling, of reasons for which the parties choose to arbitrate'[34] to arguments (such as one forwarded by Richard Naimark and Stephanie Keer on the basis of an empirical study on AAA arbitration participants and counsel[35]) that confidentiality is at most a secondary concern for the parties selecting a preferred method of dispute resolution.

2.2.3 Public interest in arbitral case law

Jean-François Poudret and Sébastien Besson remark that the lack of explicit and uniform standards in this regard in domestic laws on arbitration, as well as in the majority of institutional rules of procedure, deepens this state of ambiguity. The controversy as to whether the parties to arbitration have an implied right to confidential arbitral proceedings if they have not explicitly agreed so has been addressed by case law, particularly by a series of decisions made by English courts. An evolution in their approach can be traced from *Dolling Baker v. Merrett*,[36] where the Court of Appeal relied expressly upon the 'essentially private nature of an arbitration, coupled with an implied obligation' of confidentiality, which bound the parties, to *Hassneh Ins. Co. of Israel v. Mew*,[37] where the assertion of the existence of such duty was modified in regard to the use of a previous, reasoned award, which was considered to be a practice consistent with the ordinary course of commerce, as well as procedurally legitimised.

Notably, the issue of transparency has been approached in recent years in investment arbitration, including such developments as the 2006 amendments to the ICSID Rules and the introduction of the 2014 UNCITRAL Rules on Transparency in Treaty-based Investor-State Arbitration, as well as in case law, such as the widely commented upon ICSID case *Biwater Gauff (Tanzania) Ltd.* v. *United Republic of Tanzania*,[38] in which the issue of balancing the values of transparency

[33] cf. Gary Born, *International Arbitration: Cases and Materials* (Aspen: Wolters Kluwer/ Aspen Publishers. 2011), 791–792.

[34] Noussia, *Confidentiality*, 1.

[35] Richard W. Naimark and Stephanie E. Keer, 'What Do Parties Really Want from International Commercial Arbitration?', *Dispute Resolution Journal*, vol. 57 (2003).

[36] *Dolling-Baker* v. *Merrett* [1990] 1 WLR 1205.

[37] *Hassneh Insurance Co. of Israel & Others* v. *Steuart J Mew* [1993] 2 Lloyd's Rep 243.

[38] ICSID Case No. ARB/05/22 *Biwater Gauff (Tanzania) Ltd.* v. *United Republic of Tanzania* – Procedural Order No. 3, 29 September 2006, https://icsid.worldbank.org

with the protection of arbitral procedural integrity was addressed in much detail. However, public interest as a circumstance justifying disclosure in the commercial – and not investment – context was already considered in 1996 by the Australian High Court in *Esso Australia Resources Ltd.* v. *Plowman*,[39] upon the action of the Australian minister for energy and minerals. The court considered that the outcomes of pending arbitrations would affect the prices of energy supplied to the public; thus, the proceedings were an object of genuine public interest. The court stated that it would be 'unduly narrow' not to acknowledge that 'there may be circumstances, in which third parties and the public have a legitimate interest in knowing what has transpired in an arbitration, which would give rise to a "public interest" exception.'

3 Interpretation and possible future developments

This section focuses on the consequences of greater openness in WTO law and international commercial arbitration and the degree to which further openness is possible.

3.1 WTO

This section will analyse the consequences of the movement towards greater openness from different perspectives. First, an analysis of the role of non-state actors in *jus gentium* is set out, with a special focus on the DSM of the WTO. This analysis also includes an evaluation of whether and how further participation is possible for 'global citizens.' Second, an analysis of whether the openness of the WTO system has developed to such a degree that codification is needed, how amendments to the rules could be made to further ensure broader participation, and what the consequences of this action may be is presented. This is thus the thesis or argument of this chapter: more openness in the WTO system may in effect lead to forum shopping and to more frequent use of a more closed system, such as international commercial arbitration.

/ICSID/FrontServlet?requestType=CasesRH&actionVal=showDoc&docId=DC1583_En&caseId=C67.

[39] *Esso Australia Resources Ltd* v. *Plowman* [1996] XXI Y.B.Comm. Arb. 137 (Australian High Court 1995).

3.1.1 Non-state actors in state-to-state relations

Legal positivism and legal formalism in international law focus on the issue of legal subjects.[40] Thus, although running the risk of being overly formalistic and stating the obvious, it is important to build the analysis on a solid foundation; States are the primary subjects in *jus gentium* in the sense that they are legal personalities capable of holding rights, duties and capacities. In addition, IGOs such as the WTO have legal personality. However, IGOs' legal personality is limited in comparison to that of the state. The focus of this chapter is on international courts or arbitral mechanisms, and in this setting, IGOs may be able to provide a venue, procedural rules, etc., but the IGO cannot itself be an actual party to a dispute. Exemplified in the WTO context, the WTO cannot bring a case against a member to ensure compliance with the rules. Compared to the EU system, the EU Commission can for example bring cases against the EU member states to ensure compliance. This action is possible because it is part of a supranational system where the EU Commission has been granted powers to oversee compliance with the rules. While it remains possible to set up a similar function with an independent division at the WTO, it is probably difficult to ensure continued support for the WTO by members when they themselves are being sued by an IGO, as they can withdraw at will. Of course, EU members can also withdraw, but because the European project is so inherently different and more advanced in integration and consists of a more homogeneous group of states, such withdrawal is more unlikely.

Even if one speculates on whether IGOs could be third parties to a WTO dispute, which could easily be provided for by a slight amendment of the rules, the underlying premise of IGOs becomes apparent: IGOs are set up by the states. If an IGO is set up by a subgroup of states that may have an interest in a trade dispute, why should that IGO hold views that differ from the parties to the dispute? However, if one thinks of an IGO with broad participation, it is also difficult to tackle a situation in which e.g. the IMF and UNCTAD hold their own views concerning interpretations of WTO law; an in-fight amongst IGOs is certainly an element to consider before providing for such access to IGOs.

When one starts adding private parties to the equation, the limitations of the international legal system become even more apparent. One may even go so far as to posit that it is inherently contradictory to attach legal capacity to others than states in state-to-state dealings, apart from the

40 See e.g., Jean d'Aspremont, 'Non-State Actors from the Perspective of Legal Positivism' in D'Aspremont, *Participants*, 23.

limited mandate granted to IGOs to perform their duties. Including private parties in the legal system of state-to-state relations poses similar legal and practical challenges as it did when the discussion on trees having standing in the United States began. A frustrated attorney so eloquently highlighted the challenges after Justice Douglas accepted the independent standing of trees in a dissent in *Sierra Club v. Morton*[41]:

> If Justice Douglas has his way –
> O come not that dreadful day –
> We'll be sued by lakes and hills
> Seeking a redress of ills.
> Great mountains peaks of name prestigious
> Will suddenly become litigious.
> Our brooks will babble the courts,
> Seeking damages for torts.
> How can I rest beneath a tree
> If it may soon be suing me?
> Or enjoy the playful porpoise
> While it's seeking habeas corpus?
> Every beast within his paws
> Will clutch an order to show cause.
> The Courts, besieged on every hand,
> Will crowd with suits by chunks of land.
> Ah! But vengeance will be sweet
> Since this must be a two-way street.
> I'll promptly sue my neighbor's tree
> For shedding all its leaves on me.[42]

Comparing this situation to when the tables are turned and the states give mandate to an international court to prosecute private persons for international crimes, the situation is thus much less complicated, and one should not forget that *enforcement* against a private person is much easier than enforcement against a state (i.e., the private person goes to prison).

Below is an account of the different aspects of non-state participation in the WTO DSM.

3.1.2 Standing in the WTO

In the WTO system, it is not required that a member has a 'legal interest' in a case as a prerequisite to bring a case.[43] Instead, the very

41 See *Sierra Club* v. *Morten*, 405 US 727, 19 April 1972 (1972).

42 John Naff, 58 A.B.A. J. 820 (1972) (cited from Stone, *supra* note 7, xi (introduction)).

43 See Report of the Appellate Body, *European Community – Importation, Sale and Distribution of Bananas*, Appellate Body Report, WT/DS27/AB/R (adopted 9 September 1997) [hereinafter *EC – Bananas* Appellate Body Report] para. 132.

structure of the WTO Agreements dating back to the GATT 1947 provides for language that emphasises the bilateral or synallagmatic nature of the obligations when it comes to disputes – where many may agree that in principle, the obligations are owed *erga omnes partes.*[44] Article XXIII:1 of the General Agreement on Tariffs and Trade (GATT) 1994 provides:

> If any Member should consider that any benefit accruing to it directly or indirectly under this Agreement is being nullified or impaired or that the attainment of any objective of the Agreement is being impeded . . .

Interpreting this language and the language of Article 3.7 of the DSU, the Appellate Body in *EC – Bananas* held that:

> [W]e believe that a Member has broad discretion in deciding whether to bring a case against another Member under the DSU. The language of Article XXIII:1 of the GATT 1994 and of Article 3.7 of the DSU suggests, furthermore, that a Member is expected to be largely self-regulating in deciding whether any such action would be 'fruitful'.[45]

On that background, it is clear that in order to grant access to the DSM of the WTO to private parties, the entire notion of the WTO being a set of rules that are owed between states *erga omnes partes* will have to be changed because at present, no obligations are owed to private parties.[46] Moreover, operating with the concept that having a benefit accruing to it nullified or impaired as the prerequisite for a party to bring a dispute makes it even more difficult to imagine any other party than the aggrieved state being a party to a dispute. As an example, the possibility of a member bringing a claim on behalf of another country was subject to some speculation in the beginning of the *EC – Seal Products* case, when rumours held that Canada considered bringing a claim against the European Union on behalf of Greenland. In sum, operating within a system that contains obligations owed between states makes it virtually impossible to imagine granting a private party access, unless the entire founding act of the WTO changes to also include private parties as right holders in the sense that they can bring claims based on obligations owed to them by foreign states.

[44] For further discussion, see Joost Pauwelyn, *Conflict of Norms in Public International Law* (Cambridge: Cambridge University Press, 2003), 52–56.

[45] *EC – Bananas* Appellate Body Report, para. 135.

[46] Or non-nullification or other, as provided for in Article XXIII:1(b) and (c).

What is probably much easier to set up is an investor-state arbitral mechanism based on the WTO obligations, where this new treaty could accept the WTO obligations with some type of 'direct effect,'[47] which could even be part of the WTO system, perhaps as a plurilateral one, which binds only those members that have signed the agreement. This solution may be completely unrealistic from a political point of view but is nevertheless valid to analyse from a legal point of view, as it prompts some observations that would not otherwise be noted in the analysis of broader participation. We would particularly like to draw attention to the observations of Weiler, who thinks of this scenario as inherently unattractive due to a democratic deficit:

> The problem is apparent even in the EC which has far more developed political institutions than the WTO but continues nonetheless to suffer from persistent democracy deficit. How does one justify according higher law status and direct effect to norms, the democratic provenance of which is suspect? Giving individuals 'rights', even rights defensible in courts, does not make them subjects, if they have no appreciable participation in, or control over, the authorship of such rights. The bearer of such rights are no more subjects that [*sic*] the various 'subjects' of the Roman Empire who enjoyed rights granted to them by others. There is really no principle reason to grant them such rights.[48]

Another issue to consider is how to calculate any damages involved, as the WTO does not operate with damages. In the event that a WTO member does not implement a ruling, it has the option to provide compensation in the form of lowering tariffs on an MFN-basis. In case the member does neither, the opposing party may instigate retaliation in the form of suspending concessions (i.e., most commonly, raise the tariffs on a set of chosen set of sensitive products); this is not done on a retroactive basis. It may thus further complicate matters if a country is not only hit by retaliation but must also pay damages to private parties. A country may even have to pay damages retroactively, even in the case of implementation, if the investor-state lawsuit should in any way compensate the winner beyond of course implementation and WTO compliant rules going forward.

[47] For further discussion of 'direct effect' of WTO obligations in line with Van Gend en Loos in EU law, see Petros Mavroidis and Werner Zdeuc, 'Legal Means to Protect Private Parties' Interest in the WTO', *J. Int'L Econ. L.*, vol. 1 (1998), 407.

[48] J.H.H. Weiler, 'The WTO: Already the Promised Land' in Antonio Cassese (ed.), *Realizing Utopia: The Future of International Law* (Oxford: Oxford University Press, 2012), 418, 424.

3.1.3 Non-state parties

Clearly, not all private parties should be able to have standing (whether in investor-state disputes in a hypothetical WTO setting or in the WTO DSM itself), as this scenario would flood the system and lead to a potential breakdown. One idea could be to grant standing to an industry that has a specifically defined interest in a case. This standing could be granted in addition to the standing for the states in the DSM of the WTO or as a safety valve for ensuring the representation of the industry's interest in the event that the government does *not* bring a case.

While industry hardly represents 'global citizens', it is nevertheless an interesting exercise to analyse a non-state party with a direct trade interest in the case. The problems relating to this seemingly uncontroversial group of non-state actors as parties in a trade dispute illustrate exactly how difficult it would be to include 'global citizens' as parties to a dispute.

In the event that both cases could be brought simultaneously, it could be problematic if, for example, the industry disagreed with the strategy pursued by the government in the governmental case and hired their own attorney to argue a parallel case in their preferred manner. Clearly, the WTO DSM would be undermined if two cases concerning the same issue ended with two different results, not to mention the lack of *res judicata* effect (in the common law sense, where the defendant can raise the issue to preclude subsequent litigation) for the member being sued several times by what may or may not be defined as identical parties if the represented industry is also represented in the governmental case.

The possibility of industry taking a different route than the government and being enabled to do so, particularly in the scenario where the industry is permitted to bring cases where the government refrains from doing so, highlights the underlying problems in *jus gentium*. Governments are supposed to represent the people in international affairs, and governments are vulnerable when their people are granted venues to assert rights if those happen to go against the will of the government. In a modern democratic society, this issue may seem irrelevant, but it is nevertheless closely related to issues of national territoriality and the maintaining of such territory, as well as to national security in some instances. Here, the most obvious examples are particular ethnic or local groups seeking independence through litigation against the government that controls the entire territory. One example could be the Kurdish people bringing a case against Turkey or the Basque people bringing a case against France and Spain. These same concerns are present when discussing the issue of bringing cases on behalf of others. While it seems quite harmless for Canada to bring a case against the European Union on behalf of Greenland (because inter alia the Kingdom of Denmark has consented to the Faroe Islands bringing a case on its own against the European Union), it would be massively problematic if a country brought a case against Israel on behalf of Palestine in another venue. However, while these are concerns to be kept in mind, they should not impede the broadening of access to the WTO DSM for non-state parties, where it seems reasonable that the actual directly affected stakeholders should be able to directly bring cases. Industry is often the actual party in WTO cases, so why should industry not be able to influence WTO case law or assert its rights if the relevant government is not performing the task sufficiently or at all?

However, the inclusion is not thought to be limited to industry, despite the fact that this approach would seem to be the least controversial. While CSR discourse operates by holding multinational corporations responsible and including softer values than merely profits, the notion of 'global citizenship' entertains the same ideas. As alluded to *supra*, WTO law and WTO case law have the effect of influencing policies that also relate to the environment, animal welfare, social and climate change issues, etc. Why then should groups that are particularly interested in those issues not have a voice in WTO cases? When considered in the context that panellists and Appellate Body members are *trade* experts, it speaks even further for letting expertise from other areas be provided in cases that involve non-economic values, such as those of the environment, animal welfare, human rights, etc. Having analysed the problems relating to private participation (even when it is one of industry), one may probably step down from discussing *direct* participation as parties and instead settle for enhanced *indirect* participation.

However, what must not be missed is the critical approach to determining whom these NGOs really represent because while it sounds wonderful and inherently good to have friends of the environment caring about green values, and friends of the animals caring about the welfare of animals, they may not represent *all* 'global citizens', and they are not, until we have a world parliament, accountable to the population of the world, for example, by formal elections.[49] However, as suggested by Charnovitz and Dunoff, if one views NGOs as 'policy entrepreneurs'

[49] See e.g., Nehal Bhuta, 'The Role International Actors Other Than States Can Play in the New World Order', in Cassese, *Realizing Utopia*, 61, 71, describing the issue from the sense that no demos exist, and that the NGOs themselves are rarely run democratically.

rather than formal representatives, it becomes easier to accommodate NGOs in the WTO.[50]

3.1.4 Codification and further developments

It can be questioned whether the current practice that actually enables the 'global citizens' to be heard in amicus curiae briefs has gone so far that it actually requires codification, whether this is at all realistic and whatever the potential consequences may be. While this is an interesting discussion, we however find it even more relevant for purposes of this analysis to assess what could be done to ensure that more weight is given to amicus curiae briefs so that the panels and the Appellate Body cannot refrain from addressing them in the proceedings. Clearly, the parties can include the facts or legal arguments from the briefs, but if no parties advance anything from the briefs, they are likely to be there for nothing more than face value. To date and to our knowledge, no amicus curiae brief has been relied on directly by panels or the Appellate Body.

What is interesting to note for purposes of this chapter is the interplay between international commercial arbitration and WTO law at the level of 'global citizenship.' *If* the right to submit amicus curiae briefs were to be codified and were to be given mandatory weight in disputes, which may add to the legitimacy of the DSM of the WTO in particular in light of the situation with *de facto stare decisis*, this change may in turn lead the states to start forum shopping to avoid the influence of 'global citizens,' as understood in the sense of well-meaning NGOs and the like who advance ideas also as policy entrepreneurs or as representatives of relatively narrow interests in state-to-state disputes. This development may in fact lead to more disputes being brought as ICA cases, where 'global citizenship' has a divergent meaning.

3.2 ICA

3.2.1 Elite global citizens

A question thus arises concerning how the characteristics of commercial arbitration, if it is being increasingly commonly used as a pattern for DS in trade cases, can affect the relevant conceptualisation of global citizenship. Furthermore, is it possible that the states seek recourse to private arbitral mechanisms (not only the public or hybrid, but also investment arbitration-type ones) because the lack of embedded transparency

[50] See Charnovitz, 'Opening the WTO', 433, 439.

mechanisms and the accompanying limited publicity are attractive, at least in certain types of cases? The selection of arbitral proceedings would then allow for greater control by the parties over the preferred level of disclosure.

A possible answer to this question is that the concept of global citizenship, which is arguably supported by the commercial arbitration model, while quite well established in legal practice, does not recognise the representation of citizenship as a mass attribute. If global citizenship is to be understood as the existence but also as the actual consciousness of one's rights on a transnational level and the practical ability to make proper use of them, then the ICA-supported model might be prima facie interpreted as professionalised and exclusive rather than inclusive. In this chapter, we further examine whether such representation is indeed completely accurate.

The participation of third parties in arbitral proceedings on their own initiative, be it passive (through observation of the course of proceedings and access to disclosed documents), active (e.g., by entering the proceedings as amici curiae) or through active but externalised communication (such as media coverage and commentary on the pending or concluded proceedings) has been relatively modest to date. The existing procedural options, such as intervention and joinder for third parties with an established legal interest, were formally introduced to arbitral rules of procedure relatively recently, and their execution generally requires consent from the parties already involved, which suggests that the parties retain control over the composition of the actors in arbitration. Unlike investment arbitration, which is recently opening up, there seems to be no grounded practice of allowing for the introduction of amici curiae briefs that are not endorsed by the parties. However, the practice of investment arbitration tribunals in the NAFTA cases *Methanex v. United States*[51] and *UPS v. Canada*[52] accepting amicus curiae briefs on the general basis of Art. 15 of the UNCITRAL Rules might serve as an inspiration for commercial tribunals to use the same set of rules in ad hoc arbitrations or derive their powers from analogous general clauses in

[51] *Methanex Corp.* v. *United States of America*, Final award of the tribunal on jurisdiction and merits [2005], www.state.gov/documents/organization/51052.pdf.

[52] *United Parcel Service of America, Inc. (UPS)* v. *Government of Canada*, Award on the Merits and Separate Statement of Dean Ronald A Cass [2007], http://arbitrationlaw.com /library/united-parcel-service-america-inc-v-government-canada-uncitral-nafta-award-merits-and.

institutional rules, authorising arbitrators to conduct the proceedings in a manner that they deem appropriate.

The actual frequency of use of this competence in those commercial cases where public interest is also involved remains to be seen. In its current shape, commercial arbitration is indeed to a large extent a market- and competition-driven mechanism, which aims to offer pragmatic solutions to specialised and quite sophisticated class of international entrepreneurs. The global success of this mechanism has led to an increased number of practitioners worldwide who are frequently or occasionally involved in arbitral proceedings. Although the elite, truly cosmopolitan group of lawyers (arbitrators and counsel), who are able to navigate the procedural differences and nuances of substantive law application without automatically promoting solutions and preconceptions acquired in their primary legal training,[53] is vigorously expanding, the group remains relatively narrow.[54]

Such specialists are capable of fully embracing the role of 'transaction cost engineers' and can effectively handle the case on different levels, such as well-informed forum selection, conflict of laws considerations, and procedural and substantive aspects. While not limited in their choices by their original, domestic legal background, they can be characterised as global citizens, who are experts in switching among different legal systems and able to assume a transnational perspective. These individuals can also be seen as fulfilling the liberal model of citizenship, which is rooted in the enlightenment social philosophy, and oriented primarily at individualistic and economic, rather than civic and political, goals.[55] Its professional and exclusive rather than mass nature also seems to resonate with the Rawlsian concept of citizenry as a group of free and independent persons, who are endowed with equal basic liberties, with the possibility of collaboration for those who are sufficiently motivated and reasonable to undertake common initiatives.[56] Such a liberal representation of actors in international arbitration as global citizens finds further support in the essentially contractual, voluntary basis of arbitration and its private nature.

[53] Gabrielle Kaufmann-Kohler, 'Arbitral Precedent: Dream, Necessity or Excuse?', *Arbitration International*, vol. 23 (2007), 364.

[54] Joanna Jemielniak, *Legal Interpretation in International Commercial Arbitration* (Ashgate, 2014), 121.

[55] John G.A. Pocock, 'The Ideal of Citizenship since Classical Times' in Ronald Beiner (ed.), *Theorizing Citizenship* (Albany: SUNY Press, 1995), 29.

[56] John Rawls, *Political Liberalism – Expanded Edition* (New York: Columbia University Press, 2013), 48ff.

So understood, the 'global citizenship' model does not per se promote or actively seek wide participatory openness. However, the model does not necessarily oppose such openness, as indicated previously by Rawls.[57] In the context of recourse to arbitration mechanisms, as sought in the area of international trade, the question of whether those mechanisms (including their procedural framework and institutional architecture) potentially allow for expanded participation, even if they do not endorse or encourage it, becomes important. While not utilised in practice during the resolution of commercial controversies, such procedural options could be triggered when deciding cases with a component of public interest.

3.2.2 Participatory opening and the discretionary powers of the tribunals

As discussed above, the general formulation of competences of the arbitral tribunal or the sole arbitrator in relevant rules of procedure, leaving the organisation of proceedings largely to the discretion of arbitrators, can be interpreted as potentially allowing for the admission of passive or active participation of third parties in specific cases, unless the confidentiality duty prevents it. The admissibility of a public interest exception would have to be determined on the grounds of arbitration laws in specific jurisdictions, as well as relevant rules of procedure, where the confidentiality obligation might be expressed. In arbitrations conducted on the basis of those sets of standards where the confidentiality issue has been explicitly addressed (as in the LCIA Rules, Article 30), the scope of the discretionary powers of the tribunal is to be determined accordingly.

This space for the possible opening of arbitral proceedings to legitimised public interest considerations can find theoretical support in legal doctrine, pointing to the fact that in recent years, arbitration has shown many symptoms of developing from a mere *a casu ad casum* pragmatic and expeditious machinery for treating isolated cases to a system that assumes the actual role of administration of justice. Despite the limited publicity of arbitral awards, the available awards are nevertheless numerous and have been successfully accumulated over the past decades into a largely self-sustained body of case law, which as Klaus Peter Berger observes, 'may no longer be characterised as a more or less unsystematic "reservoir of examples".[58] Instead, through referencing, the preference of

[57] *Ibid.*, 205ff. [58] Berger, *Creeping Codification*, 96.

arbitral tribunals for quoting other arbitral awards rather than courts' decisions in similar cases, and the resulting development of legal doctrines through a *de facto stare decisis* (as seen in the history of modern *lex mercatoria* principles), arbitration has evolved into a 'crypto-system of precedents'.[59] In this body of case law, which is consolidated across the tribunals despite the dispersed nature of arbitral institutions, the role of *de facto* precedents has been assumed not to be due to the formal *stare decisis* force but to the persuasive force of adopted reasoning.[60]

3.2.3 Arbitration in international trade DS: possible interpretations

A **Confidentiality** The discussion of reasons for the recourse to arbitral mechanisms and the experience of ICA in international trade disputes can lead to several conclusions. Arbitration, which is traditionally perceived as confidential, can be seen by the stakeholders as a safety valve in conditions that involve too strong a push for transparency in public law proceedings. Arbitration can be sought in those types of cases where the main actors have a preference for confidentiality (e.g., due to possible economic side effects of an early disclosure or a preference for a procedurally more flexible and amicable mechanism without third-party pressure, such as excessive media coverage, which could obscure the course of proceedings). Too strong a push for transparency might in fact drive the parties towards forum shopping options, which would limit its effects. At the same time, the fact that arbitration is an adversarial method of dispute resolution, with its final outcomes based on the rules of the law, augments its legal standing and the objectively verifiable nature of the adopted solutions. This effect might make arbitration a preferred option in comparison to ADR methods and the diplomatic track when the parties intend to avoid being faced with objections about the capricious and power-dictated nature of the adopted outcomes.

B **Procedural efficiency** The opaque nature of arbitration, the usual lack of publicity accompanying the resolution of the dispute, and the highly restricted scope for recourse to the courts concerning the substance of an award can be seen as assets that enhance the efficiency of this method of dispute resolution. Internal appeal options, which are offered by some arbitral institutions as well as procedural openings for the bifurcation of proceedings and the issuance of additional awards, have also been introduced to address concerns about the substantive legal

[59] *Ibid.*, 97. [60] López Rodríguez, *Lex Mercatoria*, 82.

quality of awards without losing the advantages of avoiding domestic litigation.[61] However, these characteristics can also be seen as potentially inconsistent with the public nature of trade disputes, as the procedural standards devised primarily to befit the expectations of commercial stakeholders may not be completely adequate to states' diversified (and not necessarily primarily market-driven) interests.

The very concept of a third party, which is generally seen as an outsider to commercial arbitration proceedings unless a legal interest allowing for intervention or joinder can be ascertained, might require a reformulation for proceedings involving states as contestants. Non-state actors, such as NGOs, who represent a legitimised public interest, can be acknowledged as actual stakeholders in the dispute, and as discussed above, the current architecture of ICA, even if not actively supportive, does not necessarily preclude the possibility of the inclusion of such stakeholders in the course of such proceedings. The experience of investment arbitration in this regard, with increasingly detailed standards being established for specific types of access to proceedings and documents and for forms of active participation (such as amici curiae briefs) by non-state actors, as described in detail *supra*, can provide inspiration in this regard. However, the formalised opening of investment arbitration might also be seen as a drawback for states seeking a potentially more discreet option.

C **Neutrality of the forum** The interest of the states in arbitration as a dispute resolution track might also be explained, beyond the general preference for expanding the range of forum shopping options, by the search for a neutral forum outside of the currently existing regulatory framework for trade disputes. In particular, the involvement of the London Court of International Arbitration (LCIA), a leading international arbitral centre, in *Softwood Lumber* (rather than ad hoc arbitral mechanisms) suggests that the established, globally recognised international standing of arbitral institutions is a significant factor in parties' choices. In this context, it is remarkable that the in-built arbitration mechanism in the WTO DS system, which is based on Article 25 of the DSU, has virtually not been used by the contestants (with only one controversy addressed by means of this mechanism to date). In addition to the multilateral forum, arbitration (in the form of ad hoc panels) has also been chosen as a method of dispute resolution by the parties to a number of PTAs.[62]

61 Jemielniak, *Legal Interpretation*, 85–86.

62 Amelia Porges, 'Dispute Settlement, in Preferential Trade Agreements Policies for Development' (June 2011), 479, http://dx.doi.org/10.1596/9780821386439_CH22.

What is new in the *Softwood Lumber* awards is the recourse by the parties of this long-lasting, multifaceted and multi-fora case to the services of a private institution in a public international law controversy. It will thus be interesting to observe whether the privatisation and outsourcing of such a process of resolution of a public trade dispute was an isolated phenomenon or whether it might only be the first instance of similar actions in non-investment controversies. It might also be interpreted as a very particular variation of an observable tendency, which was characterised by Amelia Porges as a move from diplomatic or political DS towards a formal, 'rule-oriented third-party'[63] settlement (e.g., in SACU, Mercosur and EU PTAs and EPAs). Going even further, if the institutional privatisation of third-party dispute resolution mechanisms for PTA-based controversies turned out to be a lasting tendency, its consequences, from expertise considerations, through a variety of procedural issues (including transparency), to the enforceability of awards, would certainly be very far reaching. When considered in the context of the PTA trend of DS by ad hoc arbitral panels, the selection of a globally renowned, private arbitral institution might actually be seen as a move towards increased transparency and neutrality of the forum.

4 Conclusions

As we have shown in the analysis *supra*, a number of arguments speak for the further opening of the WTO DSM. While it seems problematic to allow for private parties to be direct participants in the disputes, it could be possible to make it mandatory for panels to address the legal arguments and facts set out in amicus curiae submissions. However, we argue that such attempts will lead governments to seek alternative venues to settle their disputes, such as ICA.

The turn towards arbitration in international trade DS, including its institutionalised, commercial variation, may be interpreted as an effect of the natural broadening of available DS options by a mechanism that has already proven to be highly successful in a private context. An answer to the question of how the procedural and institutional setting affects the participatory aspect of public DS and consequently, the conceptualisation of global citizenship is not obvious. When considered in the context of the WTO DS model, arbitration might seem significantly less transparent and open to external actors. The essentially contractual and private nature of arbitration has been decisive for the relevant, pragmatic shaping of

[63] *Ibid.*, 471.

procedural patterns. However, as discussed *supra*, those patterns are not necessarily stiff, and decisions about the inclusion of some participatory openings in the resolution of specific case, even if not practiced in the private context, might not necessarily be precluded in a public context.

The acknowledgement of legitimised public interest, as seen in *Esso v. Plowman*, has already been seen in the resolution of commercial cases; if the institutional and procedural apparatus of commercial arbitration was to be further put into use in trade disputes, the discussion on this issue would be likely to be vigorously revived. Moreover, when compared to the widespread practice of providing for arbitration by ad hoc panels as a method of dispute resolution in PTAs, institutional arbitration conducted under the auspices of a renowned global arbitral centre can be actually seen as a more transparent and more neutral alternative.

When analysed in terms of global citizenship, commercial arbitration appears to be a fulfilment of the liberal, contractual and economically oriented citizenship model rather than the civic and political Aristotelian one. The functioning of ICA has led to the development of a class of cosmopolitan specialists, who are capable of handling the intricacies of dispute resolution without being limited by their native legal background and are able to adopt a transnational perspective in the application of procedural and substantive rules. However, this model is not closed by definition; as a conceptual representation of the procedural participatory approach in arbitration, it encompasses both types of freedoms characterised by Isaiah Berlin: the freedoms 'from' (unnecessary intervention or coercion of the state or third parties), as well as freedoms 'to' (getting involved in collective, public undertakings). The recourse to arbitration in international trade disputes would thus not necessarily result in the abandonment of participatory values but would rather call, when needed, for a change of accents towards a more extensive exercise of freedoms 'to' within the existing regulatory framework than is being practiced in the commercial context. The processes of the autonomisation of ICA and the consolidation of its doctrinal representation as a transnational system of the administration of justice with a well-developed body of case law[64] seem to offer a solid legal, institutional and intellectual basis for such operations.

[64] Gaillard, *Legal Theory*, 5ff.

11

Proportionality analysis and international commercial arbitration – the example of public policy and domestic courts

BENEDIKT PIRKER

1 Introduction

Trade courts such as the World Trade Organization (WTO) Appellate Body or tribunals in international investment arbitration typically face the dilemma of balancing competing interests. Examples are the interest of freedom of trade or the protection of foreign investment and are typically enshrined in norms such as non-discrimination obligations or expropriation clauses, which have to be weighed against public interests pursued by states under their regulatory autonomy. As a solution, trade courts have developed balancing tests that are based upon the treaty norms they are called to interpret and apply. These tests differ, and the question arises as to how these differences can be assessed beyond a merely descriptive comparison.

The purpose of this chapter is twofold. It has been suggested that the main reason for these balancing test differences is the institutional context in which the respective test has been developed. The first purpose is to systematically examine the way in which institutional context is taken into account, thus allowing for the assessment and comparison of balancing tests and thereby formalising the theoretical grounds of this influence.[1]

The author is grateful to Markus Kern and to the participants at the iCourts Conference, in particular Joanna Jemielniak, Laura Nielsen, and Henrik Palmer Olsen, for their helpful comments on earlier versions of this chapter. All online sources were last accessed on 4 June 2015.

[1] These findings are based on an earlier study which also applied the resulting methodology to the legal regimes of WTO law and international investment law. See B. Pirker, *Proportionality Analysis and Models of Judicial Review – A Theoretical and Comparative Study* (Groeningen: Europa Law Publishing, 2013).

Second, this theoretical approach is then applied to the level of international commercial arbitration. Arbitral tribunals and domestic courts both face the question of public policy, the former in the framework of their duty to render an enforceable award, the latter when asked to consider the question of recognition and enforcement of arbitral awards. Both can be considered trade courts for our purposes, as both have to balance the interest of party autonomy against the need to ensure respect for public policy. For reasons of simplicity, this chapter focuses on the less complex institutional context of domestic courts; this does not exclude the usefulness of future study of balancing tests developed by arbitral tribunals. Some brief comparisons are then drawn between the balancing tests developed by international trade courts, the WTO Appellate Body, and tribunals in international investment law. The balancing tests of domestic courts faced with arbitral awards indeed show the influence of institutional context and, somewhat surprisingly, a more transparent approach to balancing than other trade courts. Yet there remains room for improvement, as some courts arguably refrain from balancing and favour categorical tests, despite the fact that balancing would create more transparent reasoning.

In terms of structure, the following section examines the theory behind balancing tests by calling upon the perspective of the literature on proportionality analysis. The third section demonstrates how institutional factors (i.e., the context surrounding the development of balancing tests) can influence the shaping of balancing tests. The fourth section suggests formalising this context in the framework of an exercise to balance institutional factors. The fifth section turns to the example of international commercial arbitration and analyses domestic courts applying the public policy exception in order to answer the question of the recognition and enforcement of arbitral awards. In particular, European Union (EU) law that requires that its version of public policy be respected demonstrates how a more complex context leads to more complex balancing tests. Comparisons between WTO law and international investment law lead to the conclusion that where balancing tests have been developed for international commercial arbitration by domestic courts, they appear more transparent than both the opaque balancing exercises undertaken in WTO law and the highly facts-based analysis in international investment law. Categorical approaches appear less satisfactory. Thus, balancing tests can arguably be welcomed as an improvement.

2 Formalising balancing tests and proportionality analysis

The Principles Theory is one of the main approaches used to explain balancing tests used by courts and tribunals. This section briefly introduces the Principles Theory to demonstrate how it can be used to describe balancing tests within the framework of proportionality analysis. This common framework creates a benchmark that helps to formalise balancing tests through evaluation of their deviations from this common framework.

The Principles Theory was primarily developed by Alexy and suggests that, based on their structure, two categories of norms ought to be distinguished. Rules apply by means of subsumption, while so-called principles apply by means of proportionality analysis.[2] Proportionality analysis is an ideal typus of a balancing test and Alexy highlights four phases of analysis.[3] In order to find a balance between two given principles, an adjudicator needs to first identify the pursuit of a legitimate objective by the measure at issue.[4] Subsequently, the suitability step examines whether at least one principle (i.e., the chosen legitimate objective) is furthered by the measure.[5] The following step, necessity, asks whether an alternative measure exists that is able to further the first principle to the same extent, but has less of a negative impact on the second principle at issue.[6] The last step is strict proportionality or proportionality *stricto sensu*. In this phase, an adjudicator freely weighs the competing principles based on the circumstances of the case to decide which one should prevail.

The main benefit of proportionality analysis as a balancing test is that it gives adjudicators the possibility of setting out the reasons for their decision in greater detail. Alexy describes the exercise of weighing reasons under proportionality analysis without the constraints imposed by

[2] See R. Alexy, "On Balancing and Subsumption. A Structural Comparison", *Ratio Juris*, vol. 16 (2003), 433. See also on the relationship between norm structure and norm text F. Schauer, "Balancing, Subsumption and the Constraining Role of Legal Text", *Law & Ethics of Human Rights*, vol. 4 (2010), 35.

[3] R. Alexy, *Theorie der Grundrechte* (Frankfurt am Main: Suhrkamp, 1986), 100ff.

[4] See closer M. Kumm, "Political Liberalism and the Structure of Rights: On the Place and Limits of the Proportionality Requirement" in G Pavlakos (ed.), *Law, Rights and Discourse: The Legal Philosophy of Robert Alexy* (Oxford: Hart, 2007), 142.

[5] See closer R. Alexy, "Constitutional Rights, Balancing, and Rationality", *Ratio Juris* 131, vol. 16 (2003), 135.

[6] For more on the burden of proof in such cases, see A. Barak, *Proportionality – Constitutional Rights and Their Limitations* (Cambridge: Cambridge University Press, 2012), 449.

subsumption as an "argument form of rational legal discourse".[7] Apart from the freedom that proportionality analysis gives adjudicators, it also renders decisions easier to understand for both the concerned parties and observers more generally.[8] A distinction can thus be drawn between the categorical tests that apply the subsumption model and the quantitative approach of weighing competing values proposed by proportionality analysis.

For balancing tests other than proportionality analysis, one of the central tenets of the Principles Theory is the idea that certain norms (i.e., principles) are optimization commands, which require that when there is a conflict of principles, every principle be realised to the greatest extent possible.[9] The only tool that can deliver this full optimization is full-scale proportionality analysis; the consequence of this perspective is that the Principles Theory suggests that in difficult cases, all other legal tests used by courts and tribunals are nothing but precursors that will ultimately collapse into proportionality analysis. Alexy uses the example of suitability and necessity as legal tests derived from proportionality *stricto sensu* to demonstrate this assertion.[10]

In practice, courts and tribunals do not rely on a uniform balancing test; rather, they have developed particular tests. Examples of such truncated balancing tests are suitability, necessity, a mere control of plausibility, a prohibition of gross disproportionality or the guarantee of a minimal position.[11] Thus the number of prongs of such a balancing test may vary, as can the strictness of each prong and the strictness of the test as a whole. To simply equate truncated tests with incomplete versions of proportionality analysis is somewhat unsatisfactory.[12] There may be good reasons for courts and tribunals to adapt balancing tests to their context. Some scholars have suggested that courts and tribunals rely on such truncated tests due to reasonable contextual arguments and not out

[7] R. Alexy, "The Construction of Constitutional Rights", *Law & Ethics of Human Rights*, vol. 4 (2010), 19, 26ff.

[8] See also on this advantage of balancing tests such as proportionality analysis, A. Barak, "Proportionality and Principled Balancing", *Law & Ethics of Human Rights*, vol. 4 (2010), 3, 14–15; Alexy, "The Construction of Constitutional Rights", 26ff.

[9] R. Alexy, "On the Structure of Legal Principles", *Ratio Juris*, vol. 13 (2000), 294, 297–298.

[10] Alexy, *Theorie der Grundrechte*, 101–103.

[11] See R. Poscher, "Einsichten, Irrtümer und Selbstmissverständnis der Prinzipientheorie" in J.-R. Sieckmann (ed.) *Die Prinzipientheorie der Grundrechte – Studien zur Grundrechtstheorie Robert Alexys* (Baden-Baden: Nomos, 2007), 74, or B. Pieroth and B. Schlink, *Grundrechte* (Heidelberg: C.F. Müller, 2005), 69.

[12] For greater detail on the topic, see Pirker, *Proportionality Analysis*, 44.

of error.[13] Although the Principles Theory includes the concept of "formal" principles to account for the influence of the institutional context, closer inspection highlights several flaws in the concept.[14]

In sum, balancing tests may be examined and compared against the benchmark of proportionality analysis that is suggested by the Principles Theory. Proportionality analysis and balancing tests that resemble it offer the advantage of more transparent decision-making, as compared to the categorical legal tests applied by subsumption. Despite this advantage, proportionality analysis should not be seen as an end to be achieved but rather as a benchmark, and there may be good reasons for courts and tribunals to deviate from this benchmark by using other balancing tests that have been adapted to their institutional context.

3 The influence of institutional context

Based on the observation that courts and tribunals develop different forms of balancing tests, this section examines the possible reasons for such differences. While it may be possible that differences are at least partially shaped by the historical legal background of a particular legal regime,[15] there are arguably more substantive contextual reasons for the shaping of a particular balancing test, too.

In that regard, a central question is the legitimacy of choosing a particular balancing test. The ability of courts and tribunals to exercise their judicial review functions may be specified in advance, for example within an international treaty. Nonetheless, a minimum level of legitimation while exercising this function appears indispensable for the proper long-term functioning of a legal regime.[16] Consequently, it is necessary to question the basis on which courts and tribunals can exercise their function of judicial review.[17]

[13] J.P. Trachtman, "Trade and ... Problems, Cost-Benefit Analysis and Subsidiarity", *European Journal of International Law*, vol. 9 (1998), 32, 39, argues that proportionality analysis is nothing but a heuristic to replace cost-benefit-analysis, for which courts and tribunals typically do not have the resources.

[14] See Section 4.

[15] For more on this argument, see J. Bomhoff, "Genealogies of Balancing as Discourse", *Law & Ethics of Human Rights*, vol. 4 (2010), 109, 112–113.

[16] For greater detail, see Pirker, *Proportionality Analysis*, 73ff.

[17] As J. Rivers, "Proportionality, Discretion and the Second Law of Balancing" in G Pavlakos (ed.), *Law, Rights and Discourse: The Legal Philosophy of Robert Alexy* (Oxford: Hart, 2007), 169, shows, the Principles Theory has also moved from a "substantial theory of

This is of particular importance in cases of conflicting values (i.e., the "principles" specified within the Principles Theory), for example when a legislator adopts a law that codifies a particular solution to this value clash. In such cases, the balancing test adopted by a court can lead to judicial "second-guessing" of the compromise that became enshrined in the law in question. Full-scale proportionality analysis aims to optimise both sets of values and therefore enables a court to weigh the competing values freely, thereby questioning the compromise between the values enshrined in the law. If, on the other hand, a balancing test such as a necessity test is embraced, the court instead asks a more limited question. Rather than proceeding to optimisation itself, the court merely asks whether there exist less restrictive alternatives, i.e., whether the law is the best measure with which to achieve a certain positive effect on the first set of values while simultaneously producing the least detrimental impact to the second set of values.[18] Nonetheless, this can also call into question the solution found by the legislator that was then formulated into law.

The basis for courts and tribunals to exercise their review powers thus ought to provide reasons for courts and tribunals to be able to choose the balancing tests that they use. A theory assessing the justification of judicial review can thus provide the framework to assess and systematise these reasons. There are indeed theoretical proposals that supply reasons for this purpose.

As a matter of principle, some scholars suggest that judicial review using balancing tests should not be seen as "second guessing" legislative choices, but rather as furthering a "culture of justification".[19] In contrast, the classic argument against judicial review constitutes the countermajoritarian objection. In a well-functioning democracy with functioning institutions and members of society who are committed to the ideas of democracy, reasonable debate and disagreement on rights in which they have a true interest, there seems to be no justification for a court to overthrow the decisions that are made by a majority.[20] However, in practice democratic systems do not correspond to this ideal. The protection of certain specific values against purely majority-based

legal decision-making" towards a "theory of constitutional review", as a reaction to this very line of questioning.

[18] *Ibid.*, 172.

[19] For more on this notion, see M. Cohen-Eliya and I. Porat, "Proportionality and the Culture of Justification", *American Journal of Comparative Law*, vol. 59 (2011), 463.

[20] J. Waldron, "The Core of the Case against Judicial Review", *Yale Law Journal*, vol. 115 (2005), 1347, 1360.

decision-making proves thus indispensable. A number of theories have thus been developed to overcome the countermajoritarian objection, and to flesh out the need to protect certain values and the reasons why this protection should take the form of judicial review.[21] Ely's procedural democracy doctrine can provide further grounding on this point, and is one of the most promising approaches.[22]

Ely suggests that the reasonableness of democratic (i.e., majority-based) decision-making should be verified by looking primarily at the functioning of the democratic process. Judicial review ought to intervene only where there are major defects such that quality and legitimacy are corrupted. In the US context, there are two signals that suggest that such malfunctioning has occurred: (1) serious neglect of either electoral rights or the freedom of expression as central elements of the democratic process, and (2) outcomes which systematically treat the interests of specific groups less favourably, typically because the process is defective due to prejudice by a given legislator who in turn neglects the interests of these groups.[23]

Ely's thesis is focused on US constitutional law and the protection of fundamental rights, but nonetheless provides valuable lessons that can be transposed to the realm of international courts and tribunals.[24]

Judicial review is justified when it is based on certain important values or neglect of certain important values, the latter resulting from systematically biased results that were created by the democratic process. Courts

[21] See e.g., M. Kumm, "The Idea of Socratic Contestation and the Right to Justification: The Point of Rights-Based Proportionality Review", *Law & Ethics of Human Rights*, vol. 4 (2010), 140, 171, who suggests that the right to contest a legislator's choices before a court has to be understood as "Socratic contestation", and as inextricably linked to the individual right to vote.

[22] There are, of course, other possible approaches. As two examples, the focus can be put on the institutional advantages judicial review can provide, (see e.g., A. Walen, "Judicial Review in Review. A Four-Part Defense of Legal Constitutionalism", *International Journal of Constitutional Law*, vol. 7 (2009), 329) or on the possibility of legitimising judicial review as a process of deliberative dialogue between courts and legislators (see e.g., P.W. Hogg and A.A. Bushell, "The Charter Dialogue between Courts and Legislatures (Or Perhaps the Charter of Rights Isn't Such a Bad Thing After All)", *Osgoode Hall Law Journal*, vol. 35 (1997), 75.

[23] J.H. Ely, *Democracy and Distrust – A Theory of Judicial Review* (Cambridge: Harvard University Press, 1980), 103.

[24] For a more comprehensive discussion, see B. Pirker, "Democracy and Distrust in International Law – The Procedural Democracy Doctrine and the Standard of Review Used by International Courts and Tribunals" in L. Gruszczynski and W. Werner (eds.), *Deference in International Courts and Tribunals – Standard of Review and Margin of Appreciation* (Oxford: Oxford University Press, 2014), *passim*.

and tribunals thus ought to use these insights to reflect about their review powers and determine the intrusiveness of their review (i.e., the balancing test they use) accordingly. They should "balance balancing".[25] They ought to reflect what precise values they are called to protect, and the extent to which they are called to protect them by the context in which they adjudicate, which is typically the broader context of the international treaty they are called to adjudicate upon. While international courts and tribunals may not be called upon to ensure the functioning of a domestic process, they are still in charge of judging severe violations of the values they are called to uphold. The second prong of Ely's theory (i.e., violations of fundamental values that prove bias in the procedure) is thus the most relevant one. Adjudicators ought to reflect what balancing test is most helpful to weed out severe violations of the central values they have identified first.

At this stage, contextual, institutional arguments enter the reasoning process. These arguments should be weighed by adjudicators to determine which values are most central to a particular legal regime and thus require the greatest protection with judicial review. Typically, these central values could be deduced from a mere analysis of the legal texts to be interpreted. However, the often ambiguous wording of the relevant treaty provisions renders this task highly difficult, as do debates in the doctrine and practice on what rationale such treaty regimes truly pursue. There is, consequently, a need to go beyond such black letter analysis.[26] Arguably, the broader context includes elements such as history, political economy or institutional features of treaty regimes, all of which can sharpen the analysis that is undertaken for the development of a balancing test. Using the broader context also helps adjudicators to go beyond the only marginally instructive calls for the use of appropriate deference which are typical of much of the literature on balancing tests.[27]

International courts and tribunals thus ought to devise balancing tests based on the institutional context, as a generalisation of Ely's procedural democracy doctrine. Ideally, they should reflect upon the central values they are called to protect as the justification of their judicial review, and

[25] See also Pirker, *Proportionality Analysis*, 70–71.

[26] As but one example, for more on the blurry notion of the public interest in international investment law and arbitration, see A. Kulick, *Global Public Interest in International Investment Law* (Cambridge: Cambridge University Press, 2012).

[27] See e.g., G. Sartor, "A Sufficientist Approach to Reasonableness in Legal Decision-Making and Judicial Review" in G Bongiovanni, G Sartor and C Valentini (eds.), *Reasonableness and Law* (Dordrecht: Springer, 2009), 55; or Barak, *Proportionality*, 417.

then adapt a balancing test so as to evaluate how they can best counter severe violations of these values in their specific institutional context, while avoiding second guessing (e.g., second guessing legislative policy-choices where it is not required).

4 Formalising the development of balancing tests

With this conceptual setup in mind, it becomes possible to move beyond mere description and instead use a critical-comparative approach to assess the different balancing tests chosen by courts and tribunals. This enables the assessment of the extent to which the weighing of the arguments taken from the context has taken place and whether it has led to a convincing solution.[28]

As mentioned, the Principles Theory introduced the notion of formal principles to formalise the development of balancing tests and the issue of due deference by courts and tribunals.[29] The principled idea behind judicial review is argumentative representation, which is a connection between a parliament and the people "by argument".[30] Formal principles become part of the balancing process of proportionality analysis, in particular the stage of proportionality *stricto sensu*, and ought to ensure appropriate deference to the legislator's choices.[31] However, apart from a number of other criticisms,[32] it remains unclear why a competence element should become part of the substantive weighing exercise of competing principles.[33] The introduction of the concept of formal principles thus cannot provide a convincing answer.

28 For an early attempt, see Trachtman, *passim*.

29 See R. Alexy, *A Theory of Constitutional Rights (translated by* Julian Rivers*)* (New York: Oxford University Press, 2002), 82; M. Borowski, "The Structure of Formal Principles – Robert Alexy's 'Law of Combination'" in M Borowski (ed.), *On the Nature of Legal Principles* (Stuttgart: Franz Steiner Verlag, 2010). The underlying idea had already been present in Dworkin's concept of legislative supremacy, see R. Dworkin, *Taking Rights Seriously* (Cambridge: Harvard University Press, 1978), 37–38.

30 R. Alexy, "Balancing, Constitutional Review and Representation", *International Journal of Constitutional Law*, vol. 3 (2005), 572, 579.

31 M. Borowski, *Grundrechte als Prinzipien* (Baden-Baden: Nomos, 2007), 128.

32 See e.g., M. Jestaedt, "Die Abwägungslehre – ihre Stärken und ihre Schwächen" in O Depenheuer et al. (eds.), *Staat im Wort: Festschrift für Josef Isensee* (Heidelberg: C.F. Müller, 2007), 274; M. Klatt and J. Schmidt, *Spielräume im Öffentlichen Recht – Zur Abwägungslehre der Prinzipientheorie* (Tübingen: Mohr Siebeck, 2010), 62.

33 S.P. Hwang, "Verfassungsgerichtliche Abwägung: Gefährdung der gesetzgeberischen Spielräume? Zugleich eine Kritik der Alexyschen formellen Prinzipien", *Archiv des öffentlichen Rechts* (2008), 606, 621.

Instead, it seems more appropriate to formalise the influence of contextual factors at an independent level without jeopardising the substance of the balancing process undertaken by courts and tribunals.[34] Formal principles influence the substance and outcome of a balancing test. Instead, courts and tribunals ought to strive for the use of an appropriate balancing test first, and only afterwards apply this test to the case in question, balancing only the substantive values at issue. Therefore, instead of factoring contextual elements into the main balancing test, these elements should be examined independently; the result of weighing them ought to serve international courts and tribunals to devise their balancing test at the outset before using the test they have found.

This approach is useful not only for courts and tribunals themselves, but also for comparative studies of balancing tests, as is shown subsequently. First, the influence of EU law on the courts of EU member states provides a useful illustration of the ways in which additional contextual values can be factored into the balancing tests used by courts. Second, the examination of balancing tests by domestic courts under the public policy exception in international commercial arbitration can serve as a comparative assessment with other legal regimes of international economic law, here WTO law and international investment law.

5 The example of international commercial arbitration

The setting chosen to examine the development of balancing tests in international commercial arbitration is that of the public policy exception as interpreted by domestic courts, which serves as a justification for the refusal of recognition and enforcement of an arbitral award. A central provision is Article V(2)b of the 1958 UN Convention on the Recognition and Enforcement of Foreign Arbitral Awards, better known as the New York Convention (hereafter NYC).[35] The focus lies on this provision mainly for the sake of simplicity, but also to be able to appropriately compare the balancing tests developed by diverse domestic courts from different countries.[36] Future studies may shed light on

[34] Pirker, *Proportionality Analysis*, 66. [35] 330 U.N.T.S. 38 (1959).

[36] Article V of New York Convention is not the only pertinent provision. There is also Article 34(2) of the UNCITRAL Model Law on International and Commercial Arbitration (UNCITRAL Model Law on International Commercial Arbitration, 21 June 1995, adopted by the UN Commission on International Trade Law; texts of the original 1985 version, and the version with amendments made in 2006, both available at www.uncitral.org/uncitral/en/uncitral_texts/arbitration/1985Model_arbitration.html).

balancing tests in other contexts, notably the role played by public policy in the interpretation and development of balancing tests by arbitral tribunals. The focus of this chapter, however, deliberately does not extend to arbitral tribunals themselves, as there is much debate about what notion of public policy they have to take into account and what the extent of this duty to take into account public policy is.

The public policy clause, as interpreted by domestic courts, provides the setting to examine the balance between competing interests of a public nature. On the one side, there is an interest in having party autonomy to choose a means of dispute settlement outside of the public courts; the extent to which such autonomy is granted can certainly be framed as a public choice. On the other side, there is the public interest of upholding a minimum guarantee of procedural safeguards (e.g., fairness, due process) in the particular legal order of the state where recognition and enforcement are sought. The focus thus lies on the judicial review of arbitral awards by domestic courts that have to grapple with these competing public values. This setting offers a rich playground for examining the balancing tests developed by these courts.

In this case study, when examining international commercial arbitration, the first step is to provide general, non-normative elements of context (Subsection 5.1). These elements will subsequently become relevant background knowledge to assess what values are specifically protected in a norm like Article V(2)b NYC as part of international commercial arbitration and provide justification for the exercise of judicial review, as exercised by domestic courts (Subsection 5.2). A third subsection examines the actual balancing tests developed by the courts (Subsection 5.3). The fourth subsection critically assesses the features of these tests, using the institutional background as a benchmark (Subsection 5.4). The example of the influence on balancing tests that EU law has developed in the European context demonstrates at this point the usefulness of focusing on the broader context to explain balancing tests. Finally, the balancing tests developed by domestic courts in international commercial arbitration are compared to those of other legal regimes (Subsection 5.5).

See closer on Article 34(2) and selected problems of domestic implementation L. Hsu, "Public Policy Considerations in International Arbitration: Costs and Other Issues – A View from Singapore", *Journal of International Arbitration*, vol. 26 (2009), 101, 116ff.

5.1 *Contextual elements of judicial review in international commercial arbitration*

International commercial arbitration, in particular international treaty-making in this area, developed alongside efforts to support international economic cooperation of the twentieth century.[37] Arbitration offers a number of advantages to commercial actors over litigation in public courts because it allows for party autonomy. Advantages such as secrecy, speed of proceedings and costs can be better controlled by the parties. At the same time, a problem may arise if party autonomy leads to a violation of fundamental rules such as due process. For example, this may lead the state where the award was handed down to set aside the award or make another state decide not to recognise and enforce such an award.

The NYC has been celebrated as "by far the most significant contemporary legislative instrument relating to international commercial arbitration",[38] and has achieved global significance due to the number of contracting parties.[39] Its two central objectives are encouraging the recognition and enforcement of commercial arbitration agreements in international contracts and unifying the standards by which such agreements are observed and by which arbitral awards are enforced.[40] The system of the convention requires that domestic courts of party states defer to valid arbitration agreements and recognise arbitral awards,[41] thereby establishing a "pro-arbitration legal regime".[42]

Based on the NYC and other instruments, international commercial arbitration has become highly popular for the resolution of transnational business disputes. This success can, to some extent, be explained by the certainty the NYC provides that an award can be recognised and enforced in another state, as there exists no other instrument of nearly universal recognition and enforcement, and none seems foreseeable in the near future.[43]

[37] Early efforts include the 1923 Geneva Protocol on Arbitration Clauses, 27 L.N.T.S. 157 (1924), and the 1927 Geneva Convention on the Execution of Foreign Arbitral Awards, 92 L.N.T.S. 301 (1929); both treaties have been replaced between the contracting parties to the NYC by the NYC (see Article VII(2) NYC).

[38] G. Born, *International Commercial Arbitration* (Austin: Wolters Kluwer, 2009), 92.

[39] As of June 2015, the NYC counts 155 countries as parties (see www.uncitral.org/uncitral/en/uncitral_texts/arbitration/NYConvention_status.html).

[40] United States Court of Appeal, *Waterside Ocean Navigation Co.* v. *International Navigation Ltd.* 737 F 2d 150 (2d Cir 1984) at 152.

[41] See in particular, Articles II and III NYC, respectively.

[42] Born, *Commercial Arbitration*, 204.

[43] H. Kronke, "The New York Convention Fifty Years on: Overview and Assessment" in H. Kronke et al. (eds.), *Recognition and Enforcement of Foreign Arbitral Awards: A Global*

At the same time, the influence of other legal regimes has grown in importance and can lead to tensions.[44] The difficulties of reconciling the demands of the legal regimes of international commercial arbitration with EU law provide an insightful example. Cases like *West Tankers* show that courts do not always find it easy to understand and account for the interests at stake in their decision. In *West Tankers*, the Court of Justice of the European Union (CJEU) had to interpret the Brussels I Regulation[45] on the recognition and enforcement of court judgments and its exception for arbitration agreements and awards. The CJEU held that while actions in national courts that aimed to enforce arbitration agreements and awards fell outside of the scope of the regulation, the exception did not cover cases where the jurisdiction of a court was challenged on the basis of a prior arbitral agreement as long as the case was otherwise subject to the regulation. The prohibition against member state courts using anti-suit injunctions aiming at judicial proceedings in other member states thus applied to the latter cases.[46] The decision demonstrates that good reasons in EU law supported the solution found by the CJEU: contestation of jurisdiction based on an agreement to arbitrate should not render the regulation inapplicable to an action for contract damages. However, the prohibition of anti-suit injunctions eliminated a very powerful weapon in international arbitration, and the decision therefore led to an outcry from the commercial arbitration community.[47]

The values to be protected by international commercial arbitration have thus become somewhat more complex in the European context, as the subsequent section will explore in greater detail.

5.2 *The values to be protected in international commercial arbitration*

To return to Ely's thesis, it must now be asked what values are protected in a particular legal regime like international commercial arbitration.

Commentary on the New York Convention (Austin: Kluwer Law International, 2010), 3, pointing towards the only exception of the 1968 Brussels Convention on Jurisdiction and Recognition and Enforcement, 1262 U.N.T.S. 153 (1969), which has been replaced by Regulation 44/2001, OJ L 12 [2001], 1ff., in the EU context (Brussels I Regulation).

[44] On the growing importance of actors who are active in other areas of international law such as the European Court of Human Rights, see e.g., S. Fietta and J. Upcher, "Public International Law, Investment Treaties and Commercial Arbitration: An Emerging System of Complementarity?", *Arbitration International*, vol. 29 (2013), 187.

[45] See footnote 44. [46] Case C-185/07 *West Tankers* EU:C:2009:69 (CJEU), para. 24.

[47] G. Bermann, "Navigating EU Law and the Law of International Arbitration", *Arbitration International*, vol. 28 (2012), 397, 403.

The answer to this question sets out how judicial review should be shaped in this regime. Outcomes that severely violate these values would thus hint that the underlying process has malfunctioned, thereby justifying more intrusive judicial review such as the development of a particularly intrusive balancing test.

5.2.1 Public policy and international arbitral tribunals

One central value that is protected in international commercial arbitration and in judicial review of arbitral awards under the terms of the NYC is the parties' autonomy, which also includes their right to finality of an arbitral award.[48] However, this principle is not an absolute value and can conflict with competing values. An award may be granted recognition comparable to a court judgment, but for this purpose the procedure of recognition must provide for certain "safety valves" that ensure sufficient respect for guarantees such as fairness and due process.[49] One such safety valve is the public policy exception. Based on this type of provision, courts can deny an award rendered in another state that is party to the NYC recognition and enforcement. For the example examined in this chapter, Article V(2)b[50] of the New York Convention reads:

> Recognition and enforcement of an arbitral award may also be refused if the competent authority in the country where recognition and enforcement is sought finds that: [...]
>
> The recognition or enforcement of the award would be contrary to the public policy of that country.

Article V(2)b NYC thus introduces public policy as a conflicting interest. But public policy is not the only safety valve between the award and the domestic legal order where enforcement is sought. Arbitral tribunals themselves are also required to take public policy into account. However, controversy surrounds the scope and content of this duty.

Arbitral tribunals are in a quite special situation compared to other "trade courts", as they are both international, yet to some extent private

[48] For more on this topic, see the example of Singaporean legislation Hsu, "Public Policy", 103.

[49] Kronke, "New York Convention", 8.

[50] Article V NYC also deals with the problem of the arbitrability of issues as a potential ground to refuse recognition and enforcement, but is not dealt with here for reasons of space; for a closer analysis of that topic, see D. Otto and O. Elwan, "Article V(2)" in H. Kronke and others (eds.), *Recognition and Enforcement of Foreign Arbitral Awards: A Global Commentary on the New York Convention* (Austin: Kluwer Law International, 2010), 348ff.

tribunals. It is well-accepted that, as part of their somewhat hybrid nature, arbitrators must take into account not only the private interests of parties, but also the relevant public interests. This is often underlined with the example of norms of competition law, which uphold the interest of maintaining competition as a necessary institution on a specific market.[51]

Among the various constraints under which arbitrators must act, one constraint that is closely linked to the problem of the public policy exception is the duty to issue an enforceable award.[52] While there may be some disagreement as to the exact source of the various obligations of arbitrators, consensus exists that the ultimate goal of arbitration is to produce an award that is enforceable at law.[53] As part of this duty, arbitrators should consider issues of public policy while rendering their award. However, the scope and content of this notion of public policy remains contested. To put it another way, the international arbitrator has no obvious *lex fori* that would also determine which legal order's public policy is to be applied.[54]

The question arises whether an arbitrator should not only apply the mandatory rules of the place of arbitration as part of the *lex arbitri*, but also the laws of possible places of enforcement. Generally, when claims based on public law fall within the arbitration agreement, arbitrators are obliged to resolve them as part of their mandate.[55] However, it cannot be expected that an arbitrator would foresee all possible places of enforcement; in all likelihood, the arbitrator would also be confronted with conflicting rules.[56]

Not even the conceptualisation of the arbitrator's duties provides a clear answer to this question. Three versions are typically distinguished. A contractual perspective sees the arbitrator's mandate as purely determined by the contract between the private parties.[57] A non-contractual account describes the arbitrator as serving in a quasi-legal capacity, with

[51] P. Tercier, "Le droit de l'arbitrage et le droit de la concurrence", *ASA Bulletin*, vol. 4 (2000), 688.

[52] See e.g., Article 32.2 of the Arbitration Rules of the London Court of International Arbitration. See with further references Born, *Commercial Arbitration*, 1621.

[53] M. Platte, "An Arbitrator's Duty to Render Enforceable Awards", *Journal of International Arbitration*, vol. 20 (2003), 307, 308.

[54] P. Lalive, "L'ordre public transnational et l'arbitre international" in G. Venturini and S. Bariatti (eds.), *Liber Fausto Pocar – New Instruments of Private International Law* (Milan: Giuffrè, 2009), 601.

[55] Born, *Commercial Arbitration*, 2181. [56] Platte, "Arbitrator's Duty", 312.

[57] This perspective, however, has hardly ever been accepted in its extreme form, Born, *Commercial Arbitration*, 2179.

a more prominent role given to the rules of the national legal order circumscribing commercial arbitration. A middle-ground view distinguishes between the contractual part of an arbitrator's relationship with their clients and the other parts where national law imposes its rules.[58] A duty to take into account the public policy of a potential place of enforcement as part of the duty to render an enforceable award cannot easily be explained under either of these perspectives. Neither is there a contractual mandate for this duty, nor does it seem plausible to derive this duty from non-contractual obligations, since the arbitration is not taking place in the country of enforcement.[59] Nonetheless, consideration of the mandatory rules of the place of enforcement could be based on the overall goal of effectiveness of the international arbitration system.[60]

Future studies of balancing tests developed by arbitral tribunals would thus need to address this complexity. For the purpose of this chapter, it suffices to address the notion of public policy in more detail.

5.2.2 The complex notion of public policy

The very concept of public policy has caused controversy since very early on[61] and has been interpreted in a variety of manners, as shown below. Nonetheless, the general tendency is to interpret public policy rather narrowly and to emphasise, by means of teleological interpretation, the main purpose of treaties like the New York Convention (i.e., to avoid obstacles to the enforcement of arbitral awards).[62] Between the competing interests of the finality of an award and the need to deny enforcement to awards in conflict with public policy, some scholars prefer the former to the latter, because arbitration is based upon the informed consent of the parties.[63] In adjudicative practice this tendency to restrict the interpretation of public policy can also be found.[64]

58 G.J. Horvath, "The Duty of the Tribunal to Render an Enforceable Award", *Journal of International Arbitration*, vol. 18 (2001), 135, 137–138.

59 *Ibid.*, 147–148. 60 *Ibid.*, 148.

61 See also the famous quote by Justice Burrough in the 1824 English case *Richardson* v. *Mellish*, Bingham's Reports 2 (1824), 229, on public policy as a "very unruly horse" that is "never argued at all but when other points fail".

62 Otto and Elwan, "Article V(2)", 367. Some authors even speak of a danger of outright "protectionism" by domestic courts in this regard, A. Changaroth, "International Arbitration – A Consensus on Public Policy Defences?", *Asian International Arbitration Journal*, vol. 4 (2008), 143, 163.

63 Kronke, "New York Convention", 9.

64 See the example of Russian courts who have moved from an initial, rather open, stance on public policy towards more frequent recognition of foreign arbitral awards: I. Nikiforov, "Interpretation of Article V of the New York Convention by Russian Courts – Due

In terms of the content of the notion of public policy, further complexity arises. On the one hand, there is some question as to whether, under Article V(2)b NYC, "domestic" or "international" public policy is to be protected. Domestic public policy would give more leeway to domestic courts, while international public policy refers to a narrower notion of internationally recognised fundamental legal principles. This "ordre public international" would thus encompass only the essential principles that govern the administration of justice in a state and that are essential to the moral, political or economic order of that state.[65] Generally, a majority of voices among courts[66] and in the literature[67] prefer the international, narrower concept of public policy.[68]

The text of Article V(2)b NYC speaks of the public policy "of that country", and this notion is typically understood to refer to important norms of national public policy, which may vary from country to country.[69] However, national recognition decisions have also attempted to interpret national public policies so that they are consistent with the NYC's objectives and the public policies of other contracting states, which has led to the recognition and application of "international public policy".[70] Nonetheless, such "international public policy" remains linked to the law of the state where enforcement is sought. Sometimes legislation has been adopted for this purpose.[71] As far as the interpretation of Article V(2)b NYC is concerned, however, commentators are sceptical whether or not the wording offers leeway for anything beyond the application of

Process, Arbitrability, and Public Policy Grounds for Non-Enforcement", *Journal of International Arbitration*, vol. 25 (2008), 787, 794–795.

65 Cour Superieure de Justice (Luxembourg), *Kersa Holding Co. Luxembourg v. Infancourtage*, 24 November 1993, *Yearbook Commercial Arbitration* XXI (1996) 617, 625.

66 See the examples in the case law T. Harris, "The 'Public Policy' Exception to Enforcement of International Arbitration Awards under the New York Convention with Particular Reference to Construction Disputes", *Journal of International Arbitration*, vol. 24 (2007), 9, 11ff.

67 See the further references listed in Otto and Elwan, "Article V(2)", 366.

68 At the same time, some flexibility has been recognised in case law. The concept of public policy thus possesses some flexibility in the sense that it may change over time. As the Court of Appeal (New Zealand), *CBI NZ Ltd.* v. *Badger Chiyoda*, New Zealand Law Reports 2 (1989) 669, 674, put it, "[c]hanges in society or attitudes prevailing internationally may show that apprehensions once seen as real and weighty are obviously no longer so."

69 Born, *Commercial Arbitration*, 2832–2833.

70 See e.g., Luxembourg Superior Court of Justice, Judgment of 24 November 1993, XXI Yearbook of Commercial Arbitration 617, 624.

71 See e.g., Article 1502 of the New Code of Civil Procedure in France.

national public policy.[72] Nonetheless, in some cases (e.g., where there is a materially close connection between an award and a foreign state), courts have applied another state's public policy to refuse the enforcement of an arbitral award.[73]

This notwithstanding, some argue that a meaning independent of any national legal order ought to be given to public policy, or "public order" as it is often referred to in this context. For some time now, part and parcel of the concept of a transnational customary law of commerce[74] has been the discussion of the existence of a body of norms that would encompass the compulsory norms of the *lex mercatoria*.[75] Based on this theory, a distinction can be drawn between the national, international and the so-called transnational public order.[76] Like national public order, the international public order finds its basis in one national legal system; the transnational public order, however, consists of principles that reflect universal values and exists completely detached from any national legal order.[77] The exact norms that form this transnational public order are difficult to discern, and some courts have suggested that they are "ungraspable".[78] Typically, it has been suggested that for rules to be accepted as part of the transnational public order, they must not be part of all legal orders but merely be respected in a large majority of legal orders; consensus is thus sufficient.[79] For example, in the case of competition law one can legitimately doubt whether the principle of a free market requiring non-distorted competition is accepted in a sufficient number of legal orders

[72] Born, *Commercial Arbitration*, 2837.

[73] See e.g., Court of Appeal, Judgment of 18 June 2007, *IPOC International Growth Fund Ltd.* v. *LV Finance Group Ltd.*, Civil Appeal No. 30 of 2006.

[74] For one foundational account, see P. Fouchard, *L'arbitrage commercial international* (Paris: Dalloz, 1965).

[75] For more on the theoretical foundations, see P. Schlosser, *Das Recht der internationalen privaten Schiedsgerichtsbarkeit* (Tübingen: J.C.B. Mohr, 1989), 146ff.

[76] See, for more on the latter term, B. Goldman, "Les conflits de lois dans l'arbitrage international de droit privé", *Recueil des Cours*, vol. 109 (1963), 347, 431–432. The notion of "ordre public réellement international" is also used in this context. See, for case law of arbitral tribunals Lalive, "L'ordre public transnational et l'arbitre international", 604ff.

[77] S. Lazareff, "L'arbitre face à l'ordre public" in P. Gauch, F. Werro and P. Pichonnaz (eds.), *Mélanges en l'honneur de Pierre Tercier* (Geneva: Schulthess, 2008), 851.

[78] "Insaisissable" in the original words of the Swiss Federal Tribunal, see Tribunal fédérale, Ière Cour civile, arrêt du 8 mars 2006, 4P.278/2005, X S.p.A c. Y. S.r.l., vol. 3 (2006) *ASA Bulletin*, 521ff.

[79] J.B. Racine, *L'arbitrage commercial et l'ordre public* (Paris: L.G.D.J., 1999), 360.

and understood in a sufficiently uniform manner to form part of the transnational public order.[80]

5.2.3 Institutional aspects of public policy relevant for domestic courts

Apart from the substantive aspects of public policy, there are also institutional issues that domestic courts face. There is the dispute over whether or not domestic courts possess a residual power under Article V(1) NYC to decide whether they will refuse enforcement of an award, where certain grounds set forth in the convention are given (e.g., the award was set aside by a court in the country where the award was made).[81] According to this provision, recognition and enforcement of an award "may" be refused under such circumstances. While some would agree that such a residual power exists due to the term "may", others point to the convention's drafting history and the French language version (which is an equally authoritative version)[82] to claim that courts have no leeway in refusing enforcement once one of these grounds is established.[83]

[80] Lazareff, "L'arbitre", 852–853.

[81] See the various grounds set out in Article V(1) (a) to (e) NYC. The NYC treats awards that have been set aside in the country under the law of which they were made in the same way as awards set aside in the country where they have been made; to facilitate discussion, this variation is deliberately left aside. For awards that have been set aside in the country where the award has been made more specifically, there are diverging views. Article VII (1) NYC is known as the "more-favourable-right provision" and allows parties to avail themselves of arbitral awards if the law or treaties in a country where an award should be relied upon are more favourable to that party's claim, A.J. van den Berg, "Enforcement of Arbitral Awards Annulled in Russia", *Journal of International Arbitration*, vol. 27 (2010), 179, 193. In France for example, the national law permits courts to ignore set-aside decisions of arbitral awards in other countries, see sceptically and with references to case law A.J. van den Berg, "Enforcement of Annulled Awards?", *ICC International Court of Arbitration Bulletin*, vol. 9 (1998), 16, 16–17. In contrast, US courts have departed from an earlier, comparable position and increasingly refuse to enforce such awards, see e.g., the decision handed down by the U.S. Court of Appeals for the District of Columbia Circuit in *Termorio S.A.E.S.P. & Leaseco Group, L.L.C.* v. *Electranta S.P. et al.*, 487 F.3d 928 (D.C. Cir. 2007). A middle position between the two extremes suggests that courts in the enforcement state should not review the vacated award but instead review the vacating decision of the court in the country where the award was made by using the internationally accepted annulment standards of the NYC, C. Koch, "The Enforcement of Awards Annulled in Their Place of Origin – The French and U.S. Experience", *Journal of International Arbitration*, vol. 26 (2009) 267, 290–291.

[82] Article XVI NYC foresees that the Chinese, English, French, Russian, and Spanish texts are to be considered equally authentic.

[83] Van den Berg, "Enforcement", 186. See also, for a draft text of a future convention or amendment to the NYC that should clarify the issue, A.J. van den Berg, "Hypothetical Draft Convention on the International Enforcement of Arbitration Agreements and

Moreover, the often-supported emphasis on protecting parties' autonomy is based on the fact that courts that review awards based on public policy are exercising "secondary" as opposed to "primary" jurisdiction.[84] Courts in the country where an award is handed down have primary jurisdiction (i.e., broader authority to set aside an award), whereas courts in other countries only possess secondary jurisdiction (i.e., the possibility to recognise and enforce such an award or not).[85] Courts exercising secondary jurisdiction are thus not entrusted with the task of reviewing an award on its merits against the benchmark of public policy, but rather on the merits of its enforcement.[86]

In contrast, Article V(2 b NYC declares that concerns over the compatibility of an arbitral award's enforcement with public policy can be taken up by a court *sua motu*, that is, of its own initiative, and shows thereby that public policy is nonetheless an important value and ground for review. The text clearly states that recognition and enforcement may be refused "'if the competent authority [. . .] finds that" there is a violation of public policy.[87]

It is in this context of a values conflict that domestic courts have to develop balancing tests. These considerations support the analysis of case law in the following section. Yet, as discussed previously, matters have become more complicated in the EU context. Elements of public policy are also based in EU law and have thus created a more complex picture.

The landmark case is the *Eco Swiss* decision by the CJEU.[88] A Dutch court had asked whether annulment of an award was required if the reason for annulment was EU public policy; in this case it was the violation of EU competition law by an agreement between the two companies in question. The Court of Justice affirmed the existence of this duty, based on the importance of the competition law provision[89] and the principle of equivalence. Based on the latter principle, member

Awards" in A.J. van den Berg (ed.) *50 Years of the New York Convention* (Alphen aan den Rijn: Kluwer Law International, 2009), 668. See, for an opposing view, J. Paulsson, "Enforcing Arbitral Awards Notwithstanding a Local Standard Annulment", *ICC International Court of Arbitration Bulletin*, vol. 9 (1998), 14.

84 See e.g., for an illustrative distinction between the two terms the United States Second Court of Appeal, *Karaha Bodas II, L.L.C.* v. *Perusahaan Pertambangan Minyak Dan Gas Bumi Negara* 500 F.3d 111 n.1 (2d Cir. 2007), para. 21.

85 Hsu, "Public Policy", 129.

86 See, with the example of Russian case law, Nikiforov, "Interpretation of Article V", 801–802.

87 See also Tribunal Fédéral, Semaine Judiciaire 1980, 65, paras. 3.c and 4.

88 Case 126/97 *Eco Swiss* EU:C:1999:269 (CJEU).

89 Para. 36.

states must ensure that claims which are based on EU law are treated no less favourably than analogous claims based on national law in terms of procedure.[90] This is particularly relevant because EU law is vested with a particular status of primacy over national law. As a consequence of this primacy, the public policy exception must be interpreted by EU member state courts to include EU public policy; it is no longer optional for a national court to take up a request by a party or act *sua sponte*, but a mandatory course of action for that court.[91]

The subsequent section turns to the balancing tests domestic courts have developed, bearing in mind this set of values that come into conflict in the realm of the public policy exception. A difference between categorical approaches and the balancing tests that resemble proportionality can be noted. This also holds true for cases where a more complex set of values must be considered due to EU law.

5.3 *The use of proportionality analysis: the example of refusal of recognition of an award based on public policy grounds*

When observing case law, it appears that courts have developed different balancing tests to assess claims that an award should not be enforced based on reasons of public policy. Noticeably, some courts tend towards categorical approaches that simply classify whether or not certain awards violate public order, or carefully examine whether there was a value that had been protected by public policy that was at stake. Other courts appear to engage in balancing tests that are rather quantitative, typically by examining whether or not the violation of a norm in a specific state was sufficiently serious to justify denial of recognition and enforcement on public policy grounds.

An example of the first group of balancing tests can be found in *Excelsior Film TV v. UGC-PH*. An arbitrator who sat on two arbitral tribunals in France and Italy for related cases had influenced the second arbitration by providing wrong information. Confronted with a challenge of the Italian award's enforcement in France based on public policy, the Cour de Cassation held that a violation of public policy by an award could concern the procedure as well as the substance of the award. The alleged irregularity had created an imbalance of power between the two parties in the arbitration, and this imbalance constituted a violation of the right of defence. Consequently, the award violated France's public

[90] Para. 37. [91] Bermann, "Navigating EU Law", 414.

order and its enforcement could indeed be refused, as the lower court had already done.[92]

In *G.W.L. Kersten & Co. B.V. v. Société Commerciale Raoul-Duval et Cie*, the respondent had submitted documents to the arbitral tribunal, but neither he nor the arbitral tribunal submitted them to the appellant. The court that reviewed the arbitral award to evaluate its compliance with public policy held that this constituted a "violation of a fundamental procedural right, namely, the principle of hearing both sides". Although the appellant had made its allegations known in advance, this could not heal the violation of the rights of the defence, and the court refused recognition and enforcement of the award based on public policy.[93]

Similarly, in *Rice Trading (Guyana) Ltd. v. Nidera Handelscompagnie BV* the respondent claimed that his rights of defence had been violated. The proceedings had been organised by the arbitral tribunal such that an oral discussion was only possible in an early meeting before any documents had been exchanged; later, the party that submitted its written statements last could submit new documents without the other party's ability to react either orally or in writing to this submission. The court held that the arbitral tribunal had "violated the fundamental right to contradictory proceedings in this case" and denied the award's recognition and enforcement.[94]

One example of the second group of balancing tests is a recent case decided by the Swiss Federal Tribunal, in which the court annulled an award on the grounds of public policy. With regard to public policy, the tribunal held that the prohibition of forced labour could be seen as such a fundamental principle of law that its violation would thus be conceived of as grounds for the annulment of an award.[95] A soccer player owed his former club a high penalty payment for having terminated his contract without sufficient cause, and his refusal to pay the requested sum was

[92] Cour de Cassation (France), *Excelsior Film TV* v. *UGC-PH*, 24 March 1998, *Yearbook Commercial Arbitration* XXIVa (1999), 643–644.

[93] Gerechtshof Amsterdam (Netherlands), *G.W.L. Kersten & Co. B.V. v. Société Commerciale Raoul-Duval et Cie*, 16 July 1992, Yearbook Commercial Arbitration XIX (1994), 708–709.

[94] Arrondissementsrechtbank Rotterdam (Netherlands), *Rice Trading (Guyana) Ltd.* v. *Nidera Handelscompagnie BV*, 2 October 1997, *Yearbook Commercial Arbitration* XXIII (1998), 731–733. Confirmed in Gerechtshof Den Haag (Netherlands), *Rice Trading (Guyana) Ltd.* v. *Nidera Handelscompagnie BV*, 28 April 1998, *Yearbook Commercial Arbitration* XXIII (1998), 731, 733.

[95] Federal Tribunal (Switzerland), *Decision no. 4A_558/2011*, 27 March 2012 (translation into English available at www.swissarbitrationdecisions.com), para. 4.1.

found to be in violation of FIFA rules. After he exhausted all means of recourse within the arbitral system without success, he thus found himself in a position where his former club could, based on FIFA rules, request that he be excluded from any form of soccer-related employment in the future. Confronted with the claim of a severe violation of the player's freedom of profession and an excessive limitation of personal freedom as enshrined in the Swiss Constitution, the Federal Tribunal held that the "free unfolding of personality" was protected as a fundamental value in the Swiss legal order not only against public, but also against private, intervention.[96] Examining the restrictions that the award effectively imposed on the player, the tribunal held that "the award under appeal would lead not only to the Appellant being subjected to his previous employer's arbitrariness but also to an encroachment in his economic freedom of such gravity that the foundations of his economic existence are jeopardised without any possible justification by some prevailing interest of the world football federation or its members."[97] The award was thus annulled as an "obvious and grave violation of privacy" and one that was contrary to public policy.[98]

A similar, more quantitative, approach can also be shown in the context of EU law. For EU member states, some complexity has been added to the notion of public policy as they need to respect notions of both EU public policy and national public policy. The ensuing difficulty for national courts of EU member states is to extrapolate clearly which norms of EU law enjoy the status of EU public policy and thus require particular respect due to their primacy over national law. Domestic courts have tried to resolve this issue by using quantitative balancing tests rather than categorical approaches. In the *Thales* case, the domestic court did not focus exclusively on the fundamental character of the norm violated by a particular award, but rather examined the severity of the violation and upheld any awards that did not manifestly disregard EU public policy (e.g., rules of EU competition law).[99] In the somewhat analogous *Renault* case that concerned the enforcement of a court judgment from another member state, the CJEU held that in order to deny recognition and enforcement to a court judgment under the public policy exception, an infringement caused by this judgment would have to constitute "a manifest breach of a rule of law regarded as essential in

[96] Para. 4.3.1. [97] Para. 4.3.5. [98] Para. 4.3.5.

[99] See e.g., Cour d'appel de Paris (France), *SA Thales Air Défense* v. *Euromissile*, 18 November 2004, *Revue de l'arbitrage* (2005), 751.

the legal order of the State in which enforcement is sought or of a right recognised as being fundamental within that legal order".[100]

5.4 *Assessing aspects of the balancing tests developed by courts*

These examples show that although in principle the balancing of competing public interests is not denied, in practice the courts in many cases apply a more categorical reasoning (e.g., *Excelsior Film TV v. UGC-PH, G.W.L. Kersten & Co. B.V. v. Société Commerciale Raoul-Duval et Cie, Rice Trading (Guyana) Ltd. v. Nidera Handelscompagnie BV*). However, in some cases balancing will be applied to determine whether or not the violation of central norms of the enforcement state's legal system is sufficiently serious to have crossed the threshold to become a public policy violation (*Decision no. 4A_558/2011, Thales, Renault*). In particular, in the Swiss Federal Tribunal's decision the explicit balancing test that was applied appears to be a version of proportionality *stricto sensu*; furthermore, this balancing test was not a step-by-step analysis as in the example of proportionality analysis presented above. Instead, these balancing tests typically are a careful examination as to whether two legitimate public interests were indeed at stake and that thus required balancing; the emphasis lies mainly on the impact that enforcement of an award would have on a particularly important norm that forms a component of "public policy".

This truncated test mirrors the institutional context that was set out previously. Based on Ely's thesis, courts would see the justification of their review power over the enforcement of arbitral awards in reinforcing the representation of the values of public policy of their state. In principle, balancing is thus not only a permissible option but necessary. However, the institutional context weighs in once courts start crafting a balancing test, because their hands are tied to a certain extent. They can only decide whether or not an award can be enforced or denied enforcement; the award itself and its contribution towards the public interest of private autonomy in dispute settlement are "fixed". This would explain the categorical approach chosen by a number of courts. For the Swiss Federal Tribunal that engaged in the balancing procedure that resembled proportionality analysis, this context proves relevant, but in a different manner. Since there are only two possibilities, namely

[100] Case C-38/98 *Régie nationale des usines Renault* EU:C:2000:225 (CJEU), para. 30.

enforcement or no enforcement,[101] it does not make sense for courts to engage in a necessity test as such a test would require courts to compare such an award's public policy violations with less restrictive alternatives. A court cannot revise an award's content and thus order the enforcement of the revised less restrictive award. This may explain the absence of necessity testing, such as in the Swiss Federal Tribunal's balancing test.[102]

Another contextual feature that is apparent in the balancing test used by the Swiss Federal Tribunal is the general weight placed on the interest of private autonomy (and therefore on the finality of arbitral awards) by commercial arbitration in general and the NYC in particular. In the case of categorical balancing tests, this leads to a narrow interpretation of the grounds available as a justification for non-enforcement under the notion of public policy; particularly important norms must therefore be violated for an award to be effectively refused recognition and enforcement.

The Swiss case, by contrast, shows that courts can also consider an increasingly broad range of values as potential violations of public policy; the Swiss Federal Tribunal accepted the effect of the award on non-procedural fundamental rights. When considering a broader set of values, it becomes more important to focus not so much on the mere quality of the norm of public order that is violated by an award, but instead to use a more comprehensive balancing test that provides room for such values, and to focus on the intensity of the violation of said norm. The Swiss Federal Tribunal thus required a "grave" violation of fundamental rights. Adopting a balancing test that is closer to proportionality analysis also enabled the courts in *Thales* and *Renault* to appropriately account for the norms of EU public policy, while at the same time giving sufficient weight to private autonomy. They did so by requiring a certain severity of the violation of a norm of sufficient importance.

Categorical approaches thus tend to primarily rely on the quality and importance of the norm violated, whereas the more quantitatively

101 To be perfectly precise, there also exists the possibility of partial recognition and enforcement; however, this remedy is only available for an award where "the good part is separable from the bad". See High Court (Hong Kong), *J.J. Agro Industries (P) Ltd.* v. *Texuna International Ltd.*, 12 August 1992, *Yearbook Commercial Arbitration* XVIII (1993), 396, para. 34.

102 At the same time, the existence of the power to order the use of a less restrictive alternative is not an impediment to using a necessity test as part of a balancing test. At the judicial reasoning stage, it may be useful to compare features of an arbitral award with possible alternatives in order to gauge the impact of that given award on public policy.

oriented balancing tests tend to look at a wider set of grounds of a public policy violation and to focus on the intensity of the interference with public policy. At the same time, it is often the same norm (i.e., typically Article V(2)b NYC) that is being interpreted. The context of balancing tests thus clearly influences the shape of balancing tests. In the case of commercial arbitration, a convincing explanation as to how courts have weighed contextual arguments can, in principle, be found. Depending on whether one perceives the justification of public policy-related judicial review of courts as very limited or as a broader authority to reinforce representation of the public interest of public policy, a court thus chooses to either employ a categorical assessment or instead employ a rather comprehensive quantitative reasoning, as the Swiss Federal Tribunal did. At least for the case discussed here, the latter approach used by that court seems, however, to do more justice to the reality that the awards handed down in international commercial arbitration can sometimes have a tremendous impact on important values such as fundamental rights. More generally, quantitative balancing tests tend to set out the reasons for the decision on recognition and enforcement in greater detail.[103] From the point of view of transparency in the decision-making process in international commercial arbitration under the public policy exception, the use of balancing tests thus seems like a welcome development. At the same time, at least based on the decision of the Swiss Federal Tribunal, more comprehensive and more quantitative balancing tests do not appear to be necessarily more or less restrictive in granting exceptions for public policy.[104]

5.5 *Comparing the balancing tests developed by other trade courts*

Having assessed the balancing tests developed by courts in international commercial arbitration, this section will briefly compare these findings with the balancing tests found in other trade courts. Some similarities and differences can be found between the two.

[103] See Section 5.2.

[104] Put another way, errors in adjudication cannot refute proportionality analysis as a concept, see M. Khosla, "Proportionality: An Assault on Human Rights?: A Reply", *International Journal of Constitutional Law*, vol. 8 (2010), 298, 306; in this regard as a reply to a more sceptical account of balancing by S. Tsakyrakis, "Proportionality: An Assault on Human Rights?", *International Journal of Constitutional Law*, vol. 7 (2009), 468, 476.

In WTO law, there is a rich but complex case law[105] (under Article XX of the General Agreement on Tariffs and Trade [GATT]) that provides for various public interests as grounds to derogate from GATT obligations. The formula developed by the Appellate Body is a test of "weighing and balancing",[106] but the use of this formula has led to disputes over whether full-scale proportionality analysis is actually at work or whether a truncated test is instead being used.[107] In international commercial arbitration, the balancing tests that are employed are less elaborate than the sometimes lengthy assessments undertaken by panels and the Appellate Body; yet where they do use balancing they convey a clearer picture of the balancing that takes place. At the same time, in terms of the institutional context of the WTO, the interest of trade is central to the justification for judicial review; it is typically not perceived as systematically hierarchically superior to the other interests enshrined in the GATT, at least in contemporary readings of WTO law.[108] In this light, the necessity-based balancing test which prevails in WTO law appears justified, as it provides the necessary weight that is given to other public interests.[109] In contrast, in commercial arbitration public policy seems to be defined as the exception rather than the rule; instead, the central objective of the legal regime is to uphold party autonomy and hence the finality of awards. Balancing that focuses on the importance of the violated norm and on the intensity of a violation of this norm has thus carried the day. Thus, the divergence between the balancing tests used in both regimes appears to be normatively justified.

In international investment law, the case law is very fact-specific and there are only a few cases where elements of a clear balancing test can be found.[110]

105 For a comprehensive overview, see I. Venzke, "Making General Exceptions: The Spell of Precedents in Developing Article XX GATT into Standards for Domestic Regulatory Policy", *German Law Journal*, vol. 12 (2011), 1111.

106 Appellate Body Report, *Korea – Measures Affecting Imports of Fresh, Chilled and Frozen Beef*, WT/DS161/AB/R and WT/DS169/AB/R (adopted 11 December 2000), para. 164.

107 For arguments in favour of the first position, see, e.g., A. Stone Sweet and J. Mathews, "Proportionality Balancing and Global Constitutionalism", *Columbia Journal of Transnational Law*, vol. 47 (2008), 73, 164; in favour of the second, see, e.g., D.H. Regan, "The Meaning of 'Necessary' in GATT Article XX and GATS Article XIV: The Myth of Cost-Benefit Balancing", *World Trade Review*, vol. 6 (2007), 347, 354–355.

108 See on the rather limited reading to be adopted for GATT obligations, P. Mavroidis, *Trade in Goods – The GATT and the Other Agreements Regulating Trade in Goods* (Oxford: Oxford University Press, 2007), 215.

109 Pirker, *Proportionality Analysis*, 330–331.

110 For an overview over the case law, see C. Henckels, "Indirect Expropriation and the Right to Regulate: Revisiting Proportionality Analysis and the Standard of Review in

At the same time, arbitrators who sit on investment tribunals appear to find it difficult to clearly spell out the public interests that are at conflict in investment arbitration cases.[111] Despite this lack of clarity, a persuasive argument to take inspiration from WTO law for relying on a necessity test rather than on full-scale proportionality can be made.[112] Although there are some similarities between commercial and investment arbitration with regard to the institutional structure of arbitration, in practice, domestic courts interpreting the public policy clause in commercial arbitration spell out balancing tests more explicitly where they use them. This would seem plausible mainly in light of the fact that the public interests at conflict in a given case are usually straightforward to identify; furthermore, courts interpreting the public policy clause are also much more embedded in the domestic institutional context, which tends to force their hand to better explain their reasoning. Arbitral tribunals in international investment law may consider the indirect precedential effect of their case law; but they are not obliged to and often instead simply focus on providing a solution to the case before them.[113] In contrast, domestic courts in international commercial arbitration are part of a judicial hierarchy and work on the assumption that not only will their decision be reviewed in case of an appeal, but also that it will have some precedential effect on lower courts. This is particularly true for the high courts. Again, features of the institutional context can be used to explain the difference in the balancing tests employed.

Compared to these two legal regimes, the case law on balancing under the public policy exception in international commercial arbitration distinguishes itself via the explicit reasoning that it employs on balancing tests, where courts dare to use them. The categorical approach to the

Investor-State Arbitration", *Journal of International Economic Law*, vol. 15 (2012), 223; E.M. Leonhardsen, "Looking for Legitimacy: Exploring Proportionality Analysis in Investment Treaty Arbitration", *Journal of International Dispute Settlement*, vol. 3 (2012), 95.

111 See A. Kulick, "Book Review, Stephan W. Schill (ed.). International Investment Law and Comparative Public Law. Oxford: Oxford University Press, 2010", *European Journal of International Law*, vol. 22 (2011), 917, 920.

112 B. Pirker, "Seeing the Forest Without the Trees – The Doubtful Case for Proportionality Analysis in International Investment Arbitration", Highly Commended Essay, Society of International Economic Law (2011)/Cambridge University Press Essay Prize 1.

113 This is not to suggest that there are no developments towards some precedential effects of awards in international investment arbitration. For more on this very topic, see e.g., S.W. Schill, "System-Building in Investment Treaty Arbitration and Lawmaking", *German Law Journal*, vol. 12 (2011), 1083; and more critical I. Ten Cate, "The Costs of Consistency: Precedent in Investment Treaty Arbitration", *Columbia Journal of Transnational Law*, vol. 51 (2013), 418.

public policy clause appears to overemphasise the interest of party autonomy, whereas the more quantitative approach to balancing (i.e., as exposed by cases such as the Swiss Federal Tribunal) provides a very adequate solution to a complex problem without opening the floodgates to public policy challenges to the recognition and enforcement of arbitral awards. In the case before the Swiss Federal Tribunal, a very serious violation of fundamental values had to be identified in order to justify the refusal of recognition and enforcement of an award. Consequently, further use of balancing tests by tribunals can in principle be welcomed, so long as it is adapted to the institutional context of international commercial arbitration.

6 Conclusion

This chapter aimed to demonstrate the influence of institutional context on the shaping of balancing tests, examined through the example of international commercial arbitration. The Principles Theory provided a framework to systematically evaluate balancing tests against the common benchmark of proportionality analysis. Ely's procedural democracy and the notion of the justification of judicial review expanded the lens to include the institutional context of balancing tests. Use of this widened perspective allowed assessment, evaluation and comparison of the reasons for a particular shape given to balancing tests in a particular institutional situation and among various legal regimes. In order to apply these theoretical findings to the case of international commercial arbitration, the example of the public policy exception was used. A typical provision enshrining this exception is Article V(2)b of the New York Convention, a norm that allows domestic courts of one state to deny recognition and enforcement to arbitral awards handed down in another state. Finding a balance between public policy and private autonomy as enshrined in the essentially contractual setting of commercial arbitration is one task of arbitral tribunals. However, because controversy surrounds the duty of the arbitrator to render an enforceable award and the public order that has to be taken into account to comply with this duty, this chapter limits its focus to domestic courts for easier comparability. The institutional context was shown to emphasise the value of private autonomy and the finality of arbitral awards, while domestic courts only have limited leeway to refuse recognition and enforcement based on the grounds of public policy. The balancing tests found in the case law mirror these features; they exhibit typically a categorical approach towards the interpretation of the notion of a state's public policy and conduct no lengthy engagement in the various stages of proportionality analysis. Courts have only undertaken a more comprehensive balancing exercise in some cases, and this has resembled proportionality *stricto sensu* to assess whether a violation concerns a norm of particular importance and consequently is sufficiently serious to qualify as a breach of public policy. These cases are more systematic in providing the reasons for the decision taken, and can thus be commended for this effort. A similar development of balancing tests is observed where the institutional context has changed through EU law. EU law has introduced its own notion of public policy, and when this is combined with the primacy of EU law, it forces the courts of member states to develop more comprehensive balancing tests to account for the more complex set of conflicting values that must be protected under judicial review of public policy violations. In comparison with other legal regimes, the balancing tests developed in international commercial arbitration under the public policy exception prove somewhat more transparent than the highly complicated and blurred balancing test embraced in WTO law, and the reluctant approach to balancing competing public interests that is found in investment arbitration. Still, in many cases domestic courts in international commercial arbitration use a categorical reasoning that does not clearly set out the actual reasons for their decision in favour or against recognition and enforcement of arbitral awards based on the public policy clause. When viewed in this light, elaborate quantitative balancing tests that are adapted to the institutional context are a welcome development in international commercial arbitration.

INDEX

For EU product safety concerns, contact us at Calle de José Abascal, 56–1°, 28003 Madrid, Spain or eugpsr@cambridge.org.

www.ingramcontent.com/pod-product-compliance
Lightning Source LLC
LaVergne TN
LVHW011527200926
848484LV00001B/182
9781107147102